Rationalism, Pluralism, and Freedom

Rationalism, Pluralism, and Freedom

Jacob T. Levy

OXFORD
UNIVERSITY PRESS

OXFORD
UNIVERSITY PRESS

Great Clarendon Street, Oxford, OX2 6DP,
United Kingdom

Oxford University Press is a department of the University of Oxford.
It furthers the University's objective of excellence in research, scholarship,
and education by publishing worldwide. Oxford is a registered trade mark of
Oxford University Press in the UK and in certain other countries

First Edition published in 2015
Impression: 2

Published in the United States of America by Oxford University Press
198 Madison Avenue, New York, NY 10016, United States of America

British Library Cataloguing in Publication Data
Data available

Library of Congress Control Number: 2014940419

ISBN 978–0–19–871714–0

Printed and bound by
CPI Group (UK) Ltd, Croydon, CR0 4YY

Acknowledgments

This book has been a very long time in the making, and draws on most of my research on a range of topics over more than a decade. It would be fair to thank everyone who has discussed any of my intellectual preoccupations with me over that time, or at least the smaller-but-still-large number of people who have responded to my related articles in formal ways. I instead let the related published work stand on its own, each piece with its own acknowledgments. I incorporate by reference the acknowledgments to that related work, especially the pieces listed in the penultimate paragraph.

Portions of this manuscript since it started to take on its present form have been presented at Princeton University's Program in Ethics and Public Affairs; UCLA's Center for British Studies; the Politics, Philosophy, and Economics workshop in the Economics Department at George Mason University; the Centre for Ethics at the University of Toronto; the "Tragedy of Liberty" conference at the Central European University, Budapest; the *Analyzes Normatives Contemporaines* workshop in the *Centre de Recherche Sens, Éthique, Société* at the University of Paris (Descartes); the Institute for Economic Affairs; the Centre for Independent Studies; the "Charles Taylor at 80" conference at the Groupe de Recherche Interuniversitaire en Philosophie Politique in Montreal; and political theory workshops at Georgetown University, American University, Nuffield College, Queen Mary, and University of London.

The book as a whole was the subject of two manuscript workshops, one at the Mercatus Center at George Mason University, organized by Claire Morgan and Peter Boettke, and led by Jack Goldstone; and one at the Center for the Philosophy of Freedom at the University of Arizona, organized by Chad van Schoelandt and David Schmidtz. I am very grateful to all those who took the time to read and discuss it. At Mercatus, Paul Dragos Aligica, Peter Boettke, Elisabeth Ellis, William Galston, Loren King, Christopher Morris, Hilton Root, Jennifer Rubenstein, and Ilya Somin all commented; I owe particular thanks to Ellis and Rubenstein for especially thorough and detailed suggestions during and after the workshop. At Arizona, Samuel Fleischacker and Eric Mack provided substantial sets of comments, and other participants included Sameer Bajaj, Taylor Davidson, Suzanne Dovi, Jerry Gaus, Ross Kenyon, Brian

Kogelmann, Matt Mortellaro, Robert Peters, Guido Pincione, Sarah Raskoff, Tristan Rogers, Danny Shahar, Stephen Stich, John Thrasher, and Steven Wall.

The project has benefited from sustained excellent research assistance from Mylène Freeman, Ju-Hea Jang, Zoë Miller-Vedam, Elisa Muyl, Emily Nacol, Diane Shnier, and Sarah Wellen; the work done by Miller-Vedam, Muyl, and Shnier was supported by McGill's Arts Research Internship Awards. Francesca Allodi-Ross, Devon Cass, Stephanie Ovens, Isaac Stethem, and Bryon Taylor-Conboy provided shorter-term research assistance.

I have presented a majority of the book over the years to the Works in Progress workshop at the Research Group on Constitutional Studies at McGill University, and am especially grateful to the members of that group who have read many chapters spread over several years. Arash Abizadeh, Mark Antaki, Evan Fox-Decent, James Gardner, Volker Heins, Hoi Kong, Catherine Lu, Victor Muñiz-Fraticelli, Andrew Rehfeld, Will Roberts, Christa Scholtz, Hasana Sharp, Daniel Silvermint, Robert Sparling, Christina Tarnopolsky, Timothy Waligore, and Yves Winter have all been part of that group at one time or another over the past several years, with my colleagues Arash, Evan, Catherine, Victor, Will, Christa, Hasana, Christina, and Yves as the core that has assembled most often in Ferrier's seminar room. Arash and Will have been especially generous with comments, criticisms, and challenges, and have not met them all, but I have benefited from trying. Victor has been an important conversation partner in that workshop and beyond it for years, as he and I have sought to work out related problems of pluralism in our various ways. While I did not present any of this manuscript at workshops of the Groupe de Recherche Interuniversitaire en Philosophie Politique, GRIPP has been a source of constant stimulation, ideas, and inspiration during the years when I was writing it.

Others who read portions of the manuscript and provided me with valuable comments include Ethan Alexander-Davey, Christine Caldwell Ames, Anthony Appiah, Mark Bevir, Richard Boyd, Sarah Mackenzie Burns, Paul Gowder, Jennie Ikuta, Jeremy Jennings, Daniel Kapust, Andrew Koppelman, Chandran Kukathas, Briana McGinnis, Michael Mosher, Emily Nacol, Andrew Sabl, Kevin Vallier, Daniel Weinstock, and four anonymous readers for Oxford University Press.

I have received funding and support for this project from the Earhart Foundation, the Mellon Foundation, the Social Sciences Division of the University of Chicago, the Social Sciences and Humanities Research Council of Canada, and visiting fellowships at the Social Philosophy and Policy Foundation and the Centre de Recherche en Éthique à l'Université de Montréal. A grant from the Templeton Foundation administered by the Atlas Foundation supported my co-teaching of a course with Susanne Hoeber Rudolph on "Freedom, State, and Society" in 2002 that was part of this project's early gestation; Professor Rudolph, the guest lecturers in the class (David Beito, William Galston, Will Kymlicka, and Vincent Ostrom), and the students in it (especially the graduate students who took part in the section set aside for them) taught me a great deal.

The Social Philosophy and Policy Center fellowship in 2001 allowed me to formulate the project; the Earhart Fellowship in 2004 supported some of the central research behind Chapters 5, 6, and 7. My debts to the Mellon Foundation's New Directions Fellowship, and to the University of Chicago Law School where I held the fellowship, are especially great. The Fellowship supported my spending 2004–5 at the Law School; that is an extraordinary academic environment and the year was perhaps the most intellectually exciting one I have ever spent. Thanks in large part to Saul Levmore, I was accorded a great deal of flexibility from day to day in acting as a visiting researcher in a world-class research environment and acting as a student who could benefit from world-class teaching. In the former capacity, Rachel Brewster, Emily Buss, Mary Ann Case, Adam Cox, Elizabeth Emens, Richard Epstein, Bernard Harcourt, Saul Levmore, Martha Nussbaum, Eric Posner, Richard Posner, Cass Sunstein, David Strauss, Adrian Vermeule, and David Weisbach provided a constantly challenging and stimulating stream of ideas in workshops, at Roundtable lunches, and in ongoing conversation. Nussbaum and Vermeule in particular, as colleagues, mentors, conversation partners, and friends, have been very important contributors to this work over many years, and most especially in 2004–5 simply because I had more opportunity to talk with them than before or since. In my capacity as student, I benefited in particular from three courses each with Douglas Baird and Richard Helmholtz. Baird's course on corporate law vastly improved my ability to think analytically about organizations and the rules governing them, while his courses on contracts gave me new ways to think about fundamental concepts in social science and political theory. Helmholtz's class on European legal history pointed me in the right direction for much of the research that went into Chapters 4–6, research that helped me see what Books XXVII–XXXI of *The Spirit of the Laws* are about and how they matter. The idiosyncratic methods in this book—the ways of thinking about individual choice, organizational forms, and state rules, the ways of thinking about the entanglement of the histories of legal and political thought—mostly derive from things I learned, ideas I began to formulate, or arguments I tried to respond to during the year of that fellowship, and I thank everyone associated with making it possible. Moreover, a follow-up fellowship from Mellon provided the crucial year of writing time during which most of this manuscript took its current form.

I am grateful to the University of Lausanne's Institut Benjamin Constant and Bibliothèque cantonale et universitaire de Lausanne for access to and assistance with the Constant archives. Additional archival work was conducted at the Bibliothèque Nationale de France and in the Franklin Collection of the Sterling Memorial Library at Yale University.

Besides the "Freedom, State, and Society" course already mentioned, a few teaching experiences stand out as having allowed me to work some of these questions through with the help of many excellent students: a graduate seminar on liberal political theory in 2001, a two-term course on eighteenth-century political thought in 2005–6, a graduate seminar on "Foundations of European Studies," co-taught with Mark Antaki, in 2007, 2008, and 2009, the Research Group on Constitutional Studies Student Fellowship reading groups of 2011–12 (Montesquieu) and 2012–13 (Constant and Tocqueville), and Institute for Humane Studies graduate seminars on "Scholarship and the Free Society" in 2009, 2011, and 2012.

Among those not otherwise named here, Charles Larmore, Patchen Markell, Patricia Nordeen, Steven Pincus, and the late Iris Marion Young have been especially important conversation partners in helping me think about this project. I owe debts and thanks of disparate kinds to Nathan Tarcov, Gerry Rosenberg, Carles Boix, Cathy Cohen, Dan Drezner, Melissa Harris-Perry, Gary Herrigel, John Holbo, Leigh Jenco, Juliet Johnson, George Kateb, Scott Kwiker, Naomi Lamoreaux, Sandy Levinson, Aaron Levy, Leonard Liggio, Chris Manfredi, Mara Marin, Wayne Norman, Callie le Renard, Fabio Rojas, Nancy Rosenblum, Rick Schultz, Susan Stokes, John Tomasi, Deborah Wais, Marshall Wais, Alexander Wendt, Bob Wieman, Gordon Wood, Libby, Indie, Justy, the cabin at Serenity, and the active community of political theorists on Facebook.

My editor at OUP, Dominic Byatt, has been a source of enthusiasm, support, advice, and suggestions as needed over the course of this project. His encouragement over the years is deeply appreciated.

This book does not join any single well-defined academic literature. The other works that seem to me most centrally about the same questions as this book only occasionally mention one another, their authors might not recognize one another (or me) as engaged in a common enterprise. Ultimately I have opted to write a book about those questions, not about those other authors. As a result, however, a few especially important books and articles are at risk of being under-acknowledged in what follows. Larry Siedentop's distinction, in his essay "The Two Liberal Traditions," between sociological and philosophical approaches is not ultimately the one I adopt here, but it was an early contribution that, I think, pointed in the right direction. Much the same is true for Charles Taylor's "Invoking Civil Society." Will Kymlicka's "Two Models of Pluralism and Tolerance," William Galston's "Two Concepts of Liberalism," and Chandran Kukathas' *The Liberal Archipelago* provided the point of departure for this project and framed its original questions. More recently, Kukathas' "Two Constructions of Libertarianism" has offered a valuable analysis of similar questions for that specific branch of liberal thought.

My teacher Nancy Rosenblum's *Membership and Morals* is a very different kind of book from this one, but has been on my mind throughout as a crucial inspiration for it. I have some important differences with Richard Boyd's *Uncivil Society*, but I owe a great deal both to his research and to conversations with him about our areas of shared interest over the years. Not the least of those debts is his alerting me to Lon Fuller's "Two Principles of Human Association."[1]

I should say a few words about F. A. Hayek's *The Constitution of Liberty*, chapter 4, "Freedom, Reason, and Tradition." As I will suggest, I think its conflation between a reason/tradition distinction and a markets/planning distinction is a mistake. Moreover, Hayek distinguishes between "British" and "French" theories construed in a way that (as he acknowledges) places Montesquieu, Constant, Tocqueville, Hobbes, and Mill on the wrong sides of the Channel. And he fails to see that there can be something authentically liberal in the rationalist view, and therefore that a rationalist liberal such as John Stuart Mill does not belong under a rubric like "totalitarian democracy." Still, there is real insight in Hayek's analysis; and I was struck many years ago by his statement that "a detailed comparison of the two traditions would require a separate book." Although I understand the traditions very differently, after a fashion I have attempted here to write that book.

The centrality I accord Montesquieu, followed by Constant and Tocqueville, in my understanding of pluralist liberalism means that the book also owes a great deal to the revival of interest in a French liberalism in which they are leading figures. A great deal of important work has been done in the past generation both on the interpretation of those thinkers and on ideas of liberalism, individualism, and pluralism in the French tradition, and my debts to the scholars who have done that work exceeds what can be listed in individual footnotes.[2] My concerns are not precisely theirs, and many of

[1] Larry Siedentop, "The Two Liberal Traditions," in *The Idea of Freedom: Essays in Honour of Isaiah Berlin*, Alan Ryan, ed. (Oxford: Oxford University Press, 1979). Chandran Kukathas, *The Liberal Archipelago: a Theory of Diversity and Freedom* (Oxford: Oxford University Press, 2003). Will Kymlicka, "Two Models of Pluralism and Tolerance," 13 *Analyz & Kritik* 33–56 (1992). William Galston, "Two Concepts of Liberalism," 105(3) *Ethics* 1995. Charles Taylor, "Invoking Civil Society." Chandran Kukathas, "Two Constructions of Libertarianism," 1(11) *Libertarian Papers* 1–14 (2009). Nancy Rosenblum, *Membership and Morals: The Personal Uses of Pluralism in America* (Princeton: Princeton University Press, 1998). Richard Boyd, *Uncivil Society*. Lon Fuller, "Two Principles of Human Association."

[2] See, among many others, Raf Geenens and Helena Rosenblatt, eds, *French Liberalism From Montesquieu to the Present Day* (Cambridge: Cambridge University Press, 2012), a volume that tellingly begins with a reprint of the Siedentop essay already mentioned. See also Lucien Jaume, *Tocqueville: Les sources aristocratiques de la liberté* (Paris: Fayard, 2008); Jaume, *L'Individu effacé ou le paradoxe du libéralisme français* (Paris: Fayard, 1997); Pierre Rosanvallon, *The Demands of Liberty: Civil Society in France Since the Revolution* (Cambridge, Mass.: Harvard University Press, 2007); Aurelian Craiutu, *Liberalism under siege: the political thought of the French doctrinaires* (Lanham, Md.: Lexington Books, 2003); Craiutu, *A Virtue for Courageous Minds: Moderation in French Political Thought, 1748–1830* (Princeton: Princeton University Press, 2012); Helena Rosenblatt, *Liberal*

them will disagree with much of what follows, but their work has done a great deal to restore both particular theorists and styles of theory on which I draw.

Chapter 9 was previously published in slightly modified form as "From Liberal Constitutionalism to Pluralism," in Mark Bevir, ed., *Modern Pluralism: Anglo-American Debates Since 1880* (Cambridge University Press, 2012). Some sections of Chapters 5, 6, and 7 are drawn from "Not so *Novus* an *Ordo*: Constitutions Without Social Contracts," 37(2) *Political Theory* 191–217, 2009, and "Montesquieu's Constitutional Legacies," in Rebecca Kingston, ed., *Modernity in Question: Montesquieu and His Legacy* (Albany: SUNY Press, 2009). I do not think that any prose from "Liberalism's Divide After Socialism—and Before," 20(1) *Social Philosophy and Policy* 278–97, 2003, survives in Chapters 1–3, but enough ideas do to warrant acknowledgment. I am grateful to these publishers for permission to use that material here.

Shelley Clark has lived with this book for as long as I have; she has also had to live with me *writing* this book. I dedicate it to her with gratitude for her support and patience.

Values: Benjamin Constant and the Politics of Religion (Cambridge: Cambridge University Press, 2008); Cheryl Welch, *Liberty and Utility: The French Idéologues and the Transformation of Liberalism* (New York: Columbia University Press, 1984); Céline Spector, *Montesquieu: Liberté, Droit, et Histoire* (Paris: Michalon, 2010); Rebecca Kingston, *Montesquieu and the Parlement of Bordeaux* (Geneva: Librairie Droz, 1996); Kingston, ed., *Montesquieu and His Legacy* (Albany: SUNY Press, 2009); Annelien de Dijn, *French political thought from Montesquieu to Tocqueville: Liberty in a Levelled Society* (Cambridge: Cambridge University Press, 2008); Jeremy Jennings, *Revolution and the Republic: A History of Political Thought in France Since the Eighteenth Century* (Oxford: Oxford University Press, 2011); Sharon Krause, *Liberalism With Honor* (Cambridge: Harvard University Press, 2002); Michael Mosher, "The Particulars of a Universal Politics: Hegel's Adaptation of Montesquieu's Typology," 78(1) *American Political Science Review* 179–88, 1984; Mosher, "What Montesquieu Taught," in Rebecca Kingston, ed., *Montesquieu and His Legacy* (Albany: SUNY Press, 2009); Melvin Richter, "Comparative Political Analysis in Montesquieu and Tocqueville," 1(2) *Comparative Politics* 129–60, 1969; Richter, "The uses of theory: Tocqueville's adaptation of Montesquieu," in Richter, ed., *Essays in Theory and History: An Approach to the Social Sciences* (Cambridge, Mass.: Harvard University Press, 1970).

Contents

Contents

Contents

"Any despotism is preferable to local despotism. If we are to be ridden over by authority, if our affairs are to be managed for us at the pleasure of other people, heaven forefend that it should be at that of our nearest neighbours."

John Stuart Mill, *Centralization*, 1862

"The man of system, on the contrary, is apt to be very wise in his own conceit; and is often so enamoured with the supposed beauty of his own ideal plan of government, that he cannot suffer the smallest deviation from any part of it."

Adam Smith, *The Theory of Moral Sentiments*, 1790

Introduction

Free persons act together. They create, join, inhabit, perpetuate, and transform all sorts of organizations, institutions, associations, and social groups in which they can jointly form and pursue their goals. They rightly seek the freedom to organize those groups as they see fit, free from outside interference, and to live according to the rules and values of the groups to which they belong. They seek religious liberty for their churches, privacy for their families, the freedom to live according to their own cultural norms and in their own languages, self-government for their clubs, societies, associations, and universities. This freedom protects their wishes to live and organize themselves as they, now, see fit. By allowing a wide range of groups to proliferate, it also protects their possible future wishes to later join meaningfully different groups. Moreover, by providing alternatives to acting through the state, and institutional resistance to expansions of state power, such intermediate groups indirectly secure freedom more broadly; they help to protect us against tyranny.

State authority in liberal democracies, at least in principle, is exercised in publicly accountable, rationally-justifiable ways. Authority wielded within other kinds of groups in a society is often quite different: resting on traditional, cultural, or religious claims about hierarchy and subordination. The consolidation of the modern state, and its gradual liberalization, has consisted in large part in the replacement of various kinds of patrimonial and local power by accountable and justifiable authority that treats persons as free and equal. Insofar as intermediate groups do *not* treat their members as free and equal, or teach their members not to view themselves and each other as free and equal, or compete with rationalized state power that upholds the constitutional order, they are suspect at best, illegitimate and despotic at worst. Intermediate groups' discriminatory rules of admission and of eligibility for leadership, undemocratic internal decision-making processes, substantively repressive rules of conduct and belief, and domineering kinds of power relations all rightly offend the liberal sense of justice and the liberal belief in each person's standing.

At the broadest level this book is about these two mindsets, these ways of looking at the triadic relationship among individual persons, intermediate groups, and states. The uneasy relationship between the two mindsets is, I will argue, an enduring and indeed necessary problem within liberal political thought. There is a deep, recurring tension within liberal political thought between seeing those groups that stand between the person and the central state as sites where free people live their diverse lives, and seeing them as sites of local tyranny that the liberal state must be strong enough to keep in check. One strand of liberalism emphasizes freedom for persons as they are, living the lives that they already lead, lives that are embedded in particular communities and partly shaped by particular cultural and religious traditions. The other looks to the importance of free persons' ability to transform or transcend those current lives. On one side of this divide lies a liberalism I will call "pluralist": skeptical of the central state and friendly toward local, customary, voluntary, or intermediate bodies, communities, and associations.[1] On the other we see a liberalism I will call "rationalist": committed to intellectual progress, universalism, and equality before a unified law, opposed to arbitrary and irrational distinctions and inequalities, and determined to disrupt local tyrannies in religious and ethnic groups, closed associations, families, plantations, the feudal countryside, and so on.

While I will suggest that *liberalism* as such necessarily faces a tension between these two strands, particular liberal *thinkers* or *theories* do not necessarily sit balanced between them. The moral, social, and political truths in the two strands are difficult to fully respect simultaneously, and so theorists who consider these questions tend to incline in one direction or the other. I illustrate this with a survey of disputes among proto-liberal or liberal theorists[2] across this intellectual divide, some stressing the threats to freedom posed by the state, some those posed by intermediate groups. A clear difference of emphasis emerges: John Stuart Mill saw the threat to freedom posed by the structure of the Victorian family, *and* by conformist intellectual cultures, but *not* by an enlightened state governing imperially over neighboring nationalities or distant lands. Tocqueville meanwhile saw the importance for freedom of voluntary associations in America and of *corps intermédiaires* in *ancien régime* France, but thought the authority of men over women within the family

---

[1] "Local," "customary," "voluntary," and "intermediate" are not synonyms; neither are "bodies," "communities," and "associations." Distinctions among words like these can be relevant and will come up.

[2] I do not think anything significant for this study turns on the precise date when the word "liberal" becomes appropriate for historical study. My own view is that the word can be fairly used starting in the mid-eighteenth century, with Montesquieu and his generation, though the word was not used to describe political doctrines until the early nineteenth century. "Protoliberal" can describe various earlier figures including Locke, some common lawyers, and the monarchomachs, but it is an awkward and telelological shorthand, and I use it sparingly.

"natural." These contemporaries and mutual admirers, among the most profound thinkers in the liberal tradition, shared a deep attachment to freedom and a fear that it would be swamped in a democratic age, but their basic sensibilities about where to find threats to it and how to defend it often pointed them in opposite directions.

Each view brings with it both insights and blind spots. Just to the degree that each one illuminates some genuine threats to freedom, it obscures others. Another example of that, from the same era, is provided by the liberal historian Lord Acton. His pluralistic commitment to checking state power, his opposition to centralization, allowed him to see more deeply than his contemporaries the danger posed by the growing identification of nation and state, to argue forcefully for multinational states as well as federalism and religious liberty. It also allowed him to believe that the most important threat to liberty at stake in the American Civil War was Lincoln's assertion of central supremacy over the states, and not the southern states' own commitment to human slavery. He understood that slavery was evil, yet protecting federalism and decentralization seemed to him more urgent.

The ideas that Tocqueville was right about associations but wrong about the family, that Mill was right about the family but wrong about imperialism, that Acton was right about nationalism and wrong about the American Civil War, and that in each case the right and the wrong are very hard to disentangle, inspire the central claim of this book. I argue not only that the tension between rationalism and pluralism within liberal thought is longstanding, but also that it is to a large degree irresolvable. We can try to be open to reasons and arguments of both sorts; we can try to reach case-by-case judgments in particular times and places. But there is no systematic way to combine all of the virtues and none of the vices of the two mindsets, and no secure middle way that would allow us to know for sure which are virtues and which are vices. I generally favor pluralist liberalism; I also think that it is the more neglected and unfamiliar of the two strands. The book therefore does much more reconstructive work with pluralist than with rationalist ideas and traditions. But the book is not a defense of pluralist liberalism, except as against the pretensions of some rationalist liberals that it should be ignored altogether. It is rather, ultimately, an argument for that claim of irresolvability. A full understanding of liberal freedom would draw on truths from both the rationalist and pluralist traditions; it would recognize that states and intermediate groups alike can oppress. And yet we cannot compromise between or combine the two accounts in a wholly satisfactory manner.

This is in part because of the kinds of social phenomena rationalist and pluralist liberalisms are concerned with. Theories of rights can aspire to fitting all legitimate claims together. Rights are a juridical moral concept, aimed at settling cases and structured to make it possible that all disputes could be rightly settled simultaneously.[3] I will argue, however, that rationalist and pluralist liberalisms are not primarily theories of rights. They are, more importantly, diagnoses of societal patterns. It's entirely normal for *both* states and intermediate groups to threaten the freedom of their members. States tend toward excessive and unjustified hostility toward group life, and groups tend toward excessive and unjustified internal power and restrictiveness, both in ways that impinge on individual persons. Moreover, the tools available to mitigate one problem often aggravate the other. The rules, institutions, and resources that protect groups and associations from state power can worsen those tendencies toward intragroup hierarchies and domination. The capacity to police intragroup life in order to protect subordinate members easily provides both tools and excuses to put that excessive hostility toward group life into effect. If theories about group life and freedom tend to bring the good and the bad together, that's in part because the social world does so, too. Or so I argue over the course of Part I, which moves from the basic contrast between rationalism and pluralism through attempts to build them up as rival theories of rights and on to an account of them as rival normatively informed social theories about the relative dangers of state intervention and group domination.

If arguments like these are sometimes absent from contemporary normative theory, depending as they do on social institutions' stubborn tendency not to do what they ought to, that is one reason for looking to the history of political thought, where a greater methodological richness can be found. Part II turns to that history: both the history of political thought, and the histories of the European state and of intermediate groups.[4] It is in large part a history of *ancient constitutionalism*, the defense of the array of intermediate institutions from the Middle Ages against the emerging absolute monarchies of early modernity. I begin with what I call the birth of intermediacy, as corporate associations proliferated starting in about 1050: universities, guilds, cities, monastic orders, and the Roman Catholic Church itself. I then trace the emergence of an early modern idea of old constitutional orders that include those bodies' corporate liberties. That ancient constitutionalism aimed to build on social and legal pluralism to keep would-be absolute monarchs in check; this was one of the sources for the eventual emergence of liberal theory, rivaling in some ways the more rationalistic and statist social contract tradition. I treat Montesquieu as the hinge figure, appropriating ancient

---

[3] I thus agree with the emphasis on compossibility in Hillel Steiner's *An Essay On Rights* (London: Wiley-Blackwell, 1994); but compossibility is a central feature of a theory of *rights* in a way that it is not necessarily a central feature of other normative theories.

[4] I discuss the restriction to Europe and its offshoots later in this Introduction.

constitutionalism and turning it into a recognizably liberal doctrine that will be developed further by such thinkers as Constant and Tocqueville. At every step I contrast these ideas with rationalist counterparts: opponents of custom, feudal privilege, and clerical power who looked to deliberate state action to free people from those inheritances.

This historical discussion has several related purposes. One is to broaden our sense of political theory's methods. The works and authors surveyed in Part II draw not only on the moral and moral-jurisprudential tools familiar in contemporary theories of rights and justice, but also on approaches ranging from moral psychological to grand historical to social scientific. They offer particular arguments we can use today, but also stand as good examples of *how* we might argue. It is reasonably well known that, say, Montesquieu and Tocqueville relied on historical and sociological as well as philosophical claims; but the same is also true of Voltaire and Mill. Some contemporary critics of liberalism, and some of its defenders, have treated liberalism very reductively: a theory of contextless individuals, abstract states, and universal rights. Abstraction has important intellectual uses, but it is very unfortunate that "abstraction" has somehow become a kind of synonym for "liberalism," as if the Kant found in Hegel's caricatures made up the whole of the liberal tradition. Montesquieu is no less concerned about freedom by being attentive to history and social relations, and Mill is no less concerned about the history and social dynamics of power by espousing a "very simple principle" about liberty.

Another goal of Part II is to provide a mental map of the past that makes the pluralist tradition within liberalism, and its relationship to rationalism, intellectually available in the present, as the Cambridge School's recovery of early modern republicanism has helped to make neo-republicanism imaginable and available to theorists today. The outpouring of work on the neo-Roman tradition that ran through much of early modernity has improved our knowledge of intellectual history; it has also helped to generate new ideas. A normative book like Philip Pettit's *Republicanism*[5] does not logically depend on historical work done by J. G. A. Pocock or Quentin Skinner; its positions could have been articulated and defended on their own. But in fact Pettit drew on the idea of republican freedom that the Cambridge historians had identified; and to many readers, the theory gained in weight and credibility because it seemed to be the refinement of a set of ideals with a substantial history. If nothing else, the historical work helped to expand the range of plausible

---

[5] Philip Pettit, *Republicanism: A Theory of Freedom and Government* (Oxford: Oxford University Press, 1997).

views, making it more likely that those of a normative bent would think to develop a philosophical defense of republicanism.[6]

Conversely, a cramped understanding of history can narrow the range of what is imaginable in the present. Brian Barry's critique of multiculturalism complained that it could not possibly be a *liberal* view, since liberalism is an Enlightenment doctrine and whatever else the Enlightenment stood for, it stood for equality before a uniform law and the abolition of group-based legal distinctions.[7] (I hope that, if nothing else, the reader will reach the end of Part II unable to believe that set of claims.) John Rawls' *Lectures on the History of Political Philosophy* offers us a history of social contract theory and the prehistory of his own theory of justice. He is explicit about this; he aims "to identify the more central features of liberalism as expressing a political conception of justice when liberalism is viewed from within the tradition of democratic constitutionalism."[8] And so he offers accounts of Hobbes, Locke, and Rousseau from within the contract tradition, Mill as the liberal exponent of individual liberty, Hume as a critic of the social contract, and Marx as a critic of theorizing about justice. This history tends to unduly focus our attention today on social contract-derived theories of rights and justice.

Ancient constitutionalism and the pluralist liberalism that grows out of it is another of the major languages of political thought in early modern Europe, rivaling civic republicanism and social contract theory (though also overlapping with them, as they overlap with each other). That is not by itself a normative argument for pluralist liberalism, any more than *The Machiavellian Moment* constitutes a normative argument for civic republicanism or a history of social contract theory makes up a normative argument for Rawls' two principles of justice.[9] But it might help make pluralist liberalism available.

Part II is quite detailed in places, sometimes about thinkers who are not of the first rank or controversies that are half-forgotten. I am very fond of both Molesworth and Destutt de Tracy, but my aim is neither to complain about their neglect in standard treatments of the history of political thought nor to make a case for their elevation to any canon. Rather, I hope to make a new map of the past available to contemporary imaginations, one that supplements (and occasionally displaces) others. A map is a stylized representation,

[6] On the idea of expanding the historical imagination, see Quentin Skinner, *Liberty before Liberalism* (Cambridge: Cambridge University Press, 1998), pp. 112–17. "The history of philosophy, and perhaps especially of moral, social, and political philosophy, is there to prevent us from becoming too readily bewitched" by how things happen to be and how our ideas happen to now stand (116).

[7] Brian Barry, *Culture and Equality: An Egalitarian Critique of Multiculturalism* (Cambridge, Mass.: Harvard University Press, 2001).

[8] John Rawls, *Lectures on the History of Political Philosophy*, Samuel Richard Freeman, ed. (Cambridge, Mass.: Belknap Press of Harvard University Press, 2007), p. xvii.

[9] J. G. A. Pocock, *The Machiavellian Moment* (Princeton: Princeton University Press, 1975).

and this is a stylized history. I mean it to provide an alternative to the existing stylized histories of liberalism's emergence: those centered on neo-Roman republicanism, possessive individualism, the wars of religion, the rise of scientific knowledge, bourgeois revolution, the Enlightenment, and so on. These have each captured something real and helped to open up intellectual possibilities in the present; I hope this one does, too.

They have done so partly by changing our sense of what lies between the especially prominent landmarks and filling in some textured detail about the surrounding terrain. Such detail makes the map more vivid and memorable. It also allows us to situate the major landmarks differently. We already think we know what the biggest pieces of the terrain look like. Readers are far more likely to have fixed views about Hobbes than about ancient constitutionalists. Studying them, however, can help us see some of his arguments in new ways. In this book I am interested in the monarchomachs partly because of how their legal theories help us situate Montesquieu's; in Molesworth partly because his ancient-constitutionalist Whiggism illuminates Locke's contractarian Whiggism by contrast; in Tracy partly because of his reaction to Montesquieu and his relationship to Constant. I do hope to spark readers' interest in those lesser-known figures in their own right; but an important aim of the detail in Part II is to make the map of the past sufficiently vivid as to compete with the maps that have already captured theorists' imaginations. That demands some unfamiliar material alongside new accounts of familiar works. Similarly, I will discuss some less-familiar events and controversies involving the familiar thinkers, when these involve group life or state centralization. Jesuits, Freemasons, and the Order of the Cincinnati sit alongside the associations studied by Tocqueville in the full story of associations and the history of liberal thought. The centralization of state power over the course of early modernity was the object of sustained theoretical engagement in a way that is hard to remember once the process ends and philosophical inquiry shifts to the question of what states should *do* with their power. The history of associational life and of state centralization help bring to light different features of the intellectual past from, say, the history of the wars of religion or of the rise of the bourgeoisie.

In particular, I hope to displace understandings of the history of liberal thought that focus overwhelmingly on social contract theory. In the contractarian model, individual persons jointly will a complete, unified state into being, and this is the fundamental fact of social organization. Intermediate, transnational, and pre-state groups are generally invisible. This, I will argue in Part II, was a deliberate and controversial position in early modernity, setting contractarianism against the whole family of ancient constitutionalist views. Contractarianism was (among other things) a particular stance in arguments about the relationships among individuals, groups, and the state. It took that stance in part by denying that groups could precede the state; individuals formed the state *ex nihilo*. But that controversial stand gradually turned into a kind of accepted mythology, one that obscures from view both ancient constitutionalist ideas and the intermediate institutions around which those ideas were organized. The resulting combination of prejudices—that liberalism straightforwardly develops out of social contract theory, that it simply is a philosophy of individuals and states—hides pluralism from view. It allows for the all too common view that intermediate groups were an idiosyncratic concern of Montesquieu's, and voluntary associations of Tocqueville's, of no particular enduring or theoretical interest. I do not deny the importance of social contract theory. But by situating it alongside ancient constitutionalism and showing that contractarians were acutely aware of intermediacy and group life, I hope to unsettle the map of the past that contractarianism has made so familiar.

In Part II I not only use history to elaborate the distinction between rationalism and pluralism; I use the ideas of rationalism and pluralism to sharpen our understandings of the thinkers surveyed. Those ideas allow us to see unfamiliar themes in some familiar works, and to see some continuities that might otherwise escape us. They point us toward some unifying ideas within the work of one author or another, and draw attention to certain points of difference between thinkers. I suggest, for example, that we can better understand Montesquieu, his relationship to contemporaries such as Voltaire, and his relationship to later liberals such as Constant and Tocqueville, with a firm grasp on ancient constitutionalism and of the possibility of pluralism.

The book's concluding chapters build on the social theories developed in Part I as well as the history studied in Part II. Chapter 10 takes as its point of departure the degree to which the theorists from Part II were arguing about intermediate bodies as actors in politics, able to shape and reshape the constitutional order; they were not only debating private religious freedom or freedom of association. In light of that, Chapter 11 asks whether associations are quite so non-state-like as we might have thought. And the Conclusion argues that all that has come before leaves unavailable any ultimate harmonization of rationalist and pluralist approaches to freedom.

In order to see even the possibility of such irresolvability, we have to resist easy narratives of harmony. The study of politics and association can easily take, and has often taken, a Panglossian turn: associations inculcate civic virtue and encourage levels of social trust which in turn mean that politics is less conflictual; such relatively consensual politics in turn is less prone to persecutionist politics toward intermediate groups, including unpopular minority groups. (This harmonious vision is sometimes called neo-Tocquevillean, but it is far from Tocqueville's own view.) Something like this might sometimes be true; virtuous cycles can exist in social life. But it is not at all the only possibility.

Associations and groups often protect the liberty of their members by taking an adversarial stance toward the state or toward other groups. The same institutional resources that make them effective defenders of their members' freedom against outsiders enhance the internal power of group elites or dominant subgroups. That very adversarial stance increases group members' suspicion of state power and of outsiders, and increases the power of group leaders. In turn, states trying to protect citizens against local or customary power often overreach (whether inadvertently or maliciously), restrict legitimate associational freedom, and leave groups less effective counterweights in the future. The virtues of group life include groups' ability to protect their members and to counterbalance against intrusive state power; but that ability depends on normative and institutional features of group life that increase the risks of internal unfreedom. Dynamics such as these are elaborated over the whole course of the book and especially in Chapter 3; together they generate good reason to doubt that Panglossian belief in the natural harmony of legitimate associations and liberal democratic states.

As I hope this overview suggests, this is primarily a book of and about political theory, but not sharply limited to that subdiscipline. The problems of how human freedom, associational and group life, and state power interrelate are problems of the social world, not only problems about how ideas hang together. The book depicts the development of liberal ideas as entangled with changes in the social and political world (not a mere effect of them, but not independent of them either), and the content of liberal ideas as involving claims about how the world works. I argue that disagreements among liberals are often disagreements about the shape of the social world rather than about first principles, and that the ultimate irresolvability of the pluralist–rationalist tension owes as much to social as to philosophical difficulties. Although the book is primarily written for political theorists, I do hope that it is accessible to other social theorists and social scientists interested in these same fundamental questions about pluralism, centralization, group life, and state power.

Boundaries

The remainder of this introduction concerns the scope of the book: which cases and kinds of language are included, which are not, and why. The reader who is interested in getting on to the argument will want to skip this section, returning to it as one concern or another arises.

On Liberalism

This is a book within and about liberal political theory. What I mean by that will mainly be explained by demonstration; the book is in part an argument about what the liberal tradition consists of. But it may help to begin with some qualifications about the uses of the idea and the word "liberal."

Contemporary political philosophers have sometimes failed to respect liberalism's boundedness. Any argument that seemed to provide a correct account of a right or a question of distributive justice might have the word "liberal" hung on it, regardless of its political content.[10] In discussions of the subdisciplinary distinction between theories that descend from so-called analytic Anglo-American philosophy via Rawls and those that descend from continental European critical theory, one sometimes sees the former described interchangeably as "liberal" and "normative," as if all normative views were liberal ones. The tendency to think that any apparently-correct normative view could be termed *liberal* sometimes goes with the thought that any apparently *incorrect* view therefore *cannot* be a liberal view. So a theorist's conclusion that, say, rationalist autonomy is rightly privileged over pluralist toleration, or vice versa, has sometimes led to the thought that one is a basic liberal value and the other is not.

In this book I will be studying the tension at the heart of liberal theory about intermediate groups. I think that the liberal tension is the right tension, and that these problems are the right problems.[11] But liberalism is, as it were, one of the party positions of western modernity, not the whole of normative thought about politics. The best working out of a question within the terms set by the liberal tradition may not be (surely will not *always* be) the best way of working it out altogether. There could be other books written about the theories of association in conservatism or socialism, to name other party ideas: a study of the conflict between guild socialism and democratic centralism, for example, or one about the choice between using religion as a pillar of conservative corporatist state order and insulating religious institutions from corrupting political entanglements.

As is true within liberalism, the socialist and conservative equivalents of the pluralist–rationalist divide might well turn on a degree of ambivalence about the modern state. Like liberalism, conservatism and socialism as party ideas

---

[10] Liberalism's boundedness can be ignored by those who reject it, as well; indeed I think that is even more common. "Liberalism" has long been a convenient name for whatever aspect of modernity or western societies one happened to dislike. Something similar has happened to the use of the word "neoliberalism," which has lost any specific meaning it once had.

[11] Compare Martha C. Nussbaum, "The Future of Feminist Liberalism," 74(2) *Proceedings and Addresses of the American Philosophical Association* 47–79, Nov. 2000, p. 68; the full quotation is given as the epigraph to Part III. I think that what Nussbaum says about the specific case of the family here is also true for the general case of associations and intermediate groups.

are *modern* ideas, situated within the state and making arguments about how its power should be deployed. But, again like liberalism, each includes some views suspicious of state power. While many socialists of course support the use of central state power to remedy economic inequality, some who look to the farmed commons before enclosure and to the medieval labor guilds emphasize the early modern state's function as the engine of capitalist primitive accumulation, and the centralized modern state's tendency to entrench the power of privileged capital. The latter wing of socialist thought thus tends toward a kind of pluralism. Conservatives are often the party of law and order, of the state's armed forces and security forces. But they are also the party of the rural, aristocratic, and church elites that find their positions seriously threatened by the bureaucratic state, of the personal relationships in village life and the local parish that the bureaucratic state seems to disrupt.[12] I mention these possible parallels only to acknowledge topics that lie beyond this book's boundaries. Within those boundaries I will often use "rationalism" and "pluralism" as shorthand for "rationalist liberalism" or "pluralist liberalism"; but the rationalist and pluralist styles are found in doctrines besides liberalism.

I will be arguing that liberalism consists of more than one thing, not that it encompasses everything. It is a particular constellation of particular goods and values; it is not every good or value. I will be examining a tension I maintain to be central to liberalism rather than studying liberalism's boundaries, edges, or rivals. But it has all of those. This also means that when I argue that the set of liberal reasons for deference to group pluralism in one case outweigh the liberal reasons against it (or vice versa), I am *not* denying that the outweighed values are liberal ones.

Europe

Another way in which I mean to openly acknowledge liberalism's particularity is this: this book is western and European. It surveys neither thinkers nor political phenomena from outside Europe or modern European-derived settler states. This is not unusual in political theory, though it is slowly and happily becoming less usual. The problems I study here are hardly alien to the rest of the world. The complex relationships among personal freedom, social group life, and political power are in many ways generic; they have probably become more so since the European model of the sovereign state was formally imposed on the whole world. The dissident seeks a freedom from custom, from an

---

[12] Robert Nisbet, *The Quest for Community* (Oxford: Oxford University Press, 1953), offers a strongly pluralist conservatism, and an analysis of state centralization and rationalization that shares a great deal with that offered by pluralist liberalism. Nisbet, however, treats those trends in state organization as basically alien to the conservative values he celebrates; there is nothing like a rationalist conservatism to be found in the book.

oppressive family, from group norms, from local power; the association or minority seeks freedom from a state that seeks to intrude on customary, religious, local, and family life. States suppress religious groups that they take to be obstacles to a kind of liberating progress, and the members of those religious groups seek liberation from that suppression. These dynamics are certainly present in, for example, many Islamic countries today. European colonialism in Africa and Asia was rife with complex interactions between the rationalizing order colonial authorities sought to impose, often in the name of freedom from local custom and hierarchy, and the norms and customs of local group life. The justifications and structures of imperial rule sometimes shifted between a rationalizing, codifying liberation from custom and a shoring up of local hierarchies through indirect rule.[13] I have not sprinkled the text with inexpert discussions of such cases. For one thing, I do not think they should be treated inexpertly; a few casual references seem worse than none at all.

More importantly, I mean to emphasize the European provenance and development of both liberal political ideas and the institutions those ideas have been about. The organizational form of corporate group life, including religious life, that emerged in the Middle Ages, and the crystallization of the modern Weberian state some centuries later were developments within Europe, indeed primarily within Catholic (later Catholic and Protestant) Europe. The medieval birth of intermediacy and the early modern emergence of the state formed the social and political setting within which modern political ideologies, including liberalism, took shape. This is not a claim about cultural relativism but about historical and geographic specificity. Genealogies or admissions of specificity are not synonymous with "debunking." The rise of a language of liberal universalism, of abstract doctrines of rights applicable everywhere, sometimes flattens our sense of what the liberal tradition has consisted of, and of what liberal ideas can consist of now. It leads us to overemphasize the dyadic relationship of individual and state, both of which seem abstract and universally necessary, rather than the triadic relations of individual, state, and a plurality of social groups that seem unavoidably locally specific. The general exclusion of non-European thinkers and facts from this book is not an assertion that the European experience can be taken as universal, but precisely an attempt to learn from its particularity.

Economic and Political Associations

The core set of associations and groups under consideration here generally does not include political parties or interest groups, secondary associations

---

[13] See Karuna Mantena, *Alibis of Empire* (Princeton: Princeton University Press, 2010).

primarily oriented toward the capture or control of the state.[14] Neither does it include labor unions or commercial corporations, bodies that aim to represent their members to the state and to the marketplace.[15] Similar boundaries are typically drawn around the concept "civil society"; it is the social sphere that is neither oriented toward the state and political activities nor toward the market and economic activities.[16] I have some worries about using the concept "civil society" in this way, but the basic boundaries around my discussion are the same. The primary normative focus of the book is not organized groups' struggle for control of *common* or *external* space—the state, the market—but their potential exercise of control over their own members. There are undoubtedly implications for, e.g., the internal governance of trade unions and their ability to compel members to pay dues or to strike. But a church, a university, a town, or a cultural group is *primarily* concerned with internal questions, whereas a union or a political party is only instrumentally so, seeking internal procedures that will aid in the pursuit of external goals. These external projects are very likely to involve normative questions far beyond how the groups treat their members.[17] A serious normative study of parties, lobby groups, and the kinds of voluntary associations that exist primarily to advocate political positions, or of corporations and unions, would take the book far into the theory of democracy or economic justice, and leave room for little else.[18]

---

[14] See Nancy Rosenblum, *On the Side of Angels: an Appreciation of Parties and Partisanship* (Princeton: Princeton University Press, 2008), for a consideration of parties' status among the associations of civil society.

[15] At this writing, cases are moving through the United States court system about whether for-profit companies can corporately exercise religious freedom; see, e.g., *Sebelius v Hobby Lobby Stores, Inc.* A full treatment of questions like that would require considering both the kinds of questions about associational religious freedom I consider in this book and the kinds of questions about justice in employer–employee relations that I don't.

[16] For a discussion and partial critique of this conception of civil society, see, e.g., Michael Walzer, "The Civil Society Argument," in *Thinking Politically* (New Haven: Yale University Press, 2007); and "Civil Society and the State," in *Politics and Passion* (New Haven: Yale University Press, 2004).

[17] This boundary marks an important difference between the present book and Richard Boyd's important study of problems of related questions, *Uncivil Society: The Perils of Pluralism and the Making of Modern Liberalism* (Lanham, M.D.: Lexington Books, 2004). He is centrally concerned with the problem of faction. More fundamentally, Boyd sees liberal constitutionalism as growing out of an anti-pluralist tradition with roots in Hobbes; I see it as grounded in the pluralist tradition that includes Montesquieu. I am greatly indebted to Boyd's work, but I think his overemphasis on Hobbes and Locke and neglect of Montesquieu leads him astray.

[18] While I do not endorse the bright-line distinction Thomas Christiano offers—"The right of association fully extends to all joint activities except economic activities . . . Economic association is characterized by the general presence of incentives to defraud and exploit others in these relationships and so they do not come under the freedom of association"—I mean to keep the argument in this book agnostic on the status of economic associations, and *compatible* with a view like his. Thomas Christiano, *The Constitution of Equality* (Oxford: Oxford University Press, 2008), p. 147. The reasons I offer for mainly excluding economic associations and political parties from consideration do not depend on such a categorical distinction.

Workplace relations often include two adversarial intermediate groups: the corporate firm that acts as employer, and the labor union that represents employees. Both constrain individual workers: to follow workplace rules and managerial directives, to become a union member and to obey union directives. Rather than the relationships among a state, a group, and the persons who inhabit both, we have relations among a state, workers, and *two adversarial groups*, both of which can regulate individual workers. A union's ability to control its members strengthens its countervailing power against firms; any state regulation of its internal rules will have to be attentive to workers' liberty as individual persons *as well as* that balance of countervailing forces. The four-body problem of states regulating intermediate groups that stand in countervailing relations to each other is extremely complicated in ways that risk confounding the analysis of other intermediate groups. Furthermore, again, states' regulation of employment relations is not (and should not be) strictly about the interests, well-being, or liberty of currently employed workers in a given firm. The interests of consumers, would-be entrants into the labor market, and all of those affected by macroeconomic conditions will also figure into the calculations, and indeed may be primary.

I have one additional reason for mostly excluding economic groups. The distinction between pluralist and rationalist liberalisms has sometimes been conflated with distinctions between normative theories of political economy. The most influential such conflation was offered by F. A. Hayek, who treated the rationalist tradition within liberalism as more or less equivalent to an attraction to economic planning, and the pluralist tradition largely equivalent to the market liberalism that values the spontaneous economic order of commercial society.[19] I have argued against this conflation elsewhere.[20] It interferes with clear understandings of *both* the welfarist/market liberal distinction *and* the pluralist/rationalist distinction. As an important aim of this book is to elaborate the latter distinction, I omit those secondary organizations that most demand to be analyzed in terms of economic justice.[21]

That said, parties, corporations, and unions come up from time to time. The development of both legal practice and liberal thought about groups was sometimes centrally concerned with parties, factions, and lobbies, or guilds,

---

[19] F. A. Hayek, *The Constitution of Liberty* (Chicago: University of Chicago Press, 1960), ch. 4.

[20] Jacob T. Levy, "Liberalism's Divide After Socialism And Before," 20(1) *Social Philosophy and Policy* 278–97, 2003.

[21] Still, it is worth noting that commercial corporations and labor unions may sometimes be neglected for some of the same reasons as associations and social groups. Normative work on political economy too often proceeds as if the relevant questions involved only individuals and states, as if an entire theory of political economy could be deduced from the morally valid claims of individuals, whether as property-owners or as persons owed guarantees of resources. Commercial corporations and labor unions are ubiquitous features of free societies, just as non-commercial associations are, and modeling those societies' political economies with only individuals and states is sure to lead to confusion.

or mercantile corporations and combinations, and it would be a distortion of that history to exclude them entirely. Indeed, the distinction I am drawing between groups that are internal in focus and those that are external can't be projected back in history indefinitely. While it might make sense to talk about the modern trade union as primarily external in orientation, the internal/external distinction is much less clear in the case of the medieval trade guild, probably so much so as to make the distinction inapplicable.

Moreover, the groups that are the focus of the project—churches and religious groups, ethnic and cultural groups, voluntary associations, universities—inevitably have an external as well as an internal face. They often externally organize as interest groups, sometimes as political parties, and sometimes as trade unions or commercial corporations or networks. Indeed, the fact that even internally focused groups engage in external power or resource competitions is highly relevant to a full analysis of power and freedom within them, as we shall see. Therefore, parties and the rest necessarily, though indirectly, arise in the course of normative as well as historical discussions.

On the other hand, levels of government below the center—towns and cities, or the provinces and states of a federation—*do* lie within the book's boundaries, for three related reasons. First, the sharp distinction between non-state groups and local governments cannot be projected backward in time through the book's historical scope. It is not until the eighteenth or nineteenth century that municipal corporations are clearly distinguishable from incorporated non-state entities; through the Middle Ages, cities, guilds, and universities were all categorically similar legal entities. Second, a clear pattern has emerged in the history of liberal and constitutional thought: suspicion of intermediate groups and support for state power means support for *central* state power and generally goes with a skepticism of decentralization, urban liberty, or federalism. Conversely, suspicion of state power and support for intermediate groups usually accompanies sympathy for cities and provinces, for federalism, for decentralization. While the pattern of pluralists' and rationalists' views on economic questions is muddy, the pattern of their attitudes toward federalism and local government is much clearer. Third, that pattern in the intellectual history turns out to be understandable and revealing. Many of the concerns rationalist liberals have about intermediate groups—local prejudices, excessive attachment to custom, conformism, a kind of insular power of in-group elites—also arise with respect to local and provincial governments. The same is true for what pluralist liberals have hoped for from intermediate groups, not least that they would provide an organized counterweight against central state power. To be sure, local and provincial governments are morally different from voluntary associations in important ways;

but there are good reasons that sympathy (or antipathy) toward group life and toward local or provincial government often go hand in hand.

Formal, Informal, and Governmental Groups

The book will be concerned with both formal, institutional groups and unstructured, unincorporated ones. It moves freely back and forth between, say, voluntary associations and cultural groups. I take my cue from the central case of religious groups, which vary tremendously in their organization. The Roman Catholic, Anglican, and Mormon churches are hierarchical and epis-copal while a Congregational church is internally democratic. But the range extends farther than that. Congregationalism still has a formal structure. Islam, or even a subset of it such as "American Sunni Islam," is quite different. An individual mosque is a corporate entity; but the larger religious commu-nity lacks institutions with, e.g., the authority to settle doctrinal questions. Individual scholars and judges issue opinions that carry greater or lesser weight, partly based on their institutional affiliations, but conflicting opin-ions are common and persistent. While Islam is populated with institutions and organizations, in most countries it is not *itself* an institution or an organ-ization in the way that most Christian denominations are. Diasporic Judaism has traditionally resembled Islam in this sense, though the American Jewish movements modeled on Protestant denominations, Reform and Conserva-tism, offer a kind of exception. If, as I think, the case of religion is paradigmatic for liberal thought about groups and the state, then that thought must include both formal incorporated groups and unincorporated ones. Any account of groups that is broad enough to encompass the whole range of phenomena at stake in debates about religious liberty cannot draw narrow boundaries about institutional form.

The sharp differentiation between associations and cultural groups some-times derives from an unstated denigration of the latter. Associations are formed by the voluntary decisions of free persons; ethnic and cultural groups are ascriptive, unchosen, pre-reflective, and a-rational if not irrational. Volun-tary associations are the stuff of a modern and liberal "civil society," which can only be formed once tribal identities are overcome. (We will return to this thought in the next section.) In the context of American political thought in particular, associations are the Tocquevillean schools of democracy; ethnic and cultural identities are the *pluribus* that must be melted into an *unum*.

The social world is not carved up so neatly. The associational sphere is pervasively ethnic and cultural; ethnic and cultural groups form partial social worlds populated by associations. The cases of Islam and Judaism mentioned previously are exemplary here. Those living within something as amorphous as an ethnic or cultural group routinely form discrete associations with which to sustain, transmit, celebrate, reform, or simply inhabit their group identities and group norms. Religious groups, too, are pervasively ethnic and cultural. In multi-ethnic and multi-religious liberal societies, Islamic mosques and Catholic churches alike are often differentiated by country of origin: one Pakistani and one Lebanese, one Irish and one Italian. Orthodox Christian churches are formally distinguished along national lines: Serbian, Greek, Russian. In the United States, many Protestant denominations are sharply (if sometimes unofficially) divided into black and white sub-denominations. And the senses in which Judaism is a cultural, an ethnic, and a religious identity are famously complicated to disentangle.

Lon Fuller plausibly argued that all intermediate groups balance an ethic of shared commitment—that is, a moral and an emotional attachment to a sense of mission and purpose and, often, a particular set of primary rules—with a principle of legality.[22] He suggested that there is an all-else-equal tendency for groups to gradually shift from the first to the second over time: they become more formal and more institutionalized, the pendulum swinging back either in response to an external crisis or because the increasingly bureaucratic organization becomes an umbrella under which new associations of shared commitment arise. Although Fuller does not invoke it, the following case perhaps epitomizes the tendency: a bureaucratic Catholic Church that had lost much of its internal religious energy to corruption and worldly affairs, faced with the external crisis of the Reformation, was internally revitalized by the growth of counter-Reformation groups of shared commitment: new seminaries, new monastic orders, and above all the new Society of Jesus (the Jesuits) and its educational institutions. Formality and informality are likely to be a spectrum rather than a dichotomy; any given intermediate group will likely move around on the spectrum. Groups tend to become populated with internal groups; ethnic and cultural groups fill up with formal associations; formal institutions bureaucratize and then fill up with less-bureaucratic and less-formal groups of shared commitment. This leaves little reason to sharply differentiate intermediate groups on the basis of their formal organizational structure, to treat more-formal and less-formal as morally or sociologically different in kind.

The Ambiguity of Civil Society

This book is mainly about what has come to be called "civil society" in the social science and social theory of the past few decades: the sphere of secondary or intermediate associations (as distinct from the primary association of

---

[22] Lon Fuller, "Two Principles of Human Association," in J. Roland Pennock and John W. Chapman, eds, *Nomos XI: Voluntary Associations* (New York: Atherton Press, 1969).

the family) that are neither primarily actors on the market like firms, nor parts of the state.

There is, however, an ambiguity embedded in the phrase "civil society," one that relates very closely to the ambiguities within liberalism we will be examining. As a result, "civil society" itself will not be a particularly clarifying category for the analysis.[23] The "civil society" to which John Locke and the early Enlightenment thinkers appealed was the civil society that found its origins in medieval cities: bounded political communities subject to the rule of law and promising equality before the law (at least compared with the surrounding feudal order). The civil society of contractarianism was the city writ large, as large as the new modern state. It trumped the barbaric feudal rules of the past, and the contentious infamy of religious jurisdictions or religious wars. Civil society was *civic* society, the society of the *civitas*, both in the medieval sense of the freestanding city and in the Renaissance sense of the republic of the ancient Roman city-state. Far from being a sphere fundamentally distinct from the state, it was a way of conceptualizing and idealizing the sphere of governance, based on the model of the city. It is this sense of "civil society" that Antony Black contrasted to the associational world of guilds in his study of medieval and modern thought, *Guilds and Civil Society*; in order to avoid terminological confusion, the book was later republished under the title *Guild and State*.[24] That civil society was an antecedent of the current use of the phrase in at least this respect: it necessarily reduced churches to something like a non-coercive role. Within a civil society, a church could not be much more than a voluntary association as we understand it. But it would have struck the thinkers of the era as perverse to *identify* civil society with institutionalized churches while *distinguishing* it from a law-governed polity.

"Civil society" in this sense suggests the self-governing city or city-state, free of feudal power or coercive religious jurisdiction. In early modernity, this urban idea of a complete political society with rough equality before the law and excluding religious violence became generalized to the much larger entities we now think of as nation-states: the Hobbesian, Weberian,

---

[23] For an account that is similar at some points to the one in this section, see Charles Taylor, "Invoking Civil Society," in *Philosophical Arguments* (Cambridge, Mass.: Harvard University Press, 1995). Taylor's L-stream (for Locke) and M-stream (for Montesquieu) in the idea of civil society generally parallel the rationalist and pluralist conceptions of liberalism, respectively.

[24] Antony Black, *Guilds and Civil Society in European Political Thought from the Twelfth Century to the Present* (London: Methuen, 1984), reissued as *Guild and State: European Political Thought from the Twelfth Century to the Present* (New Brunswick, N.J.: Transaction, 2003). This retitling exemplifies the ambiguities discussed in this section: "civil society" can mean anything from an associational sphere defined as existing outside the state to a particular kind of state defined in opposition to a private associational sphere.

Westphalian states that overpowered coercive church jurisdiction and suppressed the possibility of religious civil war. And so, in the writings of someone like Locke, civil society is *political* society, the self-contained and unified political society that can apply a general law and that excludes external (e.g. church) claims of political power. There was an important sense in which that society offered freedom—freedom from the inquisitors and their Protestant counterparts. That is, civil society-as-state *suppressed* the power of intermediate institutions.

Even Locke, who (exceptionally among contractarians) understood society to have been formed separately from the state, does not alter this pattern. Locke's society functions in his argument to choose a government, and, if needed, to reclaim the authority to do so. It is unitary and political. It is not pluralistic and extra-political, as we today think of civil society as being.

That contemporary meaning required the ability to distinguish between society and the polity: for example, the idea that Scottish society persists, in changed form, even after there is no more Scottish state, or that English society survived the regime changes of 1648, 1660, and 1688. This idea was certainly not a modern invention; medieval Christendom was a society of sorts that was not bound within any single polity, and the Italy that Machiavelli wished to see liberated was, too. But the idea had been obscured by both the rise of the absolutist state and the philosophy of contractarian civil society. Its re-emergence in eighteenth-century social thought encompassed many ideas that strike us as different: a sense of what we call cultures, including national cultures; a sense of a social order that could change by, for example, becoming progressively more polite and refined, *without* a change in political regime; and a sense of an *economic* order that could likewise change, and that was conceptually distinct from the public fisc.

All of these ideas are present in Montesquieu's *Spirit of the Laws*, which almost never uses the phrase "civil society."[25] They are imported and refined in the work of Adam Ferguson, who prominently does. His *Essay Concerning the History of Civil Society* is in large part a (partly conjectural) history of *society*, in which forms of political organization are not foundational, in which contractarianism is devastatingly rejected, and in which social–cultural–economic orders change over time and place, sometimes bringing political change in their wake. Ferguson and Adam Smith helped to pioneer the idea of social spheres distinct from political society: a society, and an economy, that could persist over time and survive regime changes. That extra-political social order

---

[25] For Montesquieu on civil society, see Melvin Richter, "Montesquieu and the concept of civil society," 3(6) *The European Legacy: Toward New Paradigms* 33–41, 1998.

could change dramatically, of course, and its changes over historical time were Ferguson's and Smith's primary interests; its conceptual independence from the political order was merely a prerequisite to clear understanding.[26]

Civil society thus became the social(–cultural–economic) order that underpins the kind of legal–political order that had once gone by that name. And therefore, in part, civil society is the market economy, and the history of civil society is the history of commercial society. This was not necessarily politically opposed to the older Lockean understanding; free contracting agents with equality before the law engaged in (among other things) market transactions. If economic civil society underpinned legal civil society, the latter also facilitated the former. The two were conjoined in Hegel's concept of civil society, described by Marx as *bourgeois* civil society—a near-redundancy, when one thinks about the *bourg* and the *civitas*, the *burgher* and the citizen. Marx and Hegel used the phrase to refer to the market, under an appropriate legal regime: the legal regime that recognizes free bourgeois citizens, legally autonomous and interacting with each other as equals.

The contemporary sense of "civil society" is as yet nowhere to be found. Locke and the contractarians, Ferguson, Hegel, and Marx, all used the phrase to include *at least one of* what we now call "state" and "market," the spheres that contemporary definitions of "civil society" ordinarily exclude at the outset. While Montesquieu, Ferguson, and Smith all recognizably analyzed aspects of social order outside the narrowly political or economic, none of them identified a pluralistic sphere of associations and organizations as constitutive of that order.

Ernest Gellner has argued for a fundamental continuity among these older meanings, and between them and our own. Thanks to the modern state's triumph over other coercive agencies, it is able to establish a social order in which individuals may detach themselves from traditional intermediate groupings: family and clan, province and county, guild and church. This frees each to act individualistically in the marketplace, and to act associationally in society.

> Modular man [Gellner's description for civil society's inhabitant] is capable of combining into effective associations and institutions, *without* these being total, multi-stranded, underwritten by ritual and made stable through being linked to a whole inside set of relationships, all of these being tied in with each other and so immobilized. He can combine into specific-purpose, *ad-hoc*, limited associations, without binding himself by some blood ritual.[27]

---

[26] See J. G. A. Pocock, "Cambridge Paradigms and Scotch Philosophers: a study of the relations between the civic humanist and the civil jurisprudential interpretation of eighteenth-century political thought," in Istvan Hont and Michael Ignatieff, eds, *Wealth and Virtue* (Cambridge: Cambridge University Press, 1983), discussing the transition "from the civic to the civil," p. 240.

[27] Ernest Gellner, *Conditions of Liberty: Civil Society and Its Rivals* (New York: Allen Lane/Penguin Press, 1994), p. 99.

Gellner insists that the triumph of the modern state was one precondition for the emergence of a truly civil society, one in which group ties may be changed "without shame or stigma . . . without formalities, ritual, trauma, or treason. This was not so in days of clans and lineages. The total national community is still very significant—or rather, it is more significant than it has ever been before— but its sub-units have lost their potency."[28] Only when group life becomes irrelevant for political and military power, because the state has trumped all sub-state competitors, can man become truly modular, able to enter, form, and leave group associations as a free agent.[29] Gellner's unified account depicts a social world of liberal agents creating new voluntary associations as easily, and with the same rules, as they create economic firms or political parties.

Gellner insists too much on the ephemerality of associations. In civil society as we know it, vast portions of the associational sphere are populated by ethnic, cultural, linguistic, and religious groups. As we noted in the previous section, religious groups are themselves routinely ethnoculturally differenti- ated. Even beyond churches, the sphere of formal associations is filled with groups that have objects besides those communal identities but are *differenti- ated* by language, culture, religion, and so on: Brandeis, Brigham Young, Bob Jones, and Howard Universities; fraternal societies such as the Knights of Columbus, the Ancient Order of the Hibernians, and the Orange Lodge; the YMCA, YWCA, YMHA, and YWHA; a vast array of ethnically differentiated professional associations; and so on. Voluntary associations routinely build on and draw from the group identities that Gellner sometimes imagines to have been superseded.

But Gellner sees, in a way that the civil society triumphalists of the past twenty years have sometimes not, that the modern pluralistic and extra- political sphere of voluntary associations is entangled with older meanings of civil society. For our purposes, Lockean and statist civil society—the tri- umph of the nation-state over religious and other sub-state coercive powers— points the way toward rationalist liberalism. Our freedom is, in part, our freedom from group power, secured by a publicly accessible and rationally determined system of state law. And our freedom is also in part the freedom of *bourgeois* civil society, the freedom of formally legally equal persons to

---

[28] Gellner, *Conditions of Liberty*, p. 88.

[29] This argument connects directly with his more famous account of nationalism. The modern industrial economy demands modular workers rather than traditional craftsmen, workers who can shift locale, sector, and job in response to changing economic conditions. This in turn requires modular, all-purpose schooling rather than specialized apprenticeships. And so there is tremendous pressure for literacy in homogenized and centralized languages, in place of an older world of constantly varying spoken regional dialects; this engenders a kind of competitive scramble to identify and demarcate whole languages that can be the foundations of whole political– economic–educational orders. See Gellner, *Nations and Nationalism* (Ithaca: Cornell University Press, 1983).

contract—a freedom that, it was eventually understood, included the freedom to form associations. Even that is enough to point toward pluralist liberalism; it lies behind the model of the pure theory of free association. What I would add is that our freedom is also, in part, the freedom to inhabit the extra-, pre-, or non-state social orders that make up "society" in the eighteenth-century sense, and that "civil" society draws on those orders as well as on the statist and the *bourgeois* traditions. In short, as between rationalist and pluralist conceptions of liberalism, we do not face a choice between the state and civil society. We face a set of mutual entanglements and complications that are reproduced within the concept of "civil society" itself.

Something similar could be said of Jürgen Habermas' treatment of civil society as the space in which public opinion can be formed. From the seventeenth-century coffee house to the twentieth-century social movement, Habermas emphasizes civil society's contribution to discussion about public questions. That is a useful way of bringing together several of the meanings of "civil society." It manages at once to emphasize the social rather than statist character of civil society and to link it to the emergence of bourgeois liberal, and eventually democratic, politics that is responsive to public discussion. But it also, necessarily, de-emphasizes the internal lives of associations: what people do in them that is *not* oriented toward policy and politics.

This genealogical mixture of contractarian politics, market economics, extra-political culture, and so on is the primary reason why, for the rest of this book, I will rarely use the phrase "civil society" to describe the plurality of associations, institutions, and groups under consideration. There is one further reason for the avoidance. Even among those who today use "civil society" to describe an associational sphere, there is sometimes sharp resistance to including churches and religious groups. This is a legacy of the old contractarian sense that "civil society" was established in part by the exclusion of religious jurisdiction and sectarian conflict. Perhaps it is the case, as Robert Putnam and his colleagues found in Italy,[30] that membership in the church and associated religious societies lacks the political and sociological benefits that membership in other associations has to offer; I have no view on that kind of question. But churches and religious associations are a part of the phenomena this book is about, and centrally so; they are not a borderline case. To avoid confusion, I will mostly avoid using a phrase that at least some readers would take to exclude them.

---

[30] Robert Putnam, with Robert Leonardi and Raffaella Y. Nanetti, *Making Democracy Work: Civic Traditions in Modern Italy* (Princeton: Princeton University Press, 1993).

Part I

"For political philosophy's habitual, and it seems ineliminable, dependence on the urgency of political questions which are not in the first instance philosophical, is of a piece with its insistence, when at all interesting, on being both normative and impure. It is normative at least in the sense that first-order moral and political disagreement with the author can relevantly motivate disagreement with his philosophy, and impure in the sense that materials from non-philosophical sources—an involvement with history or the social sciences, for instance—are likely to play a more than illustrative part in the argument."

Bernard Williams, "Political Philosophy and the Analytical
Tradition," in *Philosophy as a Humanistic Discipline*, p. 155.

1

Freedom, Associations, and Uniformity

The Setting

The most familiar subject matter of liberal analyses of freedom is a state's law. States prohibit or mandate speech, belief, or action of one sort or another, for one reason or another. The agents of the state coercively enforce those rules against individual speakers, believers, and actors, punishing them for doing or for forbearing to do. Liberal political philosophers debate when and whether such restrictions are morally problematic, politically unreasonable, or constitutionally illegitimate: whether the state may restrict liberty for the sake of the moral improvement of the person restricted; whether justified rules count as restrictions of liberty; whether liberty is centrally threatened by the content of the rules or by arbitrariness of enforcement; and so on. The questions asked by liberal theory are sometimes construed as describing moral confrontations between an abstract individual rights-bearer and the state. The lone heretic standing against a religiously oppressive state, obeying the demand of her conscience that she can do no other, is a liberal hero if anyone is.

But freedom of religion is almost always exercised in groups, no matter how individual the conscience may be; both the orthodox and the schismatic congregate. The individual who stands alone, moreover, does not confront an abstract state; he or she confronts a state that may have been captured or influenced by one church or another, using it to enforce orthodoxy.

This book is a liberal study of freedom, but it does not focus on the lone person facing a state law. At the broadest level, it studies questions of the following kind: Do the internal rules governing members of intermediate associations and non-state groups violate the freedom of their members? Do state restrictions on such groups, including those aimed at internal rules or the internal power structures that enforce them, violate the freedom of the groups' members, enhance it, or both? Do intermediate groups serve to protect the freedom of their members (or of others in society) against the state? Should the state protect persons against domination by the groups to which they belong?

Questions of this sort have become increasingly visible in politics and in various literatures in political theory and social science over the past generation. The rules and customs governing women's dress in some types of Islam have been characterized as restrictions on women's freedom, and prohibitions of various forms of *hijab* have been justified as positively liberating Muslim women from group oppression. Catholic restrictions on abortion, contraception, homosexuality, and divorce, and the limitation of the priesthood to celibate men, are perennial topics of debate, all the more so as secular norms on gender and sexuality become less conservative. Catholic and other Christian service associations seek to govern their service provision according to their religion's internal rules: not providing adoptions to same-sex couples, not offering contraception at Catholic hospitals or as part of the health insurance provided to employees of Catholic institutions, not offering spousal benefits to the same-sex partners of Salvation Army employees, refusing to perform marriages of which the particular religion's doctrine disapproves: same-sex, interfaith, interracial, remarriages. Religious and cultural groups are characterized by pervasive internal rules and norms on belief and conduct, raising the question of whether those rules and norms infringe on personal freedom.

The same is true of voluntary associations of other sorts. The Boy Scouts of America prohibit atheism, agnosticism, and homosexuality among their members (the last prohibition relaxed in 2013 for children but not adults); the U.S. Supreme Court upheld the prohibition on homosexuality as an exercise of freedom of association. Universities directly regulate students and professors in ways that have changed over time and that vary from one university to the next: mandating oaths of religious belief, prohibiting hate speech on campus, forbidding students to dance or to drink alcohol, requiring students to live on campus and in mixed-gender dormitories. Residential associations restrict the external appearance of members' homes, in ways that may be as banal as restrictions on the color one can paint a house but that can affect important expressive interests: aesthetic prohibitions on campaign posters, or flags, or *sukkots*. They moreover form exclusive communities that raise questions about social segmentation and segregation. The revitalized interest in federalism in a number of constitutional democracies has raised related questions. The self-government of provinces found in federations is often celebrated as a freedom-enhancing check on the power of central states, but many liberals point to provincial injustice at the hands of oppressive or conservative local majorities, from Québec's language laws to Jim Crow laws in the American south, as reasons to place greater trust in central states and their judiciaries.

This is a book about individual persons, intermediate groups and institutions, and states. It is concerned with the relationship between intermediate groups and freedom: whether, when, and how they impair the freedom of their members; whether, when, and how they protect it; and whether, when, and how they should be seen as manifestations or exercises of that freedom.

This book *studies* rather than *answers* questions like these. While it does aim to offer some of the resources for answering them, the book's core argument does not concern *how* these cases should be settled. Rather, I mean to make an argument about the place of problems like these within liberal political theory. I want to show that these problems of groups and freedom—the freedom of groups from the state, and the freedom of persons within groups—are not novel, anomalous, or separate from one another. What we have lately encountered as discrete odd problems about multiculturalism, religious freedom, freedom of associations, universities, and local government are just the recent manifestations of a set of deep and perennial problems. Liberalism, and the earlier theoretical frameworks out of which liberalism grew, have been centrally occupied with them for centuries.

We will follow two broad patterns and traditions of answers to these questions: one inclined toward the use of state power to protect individuals from local group power, one inclined to see groups as the results of individual free choice and the protectors of freedom against state power. I will call these patterns and traditions *rationalist* and *pluralist* liberalisms. I adopt these words for some of their connotations but not others. "Rationalism" is meant to encourage the reader to think of Weber, not Descartes: processes of bureaucratic *rationalization*, not theories of knowledge or standards of argumentation. Rationalist liberalism is sometimes associated with a kind of demand that rational accounts be given to justify customs, norms, and beliefs, demands that can perhaps never be wholly satisfied. This is obviously connected to the more abstract sense of rational knowledge and belief; but it is a demand that is made in a particular institutional context, i.e. states demanding justification of the practices of non-state groups.

"Pluralism" is meant to evoke associational, cultural, religious, and jurisdictional pluralism. In the first instance, pluralism should suggest allowing a plurality of associations, cultures, religions, and so on, to follow their own various norms. As a secondary matter, it is tied to a claim of descriptive sociology: that the sources of social organization are many, not one. It is *not* meant to be tied to the idea of moral pluralism made famous by Isaiah Berlin, though we will return to possible connections with that idea. In short, I ask the reader to keep in mind a contrast between state rationalization and the self-government of a plurality of non-state social groups, not such possibly related ideas as cognitive rationality or the supposed plurality of ultimate human ends.

These are not directly analogous categories. In describing these two tendencies within liberal thought, I deliberately oppose concepts that are not natural

27

contrasts: pluralism and rationalism, rather than, e.g., decentralization and centralization, or tradition and reform, or culture and reason, or for that matter pluralism and monism, or rationalism and sentimentalism. I do not mean to *make* rationalism and pluralism into direct contrast concepts. These strands within liberalism each encompass arguments of various kinds, many of which are not mutually exclusive. While the final chapter will offer reasons to doubt the prospects for a coherent and stable synthesis between the two views, that will not simply be because they are strictly incompatible. I mean the odd pairing of words to serve as an ongoing reminder: in any particular case, there may be rationalist reasons for constraining groups and pluralist reasons for deferring to them that might all be valid. It could be true that a church is reinforcing the power of its office-holders and taking unfair advantage of those born into its belief system, *and* be true that the state could not interfere without expanding its power over religious questions to a dangerous degree.

In this book I do not simply stand above the fray. I generally endorse the freedom of associations and groups, and sympathize with the pluralist tradition. Moreover, since I think that rationalist liberalism is most easily and most often mistaken for the whole of liberal political philosophy, that the history and the arguments in favor of pluralism are generally underdeveloped and unfamiliar in contemporary theory, I will often devote special care to explaining pluralism. Part II of the book in particular, while it traces the history of both strands, gives more emphasis to developing the less-familiar pluralist tradition and its antecedents in ancient constitutionalism. A major purpose of this book is to recover and elaborate the pluralist alternative within liberalism, to make it an available part of our sense of the history of liberal ideas.

But that purpose is not the same as the book's thesis. I do not simply maintain that pluralist liberalism offers the right answers and solutions. Both groups and states can impair freedom; both have some general tendencies to do so and general patterns of how they do so. Liberalism is not (only) a philosophical account of liberty but (also) a pair of rival but entwined social theories about where threats to freedom come from and how they can be met; and we can neither make do with just one of those theories nor easily dissolve the difference between them. The central argument of the book is that the coexistence of those two patterns and traditions is an enduring one, and for good reason. A full liberal theory of freedom cannot ignore threats to it from either the state or from intermediate groups—but there is no neat way to reconcile the appreciation of each kind of threat.

In this chapter I set the stage with some basic ideas that can motivate each of the strands, some more familiar ways of discussing related topics in contemporary political philosophy and the history of political thought, and some examples. The aim is to start to see the patterns of rationalist and pluralist ways of thought emerge, and to suggest connections where they might not have been apparent. In the next chapter I will offer more systematic accounts that try to build to rationalist and pluralist conclusions from premises about individuals and their rights. In Chapter 3 I will offer what I think are some more promising ways of thinking about these problems.

Some Sources of Disagreement

Autonomy and Toleration

One of the fundamental suspicions of group life is that members of groups do not think for themselves, whether out of conformism and traditionalism or because they are discouraged from doing so by local elites. From early modern worries about priestly power over the people's minds to current concerns about the acculturation of women in patriarchal cultures or the education of children among the Amish, we find the idea that freedom demands the ability to rationally revise or reject the norms of groups to which one happens to belong, whether by choice or by birth. Religious commitments in particular have long been seen as incompatible with thinking for oneself, especially those that seem to subsume a person's whole life. Hayek held that it was "difficult" to characterize "a Jesuit who lives up to the ideals of the founder of his order and regards himself 'as a corpse which has neither intelligence nor will'" as a free person.[1] Monastic orders and self-contained religious minorities have been viewed with the same suspicion.

In political philosophy this is often understood as an ideal of *autonomy*, and is associated with what John Rawls called "comprehensive liberalism," liberalism as a theory of the good life rather than as a strictly "political" doctrine about public justice.[2] Some theorists have claimed that such an ideal of autonomy is foundational for a liberal understanding of freedom and the self. Will Kymlicka, for example, maintained that liberal principles entail that cultural minorities have the right to maintain themselves as cultures, but also entail that they do *not* have the right to inhibit the autonomy of their members with internally illiberal norms. He identified this as the *liberal* idea of

---

[1] Hayek, *The Constitution of Liberty*, p. 14. I thank John Holbo for drawing this passage to my attention.

[2] Stephen Macedo, however, argued that even political liberalism demands something very much like a public commitment to autonomy. "Liberal Civic Education and Religious Fundamentalism: the case of God v John Rawls?" 105 *Ethics* 468–96, 1995; see also his "Community, Diversity, and Civic Education: Toward a Liberal Political Science of Group Life," 13 *Social Philosophy and Policy* 240–68, 1996. Conversely, Joseph Raz combined a strongly autonomy-based theory with considerable sympathy for group life in *The Morality of Freedom* (Oxford: Oxford University Press, 1983).

toleration, as committed to rights of conversion and apostasy as to the right to believe in traditional ways, and opposed it to non-liberal theories that did not put autonomy at the center.[3] Others emphasized certain patterns of violations of autonomy, without committing to it as a positive ideal in the way Kymlicka did. Susan Moller Okin, for example, worried about the ways that cultural and religious minorities inculcate sexist views, including among their female members, and suggested that women's freedom would be best served if these traditional communities became "extinct."[4] Building on her earlier writings on the threat the family, as currently constituted, posed to women's freedom and standing, she argued that cultural and religious groups impair the liberty of women to think for themselves.[5]

I think that in these contexts talk about autonomy—characterized by Isaiah Berlin as a species of "positive" liberty—often masks an underlying concern about intragroup power and negative freedom. Norms that subordinate some group members to others (say, subordinating women to men) help to generate practices of power and domination. If we think that those relationships are problematic and want to criticize them, we may run into the apparent obstacle that the subordination is agreed to by those in the subordinate position. *Then* the concern for autonomy is invoked: the consent doesn't count, because the norm is held heteronomously. How do we know it is held heteronomously? Because, we think, no one would, after independent critical thought, embrace a view that subordinated them. The inference may be false, but it's also argumentatively superfluous. Domination is the target of critique, and then is also used as the primary evidence for a violation of autonomy. Autonomy as such was never the point. A move like this is often made about norms of inequality; it is sometimes also made about norms that confine behavior in some way that the observer considers ridiculous or excessive enough to count as a violation of liberty.

One piece of evidence that the idea of autonomy, or the related doubt that membership in a group is genuinely voluntary, masks a concern with domination is this: secular, democratic, and egalitarian norms are rarely subjected to the same searching philosophical inquiry about whether they were arrived at autonomously or voluntarily. Often they were not; children are educated and

---

[3] Will Kymlicka, *Liberalism, Community, and Culture* (Oxford: Oxford University Press, 1989); Will Kymlicka, *Multicultural Citizenship* (Oxford: Oxford University Press, 1995).

[4] Susan Moller Okin, *Is Multiculturalism Bad for Women?* (Princeton: Princeton University Press, 1999); she later expressed ambivalence about the choice of the word "extinct."

[5] Okin, *Justice, Gender, and the Family* (New York: Basic Books, 1989). Nancy Rosenblum argues, persuasively in my view, that "equality was not [Okin's] chief concern"; rather, she was chiefly concerned about women's *subjection*, and aimed to "realize liberty in and through the family." Rosenblum, "Okin's Liberal Feminism as Radical Political Theory," in Debra Satz and Rob Reich, eds, *Toward a Humanist Justice: The Political Philosophy of Susan Moller Okin* (Oxford: Oxford University Press, 2009).

adults are socialized by other persons and institutions, and most of our norms most of the time result at least in part from those processes. But heteronomy is invoked against the customary, religious, or communal norms, and not against the secular, democratic, and egalitarian norms. This of course may be a problem. I think it often is; a double standard is often applied, one that treats background acculturation as autonomy for the majority and heteronomy for the minority. But if full autonomy is so high a standard that it could not be applied evenly, perhaps the same is not true for an underlying concern with thinking for oneself, with freedom from some kinds of power and pressure to conform.

Religious liberty is a core commitment, if not *the* core commitment, of liberal political thought. Against the ideas just discussed, pluralist liberals emphasize religious liberty in particular and toleration in general as fundamental liberal values. There is something important to life in a free society in tolerating the beliefs, norms, and practices of your neighbors, even when you disapprove of them. Chandran Kukathas defended a liberal vision defined primarily in terms of toleration and freedom of association, one that protects cultural and religious groups from almost all state intrusion, even if they refuse to educate their young, and even if the idea of questioning and rejecting them is substantially unimaginable to their members. Liberty is threatened by the state; it is realized in the societies, associations, and communities free persons join or find themselves in and do not leave. William Galston argued that a tolerant diversity is the truly liberal value, and that a demand for autonomy that justified intrusions on diversity must lie outside liberalism's boundaries.[6]

This opposition between autonomy and toleration as candidate fundamental values of liberalism ran through much of the literature on religious freedom and multiculturalism in the 1990s and early 2000s. I think that this debate was in important ways misleading: "autonomy" does not really describe the concern with in-group power that lies at the core of rationalist liberalism, nor "toleration" pluralism's concern with centralized state power. But autonomy and toleration need not be rival master values to help us see some of what is at stake in thinking about intermediate groups.

Whose Freedom?

Persons have second-order preferences; they want to want things, and want to refrain from wanting others. They have preferences about what kinds of

---

[6] Chandran Kukathas, *The Liberal Archipelago: a Theory of Diversity and Freedom* (Oxford: Oxford University Press, 2003). William Galston, "Two Concepts of Liberalism," 105(3) *Ethics* (1995). He later revised that statement, in favor of a view more like the one I elaborate here, in Galston, *The Practice of Liberal Pluralism* (Cambridge: Cambridge University Press, 2004).

persons they will become. We wish to forego short-term preferences of one sort or another, to be able to commit to uses of our time and energy that will conflict with momentary desires along the way, to be able to pursue long-term projects and aspirations at costs to our immediate-term temptations. We wish not only to restrain ourselves from pursuing the short-term temptations, but to find them less tempting; we want to *want* to eat healthy food, exercise, show up for work on time, invest the time to learn a new language, live according to our committed views about sexual morality (e.g. monogamy), and so on.

Many accounts of liberty are compatible with this fact.[7] Charles Taylor, among others, has argued that taking second-order preferences philosophically seriously will require a rethinking of the traditional liberal understanding of freedom. But most liberals at least think that their conception of freedom is compatible with the human need to govern first-order by second-order preferences. If we are not as comfortable as some followers of Plato in referring to persons as slaves to their passions, desires, appetites, and fears, neither do we believe that superegos are tyrants over enslaved egos and ids. The person who effectively governs him or herself in the pursuit of long-term or higher-order projects is not any less free, despite all of the short-term options and temptations the person might deny him or herself. The liberal theory of freedom is at worst agnostic as between the self-indulgent person and the one with self-mastery, and does not equate "self-mastery" with a politically problematic kind of masterhood. We treat the individual self as sufficiently unified, even if internally complex, not to worry about one part of the self unjustly tyrannizing over another.

Groups are not, in that sense, persons. As Taylor saw, there is a strong connection between autonomous second-order preference and collective groups. We often derive our second-order preferences from group life, structure them around group life, and pursue them in common with others. It is not only that we absorb, say, our views about right and wrong conduct from our religious or cultural societies. It is also that we often have second-order preferences precisely to be good members of our groups, to contribute to them or sacrifice for them. Whether the second-order preferences take that form or not, we will often try to live according to them through mutual commitment and monitoring, and a shared shaping of our environment so as to make our

---

[7] See Harry Frankfurt, "Freedom of the Will and the Concept of a Person," 68(1) *The Journal of Philosophy* 5–20, Jan. 1971; Charles Taylor, "What's Wrong with Negative Liberty," in Alan Ryan, ed., *The Idea of Freedom* (Oxford: Oxford University Press, 1979); Taylor, "What is Human Agency?" in *Philosophical Papers volume 1, Human Agency and Language* (Cambridge: Cambridge University Press, 1985); Philip Pettit, *A Theory of Freedom: From the Psychology to the Politics of Agency* (Oxford: Oxford University Press, 2001); Anthony Appiah, *The Ethics of Identity* (Princeton: Princeton University Press, 2005).

higher preferences easier to pursue and our lower preferences more difficult. From support-group meetings in which members help one another stay strong against addiction, to exercise clubs in which members use mutual commitment to keep themselves disciplined, to monastic orders and territorial religious communities such as the Amish, group life is strongly tied to second-order preferences, to helping members avoid temptation of one kind or another.

But when we join together in this way, when we combine with others in a frank admission that sometimes each of us might not know, or want, or do what is best for ourselves or what we (in some sense) really wish, the dynamic is very different from the individual person struggling within him or herself to follow an ideal. We wish—we really wish—to sometimes have our fellows cajole, persuade, preach to, or pressure us, when we are going to fall off the path we have chosen. We sometimes wish for our fellows to tell us what to do; and we trust them to do so. Maybe there is a permanent hierarchy, in which some are always those entrusted to tell others what to do; maybe not. But in either case, the structure is one in which there are always some saying to others, "you don't really want to do that, and you really want me to stop you or at least discourage you from doing that," and in which such a statement might be correct. But, of course, our fellows are also flawed human beings with limited knowledge of us and our circumstances and desires, with interests, biases, agendas, and pride of their own. The admitted possibility that the claim "you don't really want to do that" *could* be justified doesn't mean that it *is* justified in any particular case.

So when we see that the group of which some person is a member is exerting strong pressure for rule-compliance and conformity, or imposing sanctions for breaches, we can't immediately know (and sometimes we can't possibly know for sure even after investigation) whether this is a case in which the person really does want to be brought into compliance; a case in which the rule is irksome but strongly connected to other group goods and goals that the person does endorse; or a case in which biased or power-hungry or intrusive elites and enforcers are, in good faith or bad, constraining the person unnecessarily. And this means that the outsider concerned with a group member's autonomy may find himself *interfering* with the association, rather than respecting the ways in which collective action are usually thought of as tied to individual self-mastery.

It may therefore be that the freedom of those who wish to follow a group's norms in traditional ways and the freedom of the reformer, the dissident, or the apostate are not wholly compatible. By this I do not mean that they are logically or psychologically incompatible. No one's freedom is impaired simply by the encounter with someone who disagrees, or by the fact that some others are drawn away from what one considers the correct view. My religious

33

freedom to believe in the traditional way is not impaired by your dissent, and your freedom to dissent or apostatize is not limited by the continued existence of orthodox believers. Rather, I mean a kind of sociological incompatibility. In a world with a lumpy social fabric, spillover effects of group loyalty, and rules of law and institutional design that cannot be and should not be infinitely fine-grained, even a seamless compatibility of moral claims may generate considerable incompatibility in social practice. Institutions that permit group members to associate, incorporate, self-govern, and live their lives as they wish generate a surplus of group or group-leader power that leaves dissidents less free than they should be. Laws designed to ensure that each person within a group has full effective freedom of exit and has given full informed consent, rules to protect internal reformers and to provide refuge to those who depart, are unlikely to do so without interference with the legitimate freedom of those who wish to remain within the group as it exists. This is another potential source for the difference between rationalist and pluralist liberalism, one that is sometimes described in the language of autonomy and heteronomy, but that is really quite different. It amounts to a difference in sympathies: sympathy for the person who wants (genuinely wants, and wants to want) to live in a way that accords with existing group norms, or for the person who wants (etc.) to do otherwise.

The Sources of Law and Social Order

Associations are sources of law, or at least of law-like rules and bylaws. Formal organizations create rules that members must follow in order to remain members; they have internal procedures and authority with which to judge rule violations; and the consequences are incorporated into the legal system as a whole. But when (in Lon Fuller's example) a student is expelled from a university for violation of a dormitory parietal rule, the university's own disciplinary procedures judge the dispute in the first instance. Students who are expelled lose their legal right to live in dorms, to remain on campus, to take classes, and so on. Formal organizations from residential associations to churches share these features: they issue internal rules, judge cases arising under them, and make authoritative decisions that have standing in the legal system. Fuller suggests that it is mere linguistic prejudice that keeps us from calling this "law." He moreover suggests that we think of the rules that arise out of repeated human interactions to govern those interactions as cases of law.[8] This, he suggests, allows us to see that what has been called "customary law" and thought by some to be a matter of primitive habit, the posited rules

---

[8] Lon Fuller, "Human Interaction and the Law," in *The Rule of Law*, Robert Paul Wolff, ed. (New York: Simon and Schuster, 1971). The fact that this argument ties together various sources

governing the internal lives of secondary associations, and most of the law of states are similar in kind; they all count as part of "the enterprise of subjecting human conduct to the governance of rules."[9]

But this means that, in an associationally complex society, there is a kind of pervasive inequality before the law. We are subject to different legal arrangements, rules, and procedures in each of our groups; our rights and duties vary based on our membership status. If this is obviously true of cases of federalism or city government—the laws to which a person is subject change depending on which side of a provincial boundary they are standing on—it is also true of group life in general. Whether I have the right to make aesthetic decisions about my house depends on whether I belong to a homeowners' association; whether I have the right to a gender-equitable divorce depends on the religion to which I belong and how its marriage rules overlay on top of the state's.

This inequality is another source of liberal suspicion of group life. It seems to offend against the core value of equality before the law. Moreover, these laws and rules do not arise out of public democratic decision-making, and indeed often seem not to result from rational or deliberate decisions at all. From this perspective, even at their best, associations are internal democracies made up of a small part of the whole population, and will therefore reach decisions that are partial rather than impartial. They will not take the interests of outsiders, including outsiders who might wish to join in the future, fully into account. At worst, associations and groups' rules might be a matter of sheer custom or habit or of subservience to some hierarchy. Not only the interests of outsiders but the lives of members are then structured by norms and rules that were never evaluated or enacted by the democratic government of the whole society. A group's internal rules and decisions become a kind of law outside the state's control, at least for their members and often for others. A university's choices about student life can reshape a town; its choices about admissions policies can reshape the landscape of opportunities for a whole country. A church's rules can structure the lives of its members as profoundly as the legal system; its judgments about doctrine can affect the whole culture, including the political culture about what is and what is not moral. An association with discriminatory membership rules does not give those affected a vote; a hierarchical religion may give *no one* a vote. Decisions made by the democratic state are of course imperfect, but in principle they are made in a way that represents all, is accountable to all, and depends on the giving and evaluation of reasons. This, according to this point of view, gives the

of legal pluralism, from the customary law of indigenous peoples to the bureaucratized rule of a university, seems to me a virtue, and marks Fuller as having been considerably ahead of his time.

[9] Fuller, *The Morality of Law*, p. 74.

democratic state a fundamental legitimacy when making decisions that affect the social order, a legitimacy that intermediate groups lack.

Even the act of associating itself is a subject of dispute here. As we will see, defenders of group life have long maintained that associations are self-legitimating; they derive their rightful existence from their members, even if that is afterward *recognized* by the political authorities. But this has always been a controversial claim, and its opponents maintain that the right to associate depends on permission from those authorities, and can be structured by them as they see fit.[10]

These complaints might be made in an illiberal spirit. The sheer fact that people are doing something without the prior approval of the *demos* is not an offense; in any reasonably free society that must be the case all the time. But the specifically law-like character of groups' internal norms, the authority structures inside them, and the partial or opaque procedures for generating them strike some as setting these norms apart from ordinary private activity. The goals of accountable, representative, and equal authority encourage a rationalist skepticism of jurisdictional pluralism. Rationalists worry that the freedom that is secured by democratic procedures will be lost to lots of little unaccountable tyrannies, and that there is something unacceptably anomalous about a world in which so much law merges outside of contexts of legislative choice.

Whether this is anomalous at all depends on questions in social theory about *where social order comes from*. A traditional answer—perhaps the one most familiar to political philosophy—is that social order comes from an orderer.[11] Formal political institutions and formal legal structures make the difference between order and chaos, between social life and asocial war, between rules that generate stable expectations and rule-lessness. Many uses of the idea of a collective action problem take this form. Left to our own devices, we separate individuals will create a mess. We will be unable to live peacefully with one another, to manage our common resources without tragic overuse, to enforce rights to life or to property, to cooperate in any ongoing fashion. We will fail to generate the social order we would all prefer. And so order must be coercively imposed from above; if we are able to jointly create the right kind of coercive agent, we will do so. The subsequent coercion will transform our incentives and make it possible for us to live the orderly social lives we aspire to. Whether the public good at issue is a sustainable grazing land, an unpolluted ecosphere, a smoothly operating economy,

---

[10] This claim is not only made by defenders of *democratic* authority; as we will see, kings and emperors insisted on it as well.

[11] The familiar examples in what follows come from Thomas Hobbes, *Leviathan*, Noel Malcolm, ed. (Oxford: Oxford University Press, 2012[1651]); and Garret Hardin, "The Tragedy of the Commons," 162 *Science* 1243–8, 1968.

rights-enforcement, or peace itself, the choice is between an individualistic failure to attain it and a statist or coercive success at providing it.

In addition to emphasizing the role of coercion in solving collective action problems, this kind of answer stresses the importance of decisions and plans to social order. The social problems that are solved are those that the coercer *decides* to solve; the prohibition on killing that ends our war of all against all does not solve our tragedy of the commons, and the prohibition of overgrazing does not solve the security dilemma that leads us to kill each other. The existence of coercion is not enough; the coercer must rationally decide which private actions are to be prohibited, which ones mandated.

The rival set of answers to the question of where social order comes from involves the emergence and evolution of norms that govern group life in any particular setting.[12] The emphasis is typically on the development of rules suited to a particular group's social needs, on the stable benefits of cooperation and reciprocity under conditions of long-term coexistence, and on local knowledge of everything from the natural environment to the character of one's neighbors.

Within political theory these ideas may be best known through their development by Hayek, under the label "spontaneous order"; the associated ideas have advanced considerably in empirical content and theoretical sophistication since Hayek's time. Robert Axelrod demonstrated that repeated interactions stabilize reciprocal cooperation; in a social world where most interactions are not one-time only, the logic of prisoners' dilemmas and collective good provision does *not* drive us to perennial defection and breakdown. Elinor Ostrom has shown, empirically and theoretically, how many groups and communities develop stable norms for the management of common pool resources and avoid local tragedies of the commons, provided (among other things) that the groups are well bounded and that outsiders do not interfere with their local management strategies and self-governance. Systems of resource use and resource rights evolve that are locally stable and enforceable, making for a *polycentric* world of many social orders. Robert Ellickson has shown that, even when formal legal rules backed by coercive state power do exist to resolve local conflicts, the parties may ignore them and

---

[12] For what follows, see Avinash K. Dixit, *Lawlessness and Economics* (Princeton: Princeton University Press, 2004); Robert Ellickson, *Order Without Law: How Neighbors Settle Disputes* (Cambridge, Mass.: Harvard University Press, 1991); Elinor Ostrom, *Governing the Commons: The Evolution of Institutions for Collective Action* (Cambridge: Cambridge University Press, 1990); Robert Axelrod, *The Evolution of Cooperation* (New York: Basic Books, 1984); James Scott, *Seeing Like a State* (New Haven: Yale University Press, 1997); Scott, *The Art of Not Being Governed* (New Haven: Yale University Press, 2009). For overviews of Elinor and Vincent Ostrom's theories of polycentric social order, see Paul Dragos Aligica and Peter Boettke, *Challenging Institutional Analysis and Development* (London: Routledge, 2009); and Mark Sproule-Jones, Barbara Allen, and Filippo Sabetti, eds, *The Struggle to Constitute and Sustain Productive Orders* (Lanham, MD: Lexington Books, 2008).

develop norms that are quite different; and those norms may persistently regulate the local conflicts in preference to state legal systems that are expensive, time-consuming, and disruptive to use. And James Scott's work has shown that social orders not only emerge outside of state spheres of influence making effective use of local knowledge, but that they sometimes even develop in spite of and in resistance to such state power, gaining robustness from their opaqueness to state inquiry.

While the explosion of work on trust and on social capital in the last generation has usually been independent from this literature on polycentric order,[13] there is much overlap between them. "Trust" and "social capital" both denote possible sources of smoother uncoerced cooperation.[14] But in-group trust, cooperativeness, and social capital are often associated with the exclusion of outsiders; our ability to develop and noncoercively enforce norms governing our life depends on the stability of the group that makes up "us."

It might often be the case that locally evolved norms are seriously deficient compared with easily imaginable coercive alternatives. They may be locally expensive to maintain; they may require an undesirable level of constant mutual monitoring; they may depend on an unacceptably rigid segregation between insiders and outsiders; they may prove fragile to changes in the social environment. Coercive state laws may increase mobility and transparency; they may reduce the costs of enforcement and vastly increase the range of persons with whom cooperation is possible. A pluralist social order might be possible and still be normatively unattractive, in need of significant correction or limitation by a rationalist central state. Rationalist liberal critics of multiculturalism think something like this. They recognize fully well that cultural groups have norms that they live by, and that they provide a kind of stable social order; they think that the norms are oppressive ones, and that the social order they generate is all *too* stable. But often rationalism (inside and outside liberalism) derives in part from the sheer disbelief in a pluralistic social world. And debates about pluralism (again, liberal or otherwise) are often debates about how much of the ordering of the social world in fact does derive from rationally posited unified rules.

Assuming that the pluralists are at least sometimes right about the sources of social order returns us to the question of whether to think of the norms and rules that arise polycentrically as *law*. In various forms, this is a very old question in legal theory, often characterized as one about the legal status of *custom*, or about whether customary law is fully law. Most positive legal

---

[13] But see Elinor Ostrom, "Social Capital: A Fad or a Fundamental Concept?" in Partha Dasgupta and Ismail Serageldin, eds, *Social Capital: A Multifaceted Perspective* (Washington, D.C.: World Bank Books, 2000).

[14] They also denote possible sources of smoother *coerced* cooperation; a general culture of trust and law-abidingness makes law easier and less costly to enforce.

systems have in fact explicitly allowed for custom to carry legal force; certainly both the Roman law and the English common law did. Some positivists from Hobbes onward have found this puzzling or worse; evolved and customary norms seem never to have been posited by anybody, and explicit rules within a formal secondary association were posited by agents other than the sovereign.

In some iterations, this debate about the nature and sources of legal order has simply been one between the enactment of rationalized and codified law from a sovereign center and the preservation of a plurality of decentralized and customary legal orders. Codification is typically a project of rationalization, simplification, centralization, and normalization. It aims to undo the customary and interpretive accretions that arise over time in any legal community—and, not incidentally, to undermine the elite authority of jurists, lawyers, and scholars to make sense of such accretions, an authority that does not directly depend on the sovereign state. And so there has been a strong correlation between, e.g., arguments for the superiority of rationalized codes of statutes such as the Napoleonic code, and arguments for the centralization of legal orders, the elimination of the customary legal orders of intermediate and peripheral groups. This dispute in various ways dominated debates in legal theory in the nineteenth century, including debates about codifying German law, about reform of the common law in England, and about the recognition and incorporation of customary law in imperialistically conquered territories. In Part II we will see episodes of conflict over whether law in medieval and modern Europe was Roman or Germanic, with "Roman" meaning both codified and (often) royally enacted, and Germanic meaning customary, uncodified, and often unwritten altogether.

There are thus at least three in-principle distinct pluralist claims here. First, social orders can emerge and survive pluralistically, making effective use of localized knowledge to evolve local norms that are locally functional. Second, *law* can emerge pluralistically, whether as the internal norms of such groups or as the norms that regulate relations among them. And third, such orders are normatively attractive: perhaps they are absolutely attractive, because they are the sites for our pursuits of ethical conceptions of the good and substantive life plans thicker than the formal rules of justice, perhaps they are attractive relative to the social or legal orders enacted by deliberate state planning. The normative claim and the legal claim in particular are logically independent: whether a group's internal rules count as law is fundamentally unrelated to whether they are unjust or oppressive. But there is a strong affinity among them all. Those committed to normative pluralist liberalism often endorse all three, while those opting for rationalist liberalism often treat the first and second as anomalous and the third as false, trusting more in the uniform order created by deliberately chosen laws.

Discrimination and Diversity

The worry that groups' rules will not take the interests of outsiders or prospective new members into account is especially acute when it comes to membership rules themselves. Groups decide whom to admit and whom to refuse, and they often refuse in ways that strike liberals as pernicious: denying membership to racial or religious minorities, to women, to gays and lesbians, to holders of unpopular political opinions. Freedom of association in these moments looks like a synonym for a right to discriminate.[15] The two most important U.S. Supreme Court cases on freedom of association in recent decades have both concerned discriminatory membership rules; in one case the state's public antidiscrimination law trumped associational freedom, in the other it did not.

The suspicion of exclusion is often accompanied by claims about *diversity*: associations with exclusionary membership rules will be less diverse than the wider society, and enable their members to lead lives insulated from diversity altogether. To this, defenders of associational freedom reply that diversity can be, and often is best, an intergroup rather than an intragroup phenomenon. We will have more genuine diversity if there is a range of genuinely different organizations, communities, and institutions to choose among than if we insist that each organization must be a representative microcosm of the whole social order. Religious diversity comes from having different religious denominations, not from trying to make each sect include members of all beliefs.

Membership rules do not only apply to outsiders. Members can be expelled as well as refused: the scoutmaster who comes out as gay, the college professor whose Communist past becomes unacceptable when the political winds change. Moreover, control over membership rules is often a weapon in internal disputes, and differences about membership rules are tied up in differences about substantive beliefs. Consider the Jews' Free School case from Britain. Against the background of a general rule that religious schools may prefer to admit coreligionists, that London school prioritized for admission children it recognized as having Jewish mothers, in accordance with the traditional Jewish rule that the membership is passed matrilineally. Its policy did not recognize conversions performed outside of Orthodoxy, and so the child of a Jewish father and a mother who had converted to non-Orthodox Judaism was denied admission. Britain's courts struck the policy down as impermissible ethnic discrimination, while purporting to leave religious schools free to select applicants on a religious basis such as attendance at religious services.

---

[15] Andrew Koppelman and Tobias Barrington Wolff, *A Right to Discriminate? How the case of Boy Scouts of America v James Dale warped the law of free association* (New Haven: Yale University Press, 2009).

The case was in some ways a strange one. The admissions policy treated children of mixed marriages differently based on whether their father or their mother was Jewish, but gender discrimination was not the legal issue. "Racial" discrimination was, since a mother who was born ethnically Jewish was treated differently from one who was not. And the court's attempt to distinguish religious from non-religious tests of membership was awkward and unsuccessful, imposing Protestant norms about what it means to belong to a religion where they didn't belong. But it is worth noticing that this was not simply an insider–outsider dispute. The mother *was* recognized as Jewish by a Jewish congregation and rabbi, just not by the Orthodox rabbinate that held authority over the school. In a messy way, the state interfered in an intra-Jewish contest over the religion, and sided with the progressive dissidents against the orthodox (and Orthodox) hierarchy. Membership rules are also internal rules, and what was at stake in the case was not an outsider wishing to ignore the community's self-definition but rather disputed internal authority structures between the chief rabbinate and Liberal Judaism. This is, I think, a good case to be uncomfortable about; neither state intrusion into the definition of religious membership nor institutionally entrenched in-group power to override dissent and exclude outsiders is a result to be entirely happy with. Each side of that discomfort can be a source for a general attitude toward group life. One such attitude emphasizes that groups discriminate among potential members and limit internal diversity. The other stresses that control over membership is in part the freedom to believe and live in our own way—to be Orthodox rather than Liberal, and to be able to treat that as a meaningful distinction—and so is necessary if a society as a whole is to be genuinely diverse.

41

2

Two Approaches

In the last chapter I began to show some of the appeal of rationalist and pluralist liberal ideas. In this chapter I consider possible strategies for deriving pluralist or rationalist conclusions in a more systematic way, proceeding from claims about individual rights. I will argue that these do not succeed as complete systems. The first, although limited, does help us see something important about pluralism. The second, though often tacitly relied upon, turns out to be mainly a distraction from the best arguments for rationalism.

The Pure Liberal Theory of Freedom of Association

The first of these strategies I'll refer to as the pure liberal theory of freedom of association. Its purity lies in its lack of other elements mixed in, and is not necessarily a compliment; "pure" here is the opposite of "compounded" or "mixed," not of "corrupt." It is a way of building to pluralist conclusions from simple premises. Ultimately they are too simple, but the pure theory helps us see some of pluralism's moral force in a systematic way. The pure theory should be a moment in liberal thought about associational life; indeed I think it should often be the first moment. But it should not be the *final* moment.

The pure theory holds that, what individual persons are free to do singly, they ought to be free to do in association with one another; and rights that they are free to waive, they ought to be free to waive as against groups of which they are members.[1] The conclusion these premises generate is that persons should be free to form any associations or institutions that they wish, to

---

[1] There are standard counterexamples to each of these principles; for example, I am free to walk down the sidewalk without permission, but a thousand of us in a march create enough inconvenient externalities for other people that coordination, advance notice, and permits may be required. I set these aside, as they largely do not concern the associational character of the questions at hand. The pure theory can probably accommodate them.

structure and govern them however they wish, and to live according to the rules and norms that the associations generate. Their freedom to create associations and institutions means that the associations and institutions then take on a moral and legal existence of their own, which in effect means that associations ought to have complete freedom to govern themselves by whatever procedures and rules they wish, and to admit or refuse whomever they wish. The pure theory of freedom of association is a theory of freedom of *associations*. While associations remain restricted by the rules of justice in their interactions with outsiders—they may not break contracts, steal property, commit violence, and so on—they are substantially unconstrained in their dealings with members *qua* members and applicants for membership *qua* applicants.[2]

Substantially unconstrained does not mean *completely* unconstrained. The pure theory of freedom of association is not a theory of consent to slavery; persons cannot create an association which then has power of life and death over them, or power to hold them against their will. It need not be a theory that all rights are alienable. The usual shorthand is to say that the pure theory assumes at least a formal right of exit, encompassing rights against being killed, enslaved, or imprisoned by the group. But it is a theory that says all rights that *are* alienable may be alienated to associations, so long as one remains a member.

Volenti non fit injuria, the traditional legal rule that the consenting person is not harmed, is central to liberal thought: the person who consents, who waives the use of his or her rights in some case, has not had those rights *violated* but rather has *used* his or her freedom to make a choice. The person who sells a good has not had it stolen when the counterparty takes it away; the person who contracts for a wage-labor job is not enslaved by management's expectation of performance; neither the boxer in a fair fight nor the patient willingly submitting to surgery has suffered an assault; the person who joins a religion requiring that strange gods be forsworn has not suffered a violation of religious freedom. But for social relations not created by such clear and explicit acts as contracts, consent must be searched for and sometimes imputed, often from the fact of staying put, of accepting rather than rejecting some relationship or state of affairs. Such imputations are controversial, but one thing is clear: we may not impute such consent to someone who has no choice whether to leave.

---

[2] The idea of freedom of associations deliberately echoes *libertas ecclesiae*, the "freedom of the church" successfully asserted by the Roman Catholic Church during the Middle Ages, discussed further in Chapter 4. See Richard Garnett, "The Freedom of the Church," 4(1) *Journal of Catholic Social Thought* 59–86, 2007. See also Paul Horwitz, *First Amendment Institutions* (Cambridge, Mass.: Harvard University Press, 2013).

From this, the pure theorist derives a handful of core constraints on in-group behavior. Groups may not use or threaten violence to prevent departures. They may not commit violence against or enslave their members while they are still members, since doing so would prevent future decisions to leave. Perhaps they must provide children with a minimum of education about the ways of the world outside the group. Critics of the pure theory have argued that effective rights of exit demand far more than this. I bracket that question and examine what is attractive about the pure theory, what it means and entails—what it is that *may* be alienated to associations under it.

What persons are free to do individually, they ought to be free to do jointly; and what they are free to do or to refrain from doing, they ought to be free to conditionally promise one another to do or to refrain from doing. These together generate the freedom to combine together in a group and to agree to a decision-making procedure for the governance of the group, one with authority to decide henceforth who shall become or remain a member and under what conditions, and who shall have the authority to alter those conditions.

The conditions often take the form of what H. L. A. Hart called primary rules: they govern the conduct of members.[3] Indeed, in a sense these rules are the real business of membership; often they mark the distinctions between members and non-members. The opportunity to abide by them, among others who also do so, is one of the core meanings of joining. Such rules tell Catholics to take communion, give confession, and avoid contraception; university students not to commit plagiarism; condominium owners not to paint the outsides of their doors or hang flags from their balconies; Freemasons not to reveal lodge secrets; and club members to pay their dues. The freedom of associations to govern themselves includes their authority to regulate the conduct of their members. Such primary rules are often the real concern of those who think that groups impair the freedom of their members; the rules can be very restrictive. But the association's rules are, according to the pure theory, derivative of individual members' freedom to waive the exercise of their rights, to commit to each other that they will act or refrain from acting in particular ways.

The association once created is not the mere creature of its founders. A group of persons may form a religious group devoted to certain teachings; they may endow the religious body with land and a building and create offices of ecclesiastical governance. Once they have done so, *all* of the founders could change their minds about religious questions and leave the group, with the group surviving their departures. Assuming the governing procedures they

---

[3] H. L. A. Hart, *The Concept of Law* (Oxford: Clarendon Press, 1961).

create are not monarchical or proprietary ones—that is, if they do not declare themselves the church's owners or heads for life—they might be outvoted or excommunicated for violations of primary rules. The formal organization endures even in the face of such changes. Associations might therefore exist in perpetuity—some universities and religious orders have been in continuous existence for centuries longer than the states in which they are currently situated.

But an association need not be immortal for the point at hand to matter: associations are created as exercises of the freedom of their founders, but once created stand apart from them. Even those whose freedom was exercised in the association's creation might find themselves almost immediately constrained by it. That is a necessary consequence of having the freedom to associate: the freedom to subject oneself to constraints. Thus the pure theory holds that associations' regulation of members' conduct by primary rules does *not* impair freedom. If the rule mandates behavior that an individual person morally could engage in, or prohibits behavior that it's legitimate to refrain from, then the fact that a group of persons abide by the mandate or prohibition as a rule is simply their doing together what they would have been free to do individually. The freedom to associate just *is* the freedom to accept that entity's authority to govern one's actions.

While primary rules seem to be the primary objects of moral concern, formal associations and institutions also have secondary rules for ongoing governance, including rules for adjudicating violations of primary rules, the alteration of old primary rules, or the adoption of new ones, as well as rules that define the group's governance structure and the rules for selection of office-holders. The pure theory also argues for freedom of associations in this domain: they may govern themselves as they see fit, and part of the freedom that members have is the freedom to create or join associations that have this or that form: democratic or hierarchical, egalitarian or patriarchal, legalistic or informal, majoritarian or consensual, and so on.

Many well-known disputes about freedom and group life seem not to involve institutions with secondary rules but rather such non-institutionalized entities as *traditions* or *cultures*. From the perspective of the pure theory, this is a distinction almost without a difference.[4] These non-institutionalized

---

[4] Some might think that there is another difference: that formal associations are *joined*, while unincorporated groups are *born into*. The problem of being *born into* does not actually track the formal/unincorporated distinction very closely—a person can be born a Catholic, or born living in and heir to property in a residential association. So far as the pure theory is concerned, being "born into" does not make much difference; everyone is born *somewhere*, and even the freest person spends his or her life making choices shaped by particular contexts, the child of the most cosmopolitan urbanites no less than the Amish child. They both grow up choosing to do things that they are morally permitted to choose, and neither has meaningful access to every conceivable life choice.

groups have normative structures with primary rules that all members are under a generalized duty to follow. Conflicts of interpretation lead to divergences in practice, not to formal conflicts in adjudicative venues. Norm enforcement is radically decentralized: to local communities or congregations, to social networks willing and able to pressure their members and shun those who stray too far, or—probably especially—to families. Again, the decision to follow a norm that mandates morally permissible behavior or prohibits morally omittable behavior is simply the exercise of freedom. The decision to enforce norms—by disowning a child, breaking with a friend, refusing to marry a potential partner, or pressuring others to do those things—is, likewise, simply the choice to do something that a pure liberal theory recognizes the right to do: disassociate from another person. That the disassociation is done by many at the same time, and for norm-enforcing reasons rather than personal whim, doesn't change its moral status.

Robert Nozick, in Part III of *Anarchy, State, and Utopia*, offers perhaps the most famous approximation to the pure theory in contemporary political philosophy.[5] While the pure theory is compatible with his framework for utopias, it does not entail it, and I do not think that Nozick's vision is the most likely manifestation of even a radical and absolute freedom of association. The associations described there seem to be total, enveloping geographical communities that govern all aspects of their inhabitants' lives jointly and simultaneously. I doubt that even Nozick found this likely; it seems to have been a heuristic for the discussion of utopian communities. In any case, the pluralism that gives rise to the complex range of associations, religions, affiliations, and identities in modern life—in other words, the sociological source of associational life as we know it today—is likely to persist. This does not mean that memberships will be entirely cross-cutting; many groups will be *internally* pluralistic while still retaining substantial barriers to memberships that cut across group borders. Think of the range of associations and institutions that make up the social life of contemporary conservative white Protestantism in America: universities, private schools, home schooling associations, partly competing denominations and congregations within each denomination, competing providers of Christian-themed media programming, and so on, paralleling the associational complexity of life in the rest of American society, though still, and maybe increasingly, self-contained and separated from that society.

[5] Robert Nozick, *Anarchy, State, and Utopia* (New York: Basic Books, 1974).

Why the Pure Theory is Not Satisfactory

Nonetheless, the pure theory is built on rights-claims, not on sociological predictions; and it does not formally *exclude* the Nozickean outcome. Insofar as the pure theory stands apart from impure predictions and probabilities, it must be able to survive the analysis of mere *possibilities*. And that means that the pure theory, by itself, has the potential to be self-undermining.

It has often been noted, against attempts to strongly distinguish equality of opportunity from equality of outcomes, that inequality of outcomes in one generation becomes inequality of opportunities in the next. Pure equality of opportunity is self-undermining in the medium term. The same might be true of pure freedom of association. Freedom of association in one generation could leave the next with a social world wholly carved up into mutually exclusive groups, with no space in between.

The space that ceases to be available might be metaphorical social space, but the point is easiest to see if we begin with literal physical space. Persons who are free to own land are free to give the land they own to the associations they form. Associations are long-lived, and relatively immune to the market pressures and split-inheritance problems that tend to disperse large property holdings over time; associational ownership can act like entail laws. A world of pure freedom of association in which Nozickean total communities arise could be a world in which one generation's persons all give or bequeath their land to their associations, leaving no physical space outside the control of one or another group for their successors. That means that the succeeding generations might have, literally, no place to *go* if they wish to exit the groups into which they are born, no resources of space in which they could assemble their own dissident, hybrid, or rival associations.

The worry is not entirely fanciful; the tendency of the medieval Roman Catholic Church and its bishoprics and monastic orders to endlessly expand their land holdings by gift or bequest prompted countervailing legal responses across Europe. These statutes limited or prohibited *mortmain*, the "dead hand" of the past that would bind real property to the Church in perpetuity. In more recent times, majority-group racism and prejudice against Jews have certainly sometimes been strong enough to present a serious barrier to exit from minority communities; prejudice against the Roma remains so. For an example of a different sort, think of a gay or lesbian youth in a social world carved up among different conservative religious groups all of which forbid homosexuality, with no liberal cities of refuge in between.[6] Women suspected of sexual promiscuity have often been in a similar position.

---

[6] See my "Sexual orientation, refuge, and rights of exit," in Avigail Eisenberg and Jeff Spinner-Halev, eds, *Minorities Within Minorities* (Cambridge: Cambridge University Press, 2005).

Earlier we saw that the pure theory relies on *volenti non fit injuria* and the consent of group members, sometimes inferred from their failure to exit. But this possible exhaustive carving up of the social world into mutually exclusive communities, or the exhaustive carving up of the landscape into mutually exclusive *mortmain* holdings, would block the imputation of consent. The right of exit tacitly presumes the possibility of going someplace else. If there is no such place that will accept me, then staying put is no proof of willingness.

Some readers will notice the analogy with rights of emigration and immigration. An odd feature of the modern world is that international law recognizes a core human right to emigrate, but no duty on the part of sovereign states to accept immigrants (besides refugees and asylum-seekers). The Berlin Wall violated human rights; but once the wall comes down in the east and is re-erected in a west (or a north) that does not want to take in newcomers, human rights have ostensibly *not* been violated. This asymmetry is not some quirk of international law but a widely endorsed outcome. So, some readers may think, why should we not think the same about groups? Even if there's no place to go, mightn't a person still have a meaningful right of exit?

The analogy holds. But in the case of states, no liberals believe that the mere failure to emigrate triggers *volenti non fit injuria*.[7] Individuals still have rights against states that recognize the right of emigration, in part precisely because the right of emigration is not easily realized in a world full of states. Likewise, in a Nozickean utopia we could not impute consent to those who remained in the communities of their birth, if the social or physical landscape were already full of groups. Here, the pure theory runs aground. The imputation of consent through acquiescence only makes sense under some permutations of what everyone *else* has decided to do with *their* freedom of association. If I am a member of a minority group that is so widely despised by surrounding groups that none would take me, or if I am a dissenter in a world of orthodox communities that jointly exhaust the territory, I must stay put. Perhaps I have suffered no injustice, since no one else has a duty to take me in. But my relationship to the rules of my group may *not* be treated as one of tacit consent.

Another reason not to rest content with the pure theory concerns rule of law constraints on groups' internal procedures. Free persons may choose, without paradox, not to exercise their freedom to act in particular ways, and may do so in concert with others. Groups' primary rules are thus directly assembled from the rights of those governed by them. But subjecting oneself to arbitrary

---

[7] See, of course, David Hume, "Of the Original Contract," in David Hume, Eugene F. Miller, eds, *Essays, Moral, Political and Literary* (Indianapolis: Liberty Classics, 1987[1748]), pp. 465–87.

procedures, to ruleless rule, is a different matter.[8] Locke argued that there is a categorical moral difference between consenting to even the absolute authority of another and consenting to absolute *and arbitrary* rule; the latter would be so unreasonable that it cannot be imputed to anyone. So the reasons for wide and unsupervised latitude for intermediate institutions' primary rules do not straightforwardly carry over into their adjudicative procedures.

Systems of internal rules and bylaws, and rule-governed procedures for their adjudication and enforcement, are pervasive features of associational life. Outside of occasional temporary cult-like settings, we do not expect to see secondary groups or institutions characterized by rulelessness and arbitrary whim; and members do not expect the groups they join to be so characterized. However thick and pervasive the primary rules, the expectation of fair, impartial, and consistent application of them is widespread.[9] And since the internal system of rules routinely creates conditions that the general legal system must take notice of—the student who is expelled for violating a university's rules must vacate the dorm and forfeits tuition, and the resulting claims of property and contract must be comprehensible by the courts—occasions regularly present themselves when the general legal system must at least decide whether to decide on the fairness of internal procedures.[10] It cannot simply assume a hands-off approach. Violations of the rule of law within groups, whether because procedures are broken, corrupted, or ignored, or because the procedures themselves are gravely defective, may demand outside intervention. At least the *possibility* of that cannot be forestalled simply by the pure theory's deference to internal primary rules.[11]

---

[8] Here there is a resemblance to the distinction between non-interference and non-domination conceptions of freedom made famous in Philip Pettit, *Republicanism*. Perhaps there is a right against domination, but not a right against interference, by one's group. I find it more illuminating to think in terms of Locke's distinction between absolute and arbitrary rule, and in terms of Fuller's development of the idea of the rule of law. Non-arbitrariness was central to Locke's conception of freedom in a way that puts pressure on the commonplace that a "liberal" conception of freedom is concerned only with Hobbesian non-interference; an understanding of liberalism that includes Hobbes and excludes Locke is a sign that something has gone wrong.

[9] Indeed it is so widespread that there is often pressure to judicialize those internal proceedings to inappropriate degrees. Universities, for example, are constantly called upon to (and sometimes do) make their internal disciplinary proceedings more and more court-like. For current purposes the point is about what people think they're agreeing to when they join an intermediate institution. While the pure theory is right that we must presume consent to primary rules, matters are at least more complicated about adjudicative procedures. For the idea that associations tend to judicialize and bureaucratize over time, see Fuller, "Two Principles of Human Association."

[10] Lon Fuller, *The Morality of Law* (New Haven: Yale University Press, 1969), pp. 125–8.

[11] For a related discussion, see Michael A. Helfand, "Religion's Footnote Four: Church Autonomy As Arbitration," 97(6) *Minnesota Law Review* 1891–1962, 2013. Helfand argues that contemporary American jurisprudence on the freedom of churches is best understood by analogy with arbitration law, the primary features of which include that "parties grant arbitrators authority through consent" and "the decisions of duly appointed arbitrators, while granted substantive deference, are subject to review for misconduct, fraud, or other forms of adjudicative 'naughtiness'" (p. 1902). The presumption of consent to associations' authority generates very

These considerations—the possibility of totalizing groups, the possibility of shrinking social space between groups, and the possibility of violations of the rule of law—all contribute to the final, and in some ways overarching, reason why the pure theory is not satisfactory. *Authority generates power.*[12]

Intermediate institutions and groups have both primary rules and enforcement and adjudicative mechanisms, whether the latter are decentralized and informal or centralized and formal. This is legitimate under the pure theory; individual rights-bearers may rightfully lead their lives subject to any number of such rules and mechanisms. Indeed, anyone who lives a non-hermit life surely does so.

Authority relationships, Joseph Raz has taught us, are characterized by one person's having reason to defer to the judgments of another—a person's doing better, according to his or her own reasons, by allowing those judgments to replace their own (or at least some of their own).[13] In these cases, *even though the person submitting to authority has valid reasons to do so*, some other person or group of persons is vested with the discretion to make decisions. This relation in aggregate serves the interests of those subject to it, but that does not mean that each of the decisions reached will do so. This creates the space for the authority-holders to reach (at least some) decisions for their own reasons, in their own interests.

Locke understood that authority generates power, and that this is a source of serious concern. The absence of authority is at the core of the inconveniencies of the state of nature; we will all do better, by our own lights and in serving our own reasons, if we agree to accept the final judgments of impartial judges, even when they reach different judgments than we would if we were acting as judges in our own respective cases. So we create a government to allow us to coordinate on authoritative, impartial judges. But that government is itself staffed by human beings who are now themselves called upon to act as judges in their own case, both about the limits of their authority and about the decisions to reach using it. They will sometimes abuse that authority; they will sometimes act within its bounds to enhance their own power over others. There is a direct line from the authoritative relations we need and the power structures we have reason to fear.

---

considerable institutional autonomy on substantive questions, but comes under severe strain when confronted with procedural violations.

[12] For a closely related idea, drawing on a more rigorous social–theoretic account, see Andrew Sabl, *Hume's Politics* (Princeton: Princeton University Press, 2012), pp. 36–7. For a full development of intermediate associations as holders of authority over their members, see Victor Muñiz-Fraticelli, *The Structure of Pluralism* (Oxford: Oxford University Press, forthcoming).

[13] Joseph Raz, *The Authority of Law: Essays on Law and Morality* (Oxford: Oxford University Press, 1979).

The dynamic is somewhat different for partial authorities—authorities that, unlike the state, do not claim the final and supreme right to determine the boundaries of their own authority over every question. And liberals believe that the moral problem is at least somewhat different when authorities lack violent, coercive power with which to enforce their judgments. Nonetheless, authority relations outside the state still generate power. Precisely so far as we have reason to accept authority—because we have reasons to remain members of the relevant groups, whether those reasons concern the salvation of our souls, our friendly relations with peers, or the accomplishment of beneficent social goals—the authority figures gain power over us. They cannot, under the pure theory, *coerce* us; but we have our own good reasons for submitting, for continuing to fund the groups or volunteer for them or live in them. We are participants in the growth of the power over us; but the power is no less real for that. And the pure theory's reasons for accepting authority relations do not apply to power relations as such. Maybe the power generated by the groups' authority relations is nothing much to worry about—but we cannot know that only by analyzing the rights of those involved.

Congruence

This section will describe an idea that might be taken as the pure theory's counterpart, an attempt to build up thoroughly rationalistic, individualistic, group-skeptical conclusions from simple premises: congruence.[14] It is not often spelled out as a complete theory, but it is often reverted to or implicitly relied upon in particular cases.[15]

The core idea of congruence is that associations, groups, and intermediate bodies ought to be congruent—in their internal governance and their internal rules—with the just liberal state. They are normatively constrained to be democratic, constitutional, and rights-respecting.[16] The state ought to be governed by the consent of a majority of its members; so ought an association. The state is prohibited from passing laws that restrict basic liberties, deny equality, or impair fundamental rights; so are associations and non-

---

[14] I borrow the word from Nancy Rosenblum's treatment of recognizably the same concept in *Membership and Morals*, although I push the idea in a somewhat different direction.

[15] Russell Hardin claims to support a full doctrine of congruence, though he does not seem to see the radically anti-associational positions this commits him to. See "Special Status for Groups," *The Good Society*, vol. 6, no. 2, pp. 12–19, 1996; the discussion of "group liberalism" in *Liberalism, Constitutionalism, and Democracy* (Oxford: Oxford University Press, 1999, pp. 326–32); and "Cultural Diversity and Liberalism," in Jörg Kühnelt, ed., *Political Legitimation Without Morality?* (London: Springer, 2008).

[16] Political theories that are not liberal, democratic, or constitutionalist have their versions of congruence theory as well, as we will see.

institutionalized groups. Liberalism is concerned with the protection of individual freedom, regardless of which group or institution threatens it.

John Stuart Mill's *On Liberty* is centrally concerned with a repressive intellectual culture, with the human propensity to "like in crowds" and to succumb to (and socially enforce) the temptation of ape-like imitation; it aims to defend *individuality*, not merely—not even primarily—formal freedom from state regulation. The idea that persons are free and equal does not categorically distinguish between state and non-state *denials* of freedom and equality. The moral interests protected by liberal freedom and equality must be defended against associations and groups as well as against the state: for example, racial discrimination by private employers and schools and in private housing markets can maintain a racial caste system, and the extension of civil rights norms into the private sphere has been a major liberal triumph. Liberty, no less than equality, demands protection against non-state actors. Universities should not restrict speech; churches should not discriminate on the basis of sex in access to clerical office; residential associations should not restrict the freedom of homeowners to use their property; families should not restrict the freedom of their children to marry (or not) whomever they wish; and so on.

The congruence theory sometimes justifies importing the moral constraints on state action into the associational sphere by noting the need for the state to *enforce* the private agreements and rules of the latter sphere in case of conflicts. When Muslim women seek to protest against discriminatory treatment by praying in the space reserved for men, or Catholic dissenters take it upon themselves to elect priests and bishops who have not been consecrated and try to hold services in their traditional Catholic churches, eventually the official organization treats them as trespassers and calls for the police. The family that agrees to judge an inheritance by rabbinic or *sharia* arbitration is seeking to arrange and create property rights that eventually the civil courts will enforce. This is true for universities, residential associations, and voluntary clubs alike. Recalcitrant rules-violators will eventually be subject to state coercion to enforce their disaffiliation from the group—their expulsion from campus, the foreclosure on their condominium unit, and so on—and the operations of their rules and procedures affect the distribution of enforceable property rights. This, it is sometimes said, means that the internal rules are subject to liberal constraints on state action: the police may not be called upon to enforce internal rules that would be unconstitutional if they were public laws. A similar idea was appealed to earlier in order to shore up the idea of rule of law constraints on associations, but this version of congruence suggests that the constraints of liberal constitutionalism in general are incorporated into associational life by the need for state enforcement of associations' internal decisions. In American constitutional law, the case of *Shelley v Kraemer* apparently stands for this proposition: the prohibition on racially discriminatory *state* action was extended to the state enforcement of private restrictive covenants.[17]

Why Congruence is Not Satisfactory

Congruence cannot be generalized into a wholly coherent theory. To see why, consider the idea of freedom of religion within a church. There is *some* sense in which liberal justice prohibits churches from restricting the religious freedom of their members. For example, they may not attempt to kill apostates and blasphemers. They may refuse to recognize conversions away from the faith, but the liberal state must place sharp boundaries on what that refusal can mean; as far as it is concerned, the ex-member is outside church jurisdiction. But it does not make sense for the liberal state to tell churches that they must respect the religious freedom of their current and ongoing members in the sense that they must treat any or all religious beliefs as compatible with membership, the way that the liberal state must treat any or all religious beliefs as compatible with citizenship. Churches are, they must be, free to prohibit apostasy, blasphemy, out-conversion, and denial of the religion's claims *for those who wish to remain members in good standing*. A church that is unable to insist on adherence to its own religious tenets as a condition of membership is unable to *be* a church. Neither can the paradox be solved with the strategy mentioned in the previous paragraph. When the church calls the police to evict dissenters as trespassers, the state is not infringing on religious liberty; it is respecting the rights of the church *qua* property owner and thereby the associational freedom of the church's members.

To take a less weighty example: a homeowners' association or a condominium association just *is*, in part, an agreement to waive certain rights of use of one's property as against the association's governing board. To buy into such an association, and then assert one's unconditional freedom of property-use against its rules, is to make a basic mistake. One might coherently wish that there were no such thing as homeowners' associations; and one might certainly decide that some particular rule is unnecessarily intrusive. But one cannot without contradiction wish for homeowners' associations that leave the homeowners as free to use their property as they would be without it.

The doctrine of congruence, treated seriously, prohibits persons acting together from making any choices that would constrain their own future choices—which means that they may not make any choices of promise or commitment at all, and indeed few non-trivial choices of any sort. A group in

---

[17] *Shelley v. Kraemer*, 334 U.S. 1 (1948). This ruling is highly anomalous in American jurisprudence, and for good reason. See Chapter 11.

part consists of primary rules governing members' behavior beyond the primary rules already enforced by the state (no murder, no theft, no driving on the wrong side of the road, and so on). Joining such a group, then, is a waiver of the use of some rights. While performing the job for which I have contracted, I waive the exercise of my right to determine what to do with my time. When selling something I own, I relinquish my right to it, as against the person to whom I sell it. While sitting in the pews of a church I have joined, I waive my right to speak freely about religious matters and persuade my neighbors of my own views. Such waivers are a great deal of what we *do* with our freedom, and only confusion results if we take the "inalienability" of rights to mean that their holder cannot even for a moment waive their exercise.

A related way of expressing the idea underlying congruence is the claim that liberalism is committed to denying that groups have rights, or at the very least to prioritizing the rights of individuals over the rights of groups. These slogans mainly obstruct clear thinking on the questions at hand, and they do not form part of the best defense of rationalist liberalism, even though rationalism is indeed highly group-skeptical and attentive to the moral interests of individuals that might be impaired by group life.

The attempt to use a claim about individual and group rights as such to solve problems about freedom and group life commits a number of mistakes. It takes an unexamined opposition between individual and group rights for granted. The pure theory, whatever its other flaws, build groups' claims entirely out of the materials of individual rights. The right of freedom of association and the right to do in common what we have the right to do individually, translate capacious individual freedom into capacious group self-governance. If a group's rules compel me to do something that I have a right to do anyways, or forbid me to do something that I have a right to refrain from doing anyways, then it is a valid exercise of my individual freedom to live by the group's rules. The rights of groups play no foundational role—even though in operational terms we may observe a social world in which groups corporately make many decisions, and individuals unguided by group rules make few.

That is to say, the individual rights/group rights distinction fails to distinguish between a liberal commitment to individualist moral justification or individualist ontology and conclusions about social organization. From the fact that a particular conflict sets a person's claims in opposition to that of a group, it simply assumes that individualism demands that the claims be upheld. In fact, the gap between normative conclusions in particular cases on one hand and either social ontologies or strategies of foundational political justification on the other is wide and deep. After all, Hobbes built a political absolutism in which the claims of the state supersede those of individuals in very nearly all cases out of an individualistic ontology and justification. The interests of a group encompass (and may be reducible to) the interests of the other individuals who are members of the group, the interests of even dissident members in the group's existence and in the possibility of belonging to it, and the interests of other possible future members. That the group is standing in for those interests doesn't mean that they're not real interests of individual human beings.

The individual rights/group rights claim is question-begging. It assumes what must be demonstrated: that an individual's rights include the right not to be subject to some rule or practice at the hands of some group. The priority of individual rights is irrelevant if no individual right is impaired in the case at hand. Innocent persons have a right as against the whole world not to be deliberately killed; it follows that a group's norm of human sacrifice conflicts with individual rights (and the norm must give way). But in, say, a conflict between a dissenting member and a religious group on a norm of dress, we need to specify rights carefully. I have a basic freedom to choose my dress, and most potential state legislation on clothing choices would violate that right. Nonetheless, I may become a priest who must wear a clerical collar, I may go to a black-tie formal event that will deny me admission if I am wearing blue jeans, I may play a sport whose rules demand that I wear a helmet to protect myself. I don't have a right as against the church, the banquet organizers, or the sports league to be able to wear whatever I want and still take part in the activity. Instead, I have the right to waive the right to choose my dress for many purposes. To put it differently, I have the right to make choices about dress that comply with rules governing some setting or another, because I have the right to take part in activities that are partly constituted by agreements on such rules. To look at a Muslim woman wearing a headscarf and immediately phrase the problem as one of group rights being allowed to govern individual rights is to assume the answer: what the boundaries of the individual right to choose one's dress are, whether the right is waivable, and against whom it may be asserted. And, very often, the claim is simply wrong from a liberal perspective. There may be plausible rationalist liberal arguments to be made against veiling, but they will not rely on treating the rules about veiling as if they were statutes and analyzing them as rights-violations. The rules may impair freedom, but this must be the conclusion of a harder argument about intragroup power.

None of this is to say that intermediate groups can *never* impair the freedom of their members. It is only to rule out reaching that conclusion in the quick way described here: with a direct move from the rights liberal states must not violate to rights intermediate groups may not demand waivers of. If there is meaning in the idea that groups can threaten the freedom of their members, it is to be found elsewhere than in a simple analogy of a group's primary rules to a state's laws.

3

Reunderstanding Intermediate Groups

Treating Groups as Groups

In the previous chapter I described two arguments about the relationship among persons, groups, and freedom. Each was highly formal and abstract: a pure theory of free association that denied that the primary rules of non-state groups, provided that they are enforced only by disassociation and exclusion, can ever count as violations of the freedom of members, and a theory of congruence that held that they always did. Both were found to be unsatisfactory.

One way of understanding the problem with the pure theory and congruence is this: the pure theory treats groups as if they were individual persons, while congruence treats groups as if they were states. On the pure theory, associations wield in aggregate the rights their members hold against outsiders, and their internal rules over members are considered little-to-no different from an individual person's own reasons for action. On the congruence theory, associations' rules are considered tightly analogous to the legislation of a state, and subject to the same constraints as morally legitimate state legislation.

It also seems that both the pure theory and congruence are committed to a kind of artificial uniqueness of the state. For the pure theory, of all the rules by which we are bound in our social lives, only the state's laws should be understood as infringements on freedom. We saw this in considering the problem of exit and consent. The pure theory tells us not to consider group rules as freedom-restricting, because they are consented to or acquiesced in, as evidenced by the non-exercise of the right of exit. But this argumentative strategy is rejected by liberals as applied to the state; allowing a right to emigrate does not immunize a state from liberal criticism about the content of its laws.

The congruence theory, by contrast, treats the state as uniquely rational, abstract, and committed to justice. Social groups, if left to their own devices, will be illiberal, customary, conformist, sexist, exclusionary, and restrictive.

They should not be allowed to restrict freedom; this means that they should not be allowed *by the state* to do so. We could see this as a kind of naïve faith that the state is likely to intervene to protect freedom, but I don't think that is quite the problem. Rather, the congruence theorist treats the state's action as an object of normative philosophical attention, subject to deliberate movement in the direction of justice if only we so chose. Reflection on justice means reflection on the question "what should the state do?" Social groups only rise to the attention of political philosophy, on this view, insofar as they act unjustly; they are either uninteresting or they are problems. And once a problem has been identified, the state is looked to as the answer.

From one perspective, the pure theory and the congruence theory both treat groups as one of the more familiar categories of political philosophy: as big individuals or small states. From another, both ignore groups to focus attention on the state: the state as a unique threat to liberty, or the state as the unique locus of rationality and justice. In this chapter I adopt a different tack, one that aims to treat groups as groups, and the state as having tendencies and social characteristics of its own, just as groups do.

The problems at stake are not susceptible to dissolution by definition; what is at stake is not just what formally *counts* as a restriction of freedom. The enduring tension between pluralist and rationalist strands in liberalism is not between such absolute positions, and is not centered on such formal questions. Rather, it encompasses competing moral and social theories, claims that are sometimes in different registers altogether, and that often involve broad empirical generalizations about the behavior of particular kinds of institutions. Such generalizations rest on the thought that institutions and actors will not always behave as they should; that they tend to accumulate power, and use it for purposes beyond those that are legitimate; that they have systematic tendencies that should be taken into account in thinking about our normative principles.

Such ideas turn political theory into, in part, a branch of social theory. As Bernard Williams put it in the fuller version of Part I's epigraph,

[P]olitical philosophy's habitual, and it seems ineliminable, dependence on the urgency of political questions which are not in the first instance philosophical, is of a piece with its insistence, when at all interesting, on being both normative and *impure*. It is normative at least in the sense that first-order moral and political disagreement with the author can relevantly motivate disagreement with his philosophy, and impure in the sense that materials from non-philosophical sources—an involvement with history or the social sciences, for instance—are likely to play a more than illustrative part in the argument.[1]

---

[1] Bernard Williams, "Political Philosophy and the Analytical Tradition," in *Philosophy as a Humanistic Discipline* (Princeton: Princeton University Press, 2006), p. 155, emphasis added.

Pure theories are of limited use in political theory. And the basic disagreements between pluralist and rationalist liberalism at their best are almost entirely impure in Williams' sense.

States are not machines for dispensing justice, and we are poorly served when our theories imagine them to be. Even in normative theory, we must proceed with a sociologically plausible sense of states' behavior and dynamics. Something similar is true of groups and associations, which are not mere emanations from or expressions of their members' wills or preferences. They have dynamics of their own. States tend to be more suspicious of and restrictive toward associations than is justified: they tend to seek centralization of authority and homogenization of cultural and linguistic identities; and they tend to see local threats to freedom in minority practices that they do not understand. Those who lead intermediate groups tend to build the authority they necessarily have over internal matters into a broader power over members' lives. These tendencies are not to be idealized away; in an impure political theory, they are to be built in. And they have been built into the dynamics of interactions between states and intermediate groups—and into the arguments between pluralist and rationalist liberals.

Pure normative theories concern themselves with *what the state should do;* one virtue of impure theories is that they allow us to take theoretical account of the prediction that states will do what they shouldn't. Freedom of speech is valuable, is even demanded by justice, in part precisely because injustice happens, and ought to be exposed, denounced, and contested. Liberals reject the distinction between rights of dissent from just and from unjust order, the claim that "you needed your right to object when you lived under injustice, but now that you live under justice, freedom of speech is superfluous and harmful."

For any moral and social condition shy of seamless justice perfectly and perpetually instantiated there will always be a need for mechanisms of maintenance and improvement. A reasonably just society could protect freedom of speech to try to keep itself reasonably just, to improve where possible, to expose such episodic and particular injustices that might arise, and to hope that a wrong turn in the future might be mitigated or corrected. Moreover, the argument that the right to dissent is unneeded in a just society is so clearly ripe for opportunistic abuse that we might take its use as *prima facie* evidence that the speaker does *not* intend to pursue just policies.

There are real similarities here to the freedom of intermediate groups, which often provide a source of social and institutional resistance to the state.[2] One

---

[2] James Scott, for example, argues that a robust civil society is a crucial counterweight to the excesses of "high modernist" state rationalization. *Seeing Like A State* (New Haven: Yale University Press, 1998).

might think that this only matters in unjust societies, and cannot be a reason to allow a robust associational sphere in just ones. This has been a recurring view, especially since the French Revolution: intermediate bodies were valuable when they checked monarchies, but would be pernicious once monarchies have been replaced by democratic republics. A contemporary equivalent might say that the moral importance of a civil society that can resist totalitarianism is irrelevant to the question of what rights associations should have in liberal democracies. That which was valuable when it interfered with states' pursuit of injustice only seems, in our hypothetical just society, to interfere with its pursuit of *justice*.

While the sociological insight that a robust civil society serves as a check on state power is strictly logically compatible with the idea that only unjust states ought to be checked, the overall view would be a strange one. The reasonably just society today cannot be sure that it will remain so forever. If it takes a turn for the worse, a civil society capable of resistance can hardly be expected to spring up overnight. The minimum price to pay for the insurance policy of having robust associations when a society needs them to resist injustice could well be associations that resist the state even when it is moderately just.

If one concentrates on the mostly just state at hand or presumed to be around the corner, then the existence of sites of resistance to state power might look like a problem. If one concentrates on all states since the state form came into existence, or the whole universe of possible states, or if one takes the perspective of a particular association that needs a habit of defending its freedom across regime changes and organizational resources capable of mounting the defense, things will look quite different. While the approaches analyzed in the last chapter emphasize the moral relationship between individuals and groups, with a hypothetical state presumed to be available to enforce the correct view, this approach is often concerned with the character of states themselves. Liberalism, as a theory within and about the modern state, is concerned with what such states are like, what they do, how they act—and not only how they act *when they are liberal*.

This thought is central to the tradition of liberal constitutionalism: we should not theorize either as if men were angels, or as if angels are to govern men. As John Stuart Mill put it, notwithstanding his famous "simple principle" for deciding the scopes of state action and individual freedom,

> unfortunately it is not on the merits of either individual or government agency at its best, that the question depends, but on the imperfections and shortcomings of both in their average condition; by far the strongest arguments of each side being

drawn, not from the excellence of the kind of agency it advocates, but from the infirmities of its rival.[3]

Madison's dictum that in "framing a government which is to be administered by men over men, the great difficulty lies in this: you must first enable the government to control the governed; and in the next place oblige it to control itself"[4] applies as well when the "governed" associate into groups as it does when they are thought of as individual persons.

And so in what follows I aim to proceed symmetrically, treating states and non-state institutions and groups as similarly prone to non-angelic behavior.

While I mean the treatment to be symmetrical as between state behavior and group behavior, the consequences may not be symmetrical as between rationalism and pluralism. This is because normative political philosophy has often treated politics (and positive law) as *uniquely* subject to free and deliberate decision. The state acts, society and the economy are acted upon; we are free to think of how the state *should* act; society and the economy are determined, politics is decided. Thus, treating the state and the rest of society symmetrically, with social tendencies and dynamics of their own, will be at least somewhat deflationary of rationalism.

In place of the theories of rights we saw in the last chapter, in what follows I therefore offer normative social theories about power: reasons to expect states to exercise more power over groups than can be justified by the freedom of groups' members, and reasons to expect groups to exercise more power over their members than can be justified by their free associational choices. These are, I suggest, more secure foundations for rationalist and pluralist liberalism: rival accounts of where threats to freedom are more likely to come from, and when. They are also truer to the histories of rationalist and pluralist liberal thought that we will survey in Part II than are pure rights theories.

What follows are generalizations and tendencies, not ironclad laws. Each is a reason to normatively suspect the agent in question (states or groups). The first set of generalizations will mean that we have good reason to worry that states will restrict associational freedom and group pluralism unnecessarily, unjustly, and for reasons that have little or nothing to do with the freedom of group members even if that is used as a pretext. It will mean that even state actors sincerely trying to respect associational freedom will err systematically on the side of intrusion and limitation. When we see a state intervening in group life, we suspect that these dynamics are in play; when calling for state intervention, we should remember that it is unlikely to stop at the just-right

[3] J. S. Mill, "Centralisation," in *Collected Works of John Stuart Mill*, Vol. XIX, J. M. Robson, ed. (Toronto: University of Toronto Press, 1977[1862]), pp. 579–613.

[4] Madison as Publius, Federalist No. 51, in *The Federalist Papers*, Clinton Rossiter, ed. (New York: Mentor Books, 1961[1788]).

60

point. The second set of generalizations will mean that we have good reason to worry that internal rules, structures, hierarchies, and discriminations are not simply the result of sincere consensual commitments on the part of members.[5] But this separation of presentation is artificial. The excesses interact. State overreach forces associations and groups into a defensive posture: they raise barriers to entry, become more opaque to outside monitoring, demand more conservative and loyal behavior from their members. Local elite power, the opaqueness of intermediate social groups, and the oppositional character of many group identities make it difficult for states to regulate intra-group life in any fine-grained way, and motivate more aggressive state action. And so on.

Tendencies toward State Excess

Property and Wealth

One recurring pattern of relations between states and intermediate bodies concerns resources. To put the matter one-sidedly: political authorities recurrently expropriate the resources of intermediate bodies. This is not unique to the modern state—the medieval French monarchy crushed the Knights Templar and expropriated that order's wealth—but is strongly characteristic, indeed foundational, of the modern state as it emerged out of medieval pluralism. The expropriation of church lands and wealth and the looting of convents and monasteries stands as an important moment in the development of many west European states, from Henry VIII in England to revolutionary France to newly unified Italy. The expropriation of land from indigenous peoples—collectively organized—by settler states offers an obvious comparison.

The intergenerational continuity of intermediate bodies allows them to accumulate, invest, and compound resources over time. If intermediate institutions are more-or-less voluntarily funded by their members (at least more-voluntarily than political authorities are), then selection effects will mean that those intermediate bodies that survive over time are those that can attract relatively enthusiastic contributions and bequests. So, over time, those intermediate bodies that survive often become relatively wealthy. Moreover, some intermediate institutions benefit from international trade or from resource

---

[5] Compare Ian Shapiro, *The State of Democratic Theory* (Princeton: Princeton University Press, 2003), p. 53: "[T]he ineradicably hierarchical character of much social life makes power relations ubiquitous to human interaction. But this does not mean that domination is...Hierarchical relations are often legitimate, and, when they are, they do not involve domination." In this language, the generalizations to follow offer reasons to suspect that legitimate hierarchy will spill over into domination, or that at any given moment in time we are witnessing an example of domination and not one of legitimate hierarchy.

movements to evade local taxes and inflation thanks to their positioning across national boundaries. The Knights Templar were not a bank; but they had an institutional structure that allowed them to act as one in a fairly reliable, Mediterranean-wide way, and they grew wealthy in part for that reason.

To contemporary minds shaped by, e.g., debates about the treatment in the tax code of university endowments, the wealth of intermediate bodies may look something like a deliberate state policy. But that is not how the dynamics began. Universities, cities, nunneries and monastic orders, and transnational bodies such as the Knights Templar and Rosicrucians, were able to accumulate resources more or less to the degree that they could defend and/or conceal their resources from local political powers. During the era of relative decentralization of power in medieval Europe, that capacity to defend or conceal was relatively high. During the era of relative concentration of power characteristic of early modern absolutist Europe, that ability diminished. As state capacity increased, monasteries and convents were likely to be closed and have their wealth expropriated, in Catholic France as in Henrician England. This suggests that the earlier non-expropriation was not a deliberate policy, in the manner that the contemporary United States has a deliberate policy of allowing higher education to be supported by perpetual charitable endowments; it was simply a lack of effective ability.

Another way to look at the same dynamic is this: the resource growth in intermediate institutions over time becomes a source of social inequality, and *in extremis* of absolute deprivation in the rest of society. We associate this view perhaps most prominently with the expropriation of Church lands during the French Revolution. The Church had come to own such a large share of French agricultural land as to depress overall French wealth, and to make it difficult to accommodate population growth. But the question is older than that. Challenges to *mortmain* and to the Church's tendency to swallow up resources were common in Western Europe from the thirteenth century or so onward. Intermediate bodies may be even worse on this dimension than the aristocratic and feudal resource-holders, which in some ways they resemble. The aristocratic family will someday face a wastrel son who sells off the family estates (returning them to general circulation) to fund bad habits, or the ambitious one who sells them in order to finance commercial activity. The entail of estates is meant to prevent this but can only slow it; in the face of substantial financial pressure or opportunity costs, a way will be found (e.g. long-term leaseholds) to convert inherited dead resources into liquid capital. Churches and similar bodies seem less vulnerable to these pressures.

Secrecy and Privacy

The fear of losing resources is among the sources for the organizational habit that intermediate groups adopt norms and rules of privacy and secrecy, which in turn tends to fuel state suspicion. From a long-term perspective this could be a selection effect: the groups that endure over time are those that are able to protect themselves against outside subversion or expropriation, and this will be in part those that are able to protect their information, including the information about their resources.

Intermediate groups' reasons for preserving privacy and secrecy go far beyond the protection of assets. Groups of all sorts often act to protect their members from the legal system of the state. Intermediate groups whose purposes are overtly criminal—the Mafia with its *omertà* rules about secrecy, for example—highlight these tendencies in extreme form but are far from exhaustive. For many ethnic minorities, the bonds of local group trust are simply so much stronger than the trust of the state's agents that a norm of not revealing information about group members to the police is deeply entrenched. The pattern is common, in the face of state actions that are malicious, benevolent, or neither. Those evading conscription may seek refuge and concealment within their minority ethnic community or from a dissident church. Again, group endurance and survival are likely to be associated with this tendency. It provides a benefit to group members, discouraging them from leaving the protection of group life for the general society. It helps to protect the group against state persecution, when such persecution comes. And it builds and develops in-group trust and social capital. Indeed, the selection effects may be stronger still: what look to later eyes like clearly defined and long-lived groups could just be the accumulated populations over generations who have adopted these strategies of secrecy, evasion, and avoidance, though eventually the strategies become norms and rules for a new kind of group life.[6]

We do not, however, only have to take this evolutionary perspective. Group life *is*, in part, a barrier to outside information-gathering, and this predictably engenders state hostility. This is true whether the barrier to information is an unavoidable feature of group difference, as is true of minority languages that so often strike state officials as a kind of suspicious secret code, or a deliberately cultivated system of protection, as with associations with secret membership lists, secret handshakes and passwords, and internal mysteries revealed only to initiates. The barrier is sometimes a physical one: the highlands in which an

---

[6] See James Scott, *The Art of Not Being Governed: An Anarchist History of Upland Southeast Asia* (New Haven: Yale University Press, 2009).

ethnic minority takes refuge, the walls of a medieval city, or a church that grants sanctuary from the secular law.

The tie between secrecy and intermediate groups is so strong that conspiracy theories center on them, indeed sometimes seem to consist of little more than names of intermediate groups connected by arrows: the Trilateral Commission, the Council on Foreign Relations, the Freemasons, the Illuminati, the Rosicrucians and the Knights Templar, the Jesuits, and on and on. The basic fact that groups present a barrier to outside knowledge perpetually encourages non-members to be suspicious of them.

States necessarily rely on their ability to gather resources: financial capital, soldiers, food, and material support for the military. So states have an unavoidable organizational imperative to gather information. As Weber put it, "bureaucratic administration means fundamentally domination through knowledge. This is the feature of it which makes it specifically rational."[7] The ability of state officials to know the society they govern, to be able to see what there is to be seen in it, has been a theme of social theorists from Hayek to Foucault[8] to Scott; the last has given us the useful concept of *legibility* for what it is that states seek to impose on their societies. Taxation and conscription are core functions of state rule. But information-gathering—the census, the official map of land ownership for purposes of taxation—are barely secondary to those functions, being necessary for them. The extension of political capacity that eventually results in the sovereign modern state, and the subsequent strengthening of state capacity, is in part the process of increasing the legibility of society—knowing more and more about who is where and what they have. As the state absorbs law-enforcement functions, its need for information grows further.

That process is a conflictual one. Those under surveillance, understanding that it means their eventual conscription and taxation or their possible persecution, resist it. Those who speak a language unknown to most central state officials have an advantage in doing so. So do those who inhabit territory that is difficult to reach, map, or extend coercive force into, and those who inhabit no fixed territory at all. So do those with distinctive or fluid naming conventions; hence the imposition of intergenerationally fixed surnames by early modern states. State officials become aware of and hostile to parts of the population that are hard to count, map, conscript, tax, and police. And every kind of local shorthand, every piece of local customary knowledge that does not need to be written down, every strong local bond of trust that can

---

[7] Max Weber, "The Types of Legitimate Domination," in Hechter and Horne, *Theories of Social Order: A Reader* (Palo Alto: Stanford University Press, 2003).

[8] See, among others, Michel Foucault, *Security, Territory, Population: Lectures at the Collège De France, 1977–78*, Graham Burchell, trans. (New York: Picador, 2007[2004]).

encourage group members to protect each other and hide each other, is another informational barrier to the outside state official.[9]

The dynamics of information-gathering are fundamental to the kind of social organization that a modern state *is*. Likewise, the tendency to conceal information is a basic feature of group life, at a bare minimum because what goes on inside a group is likely to be harder for state agents to see or understand. And this predictably engenders suspicion of the group on the part of the state, regardless of whether the group is in fact concealing resources or violations of the law. The mere fact that it *could* be tends to elicit stronger suspicions and greater interventions; the ability of groups to conceal is met with attempts by states to know.

Transnationality

It is common to discuss intermediate groups as if they are wholly subsumed within one state; the word "intermediate" almost demands it. But that is misleading, and leads us to overlook another common source of state suspicion. The intermediate is often also the transpolitical or transjurisdictional, and suspect on those grounds. States routinely view their internal minorities as also (or primarily) the thin entering wedge for some external threat.[10] Sometimes the local minority or local group is seen as tied to some larger or more powerful neighbor: Anglophones in Québec as the stalking horses for Anglophone Canada or North America, Russians in the post-Soviet republics as stalking horses for Russia, Catholics within any Protestant state as owing allegiance to a foreign, Roman, prince. This is sometimes implausible to outside eyes, but revanchism does exist in the world; Czech suspicion of Sudeten Germans was not paranoid. Sometimes, however, the local group is tied to a group that is a minority, or an intermediate group, everywhere. Pre-1948 Jews, Freemasons, Jesuits, Roma, and most Protestant denominations,[11]

---

[9] Oakeshott's "practical knowledge," in other words, is a *systematic* obstacle to the desire for system-wide "technical knowledge"; the conflict between the two is not only one of temperament or education or ideology. Oakeshott, "Rationalism in Politics," in *Rationalism in Politics, and Other Essays* (New York: Basic Books Pub. Co., 1962).

[10] For a discussion about this phenomenon in Eastern and Central Europe by a political theorist sympathetic to minority claims see Will Kymlicka, "Justice and Security in the Accommodation of Minority Nationalism," in Alain Dieckhoff, ed., *The Politics of Belonging* (Lanham, Md.: Lexington Books, 2004).

[11] "Most" measured by denominations, not by adherents. Locally dominant Anglican communion churches, Lutheran churches, and Calvinist denominations make up most of the Protestants in the world. But many more Protestant denominations are not dominant in any nation-state in the world: Quakers, Amish, Mennonites, Methodists in all their variety, Baptists in all their variety, Seventh-Day Adventists, Jehovah's Witnesses, the marginal Protestant cases of Unitarians and Mormons, and so on.

to name only a few, were or are nowhere a *Staatvolk*; but their internationalism has seemed to many states no less suspicious for that.

Throughout this book I use the phrase "intermediate group," but it should always be understood that groups may be transjurisdictional, and need not be in any sense smaller than states. And this, too, predictably elicits state suspicion, making it sociologically likely that they will limit group freedom more than is justifiable.

The Centralizing Temperament and the Man of System

An important but little-noted chapter late in *Spirit of the Laws* says:

> There are certain ideas of uniformity, which sometimes strike great geniuses (for they even affected Charlemagne), but infallibly make an impression on little souls. They discover therein a kind of perfection, which they recognize because it is impossible for them not to see it; the same authorized weights, the same measures in trade, the same laws in the state, the same religion in all its parts. But is this always right and without exception? Is the evil of changing constantly less than that of suffering? And does not a greatness of genius consist rather in distinguishing between those cases in which uniformity is requisite, and those in which there is a necessity for differences? In China the Chinese are governed by the Chinese ceremonial and the Tartars by theirs; and yet there is no nation in the world that aims so much at tranquility. If the people observe the laws, what signifies it whether these laws are the same?[12]

The Burkean idea in the middle of that passage—that changes in laws are costly, and sometimes those costs are greater than the costs of an imperfect status quo—is familiar. But the surrounding argument is perhaps not. It contains at least two distinct ideas: a gesture toward a defense of pluralism, and a worry about the character of the legislator who would suppress it. The latter idea was echoed in a somewhat better-known passage from the final edition of Adam Smith's *Theory of Moral Sentiments*:

> The man of system, on the contrary, is apt to be very wise in his own conceit; and is often so enamoured with the supposed beauty of his own ideal plan of government, that he cannot suffer the smallest deviation from any part of it. He goes on to establish it completely and in all its parts, without any regard either to the great interests, or to the strong prejudices which may oppose it. He seems to imagine that he can arrange the different members of a great society with as much ease as the hand arranges the different pieces upon a chess-board. He does not consider that the pieces upon the chess-board have no other principle of motion besides that which the hand impresses upon them; but that, in the great chess-board of

---

[12] Montesquieu, *Spirit of the Laws*, Anne M. Cohler, Basia Carolyn Miller, and Harold Samuel Stone, eds (Cambridge: Cambridge University Press, 1989[1748]), henceforth *SL*, VI.29.18, p. 617.

human society, every single piece has a principle of motion of its own, altogether different from that which the legislature might chuse to impress upon it.[13]

It is easy enough (even discounting the "hand" metaphor) to see a connection with the *Wealth of Nations*, and to suppose that the man of system is what we would think of as an economic central planner, failing to see that individual persons have their own interests to pursue. But that is not the topic of this passage. In the surrounding text he discusses "confirmed habits and prejudices of the people," the rights and privileges of cities, provinces, the nobility, and long-established orders, even when these are "in some measure abusive," all contributing to the constitution that the man of system seeks to "new-model" in all its parts—the traditional rights defended by Montesquieu. To put it in a perhaps surprising way: the principles of motion of their own are *not*, or at least not necessarily, individualistic or proper to each individual. The problem is not that they each have their self-interest to pursue. Rather, they have principles of motion—rules to follow, ends to pursue—that in part derive from the habits and prejudices of their respective groups, from the rules and norms of the *corps* to which they belong.

This is ordinarily taken as Smith's late-in-life commentary on the French Revolution, though the point is expressed in general terms. If so, that is worth some attention. It appeared in the first half of 1790, before even Burke's *Reflections*, which itself was a particularly early critique of the Revolution's rationalizing tendencies. If this passage was indeed a response to events across the Channel, the trigger was not, say, the 1793 imposition of a maximum price on grain. Smith was not complaining of bad economics. Rather, the trigger had to be some combination of the abolition of feudal privileges, the replacement of traditional provinces with *départements*, the suppression of religious and monastic orders, the nationalization of church property, and the amalgamation of the Estates into the National Assembly. The text around the passage makes clear that it refers to changes in the "constitution or form of government." The reformer who would avoid the errors of the man of system is counseled to respect the "privileges" of "the great orders and societies, into which the state is divided" or "the confirmed habits and prejudices of the people."[14]

---

[13] Adam Smith, *Theory of Moral Sentiments*, Campbell and Skinner, eds (Indianapolis: Liberty Classics, 1981[1790]), pp. 233–4. Compare George Orwell: "The underlying motive of many Socialists, I believe, is simply a hypertrophied sense of order. The present state of affairs offends them not because it causes misery, still less because it makes freedom impossible, but because it is untidy; what they desire, basically, is to reduce the world to something resembling a chessboard." *The Road to Wigan Pier* (New York: Harcourt, 1958[1937]), p. 179.

[14] There is no way to be entirely sure that Smith had the French Revolution in mind rather than, say, Cromwell. (He could have been thinking of both.) The chief evidence is the timing: after five editions of the book, Smith added the "man of system" passage only in 1789, probably after the dissolution of the Estates-General and plausibly after the abolition, in August of that year, of the

Like Montesquieu, Smith suggests that the power available to the political reformer encourages a particular kind of mindset. That power will be especially attractive to those galled by the disorder of variety. The "spirit of system" "inflames" public-spirited reformism, "even to the madness of fanaticism." Like Montesquieu, Smith sees that the disorderly variety most likely to gall, in his day, is that of the inherited constitution itself, in need of remodeling by centralization and rationalization.

The psychology of the "man of system" should seem familiar to readers of Foucault on Bentham.[15] The most powerful recent account of the idea is to be found in James Scott's *Seeing Like a State*, and the best philosophical account is in Michael Oakeshott's "Rationalism in Politics."[16] The latter is concerned with the *rationalist* as a type of actor, not with "rationalism" as a free-floating gross concept. That is, like Smith and Montesquieu, Oakeshott is interested in the habits of thought, disciplines, and mindset, of the individual human beings who come to occupy positions of state power. I think these, rather than Hayek's information-based critique of economic planning, provide the closest modern analogs to Smith's "man of system."

If the diagnosis of the man of system (or the high modernist, or the rationalist) is right, then states—which is to say, state officials, with this characteristic mindset—will tend to be excessively skeptical of the jurisprudential pluralism generated by intermediate groups, of their adherence to custom or to local reasons that do not mirror the balance of reasons considered appropriate by the state. Insofar as individual humans move for reasons and in ways that reflect the moves the man of system would have them make anyway, no conflict arises. But the "principles of motion" of their own that *differ* from those desired by the state are often generated by intermediate groups—cities, provinces, religious and cultural groups, and so forth.

Congruence Again

I said in the previous chapter that there could be no general moral theory demanding that groups and associations stand in relation to their members

---

self-governing privileges of cities, provinces, guilds, along with the special privileges of the nobility and the clergy. It also seems to me that the language of Smith's indictment tracks these actions in the summer of 1789 more closely than it does the events of England's Commonwealth. Smith's discussion of the "man of system" is joined to an analysis of party competition in a way that makes it less plausible that he had in mind the absolutist monarchs with whom Montesquieu was concerned, but in a way that could encompass both the 1650s and 1789.

[15] See Michel Foucault, *Discipline and Punish*, Alan Sheridan, trans. (New York: Pantheon Books, 1977[1975]). While I do not much draw on Foucault for my understanding of the man of system in particular, the more general analysis of rationalism and the modern state is certainly indebted to him. See especially Foucault, *Security, Territory, Population*.

[16] James Scott, *Seeing Like A State*; Michael Oakeshott, "Rationalism in Politics."

strictly as just liberal states stand to *their* members. The primary rules of associations are not morally as tightly restricted in their content as are the coercive laws of the state. But this necessary lack of isomorphism between groups and states itself is an enduring source of state suspicion of groups. Tocqueville's followers have made much of the idea of associational life as the schools of democracy; but it might seem that only internally democratic associations can have that function. More generally, we find that states distrust groups whose internal governance and norms seem to inculcate values at variance with those undergirding the states' own governance.[17]

This tendency is not limited to liberal or democratic states. The internal egalitarianism of Calvinism was a source of horror to the absolutist monarch and divine right theorist James I, who famously held that "Presbytery...as well agreeth with a monarchy as God and the Devil."[18] His campaign against Scottish Presbyterianism was carried out under the slogan "No bishop, no King." One reason for early modern monarchical persecution of the Freemasons was that they were understood as subversively egalitarian and meritocratic. That is, while Freemasonry was (and is) governed by an elaborate hierarchy, social rank is officially left at the lodge door. One becomes an initiate into the higher-level mysteries for internal reasons, not by reason of wealth or status; and so an aristocrat might be lower in Masonic dignity than a commoner. The fact that some Masonic lodges admitted women as equal members was unwelcome for the same reason: internal equality that might undermine social hierarchy. Freemasonry later met persecution in the nineteenth-century United States for being aristocratic, that is, internally hierarchical and incompatible with the (white) egalitarianism of the general political culture. There had been no relevant change in the internal organization of the group, yet there is no contradiction. Internal relations of rank and status were independent of political rank and status, and monarchical and democratic states alike perceived that as a threat. Similarly, a skepticism of

---

[17] DiMaggio and Powell and their followers in organizational sociology have studied institutional isomorphism, why there is so much similarity in organizational forms and structures. Their interests are broader than mine (notably including commercial firms), but their question is connected. They postulate "three mechanisms through which institutional isomorphic change occurs...: 1) coercive isomorphism that stems from political influence and the problem of legitimacy; 2) mimetic isomorphism resulting from standard responses to uncertainty; and 3) normative isomorphism, associated with professionalization" (1983: 150). Both (1) and (3) are relevant to state-association relations of the sort I am discussing here, and they are strongly linked to each other as well. DiMaggio and Powell (1983), "The Iron Cage Revisited: Institutional Isomorphism and Collective Rationality in Organizational Fields," 48(2) *American Sociological Review* 147–60.

[18] "The Hampton Court Conference," 1604, in J. R. Tanner, ed., *Constitutional Documents of the Reign of James I* (Cambridge: Cambridge University Press, 1930), p. 67.

Anglican episcopacy featured prominently in early American republican thought. In some regions, the fear that bishops and archbishops would be created on American soil figured as prominently as complaints about parliamentary taxation in pre-revolutionary discourse about the British conspiracy to subjugate the colonists. Nineteenth-century American anti-Catholicism shared this distrust of hierarchy. English Whiggish anti-Catholicism had long been concerned with Catholics' allegiance to a *foreign* prince, but the American republican variant was concerned with their allegiance to a *prince* at all.

States tend to be hostile toward non-isomorphic associations because they fear that the groups will undermine the status relations on which the public constitutional order rests. The conception of citizens as free and equal persons that is sometimes said to be the heart of liberal democracy is here just a particular case of such status relations. If it seems so morally superior to all other kinds of status relations as to be utterly unlike them, then think again about the importance of the word "citizens" there. The suspicion of transnational groups discussed in the previous section is another particular case of this phenomenon. One group makes members believe that a commoner can outrank a king; one makes members believe that foreigners are their fellows.

The pressure toward institutional isomorphism is one reason why I propose to call the generally statist, generally centralizing strand of thought under consideration in this book "rationalism." Whatever the public view is in a given time and place of the right way to organize political life, intermediate bodies that are organized differently tend to be characterized as irrational. We have put our best understanding of the demands of reason into our public constitutional system (or we will, very soon); why do you insist on organizing your group's internal affairs differently? Hereditary rule, to those of us who live after 1800, is a clear and obvious example. But the thought that a commoner and a king, men and women, *bourgeois* and nobles, or compatriots and foreigners could be equal in status has seemed absurd to other states that sought to impose isomorphism. And if the flattening of status relations in the political sphere was absurd, their inversion was positively dangerous.

Here there is something of the social aesthetic of Scott's "high modernism," something of the man of system. Things should look consistent and alike. Non-isomorphism is disruptive; repeated patterns are pleasing. But there is a tendency to state excess at work here as well, one concerned with education and moral psychology. States systematically distrust groups that seem to teach any system of status (whether hierarchical or egalitarian) that differs from that of the political sphere, fearing that the groups will teach politically counterproductive habits of mind if not actual subversion.

Tendencies toward Group Excess

Associations and groups that are substantial enough to fulfill needs for belonging and meaning, powerful enough to check the power of the state or to organize democratic life, or institutionally complete enough to offer authoritative norm-generation for their members, are also substantial, powerful, and authoritative enough to potentially threaten the freedom of their members. That is, it is not just an unfortunate accident that groups come with features that, from a liberal perspective, are both good and bad.

The point is partly an intergenerational one. Recall from the previous chapter the idea that inequalities of outcomes in one generation become inequalities of opportunity in the next and its analog: free associations in one generation become inherited ways of life in the next. This is a necessary truth; children are born into particular times and places and social worlds that have been shaped by the choices their parents have made. This does *not* simply mean that the parents were free and the children are not; it was also true of the parents that *they* were born into particular times and places and social worlds. If the parents had some freedom to reshape their worlds in partially original ways, to join or form groups into which they were not born, then the children *also* have some such freedom. But there could be a narrowing over time; parents can join groups or adopt ways of life that leave their children with fewer choices than they themselves had.

But the point is only *partly* intergenerational. It is, more simply, a point about power, even within one generation. Robert Michels taught us that "who says organization, says oligarchy."[19] That could suffice as a statement of the problem, but I propose to instead frame it as: whoever says authority, says power—and whoever says organization, says authority.

Authority Generates Power

Associations are sources of law, or of something very like law. I think that Fuller is right that there is no good reason to withhold the word "law," and that using it clarifies the real workings of legal systems. But for current purposes it is enough if we recognize that there is something sufficiently law-like in associations to generate internal authority.

But, as noted in the last chapter, authority generates power. Associations, like states, claim and wield authority over their members, across at least some salient domains. Whatever normative system it is that unifies a group (whether as simple as the property-value-maximization of a condominium

[19] Robert Michels, *Political Parties: A Sociological Study of the Oligarchical Tendencies of Modern Democracy*, Eden and Cedar Paul, trans. (New York: The Free Press, 1962[1915]).

association or as complex as the Roman Catholic Church or a state) will generate reasons of the sort Raz has taught us to see as creating the circumstances of authority: reasons for the participants to accept the displacement of their own case-by-case reasoning with a shared decision. But when we accept the authority of another—when we accept that we have reason to abide by their decision, whatever it may be, instead of retaining recourse to our own views—we *also* create social power. We entrust authority for our own reasons, but that does not mean that the authority-holder will make decisions for our reasons. As both Hobbes and Locke in their different ways understood, the authority to offer authoritative judgments spills over into a kind of power over those affected. And if pluralist liberals have often emphasized the tendencies of really existing states to injustice, to a centralizing temperament, and to unjustified suspicion, rationalist liberals have often emphasized the parallel creation of real social power in the hands of intermediate-group authorities. This is not the complaint that the intermediate group has any primary rules *at all*. Rather, it is the observation that the secondary rules that grow up around them also create relationships of power and dominance—relationships threatening or inimical to freedom.

Sometimes the temporal relationship between authority and power is reversed, in a way that generates a slightly different tendency toward group excess. A charismatic leader—a religious prophet, say—can assemble a group where there was none before, and acquires a real sway over a growing flock of followers. It's customary to think of this as a kind of power; it was one of Weber's three ways of legitimating domination. In the early heat of the charismatic moment, the leader may well exercise power over his or her followers in all three of Lukes' senses: prevailing on in-group decisions, setting the in-group agenda, and (powerfully) shaping the norms and values of group members.[20] The difficulty (or the advantage, depending on one's perspective) is that charismatic movements come to an end: when the charismatic leader dies, or long before that when the heat of the initial moment fades. The power of the leader is directly limited by the boundaries of the followers' enthusiasm; and such enthusiasm can melt away very quickly.

The question faced by the charismatic leader who can take the long view—or by his or her immediate heirs—is whether and how to institutionalize the newly formed group. Formal organization—taking the first step from charismatic to bureaucratic-rational domination, to use Weber's categories—tends to slow things down, diminish enthusiastic passion, and limit the discretionary decision-making of the leadership. In a formal organization, at least some decisions will be made through regular and boring channels, not by the

---

[20] Steven Lukes, *Power: A Radical View* (London; New York: Macmillan, 1974).

instant decision of the person who has been gifted by the divine. This is true even when the procedures that are enacted heavily favor the authority of the leadership; that is, it does not depend on the procedures being democratic. And so charismatic leaders often resist institutionalization; and their power ends just when the followers stop following.

More interesting is what happens when the leadership does accept institutionalization and organization. For all the limits on immediate discretionary power that this introduces, it also generates a new stable system of authority. It can generate a system that is still quite hierarchical. In short, giving up a little bit of power in the short term can generate a lot of power that is entrenched in an authority structure in the long term.[21] I do not mean to suggest that decisions are consciously made in these terms; in general, I suspect that the sincere prophet does much better at gathering power than does the cynical one. But I think that this captures an important dynamic nonetheless.

The religious ferment in the early nineteenth-century United States was broadly democratic and egalitarian. Traditional religious authorities and elites saw their followers slip away. Charismatic leaders of revival meetings on the frontier did not depend on degrees from the elite East Coast training grounds of Protestant clergy. And the organizational form of the Second Great Awakening limited the power that could be accumulated by many of the preachers; they traveled from place to place, from one revival meeting to the next, while congregants largely stayed in place. And yet one of the most effective charismatic religious leaders of the era, Joseph Smith, ultimately left behind an extraordinarily hierarchical new religion. Smith established new institutions early on. He formally incorporated a new church under New York's modernized incorporation law within a year of the appearance of the Book of Mormon. Some key features of the later governance of Mormon churches (including the main Church of Jesus Christ of Latter-Day Saints) were established a few years later: a Council of Twelve with substantial governing authority including the authority to decide succession after his death, and a Quorum of Seventy members of the priesthood. A fully episcopal structure was created in the decade and a half between the church's founding and Smith's murder—a new episcopacy on American soil, just a few generations after the threat of episcopacy motivated much of the colonial resistance to Britain. With so many grandees in a young church, schisms and splits followed the death of the prophet; but the subsequent organizations largely held together

---

[21] Recall here Fuller's discussion of the tendency of voluntary associations to shift from an ethic of shared commitment to "creeping legalism" over time. Notice too that this could be a selection effect; associations that do not evolve in that direction tend to die out after the first generation of charisma, enthusiasm, and passion is exhausted.

and recreated the same governing structures, and some of them thrived. Charismatic power still infused the bureaucratic-legal structures; Brigham Young was clearly a charismatic figure in his own right. But Young inherited an organizational structure to build on; he did not have to build from the congregation up as Smith had done. And the bureaucratic-legal forms have survived uninterrupted (though occasionally schismed-from) ever since.

Without the new availability of the organizational forms—the incorporated churches and joint-stock corporations formed by the first generation of Mormon leaders—perhaps not much would have changed in this history; authority can be organized without legal recognition. But I doubt it. At the very least, the creation of legally distinct treasuries into which tithed monies could be deposited made a meaningful difference in helping to channel the first generation's charismatic power into a permanent authority structure and source of long-term power.

While the idea that authority generates power is perhaps clearest in the case of formal institutions that are strongly hierarchical, the problem, as I mentioned in the previous chapter, is not restricted to such cases. Informal, inchoate, customary, and unincorporated groups also have norms and rules, and so they also have authority relations, and so they also generate internal power. The power relations are somewhat different. Authority and power are more dispersed and decentralized, which can also mean more personalized and less impartial: the husband or father rather than the priest as the authoritative interpreter (and enforcer) of religious rules. The more inchoate kind of group perhaps does not have a strong normative commitment to some one kind of authority structure (e.g. the Apostolic Succession) and so does not imbue its authority figures with quite so much grandeur. On the other hand, the more formal and hierarchical authority structures have the advantage of reducing the number of interpretive disputes. In an informal group, these are likely to pop up more frequently, and to demand lots of moments of judgment and enforcement, i.e. many occasions for the exercise of authority and the growth of power. In an informal group it is easier to escape any one power relationship by exit, but there may be many more such relationships overall.

Pluralism Generates Power

The power wielded by group elites over members may be limited or attenuated when a group is situated within a pluralistic society. Pluralism can generate opportunities for schism and for simple exit. It can allow dissatisfied group members to reorganize and regroup without the offending leaders. It can allow for intellectual and cultural influences from outside that teach members that they can question their leaders.

But these are not the only effects that pluralistic settings can have on the internal life of groups. Consider these countervailing tendencies.

a) The availability of exit and the need on the part of members to exert effort and resources to sustain their groups affect different groups differently. Groups that are insufficiently distinct from the surrounding culture can cease to seem worth the effort to sustain them. If a group responds to the threat of exit primarily by becoming more similar to the surrounding social world—in a liberal society, if it responds by becoming internally liberal and weakening all of its internal norms and rules—then it actually hastens its own demise. The result of many groups liberalizing, one at a time, may be a sphere of group life that becomes less liberal over time. The appearance of paradox is only an appearance; it is because we are prone to the fallacy of composition.

This phenomenon is most visible in the religious sphere. In the most religiously pluralistic societies, very liberal and ecumenical denominations are losing active adherents, while very conservative ones are gaining. They offer their members a normative environment sufficiently different from the background society as to be worth active participation and support. The more liberal groups may have doctrines that are palatable to a larger number of people, but that's just to the degree that those people don't need a church to teach them those doctrines.

Moreover, the fluidity of group boundaries and the possibility of exit can reward those groups that increase their social distance from outsiders, those that put up especially high cultural barriers. The easier exit becomes at the individual level, the starker this effect at the group level. There is some tendency in a pluralist society for individuals to live at the borders between groups, through intermarriage, multiple memberships, and crossing back and forth. The groups that are best able to survive *as groups* may be those that make such partial exit and partial assimilation strategies unavailable, even though in the short run that means depriving themselves of potential members.[22]

The dynamic of group life over time thus can be one of polarization: the groups that sit next to one another in society push on one another, encouraging each to become more radically distinct from its neighbors and the wider society, more isolated and totalizing, than would be the case in a social vacuum. In one sense this is just what freedom of association looks like in a free and pluralistic society. But in another sense it is worrying and problematic. The group polarization doesn't straightforwardly reflect the desires,

---

[22] The dynamic here is substantially the same as the one I discussed in comparing federalism with more-radical decentralization in "Federalism, Liberalism, and the Separation of Loyalties," 101(3) *American Political Science Review* 459–77, 2007.

norms, values, or preferences of members. It is shaped by the external environment.

b) Relatedly, the evolutionary pressures placed on social groups *by the presence of the state* shapes which groups persist over time. Remember, for example, my suggestion that states are, more or less necessarily, information-gathering and surveilling agencies, and that the relative opaqueness of intermediate groups therefore triggers state antagonism. But that opaqueness is itself a survival strategy for groups in that environment. Too much transparency leaves their goods vulnerable to expropriation, and leaves their members vulnerable to persecution for their membership if the political winds take a hostile turn. Partial concealment from state surveillance is among the selective benefits that group life can offer to members: ethnic group kin who won't inform to the police or the conscription board, a minority language community in which one can express oneself freely, *in extremis* a network that can cooperate in smuggling one out of a jurisdiction altogether. (The normative valence here is neutral; cases range from the Mafia to Maria's nunnery in *The Sound of Music*.) And the kind of distinctness that is evolutionarily favored according to the dynamic described immediately above also tends to increase privacy and secrecy: it puts social distance between the group and the wider society or the state, making the group and its practices harder to openly understand or secretly infiltrate.

But, if it is true that privacy and secrecy are to some degree favorable traits for group survival under pluralistic conditions and under the state, that worsens internal power dynamics. Barriers to information shield abuse. That this is often an unjustified charge leveled by uncomprehending or persecuting outsiders—the charge of cultic domination is probably thrown against every new charismatic religious leader—doesn't change that it is true. Indeed, the barriers to information mean that we should expect a low correlation between when the charge is levied and when it is true.

A similar story could be told about the institutional accumulation of wealth over time. This is a survival trait for formally organized groups. It also tends to constantly increase the power differential between the group's officials, who can decide how to use its resources, and the group's weaker members, in part because they grow dependent on in-group redistribution that the officials control. The state's hunger for resources contributes to the fading away of poorer groups; and the survival of richer groups is not neutral with respect to in-group hierarchy. Again, this means that we can't simply think of in-group hierarchy as being chosen, willed, or created by group members.

c) To the degree that group members at least tacitly recognize dynamics (a) and (b), they have some reason to choose group officials who stand farther from other neighboring groups or from the background society in their norms than do the members themselves.

Members choosing a new leader know that, if the new leader proves to be more conservative than they can abide, they can exit (to the background society or to another group), while the group itself is likely to persist, perhaps remaining an option for them to return to—say, if they want their children to have a religious upbringing someday. If the leader is too moderate, however, the group's survival over time might be in jeopardy. They have reason to err on the side of leaders who are more conservative than they would ideally like, given the pluralistic setting. None of this needs to be a conscious calculation. It likely takes the form of members thinking that it's appropriate for leaders to be especially committed, especially fervent, especially devoted, even as some of them know that they themselves are mentally keeping their own options open.

This is not a point about the pool of available volunteers, though that is likely to be biased in the same direction: those willing to do associational work will be those who take the association especially seriously.[23] Rather, it is a point about the interest of group members that the group survive and thrive under pluralistic conditions. They have reason to choose officials and leaders who will pull group norms in the direction of greater distinctiveness, which will often mean greater conservatism. But that means that those with in-group authority, and power, might be systematically more conservative than the group's average members.

d) Even more directly arising from the external environment is the power elites can gain over members by acting as intermediaries, or as representatives of the group to outsiders. In a world of two monolingual communities and one bilingual go-between, the translator has tremendous power, including the ability to capture a huge proportion of the gains from trade between the two groups. If one of the communities is socially and politically subordinate to another, the effect is even more dramatic. The intermediary is the only one who can intercede with the outsiders on behalf of the group members; he can in principle extract from group members anything shy of what they fear the outsiders will extract without his intercession. *That* power is not even rooted in the group members' own desire for authority; it is not an extension of some internal good reason for hierarchy. It represents a kind of borrowing of the outside world's real or imagined power.

Those members of our group who can serve as intermediaries between us and the outside world *thereby gain power over us*. Compared with an isolated

---

[23] We will return to that problem under "Interested and invasive power" in the next section.

group, a group with a bit of contact with the outside world is not necessarily less hierarchical, and may well be more so. The contact allows some subordinated members possibilities of exit, but those who stay local may be *more* dominated than they used to be—even if they're now dominated by someone whose authority comes from the social capital they gain by bridge-building and gatekeeping rather than from a more traditional source. They may also gain power, prestige, or resources in the outside world, and those can further enhance their local power over us.[24] The power might be temporary; the local monopolist of a second language may not retain that position for long. But it might not be; when colonial authorities in the Americas or Africa decided that some particular local counted as a chief or king with whom to treat, they often created new long-lasting internal power relations.

Language, moreover, is only paradigmatic. Any source of mutual opaqueness, any social, cultural, or organizational difference between group members and the rest of society or the state (or even members of the larger group), can generate the need for intermediaries. Even mutually comprehensible and generally similar groups, if they lack overlapping social networks and personal connections, may need intermediaries who gain a degree of power over each group—though the more mutually comprehensible the groups are, the easier it will be for competing go-betweens to develop and diminish that power.

To say that go-betweens develop power is not to deny that they provide valuable services to group members. Indeed, they are essential in any pluralistic society, and they often do important work in protecting group members from members of a majority or from outside institutions including the state. It is only to say that their importance provides them with access to local monopolistic privilege which, we may expect, they will exploit for their own benefit as well, and which will generate in-group hierarchies and domination that *cannot* be justified as the expression of internal norms or values.

e) Moreover, groups can gain an excess of power over their members precisely from rules and institutions designed to reduce the excesses of *state* power described in the previous section. Guaranteed group representation; governmental or quasi-governmental power being granted to the group; state funding; inalienable land rights; the power a local majority gains by gaining control of a municipal or provincial government—all these and many more like them might be justified as counterbalancing remedies in the face of predictable state excesses. But each of them also makes a group something other than simply a voluntary association, and gives its authority structures hardened power beyond that which could be assembled out of the rights of the members.

---

[24] I came to understand this dynamic through a reading of Josiah Ober, *Democracy and Knowledge* (Princeton: Princeton University Press, 2008), ch. 3, though it is not the dynamic of primary interest to him.

Interested and Invasive Power

Finally, the power generated within groups has some distinctive and unattractive features that encourage excess. Unlike what Michael Oakeshott termed the "civil association" of the state, which in principle lacks purposes of its own and, when governed by the rule of law, provides *adverbial* rules to members about *how* to do what they do rather than rules on what is to be done, "enterprise associations" have purposes of their own to pursue.[25] To put the point in Rawlsian terms, while the state ideally puts the right ahead of the good, intermediate associations are strongly dedicated to their particular conceptions of the good. It is important not to overestimate the degree to which the wielders of state power are ever disinterested in the way the Oakeshottian rule of law of the Rawlsian priority of right demands, of course. In a reasonably just constitutional state, however, state authority can be *something* like that.

Those who wield power within intermediate groups are committed to *not* being disinterested in that way. They may be bound by procedures and rules; as I have already emphasized, intermediate groups have their own internal systems of rules, and in the normal case that means some kind of rule of law-like procedures. Canon law courts, rabbinic tribunals, university disciplinary committees, the adjudicative bodies within condominium associations, and so on all have recognizably law-like features and systems, with rule-of-law constraints. They may act only on the basis of announced rules that govern prospectively; they may forbid parties to a conflict from acting as judges over it. But they cannot govern only adverbially. They are committed to governing what is done, not only how it is done.

Moreover, there are selection effects at work that recall the dynamics drawing men of system into state positions. Those who dedicate their time and energy to rule-enforcement within intermediate associations are likely to be disproportionately attached to the group, or to its rules and norms. They must have a special degree of confidence in their ability to judge rightly. In a word, those who end up wielding the power that has been described are disproportionately likely to be busybodies.

> Of all tyrannies, a tyranny sincerely exercised for the good of its victims may be the most oppressive. It would be better to live under robber barons than under omnipotent moral busybodies. The robber baron's cruelty may sometimes sleep, his cupidity may at some point be satiated; but those who torment us for our own good will torment us without end for they do so with the approval of their own conscience... This very kindness stings with intolerable insult.[26]

---

[25] Michael Oakeshott, *On Human Conduct* (Oxford: Oxford University Press, 1975).

[26] C. S. Lewis, *God in the Dock* (Grand Rapids, MI: Wm. B. Eerdmans, 1972), p. 292. To be clear, the "tyranny" that worried Lewis was busybodies wielding the state's coercive power; but the description of the busybody's mindset and approach does not seem to be limited to that case.

When the governing procedures are *very* judicial, and call for professional role-specialization (the canon lawyer and canon law judge, for example), this need not be the case. But when either rule enforcement is very informal, decentralized, and unofficial (e.g. an unincorporated cultural group, or a religious sect without fixed judicial mechanisms) *or* when the judicial mechanisms are staffed by amateur volunteers rather than specialists (e.g. condominium associations), then we have reason to worry that intragroup power will be wielded by those who are unhealthily eager to order other people around.

John Stuart Mill, for one, was worried about the problem of the busybody—famously in *On Liberty*, but strikingly so in this passage from a later essay "Centralisation":

> Any despotism is preferable to local despotism. If we are to be ridden over by authority, if our affairs are to be managed for us at the pleasure of other people, heaven forefend that it should be at that of our nearest neighbours. To be under the control, or have to wait for the sanction, of a Minister or a Parliament, is bad enough; but defend us from the leading-strings of a Board of Guardians or a Common Council. In the former authorities there would be some knowledge, some general cultivation, some attention and habitual deference to the opinions of the more instructed minds. To be under the latter, would be in most localities, unless by the rarest accident, to be the slave of the vulgar prejudices, the cramped, distorted, and short-sighted views, of the public of a small town or a group of villages.[27]

The problem of the busybody and the problem of the man of system are just particular cases of one of the oldest and most banal thoughts about power: that those who seek it are particularly poorly suited to be trusted with it. The idea is as old as Plato and yet rarely developed, because there is no place to go with it, once we have rejected lotteries as a way of allocating positions of power. It is usually only invoked as a kind of cheap and corrosive cynicism; the trite thought that "the decision to run for office ought to disqualify you from holding office" is ultimately pointless, so long as there are offices to be filled.

I think that the worries about the man of system and the busybody are not so pointless as this, and they encourage a more-narrowly targeted skepticism rather than general cynicism. They tell us not just to distrust power, but which kinds of actions to distrust from which kinds of power-holders. The man of system is not a tyrant seeking the satisfaction of personal lusts, or a would-be slavemaster who craves a world full of slaves, or a venal character seeking office for corrupt individual benefit. He is rather someone whose understanding of what it would be to do good for others pays insufficient attention to

---

[27] Mill, "Centralisation," in *Collected Works vol. XIX*, p. 606.

their particularity and diversity; perhaps a harmless character or even a valuable social critic in many times and places, but dangerous once the social technology of the modern Weberian state has been created. And so attention to the problem of the man of system tells us, not just to worry about those who love power for its own sake, but to worry about *certain kinds of efforts to do good* using the tool of the modern state.

The busybody is the dark reflection of the man of system. The latter is all too ready to see other persons as pieces on a chessboard, or objects to be moved into patterns; he or she views other human beings too abstractly. The former is all too aware of the *particularity* of those over whom he or she exercises power, and is all too likely to use the power in personal rather than impersonal ways. Republican theorists including Rousseau and Pettit have argued that relations of personal power and dependence are especially likely to be relations of *domination*—the dominated person is ultimately subject to the will and whim of the dominator, not to impersonal rules. The person of system with too much power commits macro-level, impersonal injustices; the busybody with too much power commits micro-level, deeply personal ones. Examples should be familiar: the intensely personal power exercised within the traditional patriarchal family; the power generated by the parish priest's legitimate authority that can be turned to very personal advantage; the degree to which small-town enforcement of cultural and religious norms is entangled with spite and pre-existing grievances. One need not go along with the republicans' primary emphasis on personal dominance as *the* primary meaning of unfreedom to see that it is *a* way of being unfree, and one that is especially likely in intragroup relations.

To put the point in more technical terms, both the problem of the man of system and the problem of the busybody are hypotheses about motivational heterogeneity and self-selection.[28] The kinds of power available to the officer in the modern state, or to the authority figure in an intermediate group, are more attractive to some kinds of persons than to others. In one case, it is more attractive to those who view other persons highly abstractly, who aspire to remake messy social orders in ways that are uniform or symmetrically patterned—those who look at persons and societies in ways that align well with "seeing like a state." In the other case, the power is especially attractive to those who enjoy personal status and domination, those who derive pleasure from correcting the perceived faults and flaws of those close to them. If the

---

[28] For a useful overview of the idea of selection effects operating on motivational heterogeneity, see Adrian Vermeule, "Selection Effects in Constitutional Law," 91(4) *Virginia Law Review* 953–98, Jun. 2005. See also Timothy Besley, "Political Selection," 19(3) *The Journal of Economic Perspectives* 43–60, 2005; James D. Fearon, "Electoral Accountability and the Control of Politicians: Selecting Good Types versus Sanctioning Poor Performance," in Przeworski et al., eds, *Democracy, Accountability and Representation* (Cambridge, New York: Cambridge University Press, 1999).

hypothesis of motivational heterogeneity is false—if there is no such psychological type as the man of system or the busybody—then these are non-problems. This is tacitly the view of much of rational choice and public choice theory, which assumes motivational homogeneity and broadly trusts explanations in terms of incentives rather than in terms of selection of types of persons into particular roles.[29] But if the types are real, then those who fall into those categories will be disproportionately drawn into the appropriate offices; and so, all else equal, states (led by men of system) will distrust messy group pluralism more than they should and seek to flatten it more than is justifiable, while groups (led by busybodies) will have more intrusive enforcement of more restrictive rules than would be preferred by most group members, even though the latter do value the group's existence and distinctiveness.

The problem of the busybody is somewhat different from, though complementary to, dynamic (c) discussed under "pluralism generates power." The problem of the busybody affects the availability of candidates for leadership positions; there is some tendency for volunteers to be drawn from those with an unhealthy interest in lording it over their fellows. But under some kinds of pluralistic and competitive conditions for groups, members have good reason to *prefer* such leaders, even if they are presented with less obnoxious alternatives.

These effects—a pool of volunteers consisting of busybodies, and the group members' interest in selecting them for office—call for attention to the difference between the danger of in-group elite power, and the danger of group conformism as such. The latter diagnosis emphasizes homogeneity, not hierarchy: I find it difficult to do what I want simply because it is not what is done in my group. I am raised in a tradition and cannot easily imagine alternatives to it; my manners and morals are shaped by my community and I cannot easily act against them; my friends and loved ones are pleased by my agreement and pained by my disagreement. Violating local norms and ethics marks me as impolite, disrespectful, at least implicitly critical of how those around me live their own lives, and of uncertain character or trustworthiness. My deviation on matters that are locally important at best strains my relationships with those around me, at worst costs me those relationships altogether. Even in the absence of official hierarchies, conformism empowers the busybody; it provides an approved social license to tell other people how to live their lives.

Conversely, in-group power need not be norm-enforcing. Office-holders might be driven by the desire for status, for resources, or simply for power itself. Any of these might generate worrisome abuse or domination. Office-holders might instead be motivated by a dispassionate commitment to the

---

[29] Vermeule, "Selection Effects."

group's norms, and find enforcement a regrettable necessity. But offices and positions that carry the authority to enforce norms will be disproportionately attractive to busybodies, and under pluralistic conditions the groups that survive might be precisely those with enthusiastic norm-enforcers in power. So conformism and hierarchy may reinforce and aggravate each other, and leave us subject to in-group leadership that is much more invasive than we would willingly have chosen.

My point in this chapter is not to say that group life in a pluralistic society is *necessarily* conservative or polarized or characterized by pervasive excesses of internal power, or that states necessarily steamroll over associational life and diversity. It is rather to say that there are predictable and known social dynamics in those directions. We live under neither ideal states, concerned only with doing justice, nor ideal groups, exercising only the authority over us that tracks our own reasons and that is generated out of our own rights.

Our freedom can be threatened by states and by groups—and by each directly in response to the other. Understanding which threats are more important where and when is not a formal or philosophical exercise. And a vision of the social world that emphasizes the threat from states isn't *contradicted* by one that emphasizes the threat from groups, even when the legal and political actions the two recommend do contradict one another.

Part II

"History cannot be expected to solve the core analytical puzzles of political or economic theory. But it has its hour when the long-expected solutions of social and political science fail to materialize. History is the tool of skeptics. It helps us to ask better questions. More precisely, it can help us avoid repeating some questions again and again, running in circles unproductively."

Istvan Hont, *Jealousy of Trade* (Cambridge, Mass.: Harvard University Press, 2005), p. 156.

4

Antecedents and Foundations

Liberal ideas crystallized in the context of, and about, the early modern Weberian state. I do not think that it makes sense to talk about liberalism before about 1700, and I am quite sure that it doesn't make sense to talk about liberalism as such before the modern state took shape, even if we can sometimes identify one argument or another as more or less liberal. The core of liberal ideas includes religious toleration and freedom, in a sense that only took shape after the end of the wars of religion in Europe; the rule of law, and especially the control by law of the executive's security apparatus through *habeas corpus*, procedural rights, and prohibitions on torture and extrajudicial executions, imprisonment, or dispossession, all of which make sense only in a world of strong executive and security capacity as well as strong legislative and judicial capacity; and the desirability of commerce and international trade, in a way that was intellectually rare before the eighteenth century, and hard to conceptualize before the idea of a political-economic policy took shape in the seventeenth.[1] Political theorists like to abstract from political programs such as this to find their moral underpinnings, and then identify those underpinnings as the real doctrines. What is it that united freedom of religion, freedom from torture, and freedom to trade? *That* is the liberal idea—and moral ideas are more credibly transhistorical than political ideas are, so a liberal idea like that might be found scattered throughout history.

That kind of abstraction has its place, but it quickly slips into treating party ideas as if they are, to borrow a phrase, metaphysical not political. I do not mean to say that a political theory is nothing but a party platform; but a political theory like liberalism (or conservatism or socialism) is a bundle of

---

[1] I do not think this contradicts my use in earlier work of Judith Shklar's sense of liberalism's core meaning. The fear of cruelty, for Shklar, was a particular cluster of ideas about politics, not a free-floating principle. The restrictions on the security apparatus were central to it, and religious freedom not far behind. See Shklar, "The Liberalism of Fear," in *Liberalism and the Moral Life*, Nancy L. Rosenblum, ed. (Cambridge, Mass.: Harvard University Press, 1989); and my *The Multiculturalism of Fear*.

political ideas that hang together more or less well and stably. The move to abstraction risks excluding many who should be included, as when the abstraction includes an idea like "natural rights" that excludes Mill from liberalism, or one like "autonomy" that excludes Tocqueville. It also risks implausible over-inclusiveness—defining a political idea in terms of philosophical premises will draw in some who share the premises but (mistakenly or not) follow them to dramatically different conclusions. This is the mistake that has so often led Hobbes to be called a liberal: treating methodological individualism and contractarianism as more constitutive than, say, freedom of religion.[2]

If that's right, then the appropriate level of abstraction is low enough to be "political" not only in a Rawlsian sense but also in the mundane one. And the political program of liberalism is one about how to direct and limit the power of the modern state, in ways that are only comprehensible after the state has taken form, the wars of religion have ended, and the attractions of commerce came into focus.

While liberal ideas did not and could not crystallize before the consolidation of the modern state, the intellectual materials from which they did so were older. The early modern state did not rupture intellectual history; it was analyzed and critiqued as it was taking shape, and those analyses and critiques drew on older ideas and institutions. If it is a mistake to treat an idea like "liberalism" as existing in every era, it is also a mistake to treat it as having no relevant prehistory.

In this chapter and the next I will lay out some of that prehistory in abbreviated form. I begin with what I will call the birth of intermediacy in the European eleventh to thirteenth centuries. A number of particular institutions that we now think of as part of the intermediate sphere date to this era. More importantly, the *kinds* of institutions that we still have can be traced to this era: the university, the fraternal society, the coherent, corporate, independent, self-governing church. Coercive capacity was greatly fragmented in medieval and feudal Europe, and each of these groups was in part a legal system unto itself, albeit drawing on a shared store of legal norms.

The social and political orders of the fourteenth and fifteenth centuries saw gradually centralizing states coexisting with self-governing entities of many other kinds. When the monarchical and increasingly absolutist state of the sixteenth and seventeenth centuries gained the upper hand over these other entities, its opponents appealed to historical inheritances against it. Ascribing an anachronistic level of coherence to the medieval world, they developed the

---

[2] See Shklar on "the convoluted genealogy of liberalism that insists on seeing its origins in a theory of absolutism," the "gross misrepresentation that any social contract theory, however authoritarian its intentions, and any anti-Catholic polemic add up to liberalism." "The Liberalism of Fear," p. 24.

idea of an *ancient constitution* of Europe that had been upset by absolute kings. Liberalism in part developed out of that reaction against absolutism, an early modern reconstructed memory of the High Middle Ages.

I should emphasize that in discussing these ideas and institutions as the prehistory of liberalism, I do not mean anything teleological, or indeed anything unique to liberalism. *Whatever* ideas took shape in the European eighteenth century would have developed out of earlier-modern ideas that in turn would have developed out of Renaissance and medieval ideas. The same medieval roots might have borne very different fruit. Indeed, conservatism and socialism developed out of the same background, and share some of the same roots; there is no inexorable unfolding of liberalism here.

Much of what follows will be familiar to historians, but not, I suspect, to political theorists and political philosophers. Its importance for understanding liberal political thought is unappreciated, in part because even medieval intellectual history is relatively little known to most political theorists, medieval institutional history all the more so. Laying the groundwork for early modern political theory about group life requires attention to the legal and social practices of corporate associations in the Middle Ages, practices that were little commented on in the works that we most often characterize as medieval political philosophy.[3] This chapter therefore emphasizes legal and institutional history, not medieval political thought. We seek to understand the institutional legacies the Middle Ages left behind to the early modern world of state consolidation. In subsequent chapters we will examine how early modern theorists interpreted those legacies and that consolidation, but those theorists' arguments about these jurisprudential and social inheritances are difficult to understand without taking an earlier starting point.

The Birth of Intermediacy

The 150–200 years after about 1050 CE saw a tremendous proliferation of formal organizations that were self-created, self-governing, or (often) both. Indeed, many of these are institutionally continuous to today: European universities and cities, the Roman Catholic Church in its familiar form, and subordinate associations and orders within the Church itself. Others have not survived but spread widely during this era: independent military orders, guilds of various sorts. I describe this as the birth of intermediacy.

---

[3] "The relationship of lesser associations to the state was of interest only to jurists," and not to those we think of as political philosophers, writes Antony Black; "this was no doubt because Cicero and Aristotle had little to say except to assert the complete primacy of the state. Thus while the period was corporatist in practice, there was no theory of corporatism." Antony Black, *Political Thought in Europe, 1250–1450* (Cambridge: Cambridge University Press, 1992), p. 3.

Three features of the early Middle Ages were especially important in setting the stage for the birth of intermediacy. One was the Germanic norm in the post-Roman barbarian kingdoms that law be personal rather than territorial. In case of legal disputes, the rule to apply depended on who the parties were, not where the dispute took place. Peoples who migrated from Central Asia to Western Europe in the space of several generations had good reason to treat law in this way: group membership remained constant even as territory changed. The norm persisted once they conquered sedentary Romanized populations, sometimes much larger than their own: subjecting these populations to unfamiliar and unwritten legal customs would have been far beyond the capacity of the barbarian kingdoms, even had they seen any reason to do so.

This ended up setting the Christian clergy apart. Their status within the church came to be considered the legally relevant identity, and the law governing them was a simplified version of Roman law that gradually became the core of a new body of rules, canon law. But more generally, the jurisprudential world of post-Roman Europe was one in which the content of law was entangled with personal status and group membership, and significantly detached from political rulership or territorial boundaries.

The second was the earliest stage of feudalism and the development of lord–vassal relationships, which turned a political and military situation that was radically fractured and decentralized *de facto* and made it the *de jure* foundation of a new kind of political order. Eventually this merged with the first; being part of the web of lord–vassal political relations became a legal identity, in itself as the military class hardened into a hereditary caste.[4] Given the modern characterization of the whole system of personally differentiated privileges as "feudalism," it is worth noting that the pattern of legal differentiation preceded the special case of a distinctive law for a noble caste.

The third—perhaps the first real instance of organized intermediacy—was the founding and spread of monastic orders. Benedictine monasteries dated to the sixth century, and had become an established part of the feudal world, holding agricultural land corporately and providing enough local stability to attract neighbors. But the Cluniac Reforms beginning in the early 900s turned monasticism into a major pillar of the Church. The new order headed by the Abbot of Cluny federated a great and growing number of monasteries together, turning the order into a powerful and wealthy unified entity; the older Benedictine monasteries had generally been organizationally isolated from one another. Once the initial Cluny Abbey had gained a guarantee of independence from the local feudal lord, the order claimed such

---

[4] See Marc Bloch, *Feudal Society, vol. 2: Social Classes and Political Organizations*, L. A. Manyon, trans. (Chicago: University of Chicago Press, 1961).

independence as a general matter. Its wealth and prestige allowed it to make the claim good, providing an incentive for more monasteries to affiliate with it. The order developed into a geographically far-ranging system outside the control of the so-called secular clergy of bishops and priests (who were often more closely tied to local rulers).

I think it is useful to think of these developments as prefatory to the birth of intermediacy, beginning a few decades after the turn of the millennium.[5] This era, c. 1050–1250, saw the creation of institutions that continuously persisted until, and past, the formation of the European state, and in many cases until today. More-or-less self-created, self-governing, intergenerational corporate bodies and groups grew widespread and consequential during these centuries, fundamentally restructuring the European political world in ways that are still with us.

The Roman Catholic Church as we know it dates it to the mid-eleventh century,[6] taking shape in the events that later came to be known as the Great Schism, the Gregorian Reforms (or sometimes the Papal Revolution), and the Investiture Controversy. In the Mediterranean world of the turn of the millennium, the Pope in Rome was notionally first in dignity among equal patriarchs of the Christian church but was institutionally comparatively weak. The Patriarch of Constantinople was closely tied to the power and prestige of the Byzantine Emperor; theological questions and language divided the Western (Latin) Church from the several Eastern (Greek) Patriarchs and the *de facto* disunity of Western politics and church governance constrained the Pope's authority. Bishops, effectively feudal lords in much of Europe, grew closer to the local political system and more distant from the church; the intermittent practice of clerical marriage gave these lordly bishops legitimate heirs; and the combination of landed rule and heritability made it attractive for local feudal lords to appoint themselves or their allies to church offices. The rise of the monastic orders had to some degree strengthened the Papacy within the Western Church over the course of the 900s; their rivalry with local great bishops inclined abbots and orders to look to Rome for legitimation. Even in that case, the Benedictine order was officially answerable to the Pope but far from subordinate to him.

By 1122, things looked very different. Eastern and Western Christianity had split, leaving the Pope as undisputed head of a Western European church, not

---

[5] Here I reemphasize the cautions from earlier in the book about the idea of "intermediate." In this era the groups were certainly not intermediate between individuals and the yet-to-emerge state, and the ostensibly universal Church viewed itself as encompassing Europe's polities, not encompassed within them.

[6] For much of what follows, see Harold Berman, *Law and Revolution, volume I* (Cambridge, Mass.: Harvard University Press, 1983), though with different emphases; I think Berman would have rejected my view that both the Great Schism and the First Crusade figure into what he terms the Papal Revolution.

a weak *primus inter pares*. The church had recognized a papal right to legislate over an increasingly unified and centralized body of canon law. Papal election by cardinals alone (that is, with no say for the Emperor) had been entrenched. Clerical marriage was firmly prohibited, leaving clergy without legitimate heirs who might inherit church land, and undercutting the mingling of church governance with feudal politics. The Pope had asserted a right to depose the Emperor himself by excommunication; the First Crusade had established the Pope's effective authority to marshal the military and political power of Western Christendom.

Most importantly, the papacy had largely won an extended conflict with the Holy Roman Empire over whether the Pope or the Emperor had the authority to appoint bishops within the empire. The church by the mid-twelfth century was coherent, unified, hierarchical, legalistic, and *autonomous*, crossing all the political boundaries of Western Europe, crucially independent of feudal political orders. The *Libertas ecclesiae,* the "liberty of the church" asserted in a papal bull of that name in 1079, had been gained and made to stick.[7] By the 1160s–70s, *libertas ecclesiae* was sufficiently well entrenched that King Henry II of England could not undo it, either by appointing his own Chancellor, Thomas Becket, Archbishop of Canterbury, or by having Becket killed for his subsequent defense of the church. Thomas' rapid canonization and Henry's public penance for his assassination in 1174 confirmed the new order.

That is not to say that there was a separation of "church and state" in our sense, not only because the Empire and monarchies were not states, but also because church officials remained high political figures. For example, three of the seven members of the Electoral College that selected Holy Roman Emperors for most of the Empire's history were bishops. Still less were *religion* and *politics* separated; they interpenetrated throughout medieval Europe, and it was universally thought proper that they should. And the effective strength of *libertas ecclesiae* was to vary by time and place. In the later Middle Ages, the kings of France in particular were able to limit the church's freedom to a considerable degree, most obviously during the fourteenth-century relocation of the papal court to Avignon.

But in broad outline, by the mid-twelfth century the Catholic Church had taken on its autonomous and unified form, in a way that institutionally divided it from temporal political systems, leaving political rulers without direct governing authority within the church. This is crucial for

---

[7] Recall the idea of freedom of associations developed earlier. I would say that *libertas ecclesiae* is its most important source in the western tradition. Compare Brian Tierney, "Religion and Rights: A Medieval Perspective," 5(1) *Journal of Law and Religion* 163–75, 1987; Richard Garnett, "The Freedom of the Church," 4 *Journal of Catholic Social Thought* 59–86, 2007.

understanding the subsequent development of Western Europe—that before *states* developed as coherent, unified, self-governing, and jurisgenerative, the Church had already done so. States came into being, confronting an already-organized and independent church.

Canon law preceded this era. During the early Middle Ages, when (as noted) law was applied based on personal status, men of the Church were jurispru-dentially deemed "Romans" and governed by a descendant of Roman law.[8] But when the Western Church was highly dispersed and decentralized, canon law was as well. The Gregorian Reforms were in crucial part a Papal claim to creating a jurisgenerative legal hierarchy: centralizing judicial authority and a quasi-legislative capacity for canon law in Rome. The most important organ-ization and codification of canon law, Gratian's *Decretum*—a later name for what was originally called *Concordia Discordantium Canonum*, a reconciliation of discordant canons—was compiled *c.* 1140. Drawing on the newly redis-covered Roman Law (about which more later), it dialogically integrated a vast amount of material from many different sources: Biblical, classical, theo-logical, and canon-jurisprudential. Thousands of distinct legal rules and judg-ments were brought together, contradictions laid out and, in principle, resolved. That integrated system made possible a new level of coherence in the legal judgments of the increasingly integrated hierarchy of the church. And the public law of the church in the *Decretum* was unambiguously papalist: the Pope was identified as having the right of final appeal in canon–legal disputes, and as having authority which was superior to the opinions and judgments of theologians and scholars.[9]

This increasingly dense body of canon law was applied in a growing net-work of ecclesiastical courts. First and foremost, these courts exercised juris-diction over clergy (regular and secular alike); the privilege of clergy protected them from trial before any other courts or systems of law. They also governed disputes over the church's land and exercised considerable subject-matter jurisdiction beyond their personal jurisdiction over clergy; marriage and inheritance, for example, were governed by canon law and ecclesiastical courts, marriage being a sacrament and inheritance routinely involving bequests to the church.

It is important not to overstate the centralizing results of the Papal Revolu-tion. As Brian Tierney puts it,

---

[8] Peter Stein, *Roman Law in European History* (Cambridge: Cambridge University Press, 1999), p. 40.
[9] Brian Tierney, *Foundations of the Conciliar Theory: The Contributions of the Medieval Canonists From Gratian to the Great Schism* (Cambridge: Cambridge University Press, 1955), p. 12: "The appearance of Gratian's *Decretum* may be taken as the starting-point of the whole process of legal integration," and to understand that process of legal integration "is, in effect, to record the process by which the Church became a body politic, subject to one head and manifesting an external unity of organization." See also Berman, *Law and Revolution*, ch. 2.

In spite of the persistent tendency towards papal centralization, the whole Church, no less than the secular states, remained in a sense a federation of semi-autonomous units, a union of innumerable greater or lesser corporate bodies. Bishoprics, abbeys and priories, colleges, chantries and guilds, religious orders, congregations and confraternities all contributed to the life of the Church and, equipped with their privileges and immunities, exercised substantial rights of self-government.[10]

That is to say, the consolidated and independent Catholic Church was far more hierarchical than the old Western Church and its Pope had become far more powerful compared to both secular rulers and the rest of the clergy; but its internal associational life remained vastly complex. The Church itself may have been the most important of the institutions that came down to us as "intermediate," but it also thrived on ongoing intermediacy within itself. The late eleventh and twelfth centuries saw the creation of militant, crusading, transnational self-governing religious orders—the Templar, Hospitaller, and Teutonic orders of knights—outside any civil authority. New monastic orders proliferated starting in the early thirteenth century, the Franciscans, Dominicans, and Carmelites among them.

Under canon law, "any group of persons which had the requisite structure and purpose—for example, an almshouse or a hospital or a body of students, as well as a bishopric or, indeed, the Church Universal—constituted a corporation, without special permission of a higher authority."[11] The Church itself, the *ecclesia*, of course had an extraordinary source of legitimacy. But a *collegium* within the Church could be self-legitimating and self-creating, although it could also receive sanction *ex ante* or *ex post*.

This probably influenced the proliferation, during roughly the same era as the consolidation of the Roman Catholic Church, of other corporate associations: cities, universities, and specialized mercantile, trade, or craft guilds.[12] Black claims that developments in the Church and the growth of cities, for example, were related by more than chronological coincidence: "The development of towns coincided exactly with...the Investiture Controversy... 'Liberty of the church'...and communal liberty were related parts of the same movement for corporate self-determination."[13] The Gregorian Reforms, on this account, diminished the feudal kingdoms and opened normative space for other forms of political organization, especially those that "like the church...claimed to be champions of justice as a universal norm."

[10] Brian Tierney, *Foundations of the Conciliar Theory*, p. 90.

[11] Berman, *Law and Revolution*, p. 219.

[12] For what follows, in addition to Berman, *Law and Revolution*, see Bloch, *Feudal Society*; Black, *Guilds and Civil Society*; and Henri Pirenne, *Medieval Cities: Their Origins and the Revival of Trade*, Frank Halsey, trans. (Princeton: Princeton University Press, 1969[1925]).

[13] Black, *Guilds and Civil Society*, p. 63.

Berman likewise sees the Gregorian reforms as making the growth of the city form possible, even though cities "were wholly separate from the church."

> What made urbanization possible then and not before, and there and not else-where, were new religious and legal concepts and institutions and practices... concerning communes and other kinds of fraternal associations, collective oaths, corporate personality, charters of liberties, rational and objective judicial proced-ures, equality of rights...[14]

Cities, guilds, and universities, the *collegia* and *universitates*—the former connoting the colleagueship of the founding members, the other the univer-sal corporate whole as apart from the individual members, both ways of expressing corporate personality—were all in the first instance associations formed by mutual consent, probably deriving in part from a Germanic trad-ition of fellowship-guilds, although all came to be shaped by a juridical status expressed in canon or Roman legal terms. The relative influence of the Germanic model of unspecialized oath-societies for mutual support, of the Christian and monastic models, and of the Roman law concepts are much disputed, but these disputes need not concern us.

What matters is that self-governing societies, founded on mutual consent and holding legal personality, drawing on a common pool of conceptual and legal resources, proliferated during these centuries, creating the intermediacy that was to shape Western Europe. This intermediacy differed from the older Germanic personality principle in law, because the groups that were formed and the statuses acquired were deliberate creations, because membership in them was not immutable, and because of their independent legal status. It differed from the Church's internal pluralism because—unlike monastic orders—cities, universities, and guilds were normally outside the church hier-archy. Members of them were, *qua* Catholic Christians, subject to the Church's jurisdiction; but the groups themselves were not subject to church governance. And it differed from a strict reading of the Roman law because the groups were to a substantial degree self-creating and self-legitimating, though they often received written charters from higher authorities (again, whether *ex ante* or *ex post*) that might satisfy the Roman-law requirement of imperial permission.

When I say that cities began to appear, I do not mean only, or even primarily, that Europe's population began to urbanize in demographic terms, although that is true. From the mid-eleventh century until the outbreak of the Black Death three hundred years later, those living in concentrated settlements steadily grew in absolute numbers and as a share of Europe's

---

[14] Berman, *Law and Revolution*, pp. 362–3.

population. Of greater interest, however, is the distinct social, political, and legal form that these new cities took.

Urbanization is a process, but the medieval city was not merely a village gradually grown larger. Cities, as Berman put it, "did not simply emerge but were founded,"[15] although sometimes on spots that had previously been occupied by a church diocese, an administrative town of the Roman or Carolingian Empires, or a military outpost. The new "community endowed with legal entity [personality] and possessing laws and institutions peculiar to itself"[16] was created at a discrete moment in time. The founding act was sometimes a grant of a charter, but often—perhaps more often, and certainly more often early on—it was in the first instance an act of self-creation, only later ratified or confirmed by any external power.

It is worth emphasizing something that may be better understood by those working in traditions influenced by Marx or Hegel than by those working within contractarian or contractualist intellectual traditions: these were real foundings of new political and legal orders by real acts of mutual promise among real persons acting on their own authority.

> One act of outstanding significance generally marked the entry on the scene of the new urban community, whether in a mood of revolt or for peaceful organization: the communal oath of the burgesses. Hitherto they had been only isolated individuals: henceforth they had a collective being. It was the sworn association thus created which in France was given the literal name of *commune*.[17]

This era was long over by the time the social contract, compact, or covenant became a metaphorical way of talking about the legitimation of whole states; but the later metaphor drew on past real practice. Recall the connection I mentioned in the Introduction between the idea of "civil society" and medieval city life; the founding of what Locke called "civil society" by consent and contract drew on the founding of actual cities by actual promises.

The medieval city was walled, armed, set apart from the feudal order, domestically (by the standards of the time) egalitarian, and corporately self-governing. It was neither ruled by the church nor by the feudal nobility of the countryside.[18] This organizational form—the *commune* living within walls, defending its members against both disorganized violence and organized feudal domination—took hold and spread. Thousands of cities were founded from England to Spain to Hungary in the eleventh, twelfth, and thirteenth

---

[15] Berman, *Law and Revolution*, p. 362.   [16] Pirenne, *Medieval Cities*, p. 56.

[17] Bloch, *Feudal Society*, p. 354.

[18] There is growing interest in the political theory of the city, and some of this literature takes medieval cities and their norms admirably seriously. For an excellent example see Loren King, "Liberal Citizenship: Medieval Cities as Model and Metaphor," 14(2) *Space and Polity* 123–42 (2010).

centuries. One important dense zone of city-formation was in northern Italy; another stretched from the German Baltic coast through Flanders into northern France, and along the navigable rivers that fed into the Baltic and North Seas. Sometimes the *commune* would purchase from a local lord a piece of territory and the right to build a city on it, including the right to self-government henceforth. Some pre-existing urban settlements, such as London, were reconstituted according to the new form, but many cities shared little or nothing with any prior community in the same spot. Indeed, in what is now the Low Countries, many of the new cities were founded on new land made habitable by the dike system. Along the southern and eastern coasts of the Baltic, cities were often new in a different sense, being founded and built on newly Christianized (and sometimes Germanized) territory, whether converted by the founding of the Catholic Polish kingdom or through conquest by the Teutonic Knights.

While some of the Italian cities were to emerge as powerful sovereign city-states, and the Swiss cities were effectively able to remain free of external rule, the pattern elsewhere was one of membership in some larger polity, e.g. the kingdom of France or England, the Holy Roman Empire. Often, however, the cities belonged to the larger polity in a special way. This is easiest to see in the Empire, where Free Cities and Imperial Cities were admitted as direct members of the Empire alongside duchies, principalities, bishoprics, and so on. Leagues of cities, most importantly the Hanseatic League, were to become major powers within the Empire on the basis of their trade wealth, able to defend member cities' independence against the princes and lords. Where the central authority was more powerful than in the Empire—England, France, the Spanish kingdoms—cities often received charters or guarantees directly from the king, who saw them as a check on local lords. The cities might buy such guarantees from the center all at once, or with a pledge of recurring tax payment at a fixed rate; either way, they often thereby gained sole authority over taxation within the city walls, immunity to taxation by the feudal nobility, and immunity to taxation by the center without their consent. They had the authority to set their own toll and tariff levels, and to collect and keep the fees; to build fortifications and to arm the citizenry (even in countries where bearing arms was otherwise a noble privilege); and, broadly, to govern their own internal affairs. Some bodies of urban law, such as those of Magdeburg, Lübeck, or Frankfurt, were widely imitated and adopted—by dozens of cities each in those three cases. This sometimes involved explicitly putting the original city at the top of the chain of legal dispute resolution so as to ensure continued legal harmony among the linked cities.

Citizens (or burgesses or *burghers* or *bourgeois*) were in principle free of relations of personal dominance and servitude in the outside world: serfdom, *corvée*, conscription by local lords, the *droit de seigneur*. The legal saying that "city air makes you free" (*Stadtluft macht frei*) after breathing it for a year and a day referred to that severing of extramural bonds and obligations. Systems of domestic government varied widely, but the kind of hereditary lordly rule famously associated with the Medicis in Florence starting in the 1400s was very uncommon during this earlier era. The franchise might be restricted to descendants of the city founders, to wealthy great families, or to mercantile guilds; but on the basis of that franchise, elected councils were common, and even an individual ruler like the *doge* of Venice or Genoa was elected for life, and lacked monarchical power. Considerable importance was attached to the domestic rule of law and judicial institutions, and to protecting citizens from having to answer to judicial proceedings elsewhere. And real property was owned or leased, not held of higher lords in the feudal style.

By the thirteenth century, all of this had become part of the fabric of European society. Magna Carta guaranteed that London and "all other cities, boroughs, towns, and ports shall enjoy all their liberties and free customs"— the liberties were already traditional and customary, confirmed in part with reference to their being longstanding.

The European university dates to the same era.[19] Starting with Bologna in the 1080s, and followed over the next century and a half by Paris, Oxford, Modena, Cambridge, Salamanca, Toulouse, and Orleans, corporate bodies were formed joining together the body of students, the body of instructors, or both in a perpetual scholarly guild. As with cities, these initially self-created institutions eventually had liberties and privileges legally guaranteed by higher powers. In the mid-twelfth century, the Holy Roman Emperor created a specially protected legal status for those traveling to and from the university at Bologna for purposes of study. They had a right of free movement; they could not have their goods seized for the payment of debts incurred by their countrymen (otherwise a risk for foreigners); and they were broadly immunized from local judicial proceedings and subjected instead to the internal governance and discipline of the university. Like the clergy, scholars wore a special garb to distinguish themselves, in part to demonstrate their protected status. (Indeed, the document proclaiming these liberties was the *Authentica Habita*, from the same sense of *habitus* that now gives us the word "habit" for a nun's special form of dress.) Similar privileges were often negotiated with city authorities, such that scholars were normally subject to the university's law, or sometimes canon courts, rather than the town's.[20] Usually civil proceedings against a scholar had to take place before a university or church tribunal; the

---

[19] See Hilde de Ridder-Symoens, ed., *A History of the University in Europe, vol. 1: Universities in the Middle Ages* (Cambridge: Cambridge University Press, 1992); Charles Homes Haskins, *The Rise of Universities* (New York: Henry Holt, 1923).

[20] See Pearl Kibre, "Scholarly Privileges: Their Roman Origins and Medieval Expression," 59(3) *The American Historical Review* 543–67, 1954.

same was sometimes true of criminal proceedings; and commonly suits to which a scholar was party, whether as plaintiff or defendant, had to take place where the scholar was resident. (In other words, the scholar could not be called before a distant court as a defendant, but as a plaintiff *could* summon a distant defendant.)

The spread of cities and the development of universities reinforced one another. A university need not have a permanent set of buildings to call home, and the earliest universities sometimes did not. They were corporate assemblies of persons; wherever scholars met, there was the university. But a university must have a general location that can support a concentrated population. The scholars must be able to assemble in the same general vicinity. It is moreover dependent on commerce for food, since those spending their days lecturing or reading are not spending them farming. Like other city-dwellers, the scholars depended on not only the existence of an agricultural surplus but also its availability to those some distance from the farm. Universities in turn provided a steady stream of newcomers to the city.

While universities were of course locally specific institutions, they also came to be linked with each other. The *studia generalia* were those universities that trained students from across Europe (as opposed to a *studium particulare* which taught local students) and were registered and recognized by the Empire and the Church as belonging to the shared category, their members entitled to the associated privileges. These included the right of *ius ubique docendi*, meaning that a degreed scholar admitted to teach at one university would be authorized to teach at any of the others.

Cities and universities were both, in part, special cases of the general category of a *guild*, the Germanic fraternal societies that combined mutual defense and peacekeeping, insurance and mutual care, social functions, and shared worship.[21] These were not, to begin with, functionally differentiated. The initial *commune* oaths that formed cities seem to have been fraternal guild oaths of this sort. Once the cities were founded, however, and the division and specialization of labor advanced within them, the general fraternal guild was gradually succeeded by the trade and craft guilds that provide the most familiar meaning of the word. And so, besides the guilds of teachers and/or students that made up the initial cores of universities, guilds of merchants and of artisans, craftsmen, and skilled workers of all sorts proliferated. Again, these were self-organized and self-governing, but usually willing to negotiate with the cities for formal recognition of their corporate status. Guilds' economic

[21] Otto von Gierke, *Community in Historical Perspective*, Antony Black, ed., Mar Fischer, trans. (Cambridge: Cambridge University Press, 1990[1868]), pp. 22–8; Black, *Guilds*, pp. 3–6.

functions included training—initiation into the mysteries of each respective craft through the apprenticeship system—as well as access to costly tools and certification of quality and competence. But despite the functional differentiation, they were not simply economic actors. Rather, they continued to act as fraternal societies that provided social bonds and important insurance functions to their members. During the eleventh and twelfth centuries, these trade guilds came to organize much of the social, economic, and even political life of cities across Europe's urban zones.[22]

I have been treating cities, universities, and guilds as part of the same category, as intermediate bodies *avant la lettre*. I should briefly return to a concern raised earlier: that would now seem more natural to us to think of cities as being part of the state, not as part of the intermediate sphere. But we cannot cleanly project that distinction back to the pre-state medieval era. Cities had locally effective coercive capacity, but so did many parts of the church. Cities, guilds, and universities alike eventually acquired charters from, and privileges (often) recognized by, emperors, kings, and lords. Their internal rule-making authority, like that of church, was both effective and widely accepted as legitimate. All offered their members dispute-resolution authority that was otherwise hard to come by. All offered, in Fuller's sense, law. Whether they derived this legal and judicial authority from the social fact that they had the capacity for it, from the customary Germanic law of the guild, or from the reinterpreted rules of *collegium*-formation in a recovered Roman law that owed its own legitimacy to something very different from royal command (see the next section), none of them derived it from simple grants from a (non-existent) sovereign state. Indeed, Justinian's *Digest* treated cities and guilds as two species of the same genus. Later, as state capacity developed, the right of the cities to govern themselves was, like the similar right of guilds or universities, interpreted as an anomalous privilege, one that eventually gave way to state rationalization. As Gerald Frug puts it: "the autonomy of the medieval town was not the autonomy of a political organization in the sense which we attribute to the modern city. Rather, the medieval town was a complex economic, political, and communal association."[23]

---

[22] In some sense, the "guilds and civil society," that is, guilds and cities, opposition found in Black's book offers the familiar pattern: governmental units devoted to an abstractly rational rule of law, and groups within the city that tie people together on a thicker basis. And some of Black's own interest was in tracing a history in which a legally abstract market society coexisted with Germanic solidaristic workers' guilds. Despite that, his book clearly lays out a history of guilds and cities developing alongside one another, in similar ways and for similar reasons. The city may have been, as Black thinks, the site where an ideology developed that later became the animating spirit of something abstract and law-bound *rather than* solidaristic, but the city and guild both developed in this era as law-bound *and* solidaristic.

[23] Gerald Frug, "The City as a Legal Concept," 93(6) *Harvard Law Review* 1057–154, 1980, p. 1083.

The Roman Law

The growth of both the cities and the universities, and to a lesser degree the guilds, was deeply entwined with the recovery of Justinian's compilation of Roman law (four works collectively referred to as the *corpus iuris civilis*, hereafter simply the *corpus*), and especially the monumental *Digest*, starting in the 1070s. This is easy to see with respect to the universities, where law became one of the central topics of study. The medieval university was standardly divided into faculties of theology, medicine, philosophy, and law, with theology and law typically being the largest. At some of the earliest universities, and especially those in Italy, law was the preeminent field of study. The recovered *corpus* was not locally specific, and so could be studied by Latin-literate scholars from across Europe if they could congregate in one place. It was a large codified system of law, contained in old written texts which required organization and interpretation. It was an excellent match with the university enterprise: a system of law that could be learned only with dedicated study and education, not through apprenticeship or the thick knowledge of local customs and norms. The reconciliation of the *corpus* with the canon law was another important intellectual enterprise, also not locally specific, depending on an understanding of the two systems and on literate education. The resulting reconciled *ius commune*—the law common to the civil and canon systems—provided the basic sources of legal argument as those who studied in the universities took their learning across Europe. The civil system itself developed primarily through work done in the universities: the Glossators and Commentators who shaped it through the Middle Ages were university professors, first in Bologna and then gradually elsewhere as well. Their reorganizations and reinterpretations of the *corpus* took place within and alongside the enterprise of teaching. The university form and this very scholarly kind of law thus reinforced one another.

The relationship of the cities to Roman law is less simple but perhaps more important. The Germanic legal model of law tied to personal status—each person to be judged according to the law of his or her people—is stable and effective for locally mostly homogenous and immobile populations. It's a matter of widespread local knowledge who everyone is, and what the traditional norms are for any situation. But it is much less effective for the arms'-length interactions of strangers engaged in long-distance or urban trade, or for novel financial and commercial arrangements. The *corpus* contained rules for a complex partly urban economy that included long-distance trade, rules that served a useful purpose as cities and trade reciprocally grew starting in the eleventh century. The on-its-face strange phenomenon that the centuries-old codification of the law of a polity that had disappeared in the west even before the codification took place should be treated as law no doubt owes something to the historical luster of Rome, and something to the incentives universities had to supply legal learning. But it had to respond to demand as well. Guilds, too, found a use for the formal rules of corporate legal personality that the *corpus* made available, clarifying that a guild could own funds and a hall in its own right, and could persist over generations.

Despite these functional affinities between the recovered *corpus* on the one hand and cities and universities on the other, there was substantive tension. The default rule in the *corpus* (unlike in canon law) was that a *collegium* could only be formed with the permission of the Emperor or Senate.[24] Unsurprisingly, this was cited as needed by the Holy Roman Emperor or other central authorities in particular conflicts. But jurisprudential scholars of the Roman law worked around the apparent demand for permission of a higher power in a number of ways: for example, by treating the silence of the superior as tacit consent, or by treating lists in the *corpus* of those who were allowed to form *collegia* on their own volition as exemplary of a general type, rather than as specific exceptions to a general rule.[25] The jurists showed great creativity in adapting the *corpus* to the medieval social world; if the uptake of the *corpus* as law had to be demand-driven, then we would expect to see a strong preference for interpretations that made sense of social facts over those that demanded their reform or abolition. The twelfth-century incorporation into the *ius commune* of feudal oaths and land tenures, both wildly alien to the Roman law of contract and property, is the most dramatic evidence of this. By comparison, the accommodation of the self-creating *collegium* or *universitas* was straightforward. And once a corporation was legally legitimate, the *corpus* contained useful material about internal governance and about external corporate personality: the meaning of corporate contracts and debts, for example.[26]

Roman law eventually became politically associated with centralization, rationalism, and a kind of legal positivism. The statements that *"Quod principi placuit legis habet vigorem"* ("What pleases the prince has the force of law," *Digest* 1.4.1) and *"Princeps legibus solutus est"* ("The prince is not bound by the law," *Digest* 1.3.31) became the public law mottoes of absolute kings.[27] The imposition of Roman private law over Germanic or other customary law made the countryside legally comprehensible to the center at the expense of locally evolved legal orders. And eventually, there was no doubt an affinity between the law that required Latin literacy and educated bureaucratic elites.

---

[24] *Digest* 3.4.1.   [25] Black, *Guilds*, pp. 14–26.

[26] See P. W. Duff, *Personality in Roman Private Law* (Cambridge: Cambridge University Press, 1938).

[27] *"Solutus"* means to be untied, unbound, set free; the prince who was *legibus ab solutus* was to be free from the binding effect of law, hence "absolute."

In response to these affinities between Roman law and centralization, many early modern pluralists and constitutionalists were at pains to stress (real or imagined) Germanic and barbarian origins of their constitutional systems; they emphasized the supposed liberty of the primordial German forests, in which kings were chiefs and leaders but not rulers, and in which communal assemblies always had their say. Anglo-Saxon England, Visigothic Spain, and Frankish France were all identified with Germanic constitutional orders incompatible with this Roman imperial conception of rule. We will return to this theme in the next chapter. Later still, the basic conflict between the rule that associations relied on the permission of the Emperor and the Germanic traditions of spontaneous fellowship-formation out of which the guilds arguably first emerged was further entrenched in a vision in which Roman law was equated with centralization and legal positivism, Germanic custom with pluralism.[28]

But the *corpus* provided a vocabulary that could be called upon by more than one side in constitutional debates.[29] Public and constitutional law took up only a handful of passages in the *corpus* in any case; and the adoption of those passages by advocates of royal power was a much later development.[30] The new legal learning moreover created a class of specially trained legal professionals whose juristic knowledge was only weakly tied to any particular polity, and who were not professionally disposed to think of the local king or lord as a particularly important source of law. The *corpus* was "received" in, not posited by, medieval polities. These legal professionals gradually became a guild, a partly self-governing body in its own right with strong transnational and trans-jurisdictional ties.[31]

Facts and Norms

The self-government of the Church, the religious orders, and the various *collegia* was due, first and foremost, to the effective ability of their members and of the institutions themselves to make it stick. They emerged out of

---

[28] This view is especially associated with the nineteenth-century German legal historian Otto von Gierke, to whom we will return in Chapter 9.

[29] Daniel Lee, "Private Law Models for Public Law Concepts: The Roman Law Theory of Dominium in the Monarchomach Doctrine of Popular Sovereignty," 70 *The Review of Politics* 370–99, 2008.

[30] Later still, Roman law, or the Napoleonic Code which largely supplanted it as the foundation of codified civil law, came to represent any number of things in late modern ideological disputes. To some socialists, it was capitalist, mercantile, and individualistic. To nationalists, and eventually to the Nazis, it was an alien imposition on the customary law that truly expressed the *Geist* of the *Volk*.

[31] James A. Brundage, *The Medieval Origins of the Legal Profession: Canonists, Civilians, and Courts* (Chicago: University of Chicago Press, 2008).

struggles with emperors, kings, and feudal lords, and those struggles never ceased once and for all. The Church was likely the most powerful institution in medieval Europe; but probably no half-century passed without a serious attempt by an Emperor or a King of France or England to limit its authority—sometimes very successfully, as when France brought the papacy to heel in Avignon for two generations, and created schismatic rival popes for a third. Cities, universities, and guilds likewise faced more or less constant tests of their jurisdictional boundaries; and weakness was met with gradual encroachment. In the early fourteenth century, the jurisdictionally autonomous, trans-European, wealthy, and secretive order of the Knights Templar was suppressed by France (with the help of a captive Avignon Pope); torture, executions, and expropriation followed. Moreover, the various intermediate bodies came into repeated conflict with one another: church and town authority over universities, and city authority over guilds, were frequently asserted and contested as well.

But at a fundamental level the self-government of the Church, the orders, and the *collegia* was normative, not only a social fact arising from sheer power. Indeed, the power that they were able to bring to bear arose in part out of their normative status. Obviously, the self-government of each was *internally* normative. But I also mean that, in the centuries of and following the birth of intermediacy, the self-governing authority of these bodies was normative extramurally. Canon law and civil law affirmed it; so did repeated decrees of the Empire and the major kingdoms. While there was variation from one realm to the next in how well respected the autonomy of these bodies was, it was acknowledged everywhere in Catholic Europe. The corporate and group pluralism that came into existence during the first centuries of the millennium was a basic feature of the political world and the juridical order throughout the remainder of the Middle Ages. The European social landscape was thickly populated with such institutions before the coalescing of the modern state.

Medieval corporate pluralism was both a fact and a norm. The norm that these institutions ought to be understood as *intermediate*, of course, only took shape much later. It took a long time for uneasy *de facto* balances of power to be rationalized as desirable orders in their own right. The Church in particular often struggled with kings and Emperors for *supremacy*, not for a secure intermediate status; and the assertion of an associational right of self-government can be agnostic on whether that right should coexist with any higher political jurisdiction. The arguments for self-government for German cities were not different in kind from those for Italian cities. The former ended as "intermediate" bodies within the Empire and the latter did not because of the limits on how far imperial power could be projected, not because the German cities had a principled commitment to being intermediate rather than independent. The Church and the *collegia* could only become *corps intermédiaires*, as they were to be known in French thought, once the state coalesced. That process of state consolidation created, as a by-product, additional *corps intermédiaires* organized and legitimized in quite different terms, as we shall see in the next chapter.

5

The Ancient Constitution, the Social Contract, and the Modern State

The Emergence of the State

The processes by which medieval polities coalesced into early modern states, and the jurisdictional world of medieval Christendom became "the state system," are much studied and little agreed upon. Some combination of military technology, domestic financial and political capacity, inter-polity military competition, international law, the development of overseas empires, agricultural and commercial factors, literacy and the printing press, and the Reformation and the Wars of Religion, and the interactions among all of these, make for a thicket of causal theories that produce social science arguments that have not yet been decisively settled.[1] What matters for our purposes are the intellectual, philosophical, and ideological reactions to the social facts of state consolidation and formation.

We might think of early modern state-building as having two rough stages, one from the late 1400s through the mid-1600s, the second lasting until the French Revolution. The first corresponds to the gradual triumph of the Spanish, French, and English crowns over genuine rivals in the feudal nobility, and substantial increases in royal power vis-à-vis the Church, as well as the emergence of a powerful new state in the Netherlands. The second saw state bureaucracies built in these consolidated kingdoms, and the approximate settlement of domestic constitutional disputes: absolutist monarchy in Spain and France, parliamentary supremacy in England/Britain. The

---

[1] See, *inter alia*, Joseph Strayer, *On the Medieval Origins of the Modern State* (Princeton: Princeton University Press, 1970); Hendrich Spruyt, *The Sovereign State and Its Competitors: An Analysis of Systems Change* (Princeton: Princeton University Press, 1994); Charles Tilly, *Coercion, Capital, and European States, AD 990–1992* (Cambridge, Mass.: Basil Blackwell, 1992); Charles Tilly and Wim Blockman, eds, *Cities & the Rise of States in Europe, AD 1000–1800* (Boulder, Colo.: Westview Press, 1994); Gianfranco Poggi, *The State* (Cambridge: Polity Press, 1990).

seventeenth and eighteenth centuries saw state-building spread further east, as Prussia, Russia, and Austria engaged in self-conscious catch-up, and Denmark and Sweden turned to absolutism. Besides France, at one time or another, "absolute monarchies developed in Spain, the British Isles, Sweden, Denmark, Austria-Hungary, Brandenburg-Prussia, Russia, and Savoy-Piedmont, and formed the basis of the governance of several smaller states in Germany and Italy."[2] This second stage also saw the formalization of the inter-state system in the Treaties of Westphalia and Utrecht.

This process of state-building and consolidation came at the expense of the autonomy of the self-organized intermediate groups discussed in the previous chapter, as well as others to which we now turn: groups and bodies that drew legitimacy from other sources and that more directly contended with monarchs within the political system.

Peers, Provinces, and *Parlements*

The first is the nobility or aristocracy. The higher feudal lords in the Middle Ages, the dukes, counts, and princes, were competitors with kings. State consolidation to some degree simply *meant* their defeat or co-optation. The War of the Roses ended in England in the late 1480s, followed by more than a century of Tudor rule, most of it under the powerful reigns of Henry VIII and Elizabeth I. From the end of the Hundred Years War onward, the French kings ended the power of the most powerful and dangerous of the rival feudal domains, culminating in the 1520s when the crown absorbed the Duchy of Burgundy.

The nobilities of early modernity had thus lost status and military power relative to monarchs. While they could no longer rival kings individually, they might still balance them corporately, and they increasingly acted in politics as a group, a *corps*, an estate. Their reduction from the heights they had once occupied left them "intermediate" in one straightforward sense; their increasing reliance on the status of their *corps* or estate did so in another. Their collective organization—for example in the House of Lords or the Second Estate—did not make them a *collegium*; their sources of legitimacy were quite different from those of cities, universities, or guilds. But the nobility was a natural constituency for arguments against centralization and absolutism; and so in the constitutional debates of early modernity, many of its members self-consciously identified as an intermediate power or body. The early eclipse of the great feudal lords individually that made state consolidation possible was

---

[2] Peter R. Campbell, "Absolute Monarchy," in *The Oxford Handbook of the Ancien Régime*, William Doyle, ed. (Oxford: Oxford University Press, 2011), p. 12.

thus followed by a long, less decisive tug of war between monarchs and the aristocratic estate.

If the feudal nobility's *personnel* ended up as the Second Estate, feudalism's *places* ended up as a different sort of new intermediate entity: provinces. Again, these are a different kind of entity from the *collegia* and *universitas*. Provinces were geographically far larger than cities; a province is not surrounded by a wall. They were often primarily rural, even if they contained one or more cities within their boundaries. More fundamentally, they were not consensual deliberate creations, certainly not founded by equals committing to one another by oaths. They were in large part the leftover geography of the processes of state consolidation.

As political divisions they were largely feudal in origin: counties, duchies, principalities, and even kingdoms that were eventually absorbed as junior partners into early modern composite monarchies. They might be ruled directly by a hereditary noble, by such a figure in conjunction with a body of Estates, by a bishop, or by a junior member of the royal family. Their boundaries expanded and contracted over time through war, marriage, and dynastic politics; they were sometimes combined and sometimes divided. Some went through the Middle Ages substantially independent of any kingdom or of the Empire; some were clearly subordinate fiefs; and some moved from the orbit of one dynasty or kingdom to another.

State consolidation reduced lords into courtiers, and reduced rival polities or autonomous feudal holdings to provinces. The ducal ring of Normandy was ceremonially destroyed on an anvil in 1469 in an especially vivid symbolic demonstration that the duchy was no more.[3] Denmark and Norway's dual kingdom ended in 1536 when Denmark simply abolished Norway's status as a partner kingdom, officially making the latter a province. But these reduced fiefs or former kingdoms retained meaningful autonomy as provinces, with their own customs, languages, and inherited legal traditions, defended by local estates, nobles, and jurists. Sometimes provinces were differentiated only because a fief had been divided between two noble lines. But often provincial distinctiveness dated to the early Middle Ages and was traced to one or another of the barbarian codes of laws; different regions had, after all, been settled by different Germanic tribes, while other regions had remained mainly Roman. The Viking and Norman conquests had left their own overlay of regional variation.

Even within the same kingdom, the several provinces after consolidation might have varying degrees of autonomy or rights to retain traditional laws and usages—depending, for example, on whether the province had been

---

[3] Amable Floquet, *Histoire du Parlement de Normandie, tome 1* (Rouen: Edouard Frère, 1840), pp. 252–3.

brought into the kingdom by conquest or by marriage. In France, the *pays d'élection*, *pays d'état*, and *pays d'imposition* were quite different in their legal standing, and somewhat different in other ways as well, the latter two categories being ethnolinguistically further from the Parisian core as a rule, from Brittany to Alsace to Provence. But the Latinate "province" eventually became the generic word in France (*provincia*, in Spain) and I will use it for similar units elsewhere, except in the Empire where the duchies, principalities, and so on remained distinct lordships.

In the final decades of the 1400s, Isabella and Ferdinand joined the most powerful Spanish kingdoms by marriage and created a unified Spanish state; authorized the Inquisition (notably, an institution of the Spanish state, not a creation of the Church; its rulings could not be appealed to Rome); conquered the remaining Muslim territories in Iberia and expelled Jews and Muslims, creating a religiously homogenous Spanish state dominated by Castile; largely replaced urban self-government with rule by appointed delegates; and successfully cowed the *cortes*, the Spanish assemblies of the estates. As Montesquieu was to put it centuries later, "Ferdinand, King of Aragon, made himself Grand Master of the Orders; and that alone spoiled the constitution"—meaning, in context, to undermine its monarchical character and transform it into a despotism.[4]

Provincial autonomy and *fueros* were not ended, but they were a far cry from the power of the former separate kingdoms. Moreover, the conquest of the Americas and the extraction of precious metals reduced (without eliminating) the Spanish crown's dependence on the *cortes* for tax revenue.

These earliest modern states acquired effective coercive control over their entire territories, but were still bound by normative constraints about legislating for them, as well as by the reality that administration across long distances was time-consuming and expensive. Joined together under the rule of a single crown or dynasty, the various traditional regions were nonetheless still distinct politically and jurisprudentially; the resulting complex patterns are called "composite monarchies" and "multiple kingdoms" by historians.[5] A "multiple kingdom" is one monarchy attached distinctly to several kingdoms: Stuart rule over England, Scotland, and Ireland, or the monarchy of Castile and Aragon. A "composite monarchy," the broader category, need not have juridically distinct *monarchies*, only continuing jurisdictional pluralism within the monarchy. Spain after the establishment of the unified Spanish

---

[4] SL, I.2.4, p. 19.
[5] See J. H. Elliot, "A Europe of Composite Monarchies," 137 *Past & Present* 48–71, 1992; Conrad Russell, "Composite Monarchies in Early Modern Europe," in Alexander Grant and Keith J. Stringer, eds, *Uniting the Kingdom? The Making of British History* (London; New York: Routledge, 1995), p. 133; David Armitage, *The Ideological Origins of the British Empire* (Cambridge: Cambridge University Press, 2000), pp. 22–3.

crown in the sixteenth century, France, and England (rather than Britain) with its county-level legal variation, were composite monarchies but not multiple kingdoms. Multiple kingdoms were juridically more secure in their pluralism. When someone in a composite monarchy used the language of multiple kingdoms and characterized the monarch as separately related to the various provinces—as was occasionally done in France, and later by Americans during the pre-Revolutionary crisis—this was an especially radical attempt to shore up provincial liberties.

The Tudor kings and queens were monarchs of England (including Wales) and, separately, of Ireland. Their Stuart successors added King of Scotland to their titles. But Ireland and (until 1707) Scotland remained distinct kingdoms, with local parliaments and legal systems. Uniquely among the major composite monarchies, the British monarchy even encompassed distinct established churches. The Isle of Man and the Channel Islands were attached to the British monarchy in a similar fashion, without ever being part of England or Britain in a constitutional sense.[6] The eventual union of the crowns of Castile and Aragon founded the composite Spanish monarchy. The crown of Aragon was itself a composite of Aragon, Barcelona (that is, Catalonia), Valencia, Sicily, Naples, and others, each with their own laws and institutions.

The composite monarchy was meaningfully different from what had come before. There was no longer any question of a large powerful region of France such as Aquitaine being joined to England in matters of war and peace, as there had been during the Middle Ages. But the British and Spanish kings ruled collections of kingdoms and other units, as reflected in their lengthening titles: King of England, Ireland, and Scotland; King of Castile, Navarre, Aragon, Leon, Portugal, Naples, and Sicily.

Many French provinces retained their traditional assemblies of Estates, and eventually gained provincial *parlements*; and ordinarily the acquired provinces retained their local customary laws. Again, unified military authority did not translate into legal unification, which only formally arrived with the Revolution. In France as in Britain and Spain, the formerly distinct regions thus remained partially autonomous jurisdictions even as the modern state coalesced, even though France was *not* juridically a multiple kingdom as Britain and Spain were. And in France as in Britain and Spain, the regional institutions were quick to appeal to ancient laws, liberties, or constitutions in the face of bureaucratic or legal centralization.

---

[6] The Channel Islands were Norman possessions prior to 1066, and so remained attached to William the Conqueror's heirs—but in their Norman, not their English, capacity. When mainland Normandy fell to France, the islands remained attached to the English monarchy but outside the English state.

110

Consolidation happened more slowly in the zone to the east of France. By 1500 the Swiss confederation's independence from the Empire was *de facto* secure, and the confederation had grown to nearly the size of modern Switzerland. But it never took the path to centralization and absolutism (though absolutism replaced popular government *within* some of the cities), remaining instead a league of cities and rural communes. Neither did the Holy Roman Empire as such ever consolidate into a state; instead, Austria and Brandenburg-Prussia followed the state-building path separately, and later than the western kingdoms. The Netherlands—the United *Provinces*—jealously guarded the autonomy of the component provinces even through the era of Dutch state-building and naval supremacy. While the balance of power between the stadtholders of the House of Orange and the States (States-General at the federal level, States-Provincial within each province) varied, the office of stadtholder remained a provincial one until the mid-eighteenth century. Even a very powerful stadtholder (e.g. William III) might not be appointed to that office in all of the provinces. In the century following the recognition of Dutch independence in 1648, the most powerful group of provinces left the office empty more often than not. And Italy, of course, did not consolidate at all until much later, remaining a region of city-states ruling province-sized hinterlands, alongside the special case of the Papal States.

In Switzerland, the Empire, or the Netherlands, the medieval provinces, cantons, duchies, principalities, and cities by and large retained their authority through the sixteenth and seventeenth centuries. Ancient constitutionalists thus did not have to recall as distant a past as was the case in early modern Spain, France, and England. The defenses of provincial and urban liberties could be offered as defenses of the *status quo*, not calls for restoration; or as reforms rather than (in the old sense) revolutions.

One institution in France was especially important both as an aristocratic corporate body and (eventually) as a manifestation of provincial distinctiveness. These were the *parlements* (a word I will use untranslated to avoid confusion with parliaments).[7] The first *parlement* was a high court in Paris created in the thirteenth century. Additional *parlements* were created starting in the fifteenth century in many of the provinces; eventually there were fourteen in all. They were staffed by members of the *noblesse de robe*; that is, their judges were ennobled by virtue of being appointed to the *parlements*, though it was a sort of nobility that was often looked down upon by members of the older *noblesse d'epée*. Under France's distinctive rules, the holders of such offices could purchase the right to make the noble status heritable. Over

---

[7] See Bailey Stone, *The French Parlements and the Crisis of the Old Regime* (Chapel Hill: University of North Carolina Press, 1986); J. H. Shennan, *The Parlement of Paris* (Ithaca: Cornell University Press, 1968); Julian Swann, "*Parlements* and Provincial Estates," in *The Oxford Handbook of the Ancien Régime*, Doyle, ed. (Oxford: Oxford University Press, 2011).

the course of centuries, the *parlements* thus became mainly occupied by a (relatively) new class of hereditary aristocrats.

The *parlements* were, as Montesquieu (himself the *président* of the *parlement* of Bordeaux) would come to call them, the depositories of the laws: they served as sites where the official registries of the laws were kept. Provincial *parlements* had particular custody of the laws and customs governing their jurisdictions. In order to fulfill their function as depositories, the *parlements* had to be notified of new laws—royal edicts in particular—and to register them. If the *parlement* judged there to be a conflict between the edict and older or more fundamental law, the judges could decline to register it, and issue a remonstrance to the king explaining the conflict. The procedure operated under the fiction that the king could not *mean* to alter fundamental law, and needed only to be reminded of that which ostensibly he had overlooked. This served as something recognizably like judicial review, and occasionally generated multiple exchanges between the king and the Parisian *parlement*. Eventually, in a procedure known as the *lit de justice*—the reading of justice— the king could appear in person at the *parlement* and dictate the edict into the record, registering it himself and having the last word on the question of his intent. Whether remonstrances were still possible after he left the chamber was a contested question, the effective answer varying with royal power.

Over the course of early modernity, the process of state centralization and consolidation was to generate conflict not only with the autonomy of the corporate bodies described in the last chapter, but also with the authority of the noble estate, with the provinces, and (in France) the *parlements*.

The Ancient Constitution

With all of that in mind—the early modern consolidation of states, and the increasing power of absolute kings at the expense of the Church, cities, nobles, and provinces—we have the context for the development of a political discourse opposed to centralization and absolutism, in the name of the traditional liberties of the various intermediate bodies. The nineteenth-century French liberal Germaine de Staël famously proclaimed that in France, liberty was ancient, despotism modern.[8] This was an especially memorable statement of a widespread view in early modern European thought: that freedom had been lost within historical memory, to the centralizing kings of the age of absolutism and state consolidation. Defenders of the ancient constitution maintained that the rights, liberties, and privileges of the intermediate bodies

---

[8] Germaine de Staël, *Considerations on the Principal Events of the French Revolution*, Aurelian Craiutu, ed. (Indianapolis: Liberty Fund Press, 2008[1818]).

severally, and of the Estates or Parliament in which they were represented, were fundamental law of the various polities. The new absolutism thus not only violated tradition and restricted liberty, but also contravened the foundation of the legal and political order.

"Ancient" here—the French *ancien*, as in *ancien régime*—means "former"; it refers to the Middle Ages or early modernity, not to classical antiquity. And the early modern ideas about resisting newly the novelty of centralized monarchical power were often phrased as defenses of the "*ancient constitution*," a putative constitutional order dating to the Middle Ages. "Ancient constitution" was used approximately interchangeably with "Gothic constitution."

The latter term denotes a distinct family of claims made by many of the ancient constitutionalists. They held, broadly, that the traditional constitutional orders of Europe were Germanic in both their origins and their structures, that they owed more to the supposedly primordial liberty of the Goths and other barbarian tribes than they did to Roman imperial rule. The English constitution was that of the Angles and the Saxons, briefly disrupted by the Norman yoke but reasserting itself in Magna Carta, the common law, and a Parliament whose origins were imagined as preceding 1066. The French kingdom was that of the Frankish tribes, especially the Salic Franks, not (as the royalists were eventually to argue) a continuation of the Roman province of Gaul whose imperial rule was succeeded to by a Frankish king. In Spain, the Visigothic Code of the second half of the seventh century, the *Liber Judiciorum*, survived into the late Middle Ages as the "*Fuero Juzgo*" (largely a thirteenth-century Castilian translation of the older text) and served as the legitimating legal text for the regime of *fueros*—the corporate rights and privileges of the provinces and cities.

The appeal to Germanic traditions had different structures from place to place. In France, it sometimes amounted to a claim that the Franks had conquered the Gauls and become their lords, in time becoming a nobility that had a traditional Germanic right to govern in concert with the king. In England, the Germanic institutions were those of the *conquered*, not the conquerors. The king and high aristocracy from 1066 onward were an imported Norman yoke, on some accounts, or rapidly acculturated into the pre-existing Anglo-Saxon constitution, on others. These differences affected the political significance of the appeals. Boulainvillier's eighteenth-century version of Gothic constitutional claims excluded the Third Estate entirely; they were the conquered, and rightfully ruled by the Second Estate conquerors. But it was much more common to see assertions that assemblies of all the estates, along with provincial liberty, self-government of the towns, and autonomy of the *corps*, were somehow all alike part of a Germanic inheritance.

This explicit normative appeal to German-ness marks out ancient or Gothic constitutionalism as an atypical political discourse in European history. From

Carolingian times onward, appeals to Roman-ness in one form or another have characterized a wide range of languages of legitimation in European history. The Emperor and the Pope each claimed Rome's mantle through the Middle Ages; the recovered *corpus* exercised tremendous persuasive authority over European jurisprudence for centuries, in no small part due to the aura of Rome's prestige. Renaissance civic humanism reached, in its way, still farther back, to the Roman republic. Renaissance absolutists routinely appealed to the maxim *princeps legibus solutes est* discussed in the last chapter, combining the appeal to the *corpus* with the prestige of imperial status. Progressive theories of the seventeenth and eighteenth centuries sometimes held the moderns above the ancients; but the barbarous and Germanic medievals were considered clearly inferior to both. Ancient or Gothic constitutionalism, by contrast, claimed legitimacy derived from Germanic medieval institutions, often *against* appeals to Roman authority of one sort or another.

I prefer "ancient constitution" to "Gothic constitution," in order to emphasize not the stories about the pre-eleventh century Germanic origins of the relevant institutions, but only the understanding about their pre-sixteenth-century existence and legitimacy. Some ancient constitutionalists denied the narratives about Gothic origins, sometimes perceiving pre-Gothic immemorial law, sometimes late-medieval evolution and development. The Gothic origin stories were sufficient but not necessary for an argument to be ancient constitutionalist. The important unifying theme is that centralization and absolutism represented illegitimate innovations against older fundamental law and against the rights and privileges of the various intermediate bodies, separately as well as in representative assembly.

"Ancient constitutionalism" as a systematic way of talking was distinctively early modern, but it drew on traditional medieval discourses and concepts. The idea that custom and tradition had legal and normative force was not only a principle of common law and Roman law; it was a commonplace of politics. William the Conqueror's 1067 charter to London guarantees its "ancient liberties." In addition to protecting baronial authority and the freedom of the church, in 1215 Magna Carta guaranteed the city of London's "ancient liberties and free customs." More generally, city charters that postdated the city's actual founding routinely confirmed their "ancient liberties," however recent that "ancient" might be; the same held true for charters of guilds, monasteries, and so on. "Customs and usages," established orders and rules, were likewise reaffirmed. To show that one's *collegium* or *universitas* anciently had *libertas*, preferably guaranteed by a charter, was an important and ubiquitous type of medieval legal–political argument.[9]

---

[9] Julia Crick, "Pristina Libertas: Liberty and the Anglo-Saxons Revisited," 6(14) *Transactions of the Royal Historical Society* 47–71, 2004, discusses the frequency of twelfth- and thirteenth-century

What was novel in the early modern "ancient constitution" was, first, the attempt to turn all of the scattered ancient rights, liberties, privileges, and customs into a seamless whole; and, second, the explicit understanding that this web of liberties made for a monarchy that was legally constrained. The idea that monarchies governed according to the laws, while despotisms were lawless, is at least as old as Aristotle. But early modernity both saw a tremendous increase in what monarchs had the capacity to do domestically, and inherited a body of corporate liberties that came to be understood as part of the law according to which lawful monarchs must govern. Medieval corporate liberties were often guaranteed by kings as against more-local feudal lords; until the expansion of state capacity, the possibility of direct conflict between monarchs and the liberties of *collegia* arose more rarely. Similarly, there was little need for constitutional debates about the rights of the nobility and the liberties of provinces when the provinces were ruled by independently powerful noble lords. The conversion of monarch–noble and center–province relations to questions of fundamental law awaited the emergence of states. Indeed, the very idea of a law at stake in a dispute between absolutist and ancient-constitutional theories of a particular kingdom's public law was not entirely available to the pre-state Middle Ages. The rights of a city or a university might have been *legal* according to the *ius commune*, but describing them as part of the fundamental law of, e.g., France was a different matter. Once those arguments were made, though, they drew freely on pre-modern words, ideas, and precedents. Ancient constitutionalism was a partly novel response to partly novel facts (the coalescing of the state) and ideas (absolutism, and the emergence of public law).

Notwithstanding this turn to the language of the domestic fundamental law of each state—recall that De Staël's memorable comment referred to *France*— one common trope of ancient constitutionalism was the idea that the pre-modern, pre-absolutist constitutional orders of Europe were everywhere much the same.[10] Absolute kings threatened "the ancient constitution of Europe."

appeals by English towns and monasteries to pre-Conquest guarantees of *libertas*, indeed to the point of widespread forgery of pre-Conquest monastic charters. Already by then, the combination of antiquity and charter was understood to make a powerful tool in arguments for corporate *libertas*.

[10] Pocock's study of English ancient constitutionalism emphasizes the insularity of the common-law mindset, the concern with the distinctively good old law of *England*. Pocock, *The Ancient Constitution and the Feudal Law; a Study of English Historical Thought in the Seventeenth Century* (Cambridge: Cambridge University Press, 1957). This is an exception. The common lawyers Pocock studied were not the whole of English ancient constitutionalism. The account of the Europe-wide Gothic constitution was embraced by others, all the more so as Charles II and James II allied with, and were suspected of emulating, their cousin Louis XIV. "The English shared with other Europeans a mode of thought that resisted the attempts of modern monarchies to claim sovereign power at the expense of particularistic privileges by appealing to immemorial ancient customary law." David Resnick, "Locke and the Rejection of the Ancient Constitution," 12 *Political Theory* 97–114, 1984, p. 99.

The English writer Robert Molesworth, for example, maintained that the English constitution "in truth, is not ours only, but that of almost all *Europe* besides; so wisely restor'd and establish'd (if not introduced) by the *Goths* and *Franks*, whose Descendants we are." This justified his treating the sixteenth-century French *Francogallia* as a foundation for eighteenth-century English Whiggism, as the book "gives an Account of the Ancient Free State of above Three Parts in Four of *Europe*," England included; and a "real Whig" is "one who is exactly for keeping up to the Strictness of the true old *Gothick Constitution*."[11]

In an earlier work he said that Denmark, too, had had an "Ancient Form of Government" which "was the same which the Goths and Vandals established in most, if not all Parts of Europe . . . and which in England is retained to this day for the most part." That Gothic constitution "far excell[ed] all others that we know of in the World. 'Tis to the ancient Inhabitants of these Countries, with other neighbouring Provinces, that we owe the Original of Parliaments, formerly so common, but lost within this last Age in all Kingdoms but those of *Poland, Great Britain*, and *Ireland*." In short, "All *Europe* was in a manner a free Country till very lately, insomuch that the *Europeans* were, and still are, distinguish'd in the *Eastern* Parts of the World by the name of *Franks*." Change had come only since the turn of the sixteenth century; "slavery has within these last 200 years crept upon Europe."[12]

Montesquieu agreed. The "Gothic government," once the cities had been enfranchised, showed "such concert" among "the civil liberty of the people, the prerogatives of the nobility and of the clergy, and the power of the kings, [. . .] that there has never been, I believe, a government on earth as well tempered as *each part of Europe* during the time that this government continued to exist"; the result was nothing less than "the best kind of government men have been able to devise."[13]

Burke appealed to "the old common law of Europe" in his argument that the French ought to have rebuilt on the foundations of their own ancient constitution, borrowing as needed from contemporary English examples, since England had kept the good old law alive. And Tocqueville in the mid-nineteenth century claimed that he had studied

the political institutions of medieval France, England, and Germany, and as I progressed in my work, I was astonished at the sight of the incredible similarity to be found among their laws . . . Their laws varied constantly and almost infinitely

[11] Robert Molesworth, "Translator's Preface to *Franco-Gallia*," in Justin Champion, ed., *An Account of Denmark, With Francogallia and Some Considerations for the Promoting of Agriculture and Employing the Poor* (Indianapolis: Liberty Fund, 2011).
[12] Molesworth, "An Account of Denmark" (1694), in *An Account of Denmark*, pp. 16–17, 49–50.
[13] SL. II.11.8, pp. 167–8.

in detail, according to place, but they had the same foundation everywhere.... Among all three, government was conducted according to the same principles, political assemblies were formed from the same elements and given the same powers... The constitutions of the towns resembled each other and the country-side was governed in the same way...I think one may suggest that in the four-teenth century the social, political, administrative, judicial, economic, and literary institutions of Europe resembled each other perhaps even more than they do today.[14]

All of this was, at best, partially and approximately true. The "ancient constitution" was simply not the same from one realm to the next. No matter how much theorists of the ancient constitution emphasized shared Gothic roots and commonalities involving the rights of cities, *collegia*, estates or parliaments, and provinces, there were salient differences. France was a uni-fied kingdom, not a composite monarchy. The *parlements* had no direct analog elsewhere. England, eventually singled out by ancient constitutionalists as the model of continuity with the old European ways, was actually quite idiosyn-cratic by reason of the Conquest; 1066 placed a serious obstacle in the way of any claims of constitutional continuity running back to the Saxons. Norman rule generated an especially hierarchical and centralized order unusually early, leaving England with little tradition of provincial liberties, and greater than usual royal involvement in the founding of cities. On the other hand, the distinctive English common law placed arguments from custom and tradition at the heart of English jurisprudence, and created an unusually strong pre-sumption in *favor* of long-standing continuity. The tension that existed else-where between Roman law and local customary law was therefore mostly absent. Poland was an elective monarchy, the Empire was not a state at all, the Netherlands and Switzerland had no king, and so on—every place where ancient constitutionalist arguments were made was different, and local polit-ical arguments had to be made in local terms.

More generally, ancient constitutionalists' claims were often exaggerated at best.[15] Institutions and rules were projected back into a past in which they could not have made sense. *De facto* balances of power were reinterpreted as formal legal settlements. Long-term historical processes—say, the evolution

---

[14] Alexis de Tocqueville, *The Old Regime and the Revolution*, Volume 1. François Furet and Françoise Mélonio, eds, Alan S. Kahan, trans. (Chicago: University of Chicago, 1998[1856]), henceforth *ORR*, pp. 102–3.

[15] Indeed, modern scholars may have emphasized the problems with ancient constitutionalist historiography to a degree that has obscured the school's importance and contributions. I am thinking here especially of Pocock's influential *The Ancient Constitution and the Feudal Law*. Pocock returns to the theme of the ancient constitutionalists as bad historians when he celebrates Hume's arguments to that effect in *Barbarism and Religion* (Cambridge: Cambridge University Press, 1999). Pocock has long been centrally interested in the history of histories; it is also an important theme in *The Machiavellian Moment*.

of the English Parliament—were denied so that the desired arrangements could be said to have existed as long as the monarchies themselves. Royalist history was little better; both sides were necessarily guilty of anachronism in describing stable constitutional settlements for consolidated states into the medieval past.

The most problematic features of ancient constitutionalist history are probably the too-early start dates for Parliaments and Estates as assemblies (especially for the Commons or Third Estate), and the too-consensual account of their balance of power with kings. Fortunately these are not the most important aspects of the theory for our study of intermediate groups.

Ancient constitutionalism offered a language in which to talk about politics, a shifting and overlapping set of arguments and ideas. It was in the first instance a language for political debate, not for political philosophy. Unsurprisingly, disagreements among those I am calling ancient constitutionalists were very real. The various medieval institutions and legacies being appealed to had always been in conflict with each other to varying degrees. The cities were refuges from the feudal nobility; craft guilds sought to control and limit markets that mercantile cities sought to open; disputes between universities and the Church about doctrine and the content of university teaching were common, as were town-gown jurisdictional arguments between universities and cities. Shared distrust of the emerging absolutist state did not eliminate the differences among burghers and nobles, priests and professors, guild members and monks. Those sympathetic toward the claims of central parliaments were not always sympathetic toward those of provinces or cities. Within parliaments or Estates there could certainly be bitter rivalry between the Commons or Third Estate on one hand, and the nobility and the higher clergy on the other. Indeed, ancient constitutionalist arguments were often deployed by one group precisely when it seemed that another was being favored by the central state. And so, for example, ancient constitutionalist arguments offered by Anglicans and by Gallican Catholics often "proved" that the church had traditionally been subject to the king or the civil law in the particular kingdom. The anti-Romanism of the school, the preference for Gothic Germanic roots, was easily marshaled to undermine the claims for autonomy of the church that owed its primacy and prestige to Rome.

Similarly, over the course of the French Wars of Religion, the monarchical court and its so-called *politiques* advisors and intellectuals sought to preserve royal freedom to maneuver against both Protestant and Catholic nobles and non-state groups asserting ancient-constitutional limits. It is worth noting that the persecutionist Catholic League, associated with the Jesuits and the aristocratic House of Guise, demanded the restoration of "rights, pre-eminences, franchises, and ancient liberties such as they were in the time of Clovis, the first Christian king."[16] I am emphasizing the ancient constitutionalist tradition of resisting royal absolutism, but similar language was available and used across the political spectrum to those resisting change.

Royal coronation oaths were a frequent resource for ancient constitutionalist arguments. In the Middle Ages these had, at a minimum, routinely included a commitment to respect the rights of the Church. Language about the customs, privileges, and liberties of the kingdom as a whole were common. In France, new kings were received into cities or provinces in a formal ceremony of *entrée* in which they pledged to respect urban or provincial rights. In Poland's elective monarchy, new kings were required to sign a pact with the parliament to maintain the traditional laws, including the "ancient liberties of the palatinates [provinces]" as well as the "privileges of the university of Cracow and other cities, as well ecclesiastic as secular."[17] The formula by which Kings of Aragon and Catalonia, and afterwards Kings of Spain, were acknowledged by the *cortes* were a favorite example, widely cited in early modernity because it conditioned allegiance on respect for ancient rights: "We, who are as good as you, swear to you, who are no better than us, to accept you as our king and sovereign, provided you observe all our liberties and laws, but if not, not."[18]

Corporatism and Parliaments

The emphasis I offer here on intermediate groups as a feature of ancient constitutionalism is somewhat unusual; the two most-discussed features of ancient constitutionalism in the English-language literature are the rights of the Estates or Parliament to governing authority at the center, and the subjection in principle of royal acts to the rule of law.[19] I have already suggested, in the discussion of the *parlements*, that rule of law concerns were entangled

---

[16] J. H. M. Salmon, "Catholic Resistance Theory," in J.H. Burns, ed., *The Cambridge History of Political Thought, 1450–1700* (Cambridge: Cambridge University Press, 1991), p. 221.

[17] Luther Calvin Saxton, *The Fall of Poland* (New York: Charles Scribner, 1851), p. 607. This wording is from Augustus II's *Pacta Conventa*, signed in 1697. Also see Jean-Baptiste Desroches de Parthenay, *The history of Poland under Augustus II Which contains the great dispute between that prince and the princes of Conti and Sobieski for the Crown: with the other important transactions of his life,* John Stacie, trans. (London: W. Lewis and F. Cogan, 1734).

[18] All three of the monarchomach works discussed here cited the oath. Voltaire did likewise in *Essai Sur Les Mœurs et L'Esprit Des Nations,* Tome 2, Rene Pomeau, ed. (Paris: Garnier Frères, 1963 [1756]), p. 645. The prerevolutionary *cahiers* of grievances against Louis XVI did so repeatedly. See also Burlamaqui, *The Principles of Natural and Politic Law,* Petter Korkman, ed., Thomas Nugent, trans. (Indianapolis: Liberty Fund, 2006[1747]), Volume 2: "The Principles of Political Law," part I, ch. 7, section 4 "of fundamental laws," pp. 55–61.

[19] See Scott Gordon, *Controlling the State: constitutionalism from ancient Athens to today* (Cambridge, Mass.: Harvard University Press, 1999) for the first; and C. H. McIlwain, *Constitutionalism Ancient and Modern* (Ithaca: Cornell University Press, 1947) for the second.

with the defense of the *corps intermédiaires*; we will return to that in the next chapter's treatment of Montesquieu. The same is generally true for the authority of the Estates. The sharp distinction between the rights of the *corps* (including cities and provinces) severally and the rights of the Estates collectively at the center was slow to emerge. Ancient constitutionalist theories not only commonly defended them both, but treated them as tightly linked.

Over the course of the seventeenth century, monarchs across Europe found themselves powerful enough to rule without the participation of the Estates in their various forms, or at least (in the English case) imagined themselves to be that powerful. The French Estates-General were dormant for 175 years after 1614; Charles I of England attempted to rule without Parliament 1629–40, and his son Charles II did so 1681–5; in 1653 the estates of Brandenburg (later Brandenburg-Prussia) met for the last time, surrendering their role in authorizing taxation. In 1665 the Danish estates ceded their power to the monarchy and freed him of his coronation oath, declaring, in an especially ringing statement of absolutist principle, that the "absolute and hereditary king" "shall hereafter be, and by all subjects be held and honored as, the greatest and highest head on earth, *above all human laws and knowing no other head or judge above him, either in spiritual or secular matters, except God alone.*"[20] This diminution in estates and parliaments was a frequent occasion for ancient-constitutionalist objections; it is worth emphasizing the pluralist and corporatist character of these ideas.

Ancient-constitutionalist arguments about intermediate bodies combined three thoughts: that the *corps* should retain the right or privilege of governing themselves, according to traditional laws; that the *corps* should have a say in the government, so as to be able to protect their liberties; and that the *corps* were natural friends of legality and liberty, because their protection of their own rights was so tied up with the refusal of absolutist pretensions.

When we think about the development of parliamentary institutions, we can see that these ideas were not neatly distinguishable. The requirement that the commons or the Third Estate consent to taxation, a rule that we see in various forms across late medieval and early modern Western Europe, derives in part from the corporate right of the self-governing cities not to be taxed without their consent. We have come to think of the commons or the Third Estate as referring to the vast majority of the populace: all non-nobles and non-clergy, whether urban or rural. But reflection on which non-nobles and non-clergy held *taxable wealth* or engaged in easily taxable trade changes the picture. The coercive extractive capacity of the medieval monarchy was sharply limited, and financial assets were in any case narrowly concentrated.

---

[20] Ernst Ekman, "The Danish Royal Law of 1665," 29(2) *The Journal of Modern History* 102–7, Jun. 1957, p. 106, emphasis added.

In short, the central state could not have effectively levied a general tax on the peasant and tenant classes given state capacity at the time, and those classes could not have paid any meaningful taxes in specie or other money. Taxing the commons meant taxing the cities (and note that the French term for the self-governing cities in this era was *commune*). Cities were both an organizational form partly designed around resisting external extraction and, often, legally entitled to refuse to be taxed. Taxing the commons thus depended in a very real sense on obtaining the consent of the representatives of the cities— the *burghers* of the *burgs*.

In England, the self-governing towns were the similarly named *boroughs*, and they were corporately entitled to send representatives to the House of Commons, a fact mainly now remembered from the institution's degenerate era. Eventually, industrial cities grew up outside the traditional borough system, and some of the inherited boroughs depopulated—became "rotten boroughs." And this happened in an era when extractive capacity and taxable wealth had spread much more widely. So by the end of the eighteenth century, a skewed and unrepresentative group of boroughs sent representatives to a Parliament that could, and did, tax the entire country.

But the medieval origins were quite different: the boroughs' consent was needed for taxation precisely because it was the boroughs that were to be taxed, and because they severally had at least some degree of corporate freedom (*de jure* or *de facto* or both) to refuse to supply the king with funds. In the late Middle Ages "burgess" variously meant citizens of boroughs, those elected to govern them, and those elected to represent them in Parliament. Until the reforms of the nineteenth century, counties sent two "knights of the shire" each to the Commons; cities, towns, and universities sent burgesses to represent them corporately. The style of address to the House of Commons as a whole was "To the knights, citizens, and burgesses, of the honourable House of Commons now assembled in Parliament," where "citizens" was the equivalent of "burgesses" for the special case of the City of London. The colonial Virginia equivalent of the House of Commons was the House of Burgesses.

There is continuity between the role of the English House of Commons in consenting to taxation and later democratic theories; Locke linked representative consent and taxation as a fundamental principle of justice almost a century before the American Revolutionaries did. This might thus seem like the cunning of history, the natural unfolding of a fundamental moral truth: the burgesses were placeholders for the eventual idea of universal democratic representation. We should resist the temptation to such hindsight. In order to remind ourselves that the burgesses' presence in Parliament derived from the corporate liberties of the boroughs, consider the same dynamic in the French Second Estate. The French nobility was likewise exempt from taxation without its own consent. As with the boroughs, this right had roots in norms and power alike; the medieval king as the head of a feudal order could not unilaterally change the terms of his vassals' *feodus*, and had no power at all to tax the great lords who were not his vassals. The privilege attached to nobles as individuals, but the mechanism of consent was necessarily corporate. Consent was expressed through the Estates, and when the Estates went into abeyance, it was withheld by the *parlements*. Here, too, the need for the corporate group to consent to the taxation of its members merged into a governmental, legislative role. While we will see some ambivalence expressed by post-Revolutionary liberal thinkers as to how to judge the *parlements'* defense of the nobles' privileges regarding taxation, it is not (to say the least) generally taken as a moment in the unfolding of the logic of liberal democracy.

Focusing on these ideas at their origins and not during the eighteenth century, the important point is that ancient-constitutionalism, in the sense of preserving the corporate liberties and self-government of intermediate bodies, and ancient constitutionalism, in the sense of supporting parliaments/Estates/*cortes*, are entwined and related causes. Despite the temptation of hindsight bias, one should avoid thinking that the Commons or the Third Estate are naturally aligned with nationalist and rationalist democracy— projecting the Parliamentary supremacy of Blackstone or Dicey back into the Parliamentary cause of the 1600s, or the views of the Abbé Sièyes' *What Is the Third Estate?* into older debates about the Estates-General. Ancient-constitutionalist thought defended both the liberties of the *corps* and the authority of the Estates. The critiques of centralization and of absolutism were so closely related as to be often indistinguishable. The earliest date at which we can see them clearly come apart may be the English Commonwealth, when the Commons abolished the Lords and claimed legislative omnicompetence over the other provinces in the composite monarchy (Ireland in particular); and that disjunction was temporary. In France, the two begin to be disentangled in the thought of the *philosophes* from, say, the 1750s onward. They're not firmly and finally distinguished until Sieyès' time, in the debate about whether the Third Estate is one ancient-constitutional body among others or is instead the body politic as such. In the 1680s, say, there was no real conflict between arguing that James II's dismissal of Parliament was an attack on the ancient constitution, and saying the same of his suborning the autonomy of boroughs, universities, and the Anglican Church.[21] Absolutism threatened the ancient constitution in both senses: the corporate autonomy of the self-governing bodies, and corporate representation in Parliaments or Estates.

---

[21] See Pincus, *1688: The First Modern Revolution* (New Haven: Yale University Press, 2009).

The Theorists of the Ancient Constitution

Ancient constitutionalism was a language of political debate first and foremost, and in England a language of jurisprudence, not a style of scholarly analysis. There were nonetheless a number of important ancient-constitutionalist theoretical treatises. The most enduring of these from before 1700 are all Calvinist in origin: Althusius' *Politica*, and the writings of the French theorists of resistance known as the monarchomachs. These offered especially memorable contributions. The monarchomachs were especially influential in their own and succeeding generations. Althusius was not, being generally forgotten until the late nineteenth century, but his *Politica* has since come to be recognized as one of the most theoretically interesting works from this tradition. I will close this section with a look at Robert Molesworth, an English Whig and ancient constitutional theorist of the late seventeenth and early eighteenth century.

The Protestant Reformation in the first instance weakened intermediacy and accelerated the consolidation of state power.[22] This is most obvious in England, where the Henrician Reformation expressly made the king the head of the church, made church and state nearly coterminous, and dissolved and looted the monastic orders. Protestant churches on the continent did not recreate the system of canon law or the vigorously autonomous institutions of Catholicism. Luther and later Calvin insisted on the supremacy of civil governments, a fact which was not unrelated to the eagerness with which many German princes received Luther's views. The turn to absolutism in Denmark included an emphasis on royal supremacy over the Lutheran church. In parts of Catholic Europe, too, the outbreak of religious dissension provided an opportunity for monarchical power. With Iberia now largely free of Jews and Muslims, the Spanish crown seized on Protestants as a useful new target for its Inquisition. The 1555 Peace of Augsburg adopted the principle *"cuius regio, euius religio"* ["Whose realm, his religion"], settling the first round of the wars of religion in the Empire by allowing each local lord to define the locally established religion. Religious boundaries were aligned with sub-Imperial political jurisdictions, strengthening local rulers and providing a critical step in the long process of Imperial disintegration and domestic state consolidation.

Counter-tendencies developed quickly. England and France were more centralized than the Empire, and in neither was *cuius regio, euius religio* an immediately available solution to religious conflict. In both, religious fragmentation gave rise to calls for resistance to civil power; it endured long enough to

---

[22] See generally Harold Berman's treatment in *Law and Revolution, volume II*.

energize and justify social organization outside and against the state, as well as theoretical justifications of such organization. In France the long, intrastate wars of religion provided the occasion for an especially important ancient constitutionalism, one that infused the critique of absolutist centralization with the fervor of religious conviction: the school of the Calvinist theorists who became known as the monarchomachs.

French policy toward Protestants changed course several times over the sixteenth century, with cycles of toleration and persecution driven by court politics, shifting perceptions of the Protestants' usefulness in undermining the Empire, and factional pressure. The Huguenots were regionally concentrated in the south and west of the kingdom, at times controlling scores of cities and towns and counting a substantial share of the nobility among their ranks; the royal concessions that punctuated the rounds of warfare specified rights of the Protestant aristocrats as well as of Protestant towns. These moments of peace were vulnerable to disruption by Catholics outside the court: Jesuits declaring toleration anathema, *parlements* enforcing orthodoxy, ambitious orthodox Catholic nobles engaging in unsanctioned or only partly sanctioned anti-Protestant violence, and Catholic mobs acting on their own or with the encouragement of any of these.

In the wake of the St. Bartholomew's Day massacres (1572), a particularly bloody and sudden such disruption, a few Huguenot intellectuals came to the view that the crown's assurances were worthless and that the monarchy's power was a source of persecution, not a protection against it. The most important works to emerge from this strand of thought during the decades between St. Bartholomew and the new regime of tolerance announced in the Edict of Nantes (1598) were Francois Hotman's *Francogallia* (1573), Theodore de Beza's *On the Rights of Magistrates* (1574), and the *Vindiciae Contra Tyrannos* (1579), written under the pseudonym of Junius Brutus.[23]

Hotman, an eminent legal scholar in France and Switzerland and a leading contributor to Protestant–Catholic theological dialogue, was a key contributor to the school of thought that Donald Kelley has identified as legal humanism.[24] Like other Renaissance humanists, they sought a direct intellectual connection with the classical world, unmediated by medieval accretions. Their scholarship on the Roman law sought to recover a legal history of Rome as it had actually been, cleaning away the rearrangements and Talmudic commentaries of the preceding centuries; they aimed to better understand

---

[23] It is now generally but not universally thought to have been written by Philippe de Mornay; since the author's identity does not matter to this discussion, I will simply use the pseudonym.

[24] Donald Kelley, *The Human Measure: Social Thought in the Western Legal Tradition* (Cambridge, Mass.: Harvard University Press, 1990).

both the ancient texts and their connection to ancient society. This emphasis on a purified Roman law as an object of scholarship did not, however, mean advocacy of a restoration of it as law. On the contrary, they stressed the particularity of Roman law to its time and place. In his treatise *Anti-Tribonian* [1567], Hotman had criticized the compilation of Justinian's Code itself as distorting the law of Rome; and he had argued forcefully for the irrelevance of the *corpus* to French law, which should be fitted to French life.

Similarly in *Francogallia*, Hotman insisted that the law of France was fundamentally Frankish, and incompatible with Roman influences.[25] The Gauls had been a conquered people, never truly becoming Roman, and after the collapse of the Western Empire France became a Frankish kingdom, ruled by Germanic custom. The Frankish king was an elective chief, chosen and guided by councils, and able to be deposed by popular consent. Their duty to consult with and govern by consent of the nobles and the people of the provinces was as old as the kingdom itself.

Canon law and papal authority were of course ruled out. Hotman explicitly claimed that the Carolingian line was ordained by local council, not by papal grace. He appealed to the precedent of Philip's contest with Boniface to show that France had never accepted Vatican authority; and his discussions of the Estates simply ignored the status of the Catholic clergy, referring only to the aristocracy and to the commoners of the provinces.

But absolute monarchy was ruled out as well, just another Romanist invasion of the traditional order. The centerpiece of the French constitution as Hotman understood it was the Estates-General, the descendant of the Frankish council. This had been clear, he claimed, less than a century before. Only at about the turn of the sixteenth century had the Estates gone into abeyance and kings begun to act without constraint, although some earlier kings had sought excessive power. Before that, even when kings had overreached—as did Louis XI—they had been checked by the *parlements*, university jurists, and ultimately the Estates. Tellingly, he identified both the Empire and England as keeping up the ways of the old constitutional order.

As Harold Laski put it, *Francogallia* manages

> to buttress every dogma of the Huguenot creed by proving its origin in the facts of French history. Bad Kings may be deposed; the nobility has a special place in the political structure; [...] local autonomy is the root of political freedom—especially, as in the instance detailed by Hotman, in Languedoc, where Calvinism was especially strong; such provincial freedoms are safeguarded by fundamental law. The whole apparatus of the edifice represented a formidable weapon in the

---

[25] François Hotman, "Francogallia" (1573), in *An Account of Denmark*.

hands of Hotman's party. It made their opponents seem the innovators, while they themselves appeared as the defenders of historic constitutionalism.[26]

Francogallia's constitutional history stood as a clear denial of the legitimacy of royal absolutism, but it contained little explicit normative advice about what was to be done to resist it. That gap was filled by the other two major monarchomach works.

Beza's *On the Rights of Magistrates* proceeded along two argumentative tracks. First, it argued against absolute authority, insisting that rulers must be understood as magistrates holding a limited office for public benefit, constrained by law and by the law-articulating Estates. While Beza is friendlier to Roman precedent than is Hotman, he reiterates Hotman's account of the elective Frankish monarchy that sits at the base of the French state, and is even more forceful in drawing parallels with the Empire, England (the "most blessed" kingdom), Poland, and the rest of Europe.

Furthermore, it developed an elaborate theory of the office of "subordinate magistrates," "intermediate" between the crown and the people. In this category he includes not only the leaders of cities but also the aristocratic lords; dukes, counts, and barons are "magistrates" with duties of office as much as elected town mayors or aldermen are. And these duties of office, these responsibilities to kingdom rather than to king, include the protection of those over whom they have power. In the event that a king behaves tyrannically, the intermediate magistrates have the primary task of resistance. If they can, they should resist through regular means, in the Estates. But if they cannot—if, like the Huguenot nobles and town leaders, they face violent threats to the well-being of those for whom they are responsible, whether from the supreme magistrate or from elsewhere—then they may, indeed must, resist with the force at their disposal. They certainly must not follow tyrannical orders from above and themselves become the instruments of injustice.

Brutus likewise located the authority to resist in the intermediate magistrates severally, as well as jointly in the Estates. The Estates bring together the towns, provinces, nobles, and church (unlike *Francogallia*, the *Vindicae* acknowledges the First Estate) and together represent the whole body of the kingdom, and are therefore superior even to kings. The various officials of the towns, provinces, and church, and the nobles severally, are not individually superior to the king; but their individual allegiance is to that united whole, not to the king personally. And so they may and must act in defense of the inherited law and in opposition to acts of tyranny.

[26] Philippe de Mornay, *A Defence of Liberty Against Tyrants: A Translation of the Vindiciae Contra Tyrannos*, Hubert Languet, trans., Harold Joseph Laski, ed. (London: G. Bell, 1924), p. 36. Laski was part of the British Pluralist school, to which we will return in Chapter 9; his interest in the monarchomachs is of a piece with the Pluralists' normative and historical concerns.

Beza and Brutus both deny that private persons have the same right to resist. Centuries later this might strike us as odd, even backward. In the modern bureaucratic state, the official's duty is normally to carry out policy set from above; while theorists of resistance from Locke to Thoreau have emphasized the right of the private person to refuse or revolt. But to the sixteenth-century ancient constitutionalists, the intermediate magistrates were emphatically not bureaucrats in our sense. They have their several and various sources of legitimacy in the cities and provinces they govern, or the church they serve, or their own inherited status. They do *not* derive their legitimacy from the king, and so there is no contradiction in using their offices to oppose the king. Beza sharply distinguishes magistrates from courtiers and the king's personal appointees—the latter serve the king rather than the kingdom. And Brutus heaps disdain on those nobles who have forgotten their independent roles and become servile to the crown.

This attention to intermediate magistrates marked an important addition to, or difference from, Hotman. On the constitutional vision of *Francogallia*, when the Estates were not summoned, the king was acting in violation of customary law; but it was not clear what could be done about that. Beza and Brutus supplied an answer to that question; the inferior magistrates held office constantly, regardless of whether the Estates were called or not. They thus valued the *parlements* in particular in a way that Hotman did not. He saw the *parlements* as a kind of royal and lawyerly usurpation of the Estates' ancient constitutional role. Whether because they often sided with Catholic persecution or because of his own objections to how law was practiced, Hotman saw the *parlements* as a problem, not a solution. Beza, however, included the courts within his category of inferior magistracy charged with defending against tyranny; and Brutus endorsed the right of remonstrance as a protection of the law against royal excess. When France was well governed, only the Estates could make new law, as was true in England and elsewhere; but in the Estates' absence, the *parlements* could prevent the king from usurping the power to make law himself. In these ways, as Skinner has shown, Beza and Brutus were able to align with a broader constitutionalist tradition that might appeal to non-Calvinists, albeit with a clear view that the tyranny to be resisted included religious persecution.[27] They offered an ancient constitution whose many parts—urban and provincial, noble and common, and even Catholic and Protestant—might all recognize the threat of absolutism and use their institutional resources to resist it.

The Huguenot works inspired an important critic in the leading *politique* theorist Jean Bodin, whose doctrine of the unity and finality of sovereignty

---

[27] Quentin Skinner, *The Foundations of Modern Political Thought*, vol. 2 (Cambridge: Cambridge University Press, 1978).

ruled out not only the organized resistance the monarchomachs had sought to justify, but also the claims of persecutionist Catholics that the king *must* stamp out heresy or else lose legitimacy. Bodin was not *opposed* to "corporate associations, guilds, estates, and communities"; indeed, he insisted that it was foolish to seek to abolish them, that they provided a secure foundation for non-tyrannical monarchies as well as for popular states.[28]

> A guild can be confined to a single craft or profession, or type of merchandise or kind of jurisdiction. Or many guilds can form a single corporate association, such as a guild for all crafts, merchants dealing in all sorts of commodities, all branches of learning, or all the magistrates. Or many guilds can become a general community or university. And not only guilds and communities, but all the inhabitants of a village, a district or a province have the right of association, and can, together with the guilds and communities, assemble as Estates. Each of these can have its particular regulations, statutes, and privileges.[29]

The *collegia* organized and maintained fellow-feeling among subjects. The estates of the towns and provinces as well as the Estates-General provided a way to rapidly mobilize resources and soldiers in support of the king. Bodin adhered to the traditional rule linking representation with taxation, in part it seems for the functional reason described earlier: consent made taxation *feasible*. Similarly, he endorsed the *parlements'* right of remonstrance. The collegial associations of lawyers and magistrates he held up as the most influential and first in rank among the guilds; their members could do no less than to seek to uphold the laws.

But, Bodin continued, the guilds, monasteries, cities, and so on all derived their authority from sovereign permission and authorization, and were entirely bounded by the sovereign's rules. "We can therefore say that a corporate association or a guild is a legal right of communal organization, subject to sovereign power. The word 'legal' implies that it is authorized by the sovereign, for without his permission no guild can be instituted."[30] Although Bodin treated the *corpus'* jurisprudence about the rights of the *collegia* as a default, the sovereign had the final say on the internal rules under which they operated. They did *not* have ancient, independent, or self-generated legitimacy; they were purely concessionary on the part of the sovereign power. Likewise, if remonstrating with the king about a proposed law proved ineffective, the *parlement* corporately had no choice but to register it.

In short, Bodin recognized the reality of the institutions drawn on by ancient constitutionalists, but sought to redefine them as emanations from,

---

[28] Jean Bodin, *Six Books of the Commonwealth*, M. J. Tooley, trans. (Oxford: Basil Blackwell, 1955 [1576]); the quotation is the title of Book III ch. 7, p. 96.
[29] Bodin, *Six Books of the Commonwealth*, p. 99.
[30] Bodin, *Six Books of the Commonwealth*, p. 99.

not sources of resistance to, the sovereign. Sovereignty was offered as an alternative and a challenge to the theories of fragmented and pluralistic legal legitimacy and political authority associated with the ancient constitution in general and the monarchomachs in particular.

Bodin in turn was directly challenged on these points by the Calvinist theorist Johannes Althusius. At the time that he wrote *Politica* (1603), Althusius was an official of the self-governing city of Emden within the Empire, on the border with a confederal Dutch republic still fighting for its independence against Spain. The book was dedicated to the leaders of the States-Provincial of Friesland, with accompanying praise for the Dutch willingness to fight for the "recovery" of rights. The United Provinces had provided refuge to many Huguenots fleeing French persecution in the preceding decades, and not coincidentally, Huguenot writings were widely available. *Politica* cites Hotman, Beza, and the *Vindicae* approvingly.

Politica holds that a commonwealth is created when "many cities and provinces obligate themselves to hold, organize, use, and defend, through their common energies and expenditures, the right of the realm." It is a "mixed society, constituted partly from private, natural, necessary, and voluntary societies [families, guilds, and *collegia*], partly from public societies [cities and provinces]." The state does not create those bodies; rather, "families, cities, and provinces existed by nature prior to realms, and gave birth to them."[31] This was true in the Dutch case; the provinces had political existence prior to their decision to unite, abjure the Spanish monarchy, and create a new state. While they created a new state by promise, they remained corporately organized as provinces when they did so, and appealed to ancient provincial liberties as justification. But it is true "by nature," not just contingently in the Dutch case; private associations are prior to cities and provinces, which are prior to commonwealths. Althusius uses contractual language—but the contract is not one entered into by individuals in a prior state of nature. Indeed Althusius denies that individuals as such are members of the commonwealth at all. They are *parts* of it in the same way that boards and nails are part of a house; but "cities, urban, communities, and provinces are *members* of a realm, just as . . . roof, walls, and floor are essential parts of a house."[32]

Politica is cast at a high level of abstraction; unlike *Francogallia*, it is not the tale of some particular society's constitution. But examples are used so freely as to leave no doubt about the kind of society envisioned, and the side of contemporary disputes the book endorses. A Dutch confederation built of provinces, an Empire built of principalities and cities: these represent

---

[31] Johannes Althusius, *Politica*, Frederick S. Carney, ed. (Indianapolis: Liberty Fund, 1995[1603]), p. 66.

[32] Johannes Althusius, *Politica*, p. 67.

well-organized political societies. Absolute monarchy is intrinsically tyran-nical and unlawful, and kings everywhere are to be subject to the estates, diet, or parliament. Kings everywhere are rightfully bound by law: the Emperor may be judged by electors, as may the French king by the *parlement* of Paris.

Althusius vests primary responsibility for resistance to tyranny in the magis-trates of the realm as a whole—the Imperial Diet, the Estates—which have the duty to try to remove the tyrant from power. The magistrates who govern a city or a province may not unilaterally seek to overthrow a king, if the magistrates of the realm have not declared him a tyrant. They may, however, act defensively in order to protect their own people from tyranny, and they may withdraw their city or province as best they can from the jurisdiction of the tyrant, even to the point of secession.

> One of the estates, or one part of the realm, can abandon the remaining body to which it belonged and choose for itself a separate ruler or a new form of common-wealth when the public and manifest welfare of this entire part altogether requires it, or when fundamental laws of the country are not observed by the magistrate but are obstinately and outrageously violated...And then this part of the realm can defend by force and arms its new form and status against the other parts of the realm from which it withdrew.[33]

Althusius draws the obvious connection to the decision of the Dutch prov-inces to withdraw from Spanish rule without trying to overthrow the Spanish king. Dutch magistrates recognized the duty "not only to judge whether the supreme magistrate has performed his responsibility or not, but also to resist and impede the tyranny of a supreme magistrate who abuses the rights of sovereignty, and violates or wishes to take away the authority (*ius*) of the body of the commonwealth."[34]

Unlike Althusius and the monarchomachs, the Anglo-Irish Whig theorist Robert Molesworth is little known among theorists today. A slightly younger associate of John Locke—who thought him "ingenious and extraordinary"—and like Locke closely attached to the Shaftesbury family (the third Earl, grandson of Locke's patron and himself tutored by Locke, became in adult-hood "'Molesworth's disciple' in intellectual and political matters"[35]), Moles-worth was an important figure in post-Glorious Revolution Whig circles.[36] He influenced Frances Hutcheson and acted as a founding intellectual of the

---

[33] Johannes Althusius, *Politica*, p. 197.   [34] Johannes Althusius, *Politica*, p. 106.

[35] Michael B. Gill, *The British Moralists on Human Nature and the Birth of Secular Ethics* (New York: Cambridge University Press, 2006), p. 139.

[36] On Molesworth generally, see Steven Pincus, *1688*, especially pp. 354–63; Caroline Robbins, *The Eighteenth-Century Commonwealthman: studies in the transmission, development, and circumstance of English liberal thought from the restoration of Charles II until the war with the thirteen colonies* (Indianapolis: Liberty Fund Press, 2004), especially pp. 84–110, 151–60.

Country Whig opposition. In the years immediately following the Revolution he was sent to Denmark as Britain's ambassador. Shortly after his return he published a blistering attack on that country's descent into absolutism, *An Account of Denmark As It Was In The Year 1692*, a best-seller that was quickly translated into several other languages and which prompted sharp diplomatic complaints from Denmark to Britain.

Politically, Molesworth aimed to build interest in Britain for William's grand alliance against Louis XIV. British Tories had little appetite for entangling Britain in its new king's long-term wars, or for funding them. With the overthrow of Louis' cousin and protégé James II, they thought Britain more or less free from French threat. Like many of William's Whig supporters, Molesworth saw the struggle between William and Louis quite differently, in what we would now think of as ideological terms: the struggle over whether Europe would be ruled by the Sun King's absolutism, or by constitutional government of the sort maintained in the Netherlands and newly restored in Britain. The Revolution had been a crucial step (Molesworth had personally taken up arms against James' forces in Ireland) but, Molesworth hoped to show, French absolutism was still a menace. He openly asserts that it is Louis XIV who has pioneered absolutism in Europe, pointing especially to his destruction of the autonomy of French towns, now forced to pay for the very military presence that keeps them subdued; the "King of Denmark has been but too apt a Pupil to such a Master."[37] Denmark "has often had the misfortune to be govern'd by French Counsels."[38]

Against common British and Whig prejudice, Molesworth emphasizes that it is not Catholicism as such that makes for absolutism. Indeed, it is possible that Lutheran countries such as Denmark are even more vulnerable to it, since the church there lacks the independence from the state that might make it resist royal power. The Danish "unity of religion" deprives it of a valuable political resource for struggle against despotism, and its ecclesiastical structures are built for subservience to established authority. The comparison to Anglicanism is not lost on him. Had James II succeeded in his absolutist ambitions *without* converting the realm to Catholicism, Britain would have been reduced to a slavery all the more absolute, lacking the "clash of interests" between church and state characteristic of countries where the Catholic clergy and monasteries still fight to preserve their own autonomy. And indeed, Denmark has been reduced to a more complete absolutism than France, where not even the Sun King has been able to do away with at least the appearance of clerical freedom, provincial rights, and the authority of the *parlements*, even though in effect they now "meet for no other end, than to

[37] Molesworth, *An Account of Denmark*, p. 90.
[38] Molesworth, *An Account of Denmark*, p. 24.

verifie the King's Edicts."[39] The implication is clear: chasing the Popish James away is not sufficient to protect British freedom. The struggle of constitutional government against "French tyranny" continues, and it is properly the struggle of all of Europe.

In 1711, with British politics turning from an oligarchic Whig Junto he distrusted to a new Tory majority he feared, Molesworth translated and published the *Francogallia* under the telling title *Franco-Gallia, or, an account of the ancient free state of France, and most other parts of Europe, before the loss of their liberties*. In 1721 he published a new edition with a lengthy preface which went on to have an independent life as a pamphlet enunciating the principles of "True" (Country) Whiggism, explicitly linking Whiggism with the "Gothick" constitutionalism defended by Hotman.[40] The True Whig sought to protect "our just Rights and Liberties, together with the solid Foundations of our Constitution: Which, in truth, is not ours only, but that of almost all *Europe* besides."[41]

The True Whig must support provincial liberties; "no Man can be a sincere Lover of Liberty, that is not for increasing and communicating that Blessing to all People," including "giving or restoring it [...] to our Brethren of Scotland and Ireland" and "uniting our own Three Kingdoms upon equal Terms." This was directly linked to the cause of such protections elsewhere; Molesworth praises Queen Anne for "asserting the Liberties and Privileges of the Free Cities in Germany, an Action which will shine in History."[42]

The full platform of the British "True Whig" also includes the suppression of the monopolistic chartered trading companies; liberty of the press; a preference for a militia over a standing army, as guaranteed by the "ancient constitution"; continued war with France; and, especially, a more perfect religious liberty than that found in the Act of Toleration, one that refrains from penalizing religious liberty or conscience even of Jews or Muslims, and that can accommodate Catholic doctrine (though not political obedience to the Pope or to the Stuarts). But all of this, Molesworth maintained, was of a piece with the monarchomach theory articulated in another country almost a century and a half before. The protection of freedom necessitated the protection of the ancient constitution, at home and abroad.

---

[39] Molesworth, *An Account of Denmark*, p. 157.
[40] Molesworth writes that the preface was meant for inclusion in the first edition, but the publisher declined to do so; this seems to be true on the basis of events referred to, and not referred to, in it. Molesworth grudgingly accepts the Triennial Act of 1694, until such time as annual elections can be obtained. By 1721 it had been superseded by the—far worse from his perspective—Septennial Act, which goes unmentioned.
[41] Molesworth, *An Account of Denmark*, p. 171.
[42] Molesworth, *An Account of Denmark*, pp. 181–2.

Ancient Constitutionalism and its Neighbors

Ancient constitutionalism was a wide family of ideas, much like the two early modern families of ideas that receive far more scholarly attention: social contract theory and humanistic neo-Roman republicanism. Like them, ancient constitutionalism was neither a party nor a politically or philosophically unified doctrine. All were styles of argument, and it should not surprise us to sometimes find the same style of argument used on different sides of the same dispute. Moreover, each denotes just some of the ideas, words, and concepts a particular author might use; they were languages to draw on, not doctrines to which thinkers made monogamous commitments. Commonly, those involved in a controversy used ancient constitutionalist arguments alongside others, just as Biblical, philosophical, and legal citations sit side-by-side in many of political theory.

Still, as with social contract theory and republicanism, there are tendencies that we can identify clearly enough to make the category of ancient constitutionalism a useful one.

One of those tendencies is, in direct contrast to republicanism, anti-Romanism or at least non-Romanism about politics, and often about law and religion as well. The Renaissance was self-consciously anti-medieval and anti-Gothic, reaching around the barbarism of the preceding centuries back to Rome, whether republican or imperial. The characteristically Renaissance political theories—humanist republicanism on one hand, reason-of-state royalism on the other—both rejected feudalism, intermediacy, and the medieval jurisdictional patchwork. Ancient constitutionalists in turn reached around the Renaissance to the Gothic Middle Ages, and generally avoided reliance on Roman precedents, examples, and political categories; some even avoided relying on the *corpus*.

Republicanism of course placed great value on the life of freedom within cities, providing an area of overlap. But the paradigmatic city for humanists and republicans was a sovereign city-state, maybe sitting at the head of its own empire as Rome did but certainly not subordinate to any other jurisdiction. The *vivere civile e libero* celebrated by Machiavelli and his followers was one in which the independence of the city was a prerequisite to the freedom of its citizens. The Germanic tradition that *Stadtluft macht frei* rested on no such assumption. The city was in part a space of freedom from external overlords, and the freedom of the burghers depended on the city's ability to protect them; but that did *not* require that the cities stand jurisdictionally apart. The ancient constitution included free cities *within* the jurisdictional complexity of a province, a kingdom, the Empire, or some other polity.

One area of overlap between republican and ancient constitutional ideas drew on the tradition of the *mixed* constitution. Ancient constitutionalists

133

defended the right of Estates and Parliament to take part in governance, thereby supporting government that incorporated popular, aristocratic, and monarchical elements. But the intellectual traditions are generally distinct. Ancient constitutionalists rarely defended the Third Estate or its analogs in populist terms. The burgesses from the boroughs were not "the people" in the old Roman sense, or a stand-in for them. Cities were often represented by those who, within the city's walls, would count as aristocrats. Moreover, participation by clergy—whether, as in England, as Lords Spiritual the second House, or, as in France, as an estate of their own—belonged distinctively to the institutions of the ancient constitution, finding no equivalent in mixed-constitutional republicanism.

The relationship between ancient constitutionalism and social contract theory is closer in some respects, more radically opposed in others. Those two languages were far from being mutually exclusive. Ancient constitutionalists were happy to make use of contractarian language from time to time. The ancient laws were understood as binding both because they were ancient and because they had been anciently agreed to. If one has a conception of Gothic forbears as operating by assembly and consensus, then it becomes easy to say that they chose a chief by agreement and also agreed to the rules under which the chiefs would govern. The agreement or contract for ancient constitutionalists was literal and historical, not hypothetical; coronation oaths served as restatements of the terms of the contract. Original contracts, typically with kingships that were originally elective and mandating ongoing consultation, frequently appear in ancient constitutionalist histories. "Here, then, was a whole body of literature that turned history to the service of the rationalist notion of original contract."[43]

The monarchomachs, Althusius, and Molesworth combined the two languages in all of these fashions. So did Algernon Sidney:

> All the northern nations, which upon the dissolution of the Roman empire possessed the best provinces that had composed it, were under that form which is usually called the Gothick polity: they had kings, lords, commons, diets, assemblies of estates, cortes, and parliaments, in which the sovereign powers of those nations did reside, and by which they were exercised.[44]

It is no coincidence that Sidney, like the *Vindicae* and Althusius, offers justifications of rebellion. The contractarian overlay made the ancient constitution the foundation of the duty to obey; when it was breached, the duty lapsed. It is

---

[43] See Martyn P. Thompson, "A Note on 'Reason' and 'History' in Late Seventeenth-Century Political Thought," 4(4) *Political Theory* 491–504, 1976.

[44] Algernon Sidney, *Discourses Concerning Government*, Thomas G. West, ed. (Indianapolis: Liberty Fund, 1990), p. 167.

not only that we were freer under the old good laws, and so they should be preferred and restored; their breach is a breach of promise and of duty.

But the major social contract theorists—Grotius, Hobbes, Pufendorf, Locke, Rousseau—did *not* rely on, and often sharply criticized, ancient constitutionalism. The Gothic original contract was not the social contract of those we normally think of as contractarians.

Ancient constitutionalists sought to defend idealized medieval institutions against the increasingly centralized and rationalist modern state. The ancient-constitutional jurisdictions came into being for different reasons and at different times, many of them preceding the state as such. But contractarianism does not admit of any institutional or jurisdictional survival from before the state. "Before" was the state of nature, governed by the laws of nature but by no positive laws, perhaps having temporary and informal groupings but with no formal organizations of authority. The decision to enter into politics and law is made at one discrete moment in time, and on terms that everyone rationally could agree to, all at once. This emphasis on rational endorsability means that contractarian theories tended toward coherent, rationalized, monopolistic systems of authority. No one would rationally endorse the deliberate creation of arbitrary distinctions or authority structures with built-in conflicts; the evolved medieval patchwork of jurisdictions thus has no place in social contract theory.

And so contractarian theories were fundamentally justifications *of* the modern state, not arguments for resistance to it. I do not mean that they theorize the state as the complex social institution it turned out to be; a full understanding of the state with its permanent bureaucracy, standing army, and fiscal policy would await the eighteenth century, perhaps not arriving in full until Book V of *The Wealth of Nations*. Rather, they conceive of the created polity as having the formal properties of a state, such as unity and hierarchy of authority, properties that could hardly be said to exist before state rationalization had taken place. Before such a unitary and hierarchical structure was created, there was—from a contractarian juridical standpoint—nothing. It has been widely noticed in the last generation that this reduces much of the non-European world to a condition of political and legal nullity; if the only choices are the state of nature and the state, then (at least) most Africans and indigenous Americans seemed to belong to the state of nature. It has been less noticed that pre-state medieval Europe is also defined as outside the boundaries of the properly civil condition.

Pufendorf held that unity "is the essence of a state."[45] And "every authority by which a state in its entirety is ruled, whatever the form of government, has

[45] Samuel Pufendorf, *On the Duty of Man and Citizen According to Natural Law*, James Tully, ed., Michael Silverthorne, trans. (Cambridge: Cambridge University Press, 1991), p. 144.

the characteristic of supremacy."[46] The contract consists of "a perpetual union of wills" and "constituting some power" which will execute and enforce that union of wills.[47] And so Pufendorf wrote an entire book mocking and criticizing the "monstrous" constitution of the Empire, the most fragmented and medieval of contemporaneous polities—"monstrous" in the sense of being an unnatural organism, as with a creature with three heads. It lacked any clearly supreme power, and lacked unity of will; fundamentally, it failed to be a state.

The idea of the *pre-political* has sometimes been an important one both within liberalism and in criticisms of it. Lockean social contract theory crucially analyzes individual persons and their rights pre-politically, where "pre-" might be understood temporally or might be understood logically. That Lockean sense of pre-politicalness contributed to many subsequent understandings of the limited state; a person's pre-political rights both must be protected by the state and set boundaries on the state's scope of action. The accompanying notion that the individual person is not the mere creature of the state but has a moral status that stands apart from it has deeply influenced subsequent liberal thought on the state's limits. Critiques of liberalism routinely target the idea of the pre-political: Crusoe-style atomism, fictitious agents standing prior to disciplinary institutions, liberty and rights as natural and negative rather than civil and requiring positive state action.[48] Charges of mutual misunderstanding and of shifting levels of analysis (temporal, logical, political, ontological) are common here, and there is no shared sense of what it means to claim that persons or their moral status are, or are not, "prior" to politics. The temporal meaning is often discarded quickly, though I suspect that the philosophical meanings of "pre-" or "prior" often depend on a lingering contractarian sense of priority in time. In any case, there is rarely much discussion of what priority in time would mean, since it is taken to be a fantastic irrelevancy, of interest only to those who take state of nature theories too literally.

But contractarianism in fact leaves very *little* normative space for the pre-political. Locke's pre-political rights are only the rights of individuals; and Locke is unique among the major contractarians for allowing *any* normatively significant survival from the state of nature into civil society. In Grotius, Hobbes, Locke, Pufendorf, Rousseau, and Kant, social, civil, legal, and political institutions are all coeval with sovereign statehood. The jurisdictional pluralism and unclear lines of authority in the ancient constitution are at odds with

---

[46] Pufendorf, *On the Duty of Man and Citizen*, p. 146.

[47] Pufendorf, *On the Duty of Man and Citizen*, p. 136.

[48] See, among many others, Charles Taylor, "Atomism," in *Philosophical Papers, volume 2: Philosophy and the Human Sciences* (Cambridge: Cambridge University Press, 1985); Michel Foucault, *Discipline and Punish: The Birth of the Prison* (New York: Pantheon Books, 1977[1975]); Philip Pettit, *Republicanism: A Theory of Freedom and Government* (Oxford: Oxford University Press, 1999); Stephen Holmes and Cass Sunstein, *The Cost of Rights: Why Liberty Depends on Taxes* (New York: W. W. Norton, 1999).

contractarianism, as is the very idea of institutions having jurisdictional authority by prescription rather than by consent. The philosophically abstracted contract of the contractarians—whether or not it was understood as historically real—proceeds not by asking what *was* agreed to, but what *would have been*. Where *Francogallia* or Coke's *Reports* are filled with history (some accurate, some not), the *Second Treatise* as much as *Leviathan* is almost empty of it. At the contractarian level of abstraction, what would have been agreed to is always a unified, hierarchical, monopolistic authority structure in which clear decisions and judgments will be reached: a state, not a medieval patchwork. Althusius' sense that cities, provinces, and guilds precede the state has no place here; contractarianism follows Bodin in making them inferior and subordinate to, derivative of, the state.

Hobbes' commitment to absolutism and unity of judgment is clear, though the degree to which he took ancient constitutionalist arguments as his targets is easily overlooked. Over the course of *Leviathan*, he showed a determination to leave no assertion of right or privilege against sovereign power unrefuted and these assertions were not the creations of his own imagination. In Volume II in particular the assertions are routinely those of ancient constitutionalists of one sort or another, even setting aside the obvious attack on Parliament in Chapter 25, which redefines that body as a group of mere advisors whose counsel the king is at liberty to take or to leave. Chapter 26, "On Civil Laws," attacks the assertions of legal authority for Roman law, canon law, and, above all, common law—also the target of his *Dialogue Between a Philosopher and a Student of the Common Law of England*. Coke's argument with James I in *Prohibitions del Roy* is a special target; "It is not wisdom, but Authority that makes the Law."[49] Chapter 29 singles out universities as standing in need of externally imposed reform; left to their own devices, they will teach subversion.

Chapter 22, "Of systems subject, political, and private," offers Hobbes' most general attack on intermediate bodies and their pretensions to govern themselves.[50] By "systems" Hobbes means all groups and associations, "any numbers of men joined in one interest or one business."[51] He unsurprisingly emphasizes charters issued by the sovereign. Charters do not recognize some prior legitimate grouping; they are the primary source of legitimacy in the first place. The category of systems that are "regular, but unlawful" includes not only bands of thieves but also "corporations of men that by authority from

---

[49] Thomas Hobbes. *A Dialogue Between a Philosopher & a Student of the Common Laws of England*, Joseph Cropsey, ed. (Chicago: University of Chicago Press, 1997[1681]), p. 55.

[50] Here see Richard Boyd, *Uncivil Society*; and David Runciman, *Pluralism and the Personality of the State* (Cambridge: Cambridge University Press, 1997).

[51] Thomas Hobbes, *Leviathan*, vol. 2, p. 348.

any foreign person, unite themselves in another's dominion, for the easier propagation of doctrines," i.e. foreign churches, i.e. the Catholic Church.

The range of entities Hobbes means to include in his analysis encompasses nearly all of those that claimed ancient liberties of self-government. He expressly analogizes "an assembly for the government of a province, or a colony" to "an assembly for the government of a town, a university, or a college, or a church, or for any other government over the persons of men." The power of feudal nobles is also analyzed as a problem of systems, for such nobles are characterized by their large and armed retinues of servants. "And whereas in nations not thoroughly civilized, several numerous families have lived in continual hostility and invaded one another with private force, yet it is evident enough that they have done unjustly, or else that they had no Commonwealth"—notice the implication that a world with armed nobles is prior to and outside the state, existing in the state of nature.[52]

While I have been at some pains to deny that Hobbes was a liberal or should be taken as a unique founder of the liberal tradition, his opposition to the ancient constitution and corporate group autonomy leaves a legacy for rationalist liberalism (as the pre-liberal corporatism of the ancient constitutionalists leaves a legacy for pluralist liberalism). Hobbes' skepticism about autonomous churches, universities, and so on is tightly connected to his skepticism about ambitious elites and the power they can come to hold over ordinary people. Judges, priests, and professors set themselves above others with their unnecessarily complex and mysterious systems of knowledge. Like generals and nobles, they seek to validate their (false) sense of superiority by commanding or influencing others. This is primarily an evil because of the division that it sows and threat it poses to civil peace. But we can recognize in Hobbes a sense that it is also an evil because the elites thereby wrong their students, subordinates, or followers. The autonomy of intermediate bodies is a source of concern in part because of the in-group status hierarchies and power it generates.[53]

Politically, Hobbes was a royalist of sorts, and so his view of ancient constitutionalism seems unsurprising. This is not true of Locke, whose approach was quite unlike that of his fellow Whig intellectuals such as Molesworth. Appeals

---

[52] I therefore differ with Charles Mills, who maintains that the "tacit racial logic in the text" is one whereby "the *literal* state of nature is reserved for nonwhites; for whites the state of nature is *hypothetical*. The conflict between whites is the conflict between those with *sovereigns*, that is, those who are already (and have always been) in society." Charles W. Mills, *The Racial Contract* (Ithaca: Cornell University Press, 1997), p. 66. Here and elsewhere, I think that the post-colonialist critique of social contract theory is fair and accurate in what it finds about contractarianism and the non-European world, but that it understates the degree to which medieval Europe fell into the same category as non-Europe: outside the state, outside civil and political order, outside justice.

[53] See George Kateb, "Hobbes and the Irrationalities of Politics," 17(3) *Political Theory* 355–91, 1989.

to the common law, the ancient constitution, Coke, and Magna Carta are absent from the *Second Treatise*.[54] Natural rights do not depend on Gothic ancestry; individuals, not institutions or social groups, bear those rights (and here one might also recall Locke's individualist, anti-corporate conception of "a church" in the *Letter Concerning Toleration*); and prescription carries no weight.

Locke's refounding of Whiggism as a natural jurisprudence, social contract doctrine was obviously important in the long run for political philosophy, and shaped what eventually emerged as liberal and democratic theories. Locke bequeathed future generations a view with twin foci of individual natural rights and the general legislative authority of the representatives of a unified *people*. Both the person and the people matter; the pluralistic corporate organizations into which the people might be divided do not. And for Locke as much as for Hobbes, institutional claims did not survive from the state of nature into society. Steven Pincus has argued that, despite the language of ancient constitutionalism and restoration of traditional English liberties that was widely used about the Glorious Revolution, the revolutionary Whigs were modernizers, aiming to redirect rather than to undo the Weberian state that had taken form over the preceding generation. They, for example, had an understanding of political economy according to which commerce was wealth-creating and non-zero-sum, and a proper and intelligible area for state policy. There were Tory traditionalists who aimed to turn the clock back, but in the end they were squeezed between the rival modernizing and state-building projects of the Stuarts and Jacobites, on one hand, and the Whigs, on the other.[55]

Yet post-1688 Whigs freely appealed to Locke and to the ancient constitution both, composing hybrid arguments closer to those of the monarchomachs than to the *Second Treatise*: the original agreement of the Saxons created a limited monarchy and guaranteed both people and lords a part in political decisions. The ancient constitution was established by original agreement, and its legitimacy was both prescriptive and consent-based; coronation oaths confirmed both. The king is the creation of the contract and bound to uphold it; and the substance of that contract had, since time immemorial, been anti-absolutist, pluralist, and parliamentary. Indeed, several decades later Hume felt the need to debunk both Lockean Whig consent theory *and* the

---

[54] See David Resnick, "Locke and the Rejection of the Ancient Constitution," 12(1) *Political Theory* 97–114, 1984; Pocock, *The ancient constitution and the feudal law; a study of English historical thought in the seventeenth century* (Cambridge: Cambridge University Press, 1957); John Locke, *Two treatises of government*, Peter Laslett, ed. (Cambridge: Cambridge University Press, 1988[1689]), Introduction; Pocock, "The Myth of John Locke and the Obsession with Liberalism," in J. G. A. Pocock and Richard Ashcraft, *John Locke: papers read at a Clark Library Seminar, 10 December, 1977* (Los Angeles: William Andrews Clark Memorial Library, University of California, 1980).

[55] Pincus, *1688*.

belief that the post-Glorious Revolution order was rooted in or restored an ancient constitutional order: the former in his essay on the original contract, the latter throughout his *History of England*.

Social contract theory is often seen as the intellectual language out of which liberalism grew, whether among those who see Hobbes as the first liberal, or those who would say Locke, or those who think that Locke is the decisive source for liberal views that only crystallized later. One value of the idea that liberalism encompasses rationalist and pluralist ideas is that it widens our field of vision when looking for liberalism's history and prehistory. Locke was clearly important for the development of liberal ideas, whether or not one uses the word about him. But the ancient constitutionalists were as well. The key figure bridging ancient constitutionalism and liberalism, the one who took up the idea of the old pluralistic legal order and turned it into a doctrine about freedom within the modern state, is Montesquieu, to whom we now turn.

6

Montesquieu and Voltaire, *Philosophes* and *Parlements*

In the modified history of liberalism that I am telling in order to highlight the contrast between pluralism and rationalism, Montesquieu is the crucial figure. His *Spirit of the Laws* (henceforth *SL*) is the hinge work, appropriating and transforming the pre-state medieval inheritance and the ideas of ancient constitutionalism, making them intellectually available to the eighteenth, and indeed the nineteenth, century. More than any of his predecessors, Montesquieu directly links the rights of pluralistic intermediate bodies and groups, limits on royal absolutism, and individual liberty. And in the criticisms of Montesquieu's views by the more rationalistic thinkers of the French Enlightenment such as Voltaire, we can recognize the beginnings of the dispute that was to divide liberals thereafter. Whereas Bodin and Hotman, or Hobbes and Molesworth stood for basically opposed moral visions of politics, Montesquieu and Voltaire did not. As we will see, however, they did stand for deeply opposed accounts of *how* freedom might be protected under modern conditions, and which social forces most threatened it.

SL is the first work in the traditional canon of political theory to be published after the consolidation of the French and British states—the French during the long reign of Louis XIV, which ended in 1715, and the British from the 1688 Glorious Revolution through the 1714 succession of the House of Hanover, an era encompassing the establishment of a combined fiscal–military apparatus controlled by Parliament, the enactment of the Bill of Rights and the Act of Toleration, the creation of the Bank of England, and the Union with Scotland. *SL* is also the first such work to directly engage with the economic changes of the seventeenth and early eighteenth centuries. As a political actor, Locke was directly involved in the consolidation of the English state, and was deeply concerned with commercial development. The *Second Treatise*, however, is substantially innocent of both. Neither the organization of armed force nor economic activity after the creation of agriculture and money makes any real appearance in that work. The absence of history from the *Second Treatise*, particularly the history of the modern state or of modern commerce, contrasts sharply with *SL* as well as with later works by Voltaire, Hume, Ferguson, and Smith. Unlike the *Second Treatise*, *SL* contains hundreds of pages of historical material, yet in its treatment of politics and economics it is distinctively modern by comparison. Montesquieu aimed to understand social change over time; understanding what was new required understanding how it differed from what had come before. He did not, however, only aim to passively observe and understand such change. *SL* offers advice on choices that could be made and directions taken. "Gothic government" had been "the best kind of government men have been able to devise" "during the time that this government continued to exist."[1] The challenge Montesquieu saw for his own era was how to recover the institutional virtues of the ancient constitution under modern conditions.

The Early Eighteenth Century

The political settlements in France and Britain that took hold in the mid-1710s, and the accompanying intellectual and cultural openings, allowed the full force of those changes to become apparent.[2] The end of the War of the Spanish Succession after fifteen years reopened the two great powers to regular trade, travel, and intellectual exchange. The accession of George I in Britain was soon followed by the rise of the Whigs to power that they were to retain for decades. A stable balance of power among the consolidated states of Western Europe seemed to be established by the Treaty of Utrecht, raising hopes for long-term peace. And Louis XIV's death after more than seventy years on the throne at least raised the possibility that absolutism's zenith had passed.

Louis XIV's long absolute reign was followed by the regency of the tolerant Philippe d'Orléans, who both sympathized with the nobility and needed an alliance with them to secure his rule against Louis' illegitimate sons to whom he had tried to leave both princely status and a share in power. Orléans' reliance on the *parlement* of Paris to nullify those portions of Louis' will signaled an important difference from the Sun King's long domination over

---

[1] *SL*, II.11.8, pp. 167–8.

[2] This section draws on Pocock, *Barbarism and Religion*, vols 1 and 2; Daniel Roche, *France in the Enlightenment* (Cambridge: Harvard University Press, 1998); Jonathan Israel, *Enlightenment Contested* (Oxford, UK: Oxford University Press, 2006); Jeremy Jennings, *Revolution and the Republic: a History of Political Thought in France since the Eighteenth Century* (Oxford, UK: Oxford University Press, 2011); J. H. Shennan, *The Parlement of Paris*; Dale van Kley, *The Religious Origins of the French Revolution* (New Haven: Yale University Press, 1996).

that body; in exchange for the court's support, he restored the right of remonstrance that Louis had stripped away decades before. Censorship was relaxed, as was the persecution of Jews, Protestants, and Jansenists.[3]

The latter was a Catholic movement that inclined toward Augustinianism in its austere morality and its theology. The Jesuits were implacable opponents of Jansenism, quick to see in Augustinian ideas a crypto-Calvinism. Eventually Louis XIV had sided with them to suppress Jansenism, and even turned to the Pope in 1713 to proscribe Jansenist doctrines, breaking with the Gallican church's traditional rejection of papal interference.

As Jeremy Jennings puts it, this shocking alliance between Versailles and Rome "quickly became a metaphor for absolutism... [U]nder the weight of persecution the Jansenist cause converged with that of the *parlements* in their opposition to the arbitrary power and unlimited authority of royal absolutism and ecclesiastical hierarchy."[4] One consequence was to entrench among the *parlementaires* a long-term animosity toward the Jesuits; decades later, the *parlement* of Paris played a key role in the prohibition of that society in France.

The Jesuits, formally the Society of Jesus, were an especially important case of a transnational association that met with state suspicion and suppression. The Society was founded in the early sixteenth century as an evangelical and educational order of priests. It was unusual in a number of ways. While monks—the "regular" clergy, so-called because they live according to a rule—were customarily organized by orders devoted to some particular way of life, the secular clergy (priests, bishops, and so on) were normally not. Neither did priests take monastic vows of poverty. Priests were organized according to the normal geographical pyramid of the Church; their superiors were their local bishops and archbishops, and their primary duties were tied to a geographical diocese. The Jesuits took vows of poverty and obedience, including direct obedience to the Pope, not mediated through the hierarchy of cardinals and bishops. They also took vows of chastity at a time when the requirement of priestly celibacy was far from universally observed. They made up a transnational order, going wherever in the world the Society thought they were needed. This enabled them to be leading evangelists in parts of the world where there was no local Catholic structure, from China and Japan to North and South America. They quickly became a dominant intellectual force of the Counter-Reformation, disputing Protestant theology and simultaneously reforming and purifying the practices of a decadent Church. They founded and taught in schools, colleges, and universities, aiming to improve

---

[3] See Thomas O'Connor, "Jansenism," in William Doyle, ed., *The Oxford Handbook of the Ancien Régime* (Oxford: Oxford University Press, 2011).
[4] Jeremy Jennings, *Revolution and the Republic*, p. 302.

doctrinal knowledge among the Catholic laity and to increase the pool of literate, knowledgeable priests. In the Americas they fought against Spanish and Portuguese enslavement of the Indians.

Their activities transformed Catholicism and won them an extraordinary array of enemies. The Spanish and Portuguese governments obviously resented their activities in South America. Other European governments, especially but not only the French, were suspicious of an order of priests whose members could travel where they wished but were responsible directly to Rome rather than to the more-biddable local–national church. Those churches themselves often shared the suspicion; the local bishop would not look kindly on the infusion of priests in his jurisdiction but not under his authority. Protestants viewed them as an especially fanatical set of opponents. Philosophers were annoyed that the Jesuit educational system dressed up Catholic doctrine in the appearance of reason, thereby restoring Thomist scholasticism and casuistry to respectability. Philosophers dedicated to the priority of civil society over religious disputes found them especially distasteful; whereas local Catholic secular clergy had a stake in the peace and well-being of their respective realms, especially where they held power as an estate, the Jesuits were free to promote religious persecution regardless of the local consequences.

And the order's growth in wealth and power—Jesuits became confessors to Catholic monarchs, and rulers over Paraguay and (briefly) the Japanese city of Nagasaki—elicited the predictable suspicion that they were a dangerous conspiracy. They thus had the vigorous enmity of Protestants, deists, important parts of the Catholic Church, and both governments and theorists who wished to domesticate religion and calm religious disputes; they also had enough wealth to be an attractive target for expropriation. One member of the Freemasons—an association that almost came to match the Jesuits in the intensity of political hostility it faced on grounds of secrecy, transnationality, and worry about conspiratorial control of society—wrote that the members of his order were "friends to all the world, except to the Jesuits, whom not one master of a lodge would receive in our order."[5]

The conflict between the Jesuits and the crown on one side, the Jansenists and the *parlements* on the other, provided a wedge that the new Regent could exploit. Louis' widow and legitimized sons were considered allies of the Jesuits. While the Regent could not repeal the papal bull Louis had secured against Jansenism, he could and did suggest that he would be less than vigorous in enforcement, helping him win *parlementaire* support.

---

[5] Margaret Jacob, *Living the Enlightenment* (Oxford: Oxford University Press, 1991), p. 123.

Montesquieu

Montesquieu came of age during the Regency. In 1716 he inherited his final noble titles as well as the presidency of the *parlement* of Bordeaux, just as the *parlements* were being restored to some of their old status. He married a Protestant, perhaps giving him a personal investment in the relaxation of religious persecution, and was an active member of the recently established Academy of Bordeaux, taking part in the new openness to scientific and intellectual exchange.[6] His *Persian Letters* is set so as to span the transition: it begins in 1711 and ends in 1720. The monarchical transition is noted as an event within the novel itself by the Persian observer Usbek, the most prominent of the book's characters.

> The late king made a will, which limited the power of the regent. This wise prince went to the *parlement*, and, there laying before them all the prerogatives of his birth, he made them break the regulations of the monarch, who, desirous to survive himself, seemed to have claimed the power of governing, even after his death: The *parlements* resemble those ruins which we tread under foot, but which always recall to our mind the idea of some temple famous for the ancient religion of the people. They seldom now interfere in anything more than in affairs of justice; and their authority will continually decline, unless that some unforeseen event should arrive, to restore life and strength to it. These great bodies have followed the common course of human affairs: they yielded to time, which destroys everything, to the corruption of manners, which hath weakened everything, to the supreme, which hath overturned all things. But the regent, who wished to render himself agreeable to the people, seemed at first to respect this shadow of public liberty; and, as if he had an intention to raise from the ground the temple and the idol, he was willing that they should regard it as the support of monarchy, and the foundation of all legal authority.[7]

With its risqué, satirical humor about the major institutions of French society, it was very much literature of the more open moment whose onset it depicted. But the Persian observers Usbek and Rica are more than devices for pointed commentary on, say, the absurdity of the *parlement* and University of

---

[6] On the Academy and Montesquieu's participation in it, see Rebecca Kingston, *Montesquieu and the Parlement of Bordeaux* (Geneva: Librairie Droz, 1996), pp. 49–54.

[7] Montesquieu, *Persian Letters*, C. J. Betts, trans. (Baltimore: Penguin Books, 1993[1721]), p. 173. The sardonic edge is the voice of hindsight. By the time *Persian Letters* was written, relations between the Regent and the *Parlement* had deteriorated badly over the former's embrace of the financier John Law. Law, who preferred absolute to limited monarchies on fiscal grounds, sought to increase royal authority over taxation and money. The collapse of the speculative bubble associated with Law's "system," which we see unfold later in *The Persian Letters*, leaves Law so disreputable a figure that three decades later Montesquieu still goes out of his way to link critiques of *parlements* with him. See *SL* I.1.4, p. 19. See also Thomas E. Kaiser, "Money, Despotism, and Public Opinion in Early Eighteenth-Century France: John Law and the Debate on Royal Credit," 63(1) *The Journal of Modern History* 1–28, 1991.

Paris being involved in a dispute about the pronunciation of the letter Q in French. Usbek in particular is an important character study. He is a man of science, philosophy, and letters, committed to entering into the new world of learning that has been opened in Europe. For much of the novel, he plays the part of the rational philosopher, seeking to understand the social world as well as deeper philosophical and theological questions with a serious and critical mind. He is also, however, still the master of a household and harem in Persia, which he endeavors to control at long distance with epistolary instructions. His tone of rational discourse with his wives gradually gives way, as what appeared to be a minor subplot about trouble with the harem's eunuch guards becomes a central plot about unrest among his wives. In the novel's *denouement*, his instructions become increasingly brutal and despotic; he aims to reassert his absolute power over his household with wholesale violence.

The implications for how Montesquieu thought about the exercise of power at this stage of his life are ambiguous. On the one hand, the oriental harem is a central example in European thought of local, personalized domination. For all of his supposedly enlightened and philosophical temperament, when it comes to matters close to home, Usbek reveals himself to be every bit the stereotypical husband–master, finally preferring massive bloodshed to any threat to his own status and authority. Moreover, he is shown to suffer a localized blindness, belying his high opinion of his own judgment; his own chief slave tells him that he seems "made for nothing but to be ignorant of [his] own senses."[8] It was Roxana, the wife whom he most trusted, who was at the source of the rebellion within the seraglio. As the novel ends, she kills several guards, then commits suicide by poison, but takes the time while dying to write Usbek a letter flaunting her true inner freedom and her success in deceiving him. There is a straightforward sense in which *Persian Letters* seems to be about local tyranny. One can read it as saying that even the enlightened philosophical world-traveler and man of reason living in Paris can be a despot in his own household, and as turning on the reader's surprise that the primary point-of-view character, so initially sympathetic and modern, behaves the way that he does. One might think that the novel highlights a concern with personal and local domination that is antithetical to Parisian reason and philosophy. This in turn might suggest either a rationalist reading of Montesquieu's mature political philosophy, or a change of mind.

But I think this is too simple a reading of the novel. Usbek is only complicatedly a symbol of local power, because he spends the decade of the novel far from his wives and slaves, attempting to exercise power as a despotic monarch might over a distant rebellious province. He suffers from a shortage

---

[8] Montesquieu, *Persian Letters*, p. 280.

of information and this contributes to his increasing frustration, suspicion, and brutality; he must instruct those who do violence on his behalf with rules to follow; when order is not restored, he must change administrative personnel. While the power he wishes to exercise is personal and immediate, he must try to do so at a great distance and mediated through his eunuch slaves. And there are also suggestions—not least in Usbek's own ironic pronouncement that "men should stay where they are," that migration, colonization, and "distant conquests" weaken humanity—that the distant power-holder is especially to be feared. Usbek himself says that it is easier for him to order brutal punishments of his wives from a distance than it would be if he could see and hear them; and two wives complain about his distance while handing out judgments and punishments. It may well be that it is *especially* the enlightened philosophical world traveler, so convinced of his own intellectual greatness that he believes he can run the world from Paris, who is prone to despotism. Of the two central Persian characters, it is the more intellectual and philosophical one, the one more sure of his own powers of reasoning, who becomes a bloodthirsty tyrant; the younger Rica is unmarried and has no parallel plotline of rule at a distance.[9]

A novel, even one with a philosophical main character, is not a philosophical tract; we should not try to wring simple meanings out of a deliberately polyvocal and kaleidoscopic work of literature. But Montesquieu's magnum opus, *The Spirit of the Laws*, published almost thirty years later, sometimes seems as hard to pin down. It is a vast work that resists distillation into even a handful of theses, and any summary is necessarily very incomplete. And by emphasizing different passages or chapters, different interpreters can reach very different conclusions about Montesquieu's underlying normative commitments. This is partly because *SL* is not simply a normative work; some of its arguments are explanatory and empirical, some methodological, some historical, some interpretive; Montesquieu rarely tells the reader where one kind of argument leaves off and the next begins. I suggest that we see Montesquieu as a reformist ancient constitutionalist, hoping to restore pluralistic institutions in a legally complex modern monarchy, for the sake of protecting freedom from absolute rule. With an understanding of the ancient-constitutionalist tradition and the medieval inheritance of intermediacy, we are in a position to understand the work better than it has often been, drawing especially on the neglected final third of the book, a long legal and constitutional history of medieval and early modern France. Later in this chapter I will contrast my

<hr>

[9] For related treatments of the *Persian Letters*, see Susan McWilliams, *Traveling Back* (Oxford: Oxford University Press, 2014); Michael Mosher, "What Montesquieu Taught," in *Montesquieu and His Legacy*; Judith Shklar, "Politics and the Intellect," in Stanley Hoffman, ed., *Political Thought and Political Thinkers* (Chicago: University of Chicago Press, 1998).

view with an account of *SL* as a work of hidden republicanism, an account that I think is mistaken and that depends on not appreciating Montesquieu's pluralism.[10]

Montesquieu divided *SL* into six parts, organized into three volumes of two apiece in his preferred edition of the work.[11] Parts I and II are concerned with the analysis of regime types: the division between moderate governments and despotism, the secondary division of moderate governments into monarchies and republics (and the subdivision of the latter into democratic and aristocratic), the account of their animating principles and their possible decay, and the application of the typology to such questions as military policy, taxation, and education. Part III offers Montesquieu's arguments about climate and geography, and their effects on social, legal, and political institutions. Part IV concerns commerce, and contains his famous "*doux commerce*" thesis. And Parts V and VI offer complementary analyses of legal complexity. Part V discusses the interaction between the rightfully separate jurisdictions of religious and civil and political laws. The last part, the longest by far of the six, develops a novel constitutional history of the French kingdom, and of the legal variety that had always characterized it.

In the typology in Parts I and II, Montesquieu distinguished moderate monarchies and immoderate despotisms on the basis of the former's respect for *corps intermédiaires*. "Intermediate, subordinate, and dependent powers constitute the nature of monarchical government, that is, of the government in which one alone governs by fundamental laws."[12] The "lords, clergy, nobility, and towns" maintain a monarchy in its proper conceptual form. The most "natural" intermediate power is the nobility as a class, so much so that "nobility is the essence of a monarchy, whose fundamental maxim is: *no monarch, no nobility; no nobility, no monarch*; rather, one has a despot." Even the Church, which he sharply criticizes for intolerance and persecution, has a crucial role to play, and he suggests that ecclesiastical autonomy should be respected and legally firmly established. It provides the final check against despotism when a monarchy has otherwise abolished all of its old laws. Montesquieu's defense of the *corps intermédiaires* is a genuine theory of *intermediacy*. The aristocracy in a monarchy defends the laws; aristocratic government without a monarch to overawe the nobles tends toward lawlessness and corruption. Their privileges are "odious in themselves," but instrumentally useful in aligning their honor with the defense of the constitution.[13]

---

[10] Compare Annelien de Djin, "Was Montesquieu a Liberal Republican?" 76(1) *Review of Politics* 21–41 (2014).

[11] See Paul Rahe, *Montesquieu and the Logic of Liberty* (New Haven: Yale University Press, 2009), pp. 88–9.

[12] *SL*, II.4, p. 17.   [13] *SL*, II.11.6, p. 161.

The argument was in part conceptual, in part causal. Montesquieu both claimed that a monarchy could be identified by the presence of intermediate bodies, and that the intermediate bodies help to keep monarchies moderate. The former idea marks an unusual addition to an intellectual tradition as old as Aristotle's *Politics*. Montesquieu did not dispute the traditional view that monarchies are law-governed and despotisms lawless and arbitrary. Lawfulness and lawlessness distinguish his moderate regimes as a group from the immoderate category of despotism. But he did not simply hold that monarchies were lawful rule-by-one. He instead suggested that lawful rule-by-one would *necessarily* entail the persistence of intermediate groups.

Moreover, and more fundamentally, he held that monarchies could only *remain* moderate and lawful regimes over time because of the continued existence of the *corps*. As their liberties and privileges diminished, the monarchy would slip farther and farther toward despotism. This was because only the *corps* could have both the motivation and the power to successfully check the urge of monarchs to absolutism. Without them, there is no one to say no to the king, and certainly not to do so in the name of law. Of special importance here are those intermediate bodies he calls the "depositories of the laws," as they will have a special connection with the retention and enforcement of legality and liberties: in France, the *parlements*, which even in their weakened eighteenth-century state "do much good."[14]

Montesquieu's interest in the *corps* in Parts I and II is all too often overlooked in the Anglophone literature, which has been preoccupied sometimes with his celebration of the English constitution and sometimes with his effects on the American constitutional debates, through the ideas of a separation of powers and the proper size of republics. But Montesquieu was a skeptic about republicanism in the modern world. The famous analysis of state size in *SL*—the thesis that republics are suited only for small states, and monarchies for states of moderate size, with large states more or less inevitably being despotisms—should be understood in this light.[15] This is not simply a range of options from which one might choose; small states are not militarily viable in the era of modern states such as France and Britain. Modern states will be large; and large states will not be republics, as Cromwell's England had convincingly demonstrated.

Montesquieu identified an animating principle for each of his forms of government: civic *virtue* for democratic republics; *moderation* for aristocracies, needed to allow the aristocrats to restrain themselves collectively when there is no outside power to do so; *honor* for monarchies, to which we will return

[14] Montesquieu, *My Thoughts*, Henry C. Clark, trans. and ed. (Indianapolis: Liberty Fund, 2012), p. 192.
[15] I discuss this further in "Beyond Publius," 27(1) *History of Political Thought* 50–90, 2006.

below; and *fear* for despotisms, which govern by lawless terror. Contrary to what his American readers were to believe a generation later, Montesquieu's insistence that republics were constituted by virtue was an *indictment* of them, since the obsession with monk-like virtue and self-abnegation was anachronistic in an age of commerce. And republics were far from being intrinsically free governments. Freedom depends on, among other things, the separation of powers.

> In most kingdoms in Europe, the government is moderate because the prince, who has [the executive and legislative] powers, leaves the exercise of [the judicial power] to his subjects. Among the Turks, where the three powers are united in the person of the sultan, an atrocious despotism reigns. In the Italian republics, where the three powers are united, there is less liberty than in our monarchies.[16]

Monarchies may slip into despotism, but so long as they do not, they seem to be where the most freedom is normally found among modern states.

It is certainly true that Montesquieu admired the British constitution, the subject of extended discussions in II.11 and III.19. But enthusiasm for England's system was limited precisely by the decline of England's *corps* since the Civil War. "If you abolish the prerogatives of the lords, clergy, nobility, and towns in a monarchy, you will soon have a popular state or else a despotic state [...] In order to favor liberty, the English have removed all the intermediate powers that formed their monarchy. They are quite right to preserve that liberty," he drily concludes; "if they were to lose it, they would be one of the most enslaved peoples on earth" because of their abolition of intermediate powers.[17] This perilous state of affairs dates from the days of Cromwell: "the English nobility was buried with Charles I in the debris of the throne."[18]

---

[16] *SL*, II.11.6, p. 157.   [17] *SL*, II.4, pp. 18–19.

[18] *SL*, VIII.9, p. 118. Montesquieu does not further explain this comment, which is at first glance odd. While the House of Lords was abolished in the immediate aftermath of Charles' execution, it was restored as part of the Restoration, and in Montesquieu's own day was not a weak body. It seems to me there are two possibilities, not mutually exclusive. One is that Montesquieu understands the restored Lords not to be a restored *nobility* in his sense. This is plausible, since contemporaneously with the restoration of the House of Lords, feudal land tenures were abolished. The aristocracy's land ownership became legally indistinct from other forms of ownership—one moment from which one might date the abolition of feudalism in England. The titled aristocracy remained, but its foundation as a noble class had arguably been kicked away. The second is that, once the House of Commons had shown that it *could* abolish the House of Lords, the restored body was necessarily neutered; it could no longer serve any real oppositional function in an increasingly centralized state. This need not have been true—and I do not think it was entirely true in the mid-eighteenth century—to have been Montesquieu's understanding. I think that Montesquieu's phrasing suggests the latter account—it seems to be about 1649 rather than 1660—but the former seems very much like Montesquieu's kind of thought. And, again, the two might be complementary. Perhaps a restored Lords *could* have remained independently powerful, if its members had remained a noble class with respect to land; but with neither individual noble land relations nor clear institutional permanence, it was not.

The conviction that the *corps*, including those staffed by a hereditary nobility, are crucial to the maintenance of a lawful and balanced monarchy helps to explain Montesquieu's apparently odd identification of *honor* as the animating principle of a monarchy (one of many irritants in the book to Voltaire). Aristocratic honor, after all, does not derive directly or solely from the monarch, Hobbes' view to the contrary notwithstanding. For aristocrats who are drawn to court, i.e. Versailles, the monarch has an outsized influence on status and standing. Still, those driven by honor could not be the kinds of subservient flatterers demanded by despots. They could not help but stand up for the dignity of their own offices and authority. Indeed they could not even be counted on to obey direct royal commands; dueling, the "point of honor," had long been illegal but was still fairly common. However poorly justified a person's view of his own honor might be, it remained *his*, not only outside the direct control of the monarch but sometimes a source of the strength needed to refuse and resist oppression.[19] If the *corps* were needed to affirm and enforce legal limits on royal power and prevent despotism, honor was needed to animate the *corps*, and to keep their members dedicated to their defense. This is why, despite the "ignorance natural to the nobility, its laxity, and its scorn for civil government,"[20] that class is the *sine qua non* of lawful and moderate monarchy.

Throughout Parts I and II in particular, Montesquieu critiqued the turn to absolutism and centralization under Louis XIV, albeit always with a slight, politic opacity.[21] The recurring comparisons and contrasts between monarchies and despotisms often come just to the edge of saying that Bourbon France had crossed, or risked crossing, the line between them. The *corps* had been steadily undermined in "a great European state" over the preceding centuries. "In certain European monarchies" the autonomous provinces that govern themselves well and thus thrive are constantly threatened with the loss of "the very government that produces the good," to better allow them to "pay

---

[19] For discussions of honor as a source of strength for political resistance, though in a more democratic spirit, see Sharon Krause, *Liberalism With Honor* (Cambridge, Mass.: Harvard University Press, 2002), and Anthony Appiah, *The Honor Code* (New York: W. W. Norton, 2010).

[20] *SL*, II.4, p. 19.

[21] On Montesquieu's sensitivity to censorship, see Paul A. Rahe, *Montesquieu and the Logic of Liberty*, especially ch. 1. The fact of *ancien régime* censorship is one source of the interpretive opacity of *SL*, and what Rahe thinks happens behind that opaque barrier is very different from what I suggest here. But Rahe's discussion of the censorship itself, and of Montesquieu's concern not to test its limits too aggressively in his mature years, is clear and convincing. It is worth noting, however, that *SL* attracted controversy nonetheless: attacked by Jesuits and Jansenists alike, placed on the Vatican Index, and extensively censured by the Sorbonne. Defending the book against charges of atheism, naturalism about religion, and adherence to Spinoza and Bayle dominated the final years of his life. Either Montesquieu was not quite so concerned with avoiding offense to the established powers as Rahe suggests, or he was not terribly good at it. I incline toward the former explanation.

even more."[22] This strategy of killing the golden goose is another sign of despotism; "when the savages of Louisiana want fruit, they cut down the tree and gather the fruit. There you have despotic government."[23]

The deliberate effort to draw the aristocracy in to the court at Versailles and cut them off from the provinces likewise concerned Montesquieu. In an essay on the size of capital cities in his unpublished *Pensées*, he added that criterion to his distinctions among regimes. A great capital would destroy a republic, but was natural to despotism. In a monarchy, as usual, things were complicated and required balance. The growth of London (the capital of "a certain maritime realm") was not especially worrisome, as it arose from the attractions of commerce. But a monarchy could also grow in the capital due to onerous taxes in the provinces, or to administrative procedures that demanded a presence in the capital to settle legal questions, or to the sheer attractions in terms of honor of the monarchical court. One way to maintain balance, unsurprisingly, was to "allow cases to be concluded in the provincial tribunals, without constantly appealing them" to courts at the center.[24] But Louis XIV had sought to aggravate the imbalance rather than counteract it.

SL contains several allusions to the War of the Spanish Succession and to the illegitimacy of Louis' initial aim of creating a union between the French and Spanish thrones. In a discussion about altering lines of succession when national well-being calls for it, he says that "a great state that became secondary to another would be weakened and even weaken the principal one."[25] This is a piece of Montesquieu's broader critique of Louis' expansionism. Recall that one of the differences between lawful monarchy and lawless despotism is the size of the state. Large states such as Russia or China cannot but be governed despotically; "a large empire presupposes a despotic authority in the one who governs. Promptness of resolutions must make up for the distance of the places to which they are sent."[26] When a state expands too much through conquest, its domestic freedom will not survive. "An immense conquest presupposes despotism."[27] This is the core of Montesquieu's sense of what happened to the Roman republic, laid out at length in an earlier book on the subject and in abbreviated form in II.11. The governance of distant provinces required despotic power.[28]

---

[22] *SL*, II.13.12, p. 221. For an account of Montesquieu's defense of provincial autonomy that amounts to a kind of federalist constitutionalism for monarchies, see Lee Ward, "Montesquieu on Federalism and Anglo-Gothic Constitutionalism," 37(4) *Publius: The Journal of Federalism* 551–77, 2007.

[23] *SL*, I.5.13 p. 59.

[24] Montesquieu, *My Thoughts*, p. 540. See also Daniel Roche, *France in the Enlightenment*, pp. 209–10.

[25] *SL*, 516.   [26] *SL*, I.8.19, p. 126.   [27] *SL*, II.10.16, p. 152.

[28] While Machiavelli and the republicanism he inspired generally lie beyond the scope of this book, it is worth noting how distant Montesquieu's view here was from Machiavelli, whom he

This was an even more prominent theme in a work Montesquieu had written to accompany his book on the Romans, but decided not to publish: his *Reflections on Universal Monarchy in Europe*. In the late seventeenth century, Huguenot refugees as well as William of Orange and his allies had maintained that Louis XIV sought "universal monarchy"—the dominion over all of Europe to which Holy Roman Emperors had notionally aspired and that Charles V had seemed on the verge of attaining in the early sixteenth century. The growing conviction that this was true was a key feature of Whig thought in England before and after the Glorious Revolution that tilted England's foreign policy from an alliance with France to one with the Netherlands; and in the early eighteenth century, the War of the Spanish Succession cemented the idea in many non-French minds. Louis XIV, already commanding the most powerful kingdom on the continent of Europe, aimed to add Spain and its overseas empire to his holdings. Montesquieu connected the aspiration to universal monarchy abroad with the slide toward despotism at home.[29] Fortunately for European freedom, the aspiration to universal monarchy was doomed in the modern age; but those who did not understand this could still destroy their own countries' constitutions in their vain pursuit of military supremacy.

Parts III, IV, and V of *SL* were especially concerned with the existence of a social world autonomous of, and not created by, political rule. Geography and climate, historical and cultural change, economic forces, and religion all constrained in various ways what rulers could do—and in different ways in different places. Most of this discussion lies outside an inquiry into pluralism and intermediacy, but its striking methodological novelty is relevant. In these parts of the book we find a recurring motif of advice to legislators and rulers that they notice the particularities of their societies and govern accordingly, rather than in accordance with abstract plans. Such sociological, economic, and historical constraints were more or less invisible to the decision-based logic of seventeenth-century contractarianism, but were crucial from Montesquieu onward. The classical economists' elaboration of an economic world that transcended political boundaries, that operated according to its own discoverable rules, and that partly conditioned and limited politics—the idea, in short, of "the economy" as we now discuss it—stands out here, but it is not the only example. Montesquieu's struggle to understand the world according to differences in geography, in national or cultural or religious spirit, in historical stage, in social customs, and in economic situation was

---

much admired but frequently disagreed with. Conquest and expansion are the ruin of free governments, not the sign of their triumph.

[29] See Paul Rahe, "The Book That Never Was: Montesquieu's Considerations on the Romans in Historical Context," 26(1) *History of Political Thought* 43–89, 2005.

similarly an attempt to describe *societies* rather than simply polities.[30] The pervasive eighteenth-century concern with manners and *mœurs* can be seen in the same light; not only Montesquieu but also Voltaire, Hume, Ferguson, and Smith were deeply interested in habits and customs that, to be sure, could be affected by political decisions, but were not simple political enactments and placed constraints on the range of feasible political choices.

Besides understanding the existence of such social worlds, Montesquieu and those who followed him in this regard sought to understand their plasticity or rigidity, and the rules according to which they changed and developed. All agreed that the social worlds were not static; manners could become more polished over time, the wealth of nations could grow or decline, agricultural societies could become commercial societies, and so on. But none of these things happened by simple political decree. Governing should usually be done along the grain of such social tendencies and local particularities, occasionally in a way that might counterbalance some undesirable tendency, but never in sheer ignorance of or violence against them. The *mœurs*, manners, and customs of a society create a cultural reality that one may attempt to guide in one direction or another but that cannot be simply ruled. Montesquieu's discussion of Peter the Great's attempts to Europeanize Russia stands out here. He sought to change the "manners" of his people by laws and coercion, and disregarded their legitimate attachment to custom; the results were violence and tyranny.

Parts V and VI defended the pluralism inherited from the ancient constitution in a sense related to but distinct from the support of pluralism of political institutions and *corps* in Parts I and II: the plurality of legal norms and systems that governed modern European kingdoms, to the consternation of absolutists and reformers. "*L'Esprit des lois* was nothing short of a celebration of the diversity between and complexity within legal systems."[31] Here is where we find the critique of uniformity first mentioned in Chapter 3. While the occasional "great spirit" such as Charlemagne is attracted to uniformity in policy and laws, it is more commonly the "small ones" seized by the idea. Near the beginning of the book Montesquieu had said that when a ruler "makes himself more absolute, his first thought is to simplify the laws."[32] Then, it had appeared as something like a deliberate strategy, as the simplified state would be simpler to rule. But at the end of the book it appears rather as an unjustified

---

[30] This is the sense in which Durkheim saw Montesquieu as a founder of sociology, set apart from political philosophy. See also Taylor, "Invoking Civil Society."

[31] Sylvana Tomaselli, "Spirit of Nations," p. 31, in Mark Goldie and Robert Wokler, eds, *The Cambridge History of Eighteenth-Century Political Thought* (Cambridge: Cambridge University Press, 2006).

[32] *SL*, I.6.2, p. 75.

taste[33] or a psychological affliction of those who hold power or make laws. Shortly before the remarks on uniformity, he wrote that "it seems to me that I have written this work only to prove [...] that the spirit of moderation should be that of the legislator; the political good, like the moral good, is always found between two limits."[34] But the spirit of moderation was *not* normally that of the legislator, still less of the philosopher who imagined himself a legislator. Montesquieu names Aristotle, Plato, Machiavelli, More, and Harrington, and identifies in each case some individual preoccupation that contributed to their urge for one complete system or another. "The laws always meet the passions and prejudices of the legislator. Sometimes they pass through and are colored; sometimes they remain, and are incorporated."[35]

These statements of purpose accompany, indeed interrupt, a long study of the problems of Roman, Germanic, and feudal law in the French legal order. This large part of *SL* is obscure to the modern Anglophone reader; indeed it was obscure to some contemporaneous French readers. But it is much less so when read in light of the preceding two centuries' debate about the ancient constitution.

French political debates included three rival theses about the traditional constitution. The royal thesis saw a more or less seamless transition from Roman rule to the French kingdom, with no essential element of Frankishness introduced. The Protestant and monarchomach German thesis was one of primordial freedom and an original contract. And the view influentially put forward by the Comte de Boulainvilliers a generation before *SL* was one of Frankish conquest yielding absolute rule over the conquered, with Germanic parity between the nobles and their king.

In Part VI, Montesquieu is clearly engaged in some of the same inquiries that Boulainvilliers had made two decades before, and sometimes the two are lumped together; both, after all, were broadly supportive of the nobility, and critical of absolutism. Neither shared the later-eighteenth century enthusiasm for democratic republicanism. But Montesquieu was both a member of the *noblesse de la robe*, and a supporter of *parlements* that were filled with others in the same class—a group for which Boullainvilliers had undisguised contempt. They were, in the latter's view, *arrivistes*, not true Frankish nobles, their claims

---

[33] Montesquieu's entry on aesthetic taste in the *Encyclopédie*, his only direct contribution to that work, criticized the aesthetic vision of uniformity as well. It held that fully developed taste was attracted to a combination of order, symmetry, and variety as such; "a long uniformity renders any thing insupportable...The soul loves variety." "Essai sur le goût," (1857) in Daniel Oster, ed., *Montesquieu: Oeuvres Completes* (Macmillan Company, 1964), pp. 846–7, my translation.

[34] *SL*, VI.29.1, p. 602.

[35] *SL*, VI.29.19, p. 618. He added a complementary argument in his unpublished *Pensées*, warning against large and sudden changes in a state because, "by eliminating the respect one ought to have for the established things," such changes "serve as an example and authorize the fantasy of someone who wants to overturn everything." *My Thoughts*, p. 65.

to titles no more than two centuries old. Montesquieu's support is for the balanced monarchy that respects *corps intermédiaires* and the nobility, not for aristocracies as such—the least-discussed of his types of government. And he kept his predecessor at a careful distance:

> As work his is penned with no art, and as he speaks with the simplicity, frankness, and innocence of the old nobility from which he came [the same nobility Montesquieu had called 'ignorant' in Part I], everyone is able to judge both the fine things he says and the errors into which he falls...[H]e had more spirit than enlightenment and more enlightenment than knowledge.[36]

The Germanist account of popular government—which Montesquieu engages through the foil of the Abbé Dubos, never naming the incendiary *Francogallia*—is paired with Boulainvilliers' aristocratic thesis as comparable mistakes, one unduly privileging the Third Estate and one the nobility.[37] Moderation between these historical accounts is Montesquieu's watchword; the history of France is many things, not one thing. The Romanist historical thesis of Renaissance absolutism is, on Montesquieu's telling, simply false, not even gaining the kind of partial truth attributed to Boulainvilliers and Dubos.

Montesquieu takes a sharply unconventional approach to the disputes as to the foundations of French law. In the first place, it is directly concerned with what he terms "civil" rather than "political" law—in our terms, mainly private and criminal law rather than constitutional public law. It offers a history of laws under the French monarchy, not a history of the founding of that monarchy or of its aristocracy. The Salic Law was not a constitutional enactment; it was simply the then-extant law of inheritance of fiefs applied to the case of royal inheritance. Civil law generated political law.

Second, he declines to adopt any of the traditional sides in the constitutional dispute, neither the Romanist Gallic account of continuity with the fallen empire nor the Germanist Frankish story of primeval liberty. (By contrast, he said that English liberty was Gothic and primeval in origin.) Rather, he stressed, the civil laws in France had always been diverse and pluralistic. Insofar as the law was of barbarian Germanic origin, it was not simply imposed Frankish law—for, as he stresses here and elsewhere, the idea that conquerors should be legislators and replace the laws and customs of the conquered is a modern one. Instead, it was the laws of the Ripuarian and the Salic Franks and the Saxons, and elsewhere the relatively Romanized barbarian codes of the Burgundians and Visigoths and Lombards and so on. Roman law was retained for Romans; gradually only the clergy retained it, as others opted into one or

---

[36] *SL*, XXX.10, p. 627.
[37] Sylvana Tomaselli, "The Spirit of Nations," section 7: "The spirit of the laws: the Gothic constitution."

another of the surrounding legal codes. The independence of canon law thus appears as a foundational fact about French law. So, too, does legal pluralism more generally.

But then Montesquieu depicts a rupture in the post-Carolingian generations—he places *both* the Salic Law and the Roman Law on the far side of a deep historical divide. In place of either barbarian codes or Roman codes, the law of those outside the churches came to be primarily customary and regional. He takes care to insist that the distinction between written law and unwritten custom was *not* that between German and Roman; the barbarian written codes, like the Roman law, made reference to the ability of custom to govern where the law was silent. And all the written barbarian codes fell into disuse just as the written Roman law did from the ninth through the twelfth centuries. What took their place was a variety of territorial, regional, and eventually provincial customs. These were inflected, to be sure, with local inheritances from the old codes (Frankish, Gothic, and so on) but became detached from the old personal identities. The recovered *corpus* of Justinian was received in relatively Romanized provinces as written law, as it formalized existing practice; elsewhere, it was admitted only as *ratio scripta*. This re-writtenness of the Roman law was paralleled by a newfound writtenness of customary law in other provinces.

The rise of feudalism is acknowledged as important by Montesquieu, but not as the introduction of a unified feudal conquering race à la Boulainvilliers; rather, it is just another source of pluralism, in which each lord can hold court in his own manner. The early Middle Ages appear as a time of "prodigious diversity" in law—not indeed the same diversity that had characterized early medieval France under the barbarian codes, but one such that (as he approvingly quotes Beaumanoir as saying) no two lordships had entirely the same civil law in all of France.

Finally, Montesquieu attempts to show that this situation was not interrupted in the thirteenth century by the so-called Establishments of St. Louis (King Louis IX), a document that was sometimes appealed to as being the foundation of a unified civil code, but that he said

> was never made to serve as law for the whole kingdom ... Now, at a time when each town, borough, or village had its own custom, to give a general body of civil laws [would have been] to reverse in a moment all the particular laws under which men had lived everywhere in the kingdom. To make a general custom of all the particular customs would be rash, even in these times ... For, if it is true that one must not alter things when the resulting drawbacks equal the advantages, so much less must one alter them when the advantages are small and the drawbacks immense ... [T]o undertake to change the accepted laws and usages everywhere was something that could not enter the minds of those who governed.[38]

[38] *SL*, VI.28.37, p. 589.

Citations to the *corpus* pervade *SL* but are almost always in the service of a description of what "the Romans" did, not as an account of the development of French law. The Romans' law is perhaps the most frequently used example in Montesquieu's comparative jurisprudence; but it is still only an example to be compared with other examples. It is their law, not *the* law. The constant consideration of laws "in their relation to" climate, form of government, *esprit*, type of commerce, religion, and so on emphasizes the fitting of laws to local time and place. And toward the end of the book Montesquieu is explicit that "laws must not be separated from the circumstances in which they are made"[39] and that one should not "transfer a civil law from one nation to another" without examining "whether they both have the same institutions and the same political right." He mentions a Cretan law on robbery that was transferred to the Lacedaemonians and then to the Romans, but made no sense in the Roman context; the implication for the relevance of Roman law to modern contexts was clear, and the claims of legal continuity between Roman Gaul and modern France were dismissed.

In sum, Montesquieu's distinctive legal history in Parts V and VI rejects Romanist accounts of French constitutional origins while substantially modifying their Germanist rivals. He determinedly does not identify any particular founding moment that normatively defines the kingdom thenceforth. His ancient constitutionalism was thus more thoroughly pluralist, and further from images of original contracts, than the Gothic contractarianism sometimes found in the monarchomachs. He denies that France was simply Roman or simply Frankish, tracing instead the ebb and flow of different types of law and rules governing choice of law. The Salic Law had some pride of place, to be sure; it was the territorial law of the royal demesne. But Montesquieu refuses to indulge the fiction that this made it the law of the kingdom. He maintains that the French legal order had *always* been a pluralistic one in which different rules coexisted; and that pluralism itself evolved over time, as rules of personal jurisdiction gave way to provincial territorial jurisdiction, as the Roman law was recovered, as feudalism developed, as persons opted into one court system or another for their own various reasons. The aspiration to legal uniformity was thus at odds with the kingdom's whole history. The variety of provincial laws upheld by the provincial *parlements*, the coexistence of civil and canon law, of urban and seigniorial law—these were the complex fabric of French law, and the contemporary legislative reformer must not pretend otherwise.

---

[39] *SL*, VI.29.14, p. 611.

Voltaire

Montesquieu and Voltaire were separated in age by just five years, whereas they were more than twenty years older than the central generation of the Parisian Enlightenment, Rousseau, Diderot, D'Alembert, Helvetius, and D'Holbach, as well as Hume, Smith, and Kant. Both took formative trips to Britain in the 1720s and were impressed—in different ways—by the constitutional government, religious toleration, and commercial liveliness of the post-Glorious Revolution order. Neither was fully *of* Parisian intellectual life; willingly in Montesquieu's case and unwillingly in Voltaire's, each wrote a substantial share of his work outside of Paris. They did not live in the intense mutual engagement characteristic of the *philosophes* in the middle and later parts of the century. And the *philosophes* in turn were sometimes ambivalent about their two renowned elders, partly for the reasons that the young and ambitious are always worried about those who cast long shadows, but partly because neither seemed a sure ally for their democratic–republican enthusiasms, Montesquieu being too aristocratic and Voltaire, as we shall see, too monarchical.

They shared some strong normative commitments: a bitter opposition to religious persecution and slavery, opposition to censorship, deep skepticism about European imperialism, and commitment to judicial reform and the rule of law. Both recognized the importance of the rise of modern commerce and the advent of constitutional government in Britain, and both were basically enthusiastic about both developments, if with occasional reservations.

Nonetheless, their relationship was, at best, "strained."[40] While each had moments of demonstrated respect for the other's mind and literary talents, they had a basic distaste for one another. And this was driven in substantial part by genuine and deep disagreements.[41]

The association of Voltaire with the idea of "enlightened absolutism" is well known.[42] And if there has been exaggeration in his depiction as an uncritical advocate of "enlightened despotism"—as well as an inaccurate word choice, for he did not believe "despotism" described a real phenomenon—it is still true that he placed many of his hopes for political progress in centralizing absolute monarchs, and none at all in the institutions that kept them in check. Typical was his enthusiasm for the Danish absolutism that Molesworth had attacked: "For more than a hundred years," he wrote, "welfare [*bienfesance*]

---

[40] Jonathan Israel, *Enlightenment Contested*, p. 836.

[41] See broadly Karen O'Brien, *Narratives of Enlightenment: Cosmopolitan History from Voltaire to Gibbon* (Cambridge: Cambridge University Press, 1997); Robert Shackleton, "Allies and Enemies: Voltaire and Montesquieu," in David Wilson and Martin Smith, eds, *Essays on Montesquieu and the Enlightenment* (Oxford: Voltaire Foundation, 1988); Ian Davidson, *Voltaire: A Life* (New York: Pegasus Books, 2010).

[42] On enlightened absolutism and related ideas, see Derek Beales, "Philosophical kingship and enlightened despotism," in Mark Goldie and Robert Wokler, eds, *The Cambridge History of Eighteenth-Century Political Thought* (Cambridge: Cambridge University Press, 2006).

has been seated upon the Throne of Denmark. Happy is the nation that is so governed!"[43] Louis XIV, Peter the Great, and—for a time—Frederick the Great inspired his admiration, nobles and *parlements* his disdain, and ecclesiastical independence his fury. The worldly power, civil authority, and legal privileges of churches in Christian Europe, and especially of the Catholic Church, seemed to him an especially severe problem. The Middle Ages were a time of ignorance and feudal barbarism. While he knew very well that state authority could be used to commit great wrongs, the rise of monarchical power in modernity created the possibility that priestly and noble power could be suppressed, and that commerce, refinement, and intellectual progress could begin. Voltaire held that the historical process that supported liberty depended on a stage of accumulating and centralizing state power as seen in England, where the Henrician Reformation successfully broke the power of the church and so paved the way for the eventual development of liberty; and in Russia, which had the "advantage" of having been politically underdeveloped for centuries, leaving Catherine the Great with the ability to create as she saw fit: "it was easier to erect a building than to repair one whose ruins would still be respected."[44] This limited the force of his admiration for the British constitution. In societies where the power of the church or the nobles had not yet been broken, royal absolutism, not government by estates or parliaments, was the path to freedom.[45]

After *The Philosophical Letters* were censored in the 1730s, Voltaire wrote little by way of explicit and overt political philosophy for many years, preferring verse and plays. This was the situation when *SL* appeared in print and excited attention and controversy. Montesquieu died soon thereafter. Although the older of the two, Voltaire outlived Montesquieu by more than twenty years. So, notwithstanding some commentary in Montesquieu's correspondence (Voltaire has "too much wit to understand me," he once wrote[46]), the written debate between them was largely one-sided, carried on by Voltaire in his later political and historical writings.

[43] Voltaire, letter to M. le Comte de Bernstorff, February 4, 1767. Voltaire, *Oeuvres* (Paris: Garnier, 1881), vol. 45, p. 87.

[44] Voltaire, "Laws," in *Philosophical Dictionary*, in David Williams, ed., *Political Writings* (Cambridge: Cambridge University Press, 1994[1764]), p. 22.

[45] Montesquieu found Voltaire's understanding of history tendentious and partisan. "Voltaire will never write a good history. He is like the monks who write not for the subject they are treating but for the glory of their order; Voltaire writes for his monastery." Montesquieu, *My Thoughts*, p. 416.

[46] Montesquieu, Letter to Abbé Comte de Guasco, August 1752 in *The complete works of M. de Montesquieu* (Dublin: Printed for W. Watson, W. Whitstone, J. Williams [etc.]. 1777), p. 74. Oddly, Voltaire made a very similar complaint about Montesquieu: that *SL* was written "with great wit, while the authors of all other books on this subject are tedious"; and the wit led people to overlook how error-ridden the work was. He endorsed the comment supposedly made by an unnamed observer that the book was *"l'esprit sur les lois,"* "a joke about the laws," a pun on two meanings of *esprit*. While *SL* is occasionally funny, I confess that I find this a very strange judgment for Voltaire in particular to express. "Esprit des Lois," in *Philosophical Dictionary*, Part IV. *The Works of*

Voltaire's criticisms of Montesquieu were sometimes open, as in the entry on *The Spirit of the Laws* in his *Philosophical Dictionary*, but more often indirect, or at least, as in the "ABC" dialogue, put into a character's voice.[47] The indictment in both of those essays is cushioned in praise: *SL* is a "work of genius that makes you yearn for perfection . . . a building with poor foundations, and irregular structures, in which there are a lot of fine, well-polished, gilded apartments"[48] and a "highly defective book . . . full of admirable things." Montesquieu himself has "reminded men that they are free" and has been attacked by "fanatics . . . for those very parts that deserve the praise of the human race." He attacked tyranny, superstition, "grinding taxation," and slavery, and won the kinds of enemies that it does one credit to have. Montesquieu was "always right against the fanatics and promoters of slavery. Europe owes him eternal gratitude."[49]

But these gestures of respect do little to blunt the force of Voltaire's attack. The sentence quoted immediately above began, "Montesquieu was almost always in error with the learned, for he was not learned." He found *SL* ill-informed, unstructured, "annoying" in its lack of consistent method, and not "serious," indeed often little more than a "collection of witticisms." Montesquieu's views on the *parlements* and the French judiciary are the "tribute" that the "philosophical mind" pays to pride, nothing more than a celebration of his own position and the hat that it comes with.[50]

Above all, Voltaire complained of Montesquieu's central analysis of despotism. Montesquieu joins in the prejudice of throwing the label at "the sovereigns of Asia and Africa," attributing to oriental societies the rule by fear of one man, unconstrained by law. "Now it's quite wrong," he holds, "to think that such a government exists [or even] that it could exist."[51] Even the Pope, more despotic than the Asian sovereigns on account of his purported infallibility, governs by and under laws.

Here we find the core of the dispute that Voltaire carried on with *SL* for years. The very concept of "despotism" denoted an impossibility, and it undermined the good that could be done by enlightened absolutism. Voltaire therefore dedicated much of the 1750s and 60s to a series of historical works that challenged Montesquieu's central claims about absolutism.

Voltaire, A Contemporary Version, Vol VI, John Morley, ed., William F. Fleming, trans. (New York: E. R. DuMont, 1901[1764]), pp. 106–7.

[47] Voltaire, "The ABC" (1768), in *Political Writings*, pp. 89–99.

[48] Voltaire, "The ABC," in *Political Writings*, p. 99.

[49] Voltaire, "Esprit des Lois," in *Philosophical Dictionary*, in *Works of Voltaire*.

[50] Montesquieu's office had been *president à mortier; mortier* was the ceremonial judicial hat, a word that survives in the English "mortarboard" of academic regalia. Voltaire snickered that Montesquieu was "a high court president complete with mortar. I've never seen a mortar, but I imagine that it's a superb adornment." Voltaire, "The ABC," in *Political Writings*, p. 98.

[51] Voltaire, "The ABC," in *Political Writings*, p. 97.

His histories of Louis XIV and of Peter the Great celebrated their civilizing and enlightening accomplishments. He dismissed the idea that Louis had sought universal monarchy, claiming indeed that Louis XIV had been the one engaged in balancing behavior against Dutch naval and imperial might and deeming William "more ambitious" than Louis.[52]

Peter's efforts to modernize Russian custom and to tame the nobility and the clergy represented great progress. So too did the imposition of uniformity, happily possible because the czar could act without opposition. "Weights and measures were likewise fixed on a uniform plan, in the same manner as the laws. This uniformity, so vainly desired in states that have for many ages been civilized, was established in Russia without the least difficulty or murmuring; and yet we fancy that this salutary regulation is impractical among us."[53]

His sweeping comparative history tellingly titled *An Essay on Manners and the Spirit of Nations* is in part an answer to *SL*. It offered the extended argument against the oriental-despotism thesis that he summarized in *ABC*. Voltaire praised Russia, and denied the force of Montesquieu's criticisms of it. He defended China against Montesquieu's depiction of it as despotic and static. Likewise, he insisted that Indian and Islamic societies were civilized and law-governed—indeed often more so than Christian Europe was in the same era.

Pocock suggests, plausibly, that Voltaire's rejection of the "oriental despotism" model drew both on his concern to praise non-Christian societies in order to show that Christianity did not improve social life, and on his eagerness to forestall "neo-feudal" criticism of absolutism closer to home. The "domestic agenda" was to defend "the absolute monarchy inherited from Voltaire's hero Louis XIV"; Voltaire perhaps suspected that the very idea, "the whole construct of despotism" "had been invented to serve the *thèse nobiliaire*."[54]

In contrast to his writings on Asian non-Christian countries, Voltaire was quite viciously critical of Jews: custom-bound, irrational, particularistic, priest-ridden, primitive, and superstitious, in sum the "most detestable" nation "ever to have sullied the earth."[55] Readers of Voltaire differ over how much of this should be read as a criticism of Christianity by proxy, but

---

[52] This was not an unprecedented view. The Netherlands' naval and overseas power before 1688 was pointed to as evidence by the Stuarts and their allies in England that James II and Louis XIV were justified in defensively balancing against the Dutch. After 1688 William directly controlled two of Europe's great powers as well as holding naval dominance, making the charge that he sought universal monarchy even easier to levy.

[53] Voltaire, "The History of the Russian Empire Under Peter the Great" (1759), in *The Works of Voltaire*, vol. 18, p. 62. On Voltaire's and Montesquieu's contrasting views of Peter the Great, see Israel, *Enlightenment Contested*, pp. 315–17.

[54] Pocock, *Barbarism and Religion*, 2: 111–12.

[55] Voltaire, "Tolerance," in *Philosophical Dictionary*, in *The Works of Voltaire*, vol. 7.

most agree that the volume, venom, and specificity of such commentary over-whelms this defense. For Montesquieu, neither custom nor legalism nor par-ticularity is a criticism, and in *SL* he sympathetically discussed the persecutions and expulsions the Jews have faced. In denouncing the Spanish Inquisition he specifically puts a Jewish face on its victims. His history of commerce emphasizes that it was Christian persecution that forced Jews into the financial and trading professions which they were later resented for dominating.[56]

The last of Voltaire's substantial books of history was a study of the *parlement* of Paris, painting a picture of a corrupt judiciary that had often served the cause of religious bigotry and impeded good government.

He had good personal reason for unfriendliness to the *parlements*. The Parisian court had ordered his *Philosophical Letters* to be censored and burned early in his life, and did so again repeatedly with his other books. He jokingly likened his own experiences to those of the rationalizing finance ministers who had repeatedly found their efforts at tax reform stymied by the *parlia-mentaires*, in the *PD*'s entry on "authors":

> The most voluminous authors that we have had in France are the comptrollers-general of the finances. Ten great volumes might be made of their declarations, since the reign of Louis XIV. *Parlements* have been sometimes the critics of these works, and have found erroneous propositions and contradictions in them. But where are the good authors who have not been censured?[57]

But the *parlements* had done worse than burn books. The Protestant mer-chant Jean Calas was executed on the wheel on order of the *parlement* of Toulouse, on charges of having killed his son for planning to convert to Catholicism. Voltaire was persuaded by the family's claim that the son had committed suicide, and took up the cause. He championed Calas in print, furiously attacking the combination of religious persecution, provincial *parle-mentaire* bigotry, and torture in one of his most powerful pieces of writing, his *Treatise on Toleration*. He succeeded in winning exoneration for Calas and compensation for his family.

His history of the Parisian *parlement* was written and published near the climax of a six-year-long confrontation between all the *parlements* and the administration of Louis XV, a conflict that culminated in the dissolution of

---

[56] Arthur Hertzberg, *The French Enlightenment and the Jews: The origins of modern anti-Semitism* (New York: Columbia University Press, 1968), explains their different opinions of Jews biographically and psychologically. Hugh Trevor-Roper's very critical review of Hertzberg, "Some of My Best Friends are Philosophes," *New York Review of Books*, August 22, 1968, says correctly that the "profound difference between the philosophy of Montesquieu and the philosophy of Voltaire" suffices to explain the difference. For the best recent treatment of Voltaire in particular, see Adam Sutcliffe, *Judaism and Enlightenment* (Cambridge: Cambridge University Press, 2003). See also Pocock, *Barbarism and Enlightenment, vol. 2*.

[57] Voltaire, "Authors," in *Philosophical Dictionary*, in *Works of Voltaire, vol. 6*.

the Parisian court and the exile of its members in early 1771. In that year he continued his critique with a parody of *parlementaire* remonstrances,[58] proclaiming that the fundamental laws of the kingdom, indeed part of the Salic Law itself, guaranteed the venality of offices, the right of judges to be paid by the parties, and the privileges of office-holders all the way down to the royal dogmaster to face legal action only before the *parlements*, not before lower courts. These were, proclaimed Voltaire's *parlementaires*, the laws of which their court was the depository, pieces of the constitution second in importance only to the law governing royal succession. These pieces of nonsense, Voltaire implied, were all that was really lost with the court's dissolution, all that the *parlementaires* meant by "despotism."

The histories were the crucial site for Voltaire's arguments with Montesquieu, but he made space in his *Philosophical Dictionary* to carry on the quarrel as well. The entry on "Climate" did not name Montesquieu but clearly denied that climate affected government and religion as strongly as *SL* had suggested. In "Tyranny," he proclaims the despotism of one "less detestable" than that of many: one you might placate or else avoid. As the number of lords proliferates, the likelihood of being near one and "crushed" or "ruined" by him for personal reasons rises.

The entry on "Government" disdained the Gothic institutions:

> The barbarians, who, from the shores of the Baltic poured over the rest of Europe, brought with them the usage of estates or parliaments, about which a vast deal is said and very little known. The kings were not despotic, it is true; and it was precisely on this account that the people groaned in miserable slavery.

That on "Laws (Spirit of)" repeated and amplified the criticisms in the *ABC*, mocking the idea of Gothic origins of British constitutionalism, complaining of Montesquieu's characterization of Russia as despotic, and openly accusing Montesquieu of writing in defense of his own personal class privileges.

In the entry simply on "Laws," he delivered a quick joke about "the real spirit of the laws" being represented by brutal laws of war. More importantly, Voltaire offered a decisive rejection of *SL*'s core theses about legislation, an especially sharp statement of the rationalist view of law rejected in *SL* VI.29.

"London only became worth living in since it was reduced to ashes. Since that time, its streets have been widened and straightened. Being burnt down made a city out of London. If you want to have good laws, burn what you have, and create new ones."[59]

---

[58] Voltaire, "Très humble et très respectueux remontrance du grenier à sel," in M. Beuchot, *Œuvres de Voltaire*, Vol. 46 (Paris: Chez Lefèvre Librarie, 1832), pp. 508–15.
[59] Voltaire, "Laws," *Philosophical Dictionary*, in *Political Writings*.

In depicting Montesquieu and Voltaire as intellectually opposed in this fashion, I reject a tradition of reading Montesquieu as a hidden republican, a tradition most recently joined by Paul Rahe's treatment of what he sees as Montesquieu's and Voltaire's fundamental similarity.[60] Rahe reads *SL* as a work about the superiority of the English to the French model for a modern state; and Montesquieu's view of the English constitution as republican at its core—a new, modern, kind of republicanism, not subject to the criticism Montesquieu offers of the ancient variety. Where *SL* does not appear to endorse these views, Rahe attributes this to Montesquieu's concern to avoid censorship—a concern that might have been due in part to the treatment Voltaire received for his own subversive views.

Rahe continues a reading of *SL* that has been offered from time to time for more than two centuries. Thomas Paine held that "Montesquieu . . . went as far as a writer under a despotic government could well proceed; and being obliged to divide himself between principle and prudence, his mind often appears under a veil, and we ought to give him credit for more than he has expressed."[61] Rahe characterizes ancient-constitutionalist readings of Montesquieu as a kind of insult to him, a way of saying that he was nothing but "a man of his time" and was motivated by a desire to uphold the privileges of his class.[62] By reading ancient constitutionalism entirely out of the respectable history of liberal thought, he attempts to force readers to choose between Montesquieu the rationalistic republican and Montesquieu the disreputable defender of feudal privilege.[63]

---

[60] My reading of Montesquieu in particular genuinely differs from Rahe's. By contrast my differences with Dennis C. Rasmussen, *The Pragmatic Enlightenment: Recovering the Liberalism of Hume, Smith, Montesquieu, and Voltaire* (Cambridge: Cambridge University Press, 2013), are a matter of emphasis and wording more than of substance, even though he minimizes some of the passages I quote from Voltaire and emphasizes areas of agreement between the two. Rasmussen acknowledges the differences between Montesquieu and Voltaire at the level of politics, political sociology, and history. He joins them together as being opposed to "rationalism" in different senses from mine: first, a Cartesian rationalist foundationalism about ethics; second, a radicalism about the speed of political change and the likelihood of success of either revolutions or rapid technocratic reforms of the sort advocated by the Physiocrats; and, third, a simple-minded universalism of the sort critics of the so-called "Enlightenment Project" like to attack. (He is also rightly concerned to rescue Voltaire from the concept of "Enlightened despotism.") I agree that Voltaire and Montesquieu were both non-revolutionary, non-foundationalist, and pragmatic Enlightenment thinkers, which is enough for Voltaire not to be a rationalist in Rasmussen's sense of that word. In turn I think he agrees that Voltaire *is* a rationalist in my sense of the word, though he emphasizes Voltaire's prudence and pragmatism about the pace of change over his desired end of within-state legal uniformity. As I have mentioned, political and legal rationalism is detachable from claims about the grounding of philosophical rationality, just as institutional and associational pluralism is detachable from Berlinian value pluralism.

[61] *Rights of Man*, in Thomas Paine, *Rights of Man, Common Sense, and Other Political Writings*, Mark Philip, ed. (Oxford: Oxford University Press, 1995), p. 145.

[62] Rahe, *Montesquieu and the Logic of Liberty*, p. 212.

[63] In this, Rahe echoes and is perhaps influenced by a long historiographic tradition, partly but not only Marxist, that saw the *parlements* merely as self-interested and retrograde defenders of privilege against forward-looking royal ministers. In the last few decades, historians' views of the

Rahe's Montesquieu and Voltaire are both convinced that Louis XIV's monarchy has been simply replaced by England's commercial republicanism as a model for the future. In fact, neither thought England a viable direct model for constitutional reform elsewhere, though for strikingly different reasons. Voltaire held that the modern condition of English liberty had been made possible by the intervening absolutism of Henry VIII, which broke the power of the English church. Other states could not emulate English liberty if they had not first gone through that state-building process. Montesquieu considered English liberty fragile precisely because the English constitution no longer included any counterbalancing *corps*—a view for which Voltaire himself took Montesquieu to task, misunderstanding the latter's category of *corps intermédiaires* such that a bicameral central Parliament qualified.

One key for arguments like this is the anomalous place that Britain holds in *SL*. The contemporaneous government most praised by Montesquieu is also the one that does not seem to fit anywhere in his typology of regimes. It is a "nation where the republic hides under the form of monarchy,"[64] a place where the "style" of a strong monarchy is preserved "so that one would often see the form of an absolute government over the foundation of a free government."[65] His discussion of it centers on neither virtue nor moderation nor honor as animating "principles," but on "political liberty" as its "direct purpose."[66] The two chapter-length discussions of England are exceptionally odd in tone, sometimes historical and empirical but sometimes idealizing and hypothetical, as if using England as a starting point for reflections on a polity that could exist. These chapters and these oddities have generated no end of interpretive dispute about whether Britain represented Montesquieu's most-preferred constitutional order, and about how he understood the British system.

It is clear that Britain is not simply a republic as traditionally understood; it is too large and insufficiently virtuous, and so the Commonwealth was doomed to failure. It is also not a monarchy as traditionally understood; its *corps* are extinct and its nobility supposedly defunct, but it has clearly not become the despotism that Montesquieu says a monarchy without *corps* or nobility must be. It surpasses other countries in its institutionalization of the separation of powers and its embrace of modern commerce. But whether this leaves it fundamentally a new kind of republic whose monarchy is merely for show, or a new kind of constitutionalized monarchy whose hybrid nature is important to its stability, remains unclear. In his *Pensées* he gave the explicit

---

parlements have changed dramatically. See the overview of these debates in Julian Swann, *Politics and the Parlements of Paris under Louis XV, 1754–1774* (Cambridge: Cambridge University Press, 1995), pp. 28–40.

[64] *SL*, I.5.19, p. 70.   [65] *SL*, III.19.27, p. 330.   [66] *SL*, II.11.5, p. 156.

answer missing from *SL*: "What then is the constitution of England? It is a mixed monarchy," to be contrasted with the mixed aristocracy of Lacedaemon and the mixed democracy of the later Roman republic because "England, as we have seen, inclines more toward monarchy."[67] But the aphoristic and unpublished *Pensées* do not necessarily resolve interpretive questions about *SL*, and what kind of regime Montesquieu thought England to be is a question that continues to divide interpreters.

That dispute connects directly to the questions at stake here. Those who read Montesquieu as an admirer of an effectively republican England deny that he was the kind of pluralist ancient constitutionalist I depict here. In part, I think, they do so because the idea of a pluralist liberalism is unfamiliar. They therefore think if Montesquieu favored freedom, as he clearly did, he must have rejected the world of *corps intermédiaires* and their privileges.[68] But if he was a skeptic of republican government and inclined toward mixed monarchies, then he was indeed a pluralist; the way to prevent the French monarchy from becoming despotic was to revive its *corps*, and in the absence of any *corps* even the British monarchy seemed fragile.

As I see it, the reformist agenda of *SL* is one of restoring the long-since weakened limits on the monarchy, especially though not only in France. Strikingly, Montesquieu does not include among these the Estates-General, which are never even mentioned in the book, though some of their institutional ancestors are alluded to in discussions of the distant past. It is possible that he considered the Estates such a potentially subversive body that they could not even safely be named. Perhaps Montesquieu admired the British Parliamentary regime but understood its complete incompatibility with the French monarchy, and so was deliberately, conspicuously silent about the French equivalent of the British Parliament that he hoped would supplant the monarchy someday. This would be a republican reading.

It seems to me more likely, first, that the long desuetude of the Estates (more than a century at the time of *SL*'s publication) meant that they struck him as an unlikely and unavailable source for effective counterbalancing; and, second, that he trusted pluralistic and decentralized bodies such as the *parlements* more than he trusted a unitary and centralized British-style parliament. He might well have sympathized with the next generation's calls to summon the Estates; but they were not the centerpiece of the ancient constitutional limits on royal authority he hoped to restore.

---

[67] Montesquieu, *My Thoughts*, p. 519.

[68] In addition to Rahe, for the view that Montesquieu saw and admired Britain as fundamentally republican, see Mark Hulliung, *Montesquieu and the Old Regime* (Berkeley: University of California Press, 1976).

Certainly, Montesquieu must have worried about censorship and offending the established authorities. But to read him as a secret British republican hoping for the end of the French monarchy is doubly odd. First, it makes Parts V and, especially, VI extremely difficult to understand. A purely modern–commercial–republican would have no reason to build up such an elaborate and distinctive variant of ancient constitutionalism.

Second, it would be strange to hide impermissible republicanism beneath a surface of equally impermissible religious heterodoxy and *parlementaire* constitutionalism, a kind of wolf-in-coyote's-clothing strategy. *SL* is all but explicitly subversive in its account of the *corps*; it all but explicitly describes the Bourbon monarchy as despotic because the *corps'* privileges have been eroded and attacked. He exercises some caution; he does not say that France *is* a despotism, and in several crucial passages he declines to name France even when it is conspicuously being singled out. But the indictment of the centralized monarchy is barely disguised; and it might have been sufficient to call down official disapproval. Why bother exposing the book to that risk, if the constitutionalized monarchy with its pluralistic institutions was not his goal?

In discussing England, Montesquieu disavows any intention "to disparage other governments, or to say that this extreme political liberty should humble those who have only a moderate one. How could I say that, I who believe that the excess even of reason is not always desirable and that men almost always accommodate themselves better to middles than to extremities?"[69] This very deliberate mentioning of the view he is not going to mention, so as to disparage without offending the censor, tempts many readers to suspect Montesquieu of irony. If the extreme liberty of England is compared to reason, then we should surely read Montesquieu as embracing it. After all, how could a philosopher genuinely worry about an excess of reason itself? For later readers used to thinking of mid-eighteenth-century France as the age of enlightened reason, nothing could seem more at odds with the spirit of the era. But I think *SL* makes more sense if we take this passage at face value. It directly anticipates the defense of the legislative spirit of moderation over those of uniformity and philosophy later in the book. For Montesquieu, rational unity, even the rationality of a unified system of liberty, is far from being the only virtue a legal system might have, and institutional pluralism, legal pluralism, and the pluralism of customs and norms is often preferable to it.

In any case, the pluralist, constitutionalist, monarchist *SL* was the book that inspired pluralist liberalism in the century that followed, regardless of whether that *SL* is the real book or a deceptive surface. Similarly, that *SL* inspired the indignation of Voltaire and of many later rationalist and *philosophe* readers.

---

[69] *SL*, II.11.6, p. 166.

It also helped to inspire *parlementaire* constitutionalism from the 1750s–80s in a series of confrontations with Louis XV. The first, shortly after *SL* was published, centered on the prohibitions on Jansenism, then being enforced with renewed vigor. The *parlement* of Paris issued a "Grand Remonstrance" on the prohibition's incompatibility with the fundamental laws of the kingdom, quoting Montesquieu and emphasizing the duty of the king to obey the laws, denying that the *"Quod principi placuit legis habet vigorem"* model of arbitrary rule was part of the French constitution. Louis XV rejected the remonstrance, the *parlement* went on strike, and he exiled the judges and tried to replace the body before backing down a year later.

Over these decades the Parisian and provincial *parlements* began to articulate a doctrine of *parlementaire* unity and solidarity, aligning the powerful court in the capital with the defenses of provincial autonomy in the *pays d'états*. The rule of law, judicial independence, and provincial self-rule thus came together in the La Chalotais affair that began in Brittany in 1765 and culminated with the dissolution of the Parisian *parlement* in 1770 that so pleased Voltaire.[70] A conflict between the Breton *parlement* and the province's royal *intendant* led to the resignation of the court's judges and the arrest of La Chalotais, an official of the *parlement*. The Parisian court invoked the idea of *parlementaire* unity and issued remonstrances to the king, who rejected them; in a personal *lit de justice* (the reading of an edict directly into the *parlementaire* record discussed in the previous chapter) he denounced *parlementaire* constitutionalism and insisted on his own sovereignty. The Breton *parlement* was restored but the conflict continued, and the *intendant* eventually stood trial before the Parisian *parlement*, over Louis XV's attempts to stop the proceedings. A flurry of remonstrances, edicts, and *lits de justice* followed, until the king stripped the judges of their offices altogether and exiled them from Paris.

Voltaire was probably surprised to find himself relatively isolated in his view of these proceedings. Reformist liberals such as Lafayette saw the destruction of the *parlement* as a triumph for lawless absolutism. So too did *philosophes*. Diderot did not admire the *parlements*—"Gothic in their usages, opposed to every good reform, too enslaved to forms, intolerant, bigoted, superstitious, jealous of the priest, and enemy to the philosopher, biased, and sold to the great,"—but called their dissolution "a very great misfortune" that abolished a proud and independent court leaving nobody that could refuse the sovereign will.[71]

---

[70] See Le Roy Ladurie, *The Ancien Régime: a history of France, 1610–1774* (Oxford: Blackwell Publishers, 1996), pp. 433–6; Shennan, *The Parlement of Paris*, pp. 316–19.

[71] Diderot, "Essai historique sur la police de la France depuis son origine jusqu'à son extinction actuelle," in Diderot, *Œuvres politiques*, Paul Verniere, ed. (Paris: Garnier, 1963[1773]), pp. 221–41, at p. 238, 239. See also Rasmussen, "Burning Laws and Strangling Kings? Voltaire and Diderot on the Perils of Rationalism in Politics," 73(1) *The Review of Politics* 87–8, 2011.

Public opinion rallied so strongly to the *parlementaire* cause that when Louis XVI came to the throne in 1774 he restored the court, distancing himself from his predecessor. Notwithstanding that move on his part and his shift toward tolerance of Jansenism, the *parlement* remained intransigently opposed to royal absolutism and insistent on constitutional forms. This, of course, came to define Louis XVI's reign, as the *parlements* refused to submit to noble taxation or otherwise to allow fiscal rationalization on the basis of royal or ministerial edict, insisting that only the Estates-General could change such fundamental laws. In 1788 he finally agreed to summon the Estates; neither the monarchy nor the *parlements* survived the events that followed.

7

The Age of Revolutions

In this chapter we will follow intellectual and political developments from the 1770s to the 1820s—the era in which "liberal" as a name for a party-idea or political ideal emerges. Our interest here is not in the central events of the French and American Revolutions, nor in the general course of American or French political thought during and after them. The liberal–republican debate in the historiography of American political thought, for example, is beyond our scope, as are questions about whether the Terror emerged for reasons internal to the French Revolution or as a response to external threat. Our interest is rather in the further development of the ideas described in the last two chapters: how associational and institutional pluralism mattered in the emergence of liberal thought on both sides of the Atlantic; how the democratizing revolutions drew on rationalist and pluralist, contractarian and ancient-constitutionalist, resources; and how political thinkers understood the relationships among central states, corporate social groups, and individual freedom in the revolutionary and post-revolutionary societies. Over the course of these decades, liberal sympathy for enlightened absolutist monarchies was more or less crowded out by the idea of a rational unitary *democratic* sovereign state. Rationalist liberals were henceforth absolute democrats, not absolute monarchists. Pluralism was transformed as well: the institutions on which ancient constitutionalists had pinned their hopes were swept away, leaving a great puzzle as to how associational and group life could be protected against an increasingly powerful state.

In its first two years, the French Revolution decisively broke with the French ancient constitutional tradition and abolished the rights and privileges of the *corps*. The merging of the Estates-General into the National Assembly and the abolition of feudal and clerical privileges in 1789 were followed by the nationalization of Church property, the suppression of monasteries and ecclesiastical orders, then by the Civil Constitution of the Clergy, which turned the clergy into state employees and demanded oaths of political loyalty from them. The preamble of the 1791 Constitution is devoted to announcing the end of a long list of "institutions which were injurious to liberty and equality of rights," but this was already the formalization of what had been legislated with astonishing rapidity. Provincial languages were eventually encompassed in the revolutionary attack on pluralism.

In later years, the unity of the (by then) Republic became increasingly dominant as a revolutionary theme. The Jacobin fusion of republican suspicion of faction with nationalist fervor generated a toxic view that pluralism was, as such, treasonous. But this was not, it seems to me, so central in 1789–91. Feudal and clerical privilege were hated for the power they gave nobles and bishops over others. Monastic vows were seen as demanding an unnatural forfeit of human liberty. The provinces came to be seen as tied to noble power, through the provincial Estates or the *parlements*. The abolition of privileges was motivated by a concern for liberty continuous with the concerns of Voltaire and the encyclopedists, not the Jacobins' republican–nationalist passion for collective unity.

But even in the first two years some observers worried about the concentration of state power necessary to remake society so quickly and radically, and about the resulting loss in institutions that could oppose that power. The treatment of the Church in particular—lands seized, monasteries suppressed, clergy forced to swear loyalty oaths and cut off from the magisterium they served—struck them as incompatible with religious liberty. In the years and decades after the Terror, even many who supported the liberal aims of 1789 grew to share these concerns. Debates about intermediacy and pluralism or centralization and rationalism in France were, for more than a century, hopelessly entangled with bitter quasi-partisan left–right disputes about the legacy of the Revolution.[1] But for some of those in the liberal center, support for 1789 coexisted with serious reservations about the turn to centralization and uniformity and concerns about despotism. Others lacked these reservations, and saw in the abolition of the *corps* the emergence of equal liberty.

Smith, Burke, and Paine

We begin in Britain. Burke's early reaction to the Revolution was more pluralist and ancient-constitutionalist in sensibility than has sometimes been noticed; in Paine's reply we see a classic statement of social contractarianism,

---

[1] See Jeremy Jennings, *Revolution and the Republic*, and Pierre Rosanvallon, *The Demands of Liberty: Civil Society in France since the Revolution* (Cambridge, Mass.: Harvard University Press, 2007) for the most important recent contributions to a massive literature.

with all the skepticism about pluralism that entails. Even before Burke, though, it seems that Adam Smith looked at the Revolution through Montesquieuian lenses.

Smith's writings show a striking skepticism about centralized states and intermediate *corps* alike. More than either Montesquieu or Voltaire (indeed, more than most of the theorists discussed in this study) he recognized the ways in which states and corporate groups might collude rather than compete, to the disadvantage of ordinary people. This was true in his own day of mercantilist collaboration between imperial states and the great monopolistic trading companies, the most important target of critique in *The Wealth of Nations*. But the dynamic was not a new one. His analysis of the guild system is mainly a critique of local power: the power of the master over the apprentice, who should have the liberty to enter a trade without years of servitude; the power of the guild over consumers as well as competitors; the power of the incorporated towns to protect their guilds, to everyone else's detriment.[2] However, he notes that the formal difference between the continental rule that guilds could self-organize and the rule in England requiring crown permission did not in fact restrain them. The state did not prevent guilds from arising or operating; it only extracted payment from them for the privilege. The central state was not somehow different in kind from the governments of the towns; both could be swayed to entrench the power of particular local groups.

Similarly, Smith argued that the Poor Laws allowing local parishes to exclude newcomers who might be indigent—enacted after Henry VIII abolished the monasteries on which many depended for charitable support—amounted to unjust local community power over the natural liberty of workers seeking work. Indeed, the restrictions placed on workers' ability to sell their labor by the Poor Laws and by the master–apprentice system are the two cases in *Wealth of Nations* in which Smith clearly moralizes the individual liberty to engage in economic activity.

Smith's analysis of religious competition—discussed later—was likewise attentive to the potential for collaboration between central state power and social group power. Unlike both Hobbes and Hume, Smith thought that civil war was driven by political contestation that drew in and made opportunistic use of religious factions, not by religious pluralism itself. And after such conflict, the victorious religious faction given establishment privileges by its

---

[2] This is where Smith makes his famous comment that "people of the same trade seldom meet together, even for merriment and diversion, but the conversation ends in some conspiracy against the publick, or in some contrivance to raise prices." Adam Smith, *An Inquiry Into the Nature and Causes of the Wealth of Nations*, Campbell, Skinner, and Todd, eds (Indianapolis: Liberty Fund, 1981[1776]), p. 145. When such people are corporately organized into a guild, they *must* meet together; and so towns that grant guild privileges are guaranteeing such conspiracies.

political coalition partners will become triumphantly vengeful, even if the sect had been a calm one beforehand. Smith's critique of religious establishments was thus partly a defense of the liberty of rival sects. It was also an analysis of the relations among groups of the powerful. The hazards of clerical power arose from church establishment, not from religious life as such; in turn the expansion of state power needed to control the clergy resulted from the authority religious establishment accorded them.

If Smith was especially concerned with cooperation between state and other power-holders, he nonetheless offered critical analyses of each separately.

The moral psychology of Smith's *Theory of Moral Sentiments* (henceforth *TMS*) suggests that we find it difficult to hold the powerful to proper moral account. *TMS* depends on a tacking back and forth between observed praise and abstract praiseworthiness, between normative judgments we observe and normative judgments we imagine being made by an impartial spectator. But those who are highly socially visible, and seem to enjoy a great deal of social approbation and esteem, distort that procedure.[3] The fact that they are esteemed makes them seem more estimable than they really are. They are flattered for being fashionable; they are admired for their wealth; they flout ordinary rules of morality and prudence, and seem only to rise in status as a result. He refers to this as a "corruption" of our moral sentiments—an unusual phenomenon in *TMS*, which is in large part an account of the beneficent moral learning that human beings naturally acquire through social interaction.

Though it is not quite Smith's intended point, we can see here an idea about a source of social power.[4] Non-elites tend to hold the elites they observe in undeservedly high regard; this will lead them to be insufficiently skeptical of their actions, and excessively compliant with norms they set. In turn, the high regard in which they are held will encourage elites to think undeservedly highly of *themselves*, and so to pay insufficient attention to the legitimate interests of others. Visibility and observation matter for this dynamic, as for much of moral learning in Smith. While distant elites may be more famous, and so more observable by more people, I think that on balance it is local elites Smith gives us the greater reason to distrust here. Personal observation, and personal knowledge of being observed, are especially powerful, and status comparisons with nearby persons are felt especially sharply. If, as Smith argues later in the book, we spontaneously feel greater attachment to closer communities than to more distant and abstract ones, the same would seem to hold true for those who stand high within those communities. For the "great mob

[3] Smith, *Theory of Moral Sentiments*, Part I Section III, and especially ch. III.
[4] Smith's primary concern here is with the bad behavior into which non-elites are drawn by seeking to emulate those who should not be emulated.

of mankind [who] are the admirers and worshippers...of wealth and greatness,"[5] it seems likely that the wealthy and great can thereby gain personal sway over them.

All of that said, Smith was also a sharp critic of power exercised at a great distance. By now it should be clear that Smith's portrait of the "man of system" has much in common with Montesquieu's account of the spirit of uniformity, and that the underlying idea is an important one for the pluralist tradition. And indeed Smith emphasizes that the man of system is most to be feared when in control of centralized political power:

> But to insist upon establishing, and upon establishing all at once, and in spite of all opposition, every thing which that idea may seem to require, must often be the highest degree of arrogance. It is to erect his own judgment into the supreme standard of right and wrong. It is to fancy himself the only wise and worthy man in the commonwealth, and that his fellow-citizens should accommodate themselves to him and not he to them. It is upon this account, that of all political speculators, sovereign princes are by far the most dangerous. This arrogance is perfectly familiar to them. They entertain no doubt of the immense superiority of their own judgment. When such imperial and royal reformers, therefore, condescend to contemplate the constitution of the country which is committed to their government, they seldom see any thing so wrong in it as the obstructions which it may sometimes oppose to the execution of their own will. They hold in contempt the divine maxim of Plato, and consider the state as made for themselves, not themselves for the state. The great object of their reformation, therefore, is to remove those obstructions; to reduce the authority of the nobility; to take away the privileges of cities and provinces, and to render both the greatest individuals and the greatest orders of the state, as incapable of opposing their commands, as the weakest and most insignificant.[6]

If this is true of the sovereign prince ruling over his own state, it is probably even more true of those who hold despotic power over *other* societies, societies with which they lack enough social connection to have even sentimental attachment to cities, provinces, or orders. This seems a fair description of the imperial rulers attacked in Book IV of *Wealth of Nations*, including the calculating merchants who rule over distant lands through the imperial trading companies. The officers of the British East India Company surely see that country as made for themselves and their instrumental use, not they for it; and any local nobles, provinces, or orders who might oppose their commands are so many obstacles to be removed.

The analysis of the man of system is Smith at his most negatively pluralist, driven by a distrust of rationalistic state power. But he offered a positive account of pluralism as well. Indeed, Smith's analysis of religious sects in

[5] Smith, *Theory of Moral Sentiments*, p. 62.   [6] Smith, *Theory of Moral Sentiments*, p. 234.

Book V of *WN* is perhaps the first great analysis of associational pluralism in liberal social theory.[7] Smith's friend David Hume had wryly suggested that the most "decent and advantageous thing" a statesman could do with priests was to "bribe their indolence" with public subsidy and establishment, in order to prevent the spiral of fanaticism that could arise from a competition of enthusiastic clergy seeking to make their living from the contributions of their flocks. The competitive religious market rewards those preachers who can instill fervor, attracting both more and more-devoted followers; the employees-of-the-cloth of a public religious establishment have no such incentive structure. Since the combination of religious fervor and religious disagreement provides the seeds of religious–civil conflict, the lesson is clear.

Smith quoted this argument at substantial length, then dissented from it in a number of ways. Most importantly, he insists upon the difference between a society with two or three religious sects, and one with many. The latter will certainly induce a competition among sects and among clergy, but the competition is much less like a civil war.[8] Smith viewed the enthusiasm likely to be encouraged by competition with much more sympathy than did Hume. Perhaps thinking of the then-burgeoning Wesleyan and Methodist revival, Smith suggested that a proliferation of vigorous, active churches could provide socialization and moral community for increasingly anonymous, and (therefore, on *TMS*'s argument) increasingly vice-prone, city life. The mobility defended earlier in *WN* as the exercise of natural liberty would detach persons from the community of personal acquaintances, and so discourage moral learning. The excessively enthusiastic and austere churches likely to find favor in a competitive environment could counterbalance those dangers.

My aim in Part II is to follow the development of rationalist and pluralist ideas, and their tendency to cluster, not to make lists of thinkers who fit under one category or the other. Although, from Montesquieu onward, we do not find theorists who are ever purely and simply one or the other, for the most part we do find one preponderant tendency, brought out by contrasting each theorist with one or more contemporaries. Smith is the exception. He advances the liberal social theory of group power, state power, and their collaboration in an unusually balanced way, and I do not pair him with any interlocutor because he develops his own contrasts so effectively.

Even the critique of the "man of system" is more complicated than it first appears, coming as it does in a discussion of problems of political faction. The spirit of system is not simply a flaw of rulers who imagine themselves to be

---

[7] Smith, *Wealth of Nations*, V.i.g, article iii, pp. 788–814.

[8] Compare Voltaire, "Presbyterians," in *Letters on England*, Leonard Tancock, trans. (Harmondsworth: Penguin Classics, 1980[1726–9]); and Madison, "No. 10," in *The Federalist Papers*. See also Richard Boyd, *Uncivil Society*.

great; it is a tendency that might be selected for by partisan contestation. At a moment when the need for reform is widely felt, moderate men of "humanity and benevolence" inclined to proceed carefully and ameliorate the worst harms, will lose out to the man who is "wise in his own conceit." Even here, in explaining the emergence of rationalistic planners, Smith is attentive to the unplanned dynamic and competitive effects he analyzes in commercial markets, religious pluralism, judicial systems, and state consolidation.[9]

It is noteworthy that Smith discusses, in the same argument, *both* the "sovereign prince" model of the rationalist man of system and the factional competition model that he, presumably, thought explained the early stages of the French Revolution. This is an especially early case of a theorist drawing a connection between the kind of aspirationally absolute monarch Montesquieu had criticized and the rationalism of the democratic centralizing state.

If there is a natural contrast figure for him it is perhaps Hegel, who aims to harmonize group and state power in a way that incorporates but transcends Smithian commercial society, and that finds liberty in that harmony. But that makes Hegel in an important sense a contrast to the whole dialectical narrative of Part II, and so we will defer consideration of his proposed synthesis to the concluding chapter.

Edmund Burke's and Thomas Paine's reactions to the French Revolution pose few such difficulties.

It is less controversial than it once was to think of Burke, a friendly acquaintance of Smith's, as a figure within the history of liberal thought.[10] It is certainly not *un*controversial. As Conor Cruise O'Brien notes, "several modern writers still cling to the position popularized in the 1790s by the Painite radicals and the Foxite Whigs: that Burke's hostility to the French Revolution made him an apostate from his previous liberal position."[11] But there is now a

---

[9] For Smith's pluralist-competitive account of legal and judicial systems, see *Wealth of Nations*, V.i.b, "Of the expense of Justice," especially pp. 718–20 on the relationships between, e.g., common law courts and the court of exchequer: "The fees of court seem originally to have been the principal support of the different courts of England. Each court endeavoured to draw to itself as much business as it could, and was, upon that account, willing to take cognizance of many suits which were not originally intended to fall under its jurisdiction... it came, in many cases, to depend altogether upon the parties before which court they would chuse to have their cause tried; and each court endeavoured, by superior dispatch and impartiality, to draw to itself as many causes as it could. The present admirable constitution of the courts of justice in England was, perhaps, originally in great measure, formed by this emuation, which antiently took place between their respective judges...," p. 720. See also Adam Smith, *Lectures on Jurisprudence*, Meek, Raphael and Stein, eds (Indianapolis: Liberty Fund, 1982), pp. 275–82, 422–6. For state consolidation, see Smith, *Wealth of Nations*, Book III, and much of the historical discussion in Smith, *Lectures on Jurisprudence*, e.g. 245–65.

[10] For a sharp and sophisticated treatment, and criticism, of Burke that considers him as fundamentally conservative, see Don Herzog, "Puzzling through Burke," 19(3) *Political Theory* 336–63, Aug. 1991.

[11] Conor C. O'Brien, *The Great Melody: A Thematic Biography and Commented Anthology of Edmund Burke* (Chicago: University of Chicago Press, 1992), p. 595.

general recognition that Burke was not simply a "reactionary," as Isaiah Berlin once called him.[12] Over the past 20 years the combined force of O'Brien's exposition of Burke as a pluralist Whig and the increased attention to colonialism and imperialism in the history of political thought have, at least, highlighted the side of Burke that is interesting for our purposes.[13]

Burke, like Montesquieu, was an ancient constitutionalist facing a modernizing world.[14] But for Montesquieu writing in France after Louis XIV, ancient constitutionalism had to be a reformist position. For Burke in Whig Britain, there could be, and was, a stronger sense of satisfaction with the status quo. The Stuarts, unlike Louis XIV, had been defeated, and the domestic British constitution largely (by Burke's lights) preserved and defended. That is not to say that Burke was content with British politics of his day. The constitutional settlement of 1688 was, he feared, jeopardized by the corruption of Parliament made possible by the trading companies' influence and wealth. And outside England itself, the British state often acted in defiance of traditional liberties. In America, India, and Ireland, imperial policy disrupted the freedom of subject peoples to live according to their own usages. In the debates before the American Revolution, Burke had depicted the Americans as common lawyers standing on traditional English rights. The innovation came from a Parliament set on uniformity and abstract rational principle: the principle of its own sovereign, absolute, undifferentiated right to legislate over the whole empire. Indeed, a central theme throughout his career is a distrust of "abstractions and universals."[15]

In the *Reflections*, Burke attacks the early stages of the Revolution in a number of ways that may not ultimately cohere. His celebration of Marie Antoinette, his evident fury at the forced removal of the royal family from Versailles, and his insistent disavowal of the supposed right to choose one's own kings leave an impression of monarchism that is at least partly misleading; and much of the book is best understood in a more Montesquieuian light. More of the book is devoted to the acts of suppression and nationalization taken against the Church, the monasteries, the provinces, and the *parlements*. The latter, "like the rest of the old government, stood in need of reform," but they were independent and "had furnished ... some considerable corrective to the vices and excesses of the monarchy." In traditional language, Burke

---

[12] See the exchange between O'Brien and Isaiah Berlin about whether and how to consider Burke a liberal pluralist—in Berlin's sense, related to but not the same as my sense in this book—O'Brien, *Great Melody*, pp. 612–18.

[13] See Jennifer Pitts, *A Turn to Empire* (Princeton: Princeton University Press, 2005), ch. 3 generally, and p. 277, fn 3 and 4, for a balanced account.

[14] See J. G. A. Pocock, "Burke and the Ancient Constitution—A Problem in the History of Ideas," 3(2) *The Historical Journal* 125–43, 1960.

[15] "Speech on the Petition of the Unitarian Society," in *Edmund Burke: Selected Writings and Speeches*, Peter J. Stanlis, ed. (Washington: Regnery Gateway, 1963[1792]), p. 313.

maintains that "[t]hey had been a safe asylum to secure these laws in all the revolutions of humor and opinion. They had saved that sacred deposit of the country during the reigns of arbitrary princes and the struggles of arbitrary factions. They kept alive the memory and record of the constitution."[16]

The abolition of the provinces Burke saw as, first, an act of the simple-minded "geometrical" mindset that preferred newly designed *départements* to traditional jurisdictions with traditional privileges; and, second, a deliberate elevation of centralized, Parisian power. Now that the provinces have been torn apart and replaced with too many tiny "square" units that lack any traditional authority, they cannot counterbalance against Paris' wildly dispro-portionate influence. The deliberate shattering of all regional identities will, Burke suggests, succeed too well. Once the Gascon, Picard, Breton, and Nor-man are destroyed, what will remain will not be devoted Frenchmen, but alienated subjects with no love of country at all. The traditional love of France was mediated through the provincial country.[17] The local square on the new administrative checkerboard will never inspire the same affection, and detach-ment will be the only result. Paris will gain in relative strength, as intended; but France as a whole will be weakened terribly.

Burke describes the dissolution of the *parlements* and the provinces as acts of foolish rationalistic hubris; but it is the destruction of traditional ecclesiastic institutions that rouses his passionate anger. It is both spoliation and sacri-lege, undermining security of property and freedom of religion. He expresses great sympathy for the charitable activities of the French monasteries. Such "corporate bodies" with "perennial existence" and staffed by devoted, selfless, benevolent men are a rare social resource.[18] They could not be called into being on demand; but where they have developed out of particular commit-ments, the wise statesman would draw on rather than dissolve.

Here as elsewhere, Burke sometimes dances around England's own history and sometimes distorts it. The looting and closing of the monasteries under Henry VIII is unmentioned, and he insists that no one in England would ever dream of nationalizing church property for state purposes. Indeed, he makes the astonishing claim that "little alteration" has been made in English eccle-siastical government "since the fourteenth or fifteenth century."[19] Ancient-constitutionalist Whigs tended to overstate the smooth continuity of the English past, and the Irish-descended Burke who defended Catholic liberty

[16] Edmund Burke, *Reflections on the Revolution in France* (Oxford: Oxford University Press, 1993 [1790]), p. 207.
[17] Burke, *Reflections*, pp. 174, 198. Compare this to Charles Taylor's notion of "deep diversity," and his discussion of the strength of belonging to a larger state in a way that is mediated through belonging to a minority nation. Charles Taylor, "Shared and Divergent Values," in *Reconciling the Solitudes* (Montreal and Kingston: McGill-Queen's University Press, 1993), p. 183.
[18] Burke, *Reflections*, p. 158.   [19] Burke, *Reflections*, p. 100.

in Ireland was careful not to offend sensibilities about England's own religious history, but eliding the Henrician Reformation altogether is especially egregious. But in a way he had no choice; he could not denounce the founding acts of Protestant England, but he would not excuse, pardon, or justify them. So he ignored them.

The *parlements*, the provinces, the Church and monasteries, and the Estates that brought them together had served as the core of an ancient constitution that wiser reformers would have recovered instead of overthrowing.

> Your privileges, though discontinued, were not lost to memory. Your constitution, it is true, whilst you were out of possession, suffered waste and dilapidation; but you possessed in some parts the walls and in all the foundations of a noble and venerable castle. You might have repaired those walls; you might have built on those old foundations. Your constitution was suspended before it was perfected, but you had the elements of a constitution very nearly as good as could be wished.[20]

The Estates featured properly incorporated "opposed and conflicting interests" in the same structure in a way that forces "compromise" and "moderation." Such "action and counteraction... from the reciprocal struggle of discordant powers, draws out the harmony of the universe," in politics as much as in physics. But the revolutionaries treated such counterbalancing of interests as "so great a blemish in your old and in our present constitution."

Instead of recovering their ancient constitution, the revolutionaries proceeded in contractarian fashion; "you chose to act as if you had never been molded into civil society and had everything to begin anew." And if it had proven too difficult to reclaim "ancient privileges" and "the almost obliterated constitution of your ancestors," other options remained. One was to imaginatively reach further back in time to "a more early race of ancestors," i.e. to reclaim a Gothic constitution. The other was to look to England, which "had kept alive the ancient principles and models of the old common law of Europe meliorated and adapted to its present state." Any of these could have left France with "a free constitution, a potent monarchy, a disciplined army, a reformed and venerated clergy, a mitigated but spirited nobility to lead your virtue [... and] a liberal order of commons."

This account of the path not taken is odd at first glance. If the old constitution was in fact too decayed to conserve and rebuild, if incremental reform was not an option, then why imagine oneself to be recovering it? If there were useful lessons to be learned from England's constitution, why not simply learn them, rather than pretending that England was being used as an epistemic shortcut to learn about France's own ancient constitution? A part of Burke's

---

[20] Burke, *Reflections*, p. 35. The quotations in the next two paragraphs are all from pp. 35–7.

answer is that such imaginative discipline would have moderated rationalistic hubris. In his retelling of the Glorious Revolution, the men of 1688 seem to have found themselves with the power to remake the constitution, and wisely rid themselves of it. The pretense of restoring an old order, even if innovation was in fact unavoidable, limited their *awareness* of the power they held, and so limited the danger that they would use it to its full extent.

Cultivating an attitude of veneration for custom and tradition thus would have weeded out those who were especially not to be trusted with reforming power: the "turbulent, discontented men of quality...puffed up with personal pride and arrogance, [who] generally despise their own order." Those whose sentiments tied them to a local unit rather than alienating them from it were more to be trusted with governance of general affairs. As he famously put it, "To be attached to the subdivision, to love the little platoon we belong to in society, is the first principle (the germ as it were) of public affections. It is the first link in the series by which we proceed towards a love to our country, and to mankind."[21]

The other part of Burke's answer is that pluralistic institutions are difficult to either commit to rationalistically or to attach oneself to sentimentally. I am attached to my little platoon and you to yours, and we might each fight to protect our own, whether it be a privileged class or a province. This, however, doesn't tie either of our affections to the whole system in which your platoon and mine coexist; the localist is not a committed pluralist. Under a well-functioning system this might not matter, as the various local attachments would balance out, generating moderation and liberty. But in times of constitutional choice it poses a real problem. The history and tradition of the whole constitutional order, the wisdom of our ancestors in developing such a balanced system, the identification of the pluralistic order with the overall *patrie*, can supply the missing motivational commitment. So the constitutional chooser who imagines himself recovering a long-lost system, out of love and veneration for what has come before, will be more likely to choose a balanced and pluralistic order. Burke thinks that such orders are what is to be found in the past, if one looks; the "harmony of the universe" tends to encourage them. But historical truth is not the chief commitment, any more than it is for domestic English ancient constitutionalism. If, when one looks to history, one finds an absolute monarchy, one should keep looking, deeper and farther back, for a free and pluralistic constitution.

Thomas Paine united ideas in a powerful combination that came to seem natural to later Americans, but that no one else had put together in quite the same fashion: the social contract, natural rights, representative democratic

---

[21] Burke, *Reflections*, pp. 46–7.

government, and enacted constitutions. He held that enacted constitutions literally *were* social contracts, so that between the severing of ties with Britain and the adoption of the several state constitutions, Americans were returned to the state of nature and resumed their natural rights. And enacted constitutions on the new American model were the only constitutions worthy of the name. While Paine did not inaugurate the American idea that Britain lacked a constitution because it lacked a written text of that name, he did more than anyone to transform it from a debating point specific to the American Revolution into a general principle. This left no room whatsoever for ancient constitutionalism.[22]

His ideas in *Common Sense* and *The Rights of Man* undoubtedly owe something to Locke, but the debt was likely indirect; there is little evidence of Paine being well-read in law and philosophy in the way that the other leading intellectuals of the American Revolution and founding were. He proceeded from simple, foundational principles—discernible, after all, to mere "common sense"—and embraced the idea of an emerging "age of reason" more passionately and uncomplicatedly than perhaps any other political thinker of his era. What followed was a celebration of rational simplicity in governing forms, and a disdain for both tradition and complication.

Paine detested monarchy as a form of government. The radicalism of *Common Sense* lay not only in its early call for American independence from the British crown, but also in its transformation of the American cause into an ideological rejection of monarchy as such. It was a ridiculous system, guaranteeing regular succession by children or the incompetent, and leading to recurring, devastating wars between rival claimants. But, as with Burke, his memorable rhetoric about monarchy can mislead. He accepts Burke's claim that Louis XVI had been a "mild" king. *The Rights of Man* has no venom for Louis, whose execution Paine was to oppose a few years later, at his own peril. Indeed, he held that the despotism of the old regime had not really been a matter of central royal power.

> Every office and department has its despotism, founded upon custom and usage. Every place has its Bastille, and every Bastille its despot...There were, if I may so express it, a thousand despotisms to be reformed in France...Between the monarchy, the parliament, and the church, there was a *rivalship* of despotism; besides

---

[22] See James Tully, *Strange Multiplicity* (Cambridge: Cambridge University Press, 1995). Tully treats Paine as an exemplar of the central ideas of modern liberal constitutionalism; I think he was an outlier in his thoroughgoing rationalism. Post-revolutionary liberal constitutionalism did not in general radically break with pluralist ancient constitutionalism. But Tully is certainly right that *Paine* so broke; and if there was a radical rupture, Paine is the right thinker to choose as its personification.

the feudal despotism operating locally, and the ministerial despotism operating everywhere.[23]

As with Burke's distrust of principles and abstraction, Paine's distrust of normative or institutional complexity predated the French Revolution. In *Common Sense* he wrote that "the more *simple* any thing is, the less likely it is to be disordered, and the easier repaired when disordered."[24] Absolute monarchy, however "ridiculous," at least had the virtue of making clear who was responsible for oppression; under the British hybrid constitution, no such clarity was possible.

The defense of simplicity in government was strong enough to be picked up by defenders of the Bourbon state. The first French translation of *Common Sense* appeared within months of its American publication—in an anti-English propaganda journal secretly funded by the French foreign ministry, *Affaires de l'Angleterre et de l'Amérique*.[25] The journal's editor (Edmé-Jacques Genêt, father of the future controversial ambassador to the U.S., writing under the pseudonym "a London banker") interrupted the translated text at several points with long commentary of his own—praising Paine's indictment of the British mixed constitution as a confused kind of anarchy, and assimilating Paine's endorsement of simplicity in government to the doctrine of unlimited monarchy. When Paine says that in America the law will be king, Genêt is happy to point out the similarities this has to the anti-*parlementaire* view that in France the King is the law. Indeed, Genêt suggests that "the author of *Common Sense* [...] does not at all believe in the possibility of the democracy he proposes. There may be no American better disposed than he for a hereditary monarchy. It follows naturally from his principle of simplicity [...] That which he detests is a mixed government, a limited monarchy."[26] As further evidence that *Common Sense* supports the Bourbons in their struggle against the ancient constitutionalists, he notes Paine's endorsement of a centralized continental union and uses it as a criticism of provincial liberties.

In fact, of course, Paine always joined an anti-hereditary principle to his commitment to simplicity. While he harbored no personal fury against the French king, he was an early enthusiast for ending, not merely limiting, the monarchy, arguing against the Abbé Sieyès' Montesquieuian worries that

[23] *Rights of Man*, in Thomas Paine, *Rights of Man, Common Sense, and Other Political Writings*, Mark Philp, ed. (Oxford: Oxford World Classics, 1995[1791]), pp. 98–9.
[24] *Common Sense*, in Paine, *Writings*, p. 7.
[25] *Common Sense* was mistakenly referred to in the journal as being written by Benjamin Franklin and Samuel Adams, since Paine was an unknown. Franklin's celebrity in France encouraged Genêt to attribute a great many things to him, even before Franklin arrived in Paris as ambassador and became Genêt's most important source for documents as well as a contributor to the journal in his own right. References are to *Affaires de l'Angleterre et de l'Amérique*, Tome 1, vol. IV, 1776; consulted at La Bibliothèque Nationale de France.
[26] *Affaires*, I.IV, pp. 62–3, 1776. My translation.

France was too large to be a republic. For Paine, unlike any of the major European contractarians (even Rousseau), the theory of rational consent to sovereign government demanded politics that was democratic–republican in form, and excluded monarchy in principle. Consent was not only needed at the level of justification, as in Hobbes, or at the level of legislation, as in Locke, Rousseau, and Kant, but at the level of the choice of governors on an ongoing basis. This was a very significant change. But it did nothing to alter the institutional absolutism of social contract models, their hostility to claims of prescription and plurality.

Tracy and Constant

Antoine Louis Claude, Comte Destutt de Tracy was one of the primary intellectual forces in the group of rationalist radical liberals who came to be known as *Idéologues*. Indeed the name was derived from his own work, as he coined the term "ideology" and used it to describe his own overarching intellectual project.[27] Tracy was a noble who helped to write the *cahiers* of his region's nobility and who subsequently served as a delegate to the Estates-General (where he renounced his title and joined the Third Estate; his title was returned to him under the Restoration) and then as a member of the Constituent Assembly. There he became close to the groups surrounding Lafayette, Sieyès, and Madame Helvetius. He wrote an early reply to Burke's attacks on the Revolution, which, among other things, claimed that the provinces whose ancient liberties Burke mourned the loss of had enthusiastically surrendered them, and that the whole of the French nation was united in its desire to be politically unified. (This was both dubious as an account of political history and overoptimistic as prophecy; three years later, a provincial federalist revolt broke out.)[28]

Under the Directory, he became one of the leading lights of the *Idéologues*, a group attached to the journal *La Décade Philosophique* and personally and intellectually associated with Condorcet until the latter's death. Some members of the Coppet group around Madame de Staël regularly took part in the *Idéologues'* discussions as well, or were otherwise close to them. Constant in

---

[27] For the biographical and historical information in the following paragraphs I am indebted to Cheryl B. Welch, *Liberty and Utility*; Gilbert Chinard, *Jefferson et les Ideologues* (Paris: Les Presses Universitaires de France, 1925); Brian Head, *Ideology and Social Science: Destutt de Tracy and French Liberalism* (Dordrecht, M. Nijhoff; Boston, Hingham, MA, 1985); Jennings, *Revolution and the Republic*.

[28] Destutt, de Tracy, *M. de Tracy a M. Burke* (Paris: Imprimerie Nationale, 1790).

particular traveled easily between the two groups; Sieyès had links with both as well; and members of both groups were close to Lafayette.[29]

The *Idéologues* in general were characterized by an unflagging republicanism that endured through the Empire and the Restoration; by *laissez-faire* views in economics and a commitment to private property; by a methodology very reminiscent of Bentham's in its rationalism, its distrust of reified abstractions such as rights, and its individualist and sensationalist understanding of human interests; and by atheism and skepticism about "superstition" in general. They carried forward the intellectual projects of not only the *philosophes* but the Physiocrats as well, and were in their time France's most accomplished economists. (Jean-Baptiste Say was one of their group in later years.) Their political positions roughly tracked those of Lafayette until the latter rejected revolution and endorsed the July Monarchy in 1830; they were anti-Jacobin, antiroyalist, anticlerical, and anti-Bonapartist.

Tracy, like some other members of the *Idéologue* camp, became a Senator under Bonaparte. The latter openly disdained them, coining the description *idéologue* as a term of derision (Tracy's *idéologie* was the name of his science of ideas). Still, by providing them with status in his regime, he somewhat blunted their open criticism of him for a number of years. Tracy twice served under Lafayette in the army, and in 1802 they became in-laws: his daughter married George Washington Lafayette, the Marquis' son.

Not long afterward, Lafayette sent then-President Jefferson a copy of the first (and only then-completed) volume of Tracy's work on ideology, beginning a long service as an intermediary between the two. "No doubt it was at his [Jefferson's] request that Destutt de Tracy was admitted as an associate member" of the American Philosophical Society in 1806.[30] But Jefferson's most important services to Tracy had to await the end of the former's Presidency.

In 1811 a Philadelphia publisher close to Jefferson, William Duane, brought out a book-length *Commentary and Review of Montesquieu's Spirit of the Laws*, with no authorship attributed. A preface claimed that the author was French-born but had fled Robespierre's rule for America, where he still lived. In fact the author had never visited the United States; it was Tracy, fearful of publishing the work under his own name while Bonaparte was in power. Jefferson translated the work and arranged for its publication, calling it "the most valuable work of the present age"[31] and hoping that "it will become the

---

[29] See Lloyd S. Kramer, "Liberal Theory and the Critique of Bonapartism: Lafayette, Destutt de Tracy, and Benjamin Constant," 19(2) *Proceedings of the Consortium on Revolutionary Europe, 1750–1850*, 495–508, 1990; Lloyd Kramer, *Lafayette in Two Worlds: Public Cultures and Personal Identities in an Age of Revolution* (Chapel Hill, N.C.: University of North Carolina Press, 1998).

[30] Gilbert Chinard, *Jefferson et les Idéologues*, p. 40, my translation.

[31] Thomas Jefferson, Letter to William Duane, August 12, 1810, in Martin Segal, ed., *Thomas Jefferson, Writings* (New York: The Library of America, 1984), p. 1227.

elementary book of the youth at all our colleges." (He successfully urged its adoption as a required text at William and Mary.) It was a work that "I think will form an epoch in the science of government, and which I wish to see in the hands of every American student, as the elementary and fundamental institute of that important branch of human science."[32] In the course of reading Jefferson offered his grandson, the *Commentary* followed only Locke and Sidney as works on "general politics." His not-yet-published translation of Tracy's *Political Economy* stood alongside now-much-better-known works by Malthus and Say, and replaced *The Wealth of Nations* altogether; Jefferson considered *Political Economy* to have communicated all of Smith's truths more succinctly and to have advanced on him in important respects.[33]

Jefferson's educational writings and his plans for the University of Virginia not only show the clear mark of Tracy's arguments about knowledge, but also adopt Tracy's divisions of the disciplines. He named "ideology" as one of the basic divisions of philosophy (along with ethics; the law of nature and nations; government; and political economy)[34] at a time when few Americans had heard of the word. His draft School Bill for Virginia of 1817 similarly lists "ideology, ethics, the law of nature and nations" as forming one of the "branches of science" to be taught by the proposed new university. This arrangement persisted into his 1818 "Report of the Commissioners Appointed to Fix the Site of the University of Virginia" that laid out the plan for professorships at the university and the fields of knowledge each was to cover.

Let us return to the *Commentary*, this "most valuable work of the present age," this book that formed a new "epoch in the science of government," this now-almost-unknown work that Jefferson placed alongside Locke and Sidney and ahead of Montesquieu himself. The *Commentary* offers a book-by-book critique and reconstruction of *The Spirit of the Laws*, occasionally going through a chapter almost line-by-line, often critiquing an entire book in a few pages.[35] Often through the work Tracy purports to derive the essential truths from Montesquieu's notoriously chaotic presentation—but these "truths" are inevitably republican and libertarian truths, recognizing only the sovereignty of the people on one hand and the liberty of persons on the other. Whenever Montesquieu's views are unambiguously on the side of

---

[32] Letter to Dr. Thomas Cooper, January 16, 1814, in *Thomas Jefferson, Writings*, p. 1321.

[33] The influence of Tracy and the other ideologues on Jefferson is little discussed in American Jeffersonalia. For the two most important exceptions, see Joyce Appleby, "What Is Still American in the Political Philosophy of Thomas Jefferson?" 39(2) *William and Mary Quarterly* 287–309, 1982; and Adrienne Koch, *The Philosophy of Thomas Jefferson* (New York: Columbia University Press, 1943). See also Chinard, *Jefferson et les Idéologues*.

[34] Letter to Peter Carr, September 7, 1814, in *Thomas Jefferson, Writings*, p. 1346.

[35] Destutt de Tracy, *A Commentary and Review of Montesquieu's The Spirit of the Laws* (henceforth *Commentary*), Thomas Jefferson, trans. (New York: Burt Franklin, 1969[1811]), pp. 12–14. All further quotations will be from the Jefferson translation. The Franklin edition is a reproduction of the 1811 Duane printing, so pagination remains the same.

complexity, diversity, intermediate bodies, and balances of power, Tracy attacks them. "This system of balancing," for example, "I consider as erroneous and indefensible; it originates in imperfect combinations, which confer powers of defense on particular personages, under the idea of protecting them from the general interest."[36] For a monarchy or aristocracy established by democratic delegation Tracy admits some patience; for the British hybrid constitution almost none; and for the American constitution, tremendous admiration. Tracy has a great deal to say about representation, and offers one of the earliest full arguments on behalf of the democratic and republican merits of the practice.

About intermediate powers Tracy says much the same that he does about balances of powers or interests: if sovereignty vests in the people, then an intermediate body with rights to resist (whether hereditary or not) is necessarily an illegitimate partial interest. From Book XIX's discussion of the relationship among laws and manners of legal reform that is out of step with mores, e.g. Peter the Great's proscription of beards, Tracy claims that only one good principle can be extracted: that "for the best laws it is necessary that the mind should first be prepared by cultivation." Tracy finds in this principle yet another argument for representative democracy, which will ensure that the laws will not be out of step with the "general disposition of the nation."[37] Montesquieu's other arguments for legislative caution, for leaving habits and manners alone, for not seeking to correct all errors, are rapidly dismissed.

Montesquieu's historical analyses are unsurprisingly of no interest to Tracy. All of Part VI except for Book XXIX ("On the manner in which laws should be composed") he skips over, writing that these books are "purely historical" and so "I shall not examine them."[38] (To be sure, many other readers have been similarly indifferent to them.) In lieu of an extended commentary of his own on Book XXIX, Tracy appends a previously unpublished essay by his late associate Condorcet, "Observations on the Twenty-Ninth Book of the *Spirit of the Laws*."[39] Even more than the *Commentary* itself, this essay provides a

---

[36] Tracy, *Commentary*, p. 117.   [37] Tracy, *Commentary*, p. 203.

[38] Tracy, *Commentary*, p. 256; see also p. 259.

[39] The *Commentary* also includes two letters ostensibly written by Helvetius on the occasion of the former's reading of a draft of *The Spirit of the Laws*. One to Montesquieu himself complains that "you compromise with prejudice" and "give human genius a retrograde motion" by giving aid and comfort to "aristocrats, and our petty despots of all grades" through his endless talk of "balanced powers" and "intermediaries." Tracy, *Commentary*, pp. 285–9. The second, to a mutual friend, complained further of the book's entanglement with feudalism and barbarism. There seems to be good reason to doubt the attribution to Helvetius, and to suspect a forgery by the editor of a Revolution-era collection of Helvetius' papers. See discussion and citations in Rahe, *Montesquieu and the Logic of Liberty*, pp. 211–12. But there does not seem to be any reason to doubt that Tracy and Jefferson believed them to be genuine. The letters have sometimes been used as support for readings of Montesquieu like the one I offered in the previous chapter (and as evidence against readings like Rahe's): if a leading philosopher of Montesquieu's own day viewed him as dangerously close to the forces of aristocratic reaction, then that's reason to doubt that he was

ringing encapsulation of the rationalist case against Montesquieu's philosophy. In discussing the chapter "Of the spirit of the legislator," Condorcet simply observes that

> I do not understand what is contained in this... chapter; but I know that the spirit of a legislator ought to be justice... It is not by the spirit of moderation, but by the spirit of justice, that criminal laws should be mild, that civil laws should tend to equality, and the laws of the municipal administration to liberty and prosperity.[40]

Condorcet's greatest criticism is reserved for the chapter on uniformity. It "obtained for Montesquieu the indulgence of all the prejudiced people, of all those who detest light, of all the protectors and participators in abuse." Montesquieu's defense of allowing a plurality of systems of weights and measures can only serve dishonest businessmen. "Uniformity in laws may be established without trouble, and without producing any evil effects by the change"; and

> As truth, reason, justice, the rights of man, the interests of property, of liberty, of security, are in all places the same; we cannot discover why all the provinces of a state, or even all states, should not have the same civil and criminal laws, and the same laws relative to commerce. A good law should be good for all men. A true proposition is true every where.[41]

This is the crux of the argument for uniformity—and, necessarily, an indictment of decentralized institutions that might come to different conclusions, and of the idea that morally desirable liberty could be found in a patchwork of such institutions. Indeed I think it is one of the sharpest expressions of the rationalist philosophical distrust of institutional pluralism ever written.

And so, for all of Tracy's radical *laissez-faire* individualism, for all that he could say that "society consists only in a continual succession of *exchanges*, and exchange is a transaction of such a nature that both contracting parties always gain by it,"[42] his non-interventionism found limits. Rationalist imperatives could take priority over the commitment to liberty. During the late 1790s, when Tracy developed the ideas that would culminate in his multivolume *Elements of Ideology*, he played a leading role in the politics of education. Believing as he did that forming ideas based on the evidence of the senses would lead to rational beliefs about morality and politics, he saw the Catholic influence on education—which, of course, was founded on claims that could *not* be derived from the evidence of the senses—as deeply

---

really a republican. But I am persuaded that the letters are of sufficiently doubtful provenance that they don't add much evidentiary weight.

[40] Tracy, *Commentary*, p. 261.   [41] Tracy, *Commentary*, pp. 273–4.

[42] Tracy, *A Treatise on Political Economy* (New York: Augustus M. Kelley, 1970[1817]), pp. xvi–xvii.

pernicious. He came to argue that the establishment of republican liberty depended on aggressive action against the Church, both through an educational system that rigorously excluded it and through continued limits on its power.[43] Church superstition rendered people intellectually incapable of seeing the truths revealed by science and philosophy; in the name of freedom, state action was needed to protect them from coming under its influence.

The thoroughgoing democracy and republicanism of the *Commentary* prevented its publication in French, or Tracy's name from being attached to it, until 1818. The shared antipathy toward Bonaparte is one of few points of agreement with the roughly contemporaneous work of Benjamin Constant, the Swiss-born Protestant thinker who came to Paris in the 1790s, fled Napoleonic rule, then returned to a long career as a Restoration liberal theorist and politician, including an ill-fated collaboration with Bonaparte during the Hundred Days.

Constant and Tracy were at least friendly acquaintances during the 1790s, and their connection resumed after Constant's return to France after Bonaparte's fall. Their strongest ties were probably through Lafayette, to whom both were close and who sometimes brought them together in political causes. While Constant is now much better known in the English-speaking world than Tracy, they were, for a time, paired as probably the two most influential liberals in the world. Their works were standard references not only during the era of liberal agitation and constitutional reform in Spain, but also, indeed more so, in Latin American revolutions and constitutional struggles of the 1810s and after.

Constant's intellectual inspirations were quite different from Tracy's. His education included time in Scotland; not only the social thought of Hume, Ferguson, and Smith but also sentimentalism in moral theory seems to have left an imprint on him. Later in Germany he met Goethe and Schiller, and romanticism influenced his developing understanding of individuality and personality, an understanding quite at odds with the rational processors of sense-perception one finds in *idéologie*. A particular kind of Protestant sensibility about the individual soul remained with him his whole life.

Montesquieu's example was much on Constant's mind as he composed his works in exile: the manuscript that comes to us as *Fragments of an Abandoned Work on the Possibility of a Republican Constitution in a Large Country* as well as the writings that would become the *Principes de Politique* of 1806–10, two urtexts which together provide the substance (and most of the words) of Constant's later political writings. (The two were originally envisioned as

---

[43] See Helena Rosenblatt, *Liberal Values, Benjamin Constant and the Politics of Religion* (Cambridge: Cambridge University Press, 2008), pp. 46–8; Tracy, *Observation sur le système actuel d'instruction publique* (Paris: Panckoucke, 1801).

one *Spirit of the Laws*-style opus.) As he read Montesquieu while trying to write his own work, he wrote in his journal, "What a keen and profound eye! All that he said, even in the smallest things, proves true every day."[44]

Constant's key chapter criticizing centralization and uniformity—found in the *Principes* text and published in his anti-Napoleonic 1814 pamphlet, *The Spirit of Conquest and Usurpation* (henceforth *SCU*)—was a careful one. While he gives weight to people's attachments to custom and tradition, he insists that time can never help to sanctify abuses such as slavery. He freely admits that some kinds of local diversity may be irrational on their face and would never be constructed deliberately. But he maintains that this is not an appropriate standard of evaluation when deciding what to do with already-existing diversity.

He argues both against the spirit of system that accompanies and initiates governors' desire to rationalize, and in defense of the sentiments that attach people to their local traditions and rules. He embraces the idea of change and progress, but insists that it should be allowed to come in its own time and by free choice. Freedom of exit from monastic institutions should be allowed, rather than shutting the institutions down; an irrational winding road might prompt the construction of a straight one, but there is no need for a concomitant ban on the use of the former.

Constant offers an argument that goes a crucial step beyond either Smith's "man of system" or Montesquieu's chapter on uniformity, and lacking the attribution of deliberate malice one finds in Burke. The desire to create order and rationality in society need not be destructive in itself; but it is too-easily joined with force. "The spirit of system was first entranced by symmetry. The love of power soon discovered what immense advantages symmetry could procure for it."[45] A kind of philosophical aesthetic motivated benevolent legislators in the first instance; but the desire for uniformity led to the destruction of non-state institutions, enhancing the relative power of the center and creating a dynamic that outraced that initial public-spirited impulse.

With Montesquieu, he holds that the provincial variety of legal customs in the old regime was not a fault worth correcting.

> When I see the indignation that Voltaire and so many other writers affect to feel in the face of those numerous and opposed customs which coexisted in France, I wonder at the errors to which they were led by their love of symmetry. 'What,' they cry out, 'two portions of the same empire are subjected to different laws because they are separated by a hill or a stream of water! Is justice not the same on

---

[44] Constant, *Journaux Intimes*, January 28, 1804, in *Œuvres*, Roulin, ed. (Paris: Gallimard, 1957).
[45] Constant, "On Uniformity," in *The Spirit of Conquest and Usurpation and Their Relation to European Civilization* (1814), in Fontana, ed., *Political Writings* (Cambridge: Cambridge University Press, 1988), p. 74. Compare this thought to James Scott, *Seeing Like A State*.

the two sides of a hill, or on the two banks of a stream of water?' But laws are not justice: they were merely forms to administer it . . . [46]

Even in a post-Revolutionary world, Constant saw that there was a strong connection between pluralist freedom and traditions and customs. He rejected the impulse to constitutionally make the world anew, admitting that it would make no sense to create provincial variety in laws on a blank slate but denying that that told us anything about maintaining such pluralism where it existed.

In *SCU's* criticism of the centralization and rationalization of political life under Bonaparte, of the Napoleonic Code and the suppression of local loyalties and culture, Constant modestly suggests that there is little point in adding to Montesquieu's own writings on uniformity. But his two chapters on the subject—one in the original edition of *The Spirit of Conquest* and one added to later editions—arguably surpass Montesquieu's brief pages on the subject in their clarity and the quality of their argument. Stripped of Montesquieu's obscure references and of Burke's rhetorical excesses, and explicitly normative in a way that Tocqueville's *Old Regime* was not to be, they provide what may be the liberal canon's most effective defense of institutional diversity, cultural variety, and local autonomy—as powerful a short case for pluralism as Condorcet's response to Montesquieu is for rationalism.

I should note that there is some controversy over how much importance to assign to *SCU* in general and to these two chapters in particular. Stephen Holmes has been eager to downplay the importance of these passages from Constant in order to draw a bright line between Constant on one hand and Montesquieu, Burke, de Staël, and Tocqueville on the other.[47] He insists that they were an unfortunate result of Constant's brief 1814 attempt to make common cause with royalist exiles against Bonaparte. I find this unpersuasive, for reasons both biographical and intellectual. Biographically, the arguments in the two key chapters seem to me insufficiently different from their counterparts in the 1810 *Principes de Politique*; and we know that Constant's sympathetic engagement with Montesquieu dates to those years in exile, not to a sudden political need during the Empire's final stage.

Intellectually, while it is true that Constant was almost always an opponent of the hereditary aristocracy,[48] his relationship with the Montesquieuian tradition was closer and more complex than Holmes suggests. His views on

---

[46] Constant, *Conquest and Usurpation*, in *Political Writings*, p. 154; compare the paraphrase of Voltaire to the passage from Condorcet's "Observations."

[47] This relates to Holmes' long-term intellectual project of tying liberalism unambiguously to the modern state with its absolutist ancestry, and of distinguishing liberalism sharply from anti-statism, or ancient constitutionalism. My own view, of course, is that liberalism necessarily draws on both sources, and that Constant nicely embodies the tension between them. See Holmes, *Benjamin Constant and the Making of Modern Liberalism* (New Haven: Yale University Press, 1984).

[48] Though he was "far from approving the rigors" applied to the aristocracy during the Revolution. "De Madame de Staël et de ses ouvrages," in *Mélanges* (1829), in *Œuvres*, p. 879.

the questions at hand did change over the course of his life, but there are clear thematic continuities that mark attempts to adapt Montesquieuian constitutionalism rather than radically breaking with it.[49] I think, too, that Holmes is torn between his deep admiration for Constant and his commitment to a strong-state centralizing liberalism that owes more to Hobbes and Bodin than to Montesquieu—in a word, to rationalism.[50] He tries to save Constant for liberalism as best as he knows how, by insisting that he is no conservative. But with the idea of pluralist liberalism in mind, we can make clearer sense of Constant's views and commitments. He needs no rescuing, and the concerns in the uniformity chapters are central to his liberalism, not exceptions from it. They are indeed typical of much that he wrote on other topics and in other places.

Constant defended the proliferation of sects and denominations as a positive good, and as in any case inevitable wherever persons cared about religious questions enough to think about them, rather than mindlessly following empty rituals. Schism and proliferation tended to improve the moral purity of all sects, as the Reformation improved a previously corrupt Catholicism; it also conduced to civil peace.

In *Principes (1810)* and elsewhere he indicts the tendencies toward uniformity of centralized and metropolitan legislatures. The members of the latter tend to acquire an *esprit de corps*, identifying with each other and with the capital. So they

> lose sight of the usages, needs, and way of life of their constituents. They lend themselves to general ideas of leveling, symmetry, uniformity, mass changes, and universal recasting, bringing upset, disorder, and confusion to distant regions. It is this disposition we must combat, because it is on particular memories, habits, and regional laws that the happiness and peace of a province rest. National assemblies are scornful and careless with these things.[51]

Constant, like Tracy, wrote a work that is in an important sense a book-length response to Montesquieu, though it was never completed. It comes to us as the *Fragments of an abandoned work on the possibility of a republican*

---

[49] By contrast, Biancamaria Fontana, *Benjamin Constant and the Post-Revolutionary Mind* (New Haven: Yale University Press, 1991), appreciates much more clearly Constant's closeness to Montesquieu as well as his distance from him.

[50] Holmes' most explicit arguments on these scores postdate his book on Constant; see *Passions and Constraints* (Chicago: University of Chicago Press, 1995); and Holmes and Sunstein, *The Cost of Rights*. But I do not think that I am being anachronistic; Holmes' Constant book contains clear hints and indications of what is to come in his work from the 1990s.

[51] Constant, Book XV ch. 4, "Application of This Principle to the Composition of Representative Assemblies," in *Principles of Politics Applicable to All Governments*, Dennis O'Keeffe, trans. (Indianapolis: Liberty Fund, 2003), p. 328. "This principle" is the defense of local patriotism of city and province, of the "local interests and memories" that provide a salutary "principle of resistance" against the state, offered at the end of the immediately preceding chapter "On Uniformity."

constitution in a large state, a possibility Montesquieu famously denied and one that Constant was at pains to establish.[52] This work, dedicated to refuting one of the best-known of Montesquieu's arguments, is nonetheless steeped in Montesquieu's intellectual style and ideas; it is very little like the rationalist, philosophical *Commentary* that Tracy was composing at the same time.[53]

Constant understood that Montesquieu's skepticism was not aimed at the idea of *freedom* in a large state but at the idea of freedom in a republic. He thought that Montesquieu had looked at the virtuous, anti-commercial, unfree republics of antiquity and attributed those features to *republics*, when they were better attributed to the ancient era.[54]

This was Constant's position throughout his life: that freedom was possible in a large and extended republic, and that much of what Montesquieu attributed to the spirit of a nation or of its laws is in fact attributable to the spirit of the age. Constant's political agenda never included the recreation of the ancient constitution of Montesquieu's time. But he sympathized with Montesquieu's defense of that constitution and tried to draw appropriate lessons from it; he did not (as Tracy did) view it as a defense of local tyranny and arbitrariness. On the central claim that intermediate bodies, a hereditary class, and corporations were essential for freedom, Constant split the difference between Montesquieu's view and Tracy's. Under a free government there would be no need for such things; but Montesquieu had been right to see them as the bulwarks of freedom against the king of his era. Their irrationality and inegalitarianism did not condemn them out of hand; uniformity under a tyrannical law was, for Constant as for Montesquieu, no virtue.

Constant criticized the idea of hereditary rights of rule and the existence of a hereditary principle in a constitution. But his understanding of Montesquieu's defense of such things was that under an "abusive" government,

> heredity can be useful; where rights have disappeared, privileges offer asylum and defense. In spite of its inconveniences, heredity is better than the absence of any neutral power. The hereditary interest...creates a sort of neutrality.[55] In order to dispose of heredity, it is necessary to have an excellent constitution. Montesquieu knew this; under the pressure of despotism there is a terrible leveling equality.[56]

---

[52] The "Fragments" belong to the same era as the initial *Principes de Politique*—roughly 1806–10—and were written alongside them. I find no evidence that Constant knew of Madison's argument in *Federalist* #10 about the possibility of an extended republic, but there are strong affinities between Constant's ideas and Madison's.

[53] I am unaware of any reason to think that Constant and Tracy communicated during Constant's exile. The *Commentary* and *Republican Constitution* were written contemporaneously but probably entirely independently.

[54] Constant, "Liberty of the Ancients Compared with that of the Moderns," in *Political Writings*.

[55] The supposed neutrality of the aristocratic class was closely linked with their judicial role in the House of Lords and the *parlements*. Generating a neutral power that could take the place of the hereditary class was a long-term preoccupation of Constant's constitutional thought.

[56] Constant, *Fragments*, Henri Grange, ed. (Paris: Aubier, 1991[1810]), p. 118.

Constant agreed that a monarchy depended on an aristocracy in order to protect freedom; he insisted that the reverse was also true (a monarch might check the local tyranny of lords); and he differed from Montesquieu in maintaining that this provided an argument against monarchy altogether. He thought that the benefits of the ancient constitution's division of powers and classes could be simulated in an extended and federal republic; but he certainly agreed with Montesquieu that there had been such benefits.

As evidence that the spirit of freedom was in the air during the decades preceding the Revolution, he cites not only the lively French debates about the American "insurrection" but also the response to the Chalotais case. It was the most Montesquieuian moment of the *ancien régime*'s crisis, and by drawing attention to it as exemplary of the time when "everyone's heads were filled with the principles of liberty," Constant indicates far greater sympathies for liberal ancient constitutionalism than Tracy ever held.[57]

In the eighteenth-century quarrel between Montesquieu and Voltaire about the *parlements*, the latter's critique had three main pillars. One was the intolerability of laws varying widely from place to place, the argument responded to by Montesquieu and by Constant in their chapters on uniformity. One was the cruelty and severity of parlementary criminal punishments—and Montesquieu, Voltaire, and Constant were unified in their attacks on judicial cruelty. And one was the parlementary record on religious toleration. Some *parlements* had ferociously resisted the Edict of Nantes, most were more anti-Protestant than the crown during the wars of religion, and the Calas case in Voltaire's own lifetime confirmed his view that the *parlements* were bastions of intolerant superstition, Paris the hope for moderation.

We might expect Constant, a Protestant and the descendant of refugees, to be particularly sympathetic to this final critique. But the biographical facts are in fact indeterminate on this count; after all, the monarchomachs Beza and Junius Brutus had placed great stock in the *parlements*. And in the eighteenth century the *parlements* had been key resisters to the Jesuit–crown alliance for persecution of Jansenism. Indeed, Constant disputes both the second and the third charges, insisting that "if some of the sentences handed down by the *parlements* were atrocities," it was because "they had to carry out execrable laws," and not due to any fault in their makeup or institutional character." The "spirit of intolerance" permeated "our legislation and our entire social organization," not only the *parlements* that handed down the sentences in a few infamous cases.[58]

Constant agrees with Montesquieu that too much tranquility in a republic, too little factional strife, is a sign that freedom is absent. He of course disagrees

---

[57] Constant, *Fragments*, p. 208.   [58] Constant, *Fragments*, p. 337.

with Montesquieu about whether an aristocracy or hereditary group can provide the desirable sort of disharmony; Constant thinks that a permanent and hereditary division of that sort provides a "seed of destruction"[59] in the state. But Tracy's embrace of the general will and of the sense of a unified republican people is nowhere to be found in Constant, who instead embraces a Hume- or Publius-like account of faction. "If each [representative] is partial to his electors, the partiality of each, combined, will have all the advantages of the partiality of all." Constant argues that members of an assembly are all too likely to develop an *esprit de corps*, to become united to each other and isolated from their constituents. One symptom of this will be that they think in terms of "general ideas and theories of uniformity ... and universal reforms [re-foundings]," that they will become overly concerned with the "disorder and uncertainty" created by local variety. When he mentions the problem of legislators' temptations by theories of uniformity, Constant again explicitly and approvingly refers to Montesquieu's famous chapter.[60]

In the *Fragments* Constant distinguishes the English case over and over again; he argues that Britain has freedom for idiosyncratic reasons, and that it should not be treated as a useful example for France. But he does not follow Jefferson, Paine, and Tracy in denying that Britain was really free. His admiration of the British constitution was, and was always to be, highly qualified. But he never ceased to be an admirer, and to maintain that Britain had kept the example of free government alive in Europe.

When Constant advised Bonaparte on the creation of a new constitution during the Hundred Days, he argued (against the latter) in favor of a hereditary aristocracy. Bonaparte did not wish to be challenged, and in any event had no suitable candidates—the traditional aristocrats were his enemies. Constant, recalling Montesquieu, called a hereditary aristocracy "indispensable" for a constitutional monarchy. He would certainly have rather had a republic with no hereditary distinctions; but after the republic fell, there was a need for an aristocracy. He hoped to prevent the re-emergence of feudal privileges, but to create a hereditary house, a *corps* parallel to the House of Lords.

In the *Memoirs sur les Cent-Jours* (published during the Restoration at a time when the returned nobility had largely joined the Right), there is a passage that begins much the same way, reporting the same arguments of Bonaparte against an aristocracy. But now Constant says that his long-standing doubts about a monarchy without an aristocracy had likely arisen because he, like Montesquieu, was "seduced" by the example of the British constitution. Here Constant himself criticizes the creation of a new, imperial, aristocracy—but not on rationalist or egalitarian grounds. Quite to the

---

[59] Constant, *Fragments*, p. 143.   [60] Constant, *Fragments*, p. 310.

contrary, he maintains that "nothing is created by artifice" in politics. "The creative force in politics, like the vital force in the physical world, cannot be supplemented by any act of will or by any act of law";[61] rather, the spirit of the age and of a people would in some important way shape political developments and institutions. This is a Montesquieuian thought, and returned Constant to one of the themes of *Conquest and Usurpation*—Bonaparte's status as a usurper, the inability to create new bloodlines and institutions and traditions from scratch that would have the same legitimacy as those that had come before. It moreover recalls the comment that it would be irrational to deliberately *create* the diversity in local laws, weights, measures, and so on that Constant defended in his chapter on uniformity.

In other words, Constant was torn between two Montesquieuian impulses. He perceived the need for an intermediate and independent body of aristocrats to balance the Emperor; but such a body would be a deliberate and artificial creation, out of keeping with the spirit of the nation and of the age. In his later writings and political work under the Restoration it seems to me that we can see the same dynamic. The social background, the spirit of the society in which Constant lived, was one that had been shaped by the Revolution and what followed it. Counter-revolution no more appealed to him in the 1820s than it had in the 1790s[62]—and in both decades one of his arguments against counter-revolution was that it would be at odds with changes in social character that had taken place. The argument in *Conquest and Usurpation* that political reforms should not outpace social change and that customs should be allowed to evolve freely is no anomaly; it meshes perfectly with the view that political reactions should not attempt to undo social change that has already taken place.

And, while Constant did later change his mind about some elements of *SCU*, even in "The Liberty of the Ancients Compared With That of the Moderns" he held to the view that "the changes brought by the centuries require from the authorities greater respect for customs, for affections, for the independence of individuals."[63] Habits and affections are a crucial part of a free person's happiness and, therefore, of his or her interests. In social life, particularly but not only in religion, the liberty of the moderns was closely tied to pluralism. Free people, not joined together by ancient republican devotion to the public, would not be socially homogenous.

Although Constant never thoroughly endorsed the view that liberty was ancient (that is, medieval), his attitude toward Germanic institutions and the

---

[61] Tracy, *Commentary*, p. 317.

[62] Constant, "Des Réactions Politiques" (1797), in Charles Louandre, ed., *Œuvres Politiques* (Paris: Charpentier et Cie, 1874).

[63] Constant, "Liberty of the Ancients Compared with that of the Moderns" (1819), in *Political Writings*, p. 324.

beneficial consequences of competing local jurisdictions remained sympathetic even through his last writings. "The Treaty of Westphalia gave to the German empire a very complicated constitution; but this constitution, by dividing this immense body into a multiplicity of little particular sovereignties, brought to the German nation, with some exceptions, a century and a half of civil liberty and of moderate and gentle (*douce*) government." The multiplication of princes and powers, divided among themselves and each governing only a small territory, offered Germans "a typically peaceful existence, sufficient security, nearly-complete intellectual freedom." It offered "the enlightened segment of that society" the option to promote and pursue literary culture, the arts, and the pursuit [research] of truth."[64] If any European polity's constitution was one that no rational person operating on a *tabula rasa* would have created, it was surely that of the Holy Roman Empire, whether before Westphalia or after; recall Pufendorf's characterization of it as "monstrous." But the lack of rationality was not a disadvantage, and the weakness of the central state compared with the power of the local sovereigns had great virtues.

Constant was no rationalist or contractarian when it came to constitutions, which

> are seldom made by the will of men. Time makes them. They are introduced gradually and in an almost imperceptible way. Yet there are circumstances in which it becomes indispensible to make a constitution. But then do only what is indispensible. Leave room for time and experience, so that these two reforming powers may direct your already constituted powers in the improvement of what has been done and the completion of what is still to be done.[65]

Constant's last major commentary on ancient constitutionalism appeared in his essay on "De Madame de Staël et de ses ouvrages,"[66] a sort of elegy for his long-time friend and sometime love. Here Constant distanced himself in part from some positions famously espoused by de Staël in her history of the French Revolution: that liberty in France was ancient, and that aristocratic government helped to protect freedom, by comparison with royal absolutism. Constant remained an unapologetic friend of the early stages of the Revolution and had no patience with the Ultras of his day. And it offers an original contribution to the debate over aristocratic and monarchical government, an argument that differs from that of the *Fragments* to some degree. Constant

---

[64] "Of the Thirty Years War," in *Mélanges* (1829), in *Œuvres*, p. 895.

[65] *Principles of Politics Applicable to All Representative Governments* (1815), in *Political Writings*, p. 172, fn 1. Note that this much shorter work has a different name, specifying *representative* governments, than the 1806–10 ur-text from which it was partly drawn.

[66] "De Madame de Staël et de ses ouvrages," in *Mélanges* (1829), in *Œuvres*, pp. 859–86, my translation. Holmes relies in part on this work to support his claim that Constant abandoned the pluralism of *SCU*.

claimed that genuine despotism, real monarchical power concentrated in one person, was impossible in a modern age of commerce and learning. Aristocratic bodies could moderate and liberalize a monarchy enough to make it tolerable for a modern commercial society; it was in this way that one could say that aristocratic rule was preferable to despotic absolute monarchy. But, ultimately, the latter could not survive modernity and so the choice between the two is a false one. He therefore attributed de Staël's view to a "confusion of epochs,"[67] just as he had said of Montesquieu in "Liberty."

"The English Constitution," Constant says, "was the object of Madam de Staël's constant admiration." For himself, Constant continued to offer a moderated view much like that of the *Fragments*: France under the Charter was freer than Britain, and the British order was marred by excessive inequality of privileges, rotten boroughs, and so on. But he did not wish to "commit the least wrong against a people who offered the world such a fine example for a hundred and forty years"; "I do not at all misunderstand how much we owe to that constitution; its name alone has rendered great services to liberty."

But Constant agrees with de Staël completely in her evaluation of the would-be absolutists; and here his view converged with Montesquieu's as well. It was the Bourbons who were the true authors of the Revolution, and life under them was not the idyll then being depicted by the Ultras. He concurs with her attribution of religious persecution and murder to the monarchy (and not, as already noted, with Voltaire's attribution of it to local prejudice embodied in the *parlements*). The kings' useless wars and the taxation that accompanied them, Richelieu's successful evisceration of the nobility, and the (doomed) desire to maintain despotic rule were the source of eighteenth-century France's ills. Tocqueville is foreshadowed here, and if Montesquieu is not precisely echoed, he is argued to have been on the side of freedom.

None of this is to say that Constant endorsed all of the group privileges of the ancient constitution. He admired Montesquieu deeply but always saw him from across a deep Revolutionary break, and did not wish to return to the *ancien régime*. He was keenly aware of the costs to individual freedom of state-sanctioned group privileges. For example, he wrote against the guild system and chartered monopolistic corporations with a concentrated fury not seen even in Smith, whose arguments he relied upon and cited freely.[68] Constant moralized Smith's "system of natural liberty" to a stronger degree than did

---

[67] "De Madame de Staël et de ses ouvrages," in *Mélanges* (1829), in *Œuvres*, pp. 859–86, my translation.

[68] "Of Privileges and Prohibition," in Book XII: On Government Jurisdiction over Economic Activity and Population, in *Principles of Politics*.

Smith himself; for Constant, the economic arguments for freedom of trade dovetailed with the natural right of persons to engage in commercial activity.

Likewise, but more profoundly for understanding Constant: his religious sensibility was a romantic Protestant individualism.[69] While he entirely lacked Tracy's contempt for religion, he was instinctively unsympathetic to Catholicism and skeptical of all sacerdotal corporations: organized churches, a privileged priesthood, monastic orders. The religion to which he was so concerned to preserve free access was a religion of individual spirituality that develops the soul and the mind.

Yet he recognized that for many people their religious sentiments came to be tied up in external "forms," and that this was a reason for freedom of religious practice with respect to those forms—a freedom that had been violated under the Revolution. He supported the liberty to form and live in sacerdotal corporations such as monasteries. Provided that freedom of exit was protected, life within such corporations was an option legitimately open to free persons.

> There are two ways of suppressing monasteries; you may open their doors; or you may drive out their occupants. If you adopt the first solution, you do something good without causing any harm; you break chains without violating refuges. If you adopt the second, you upset calculations based upon public faith; you insult old age, which you drag languishing and unarmed into an unknown world; you violate an incontestable right of all individuals in the social state, the right to choose their own way of life, to hold their property in common, to gather in order to profess the same doctrine, to enjoy the same leisure, to savour the same rest.[70]

Constant's pluralism had to differ from Montesquieu's; the post-revolutionary world he inhabited differed too greatly from the *ancien régime*. But it is a reasonable assessment to say that "Montesquieu's dread of uniformity resonated in the writings of his nineteenth-century followers, especially Benjamin Constant, in response to the imposition of the *Code Napoléon*, and Alexis de Tocqueville, in the face of what he perceived to be increased political centralisation."[71]

In the politics of the Restoration, Constant was generally more moderate than the *Idéologues* but was still considered a liberal of the left—unlike the liberals of the center, the Doctrinaires. The leading intellectual light of

---

[69] For Constant on religion, see Helena Rosenblatt, *Liberal Values: Benjamin Constant and the Politics of Religion*; Bryan Garsten, "Constant on the Religious Spirit of Liberalism," in Helena Rosenblatt, ed., *The Cambridge Companion to Constant* (Cambridge: Cambridge University Press, 2009); Garsten, "Religion and the Case Against Ancient Liberty: Benjamin Constant's Other Lectures," 38 *Political Theory* 4–33, 2010.

[70] "On innovation, reform, and the uniformity and stability of institutions;" ch. 1 of the material added to the fourth edition of *Conquest and Usurpation*, in *Political Writings*, p. 153.

[71] Tomaselli, "Spirit of Nations," pp. 30–1.

the latter group—and eventually their political leader as well—was Francois Guizot, whose tremendously influential 1820–2 lectures on the history of political institutions in Europe helped to transmit ancient-liberty ideas to Restoration-era liberals. He did see gradual centralization and rationalization as something like the natural course of events, a view of history that influenced Tocqueville's. Modern free societies would have centralized representative institutions, but that freedom depended on not taking the centralization to excess. Over the course of the preceding centuries, Guizot argued that the absolutist monarchs had undermined both representative institutions and local liberties, while both elements of the ancient constitution had been successfully defended in Britain.[72]

The Doctrinaire argument about ancient and modern constitutionalism was made more directly and explicitly in Barante's 1829 *Des Communes et de l'Aristocratie*.[73] Barante argued that the *parlementaire* cause had been, roughly, in the right, but that its particular institutional solutions were no longer applicable. "Refusing the *parlements* their right of remonstrance was an act of despotism. Liberty had taken shelter in them; it had chosen an irregular method of expressing itself; but since no one had given it another method, it was necessary to allow it that one." Nonetheless, introducing any *contemporary* equivalent, the creation of a right of remonstrance by a hereditary body, would have been a "disorder," inappropriate to the age.[74] Instead, constitutional reform in Restoration France should emphasize the full conversion of the traditional nobility into an English-style constitutional aristocracy; the restoration and reinvigoration of the rights of cities and *communes* ("the ties that unite the inhabitants" of which "are more real than is imagined. It is outside the power of the laws to entirely destroy this division of French soil, and to set arbitrary boundaries to these small units"); and the granting of province-like self-government to the centrally administered *départements*.

For the Doctrinaires as for de Staël and Constant, it was perfectly possible to perceive freedom in the ancient constitution without hoping for its resurrection, to see aristocratic privileges and particular liberties as having helped to protect liberty from monarchs without proposing that they be restored. But the non-*Idéologue* liberals held that there were crucial lessons to be learned from the ancient constitution, and there was a need to undo the excesses of Revolutionary and Bonapartist centralization and rationalization. Institutions that might not have been rationally justifiable from first principles could

---

[72] François Guizot, *The History of the Origins of Representative Government in Europe*, Andrew Scoble, trans. Aurelian Craiutu, ed. (Indianapolis: Liberty Fund, 2002[1861]), p. 34. On the Doctrinaires generally see Aurelian Craiutu, *Liberalism Under Siege: The Political Thought of the French Doctrinaires* (Lanham MD: Rowman and Littlefield, 2003).

[73] M. de Barante, *Des Communes et de l'Aristocratie* (Paris: Librairie Française De L'advocat, 1829).

[74] Barante, *Communes*, p. 186, my translation.

nonetheless provide desirable constitutional counterbalances to the concentration of power. For Tracy as for Paine, the rational unjustifiability of the institutions was all that was needed to condemn them. But the others held, with Burke, that such institutions could not be recreated at will; their desirable effects stemmed in part from their appearance of permanence and from the sentiments of attachment that had developed around them. New protections of diversity, new kinds of decentralized power, would be necessary for an age in which the ancient constitution had been swept away. Jennings calls this

> one of the central themes of French liberalism in the nineteenth century: the preservation of local independence as a means of restricting the power of despotic, central government. This argument was an updated supplement to Montesquieu's defence of the rights of the provincial nobility. The French liberals [...] became obsessed by what they saw as the systematic destruction of all intermediary powers and the consequent subjection of an undifferentiated and amorphous population at the hands of a highly organized, centralized bureaucratic power.[75]

The United States

The political thought of the revolutionary and founding eras in (what were to become) the United States was complex and often contradictory. In retrospect we identify an ebb of traditional republicanism and a flow of various kinds of liberalism and liberal republicanism. Constitutional theories were worked out in the midst of new experiments in constitutional practice. The debate over the ratification of the 1787 Constitution and that between Federalists and Republicans in the 1790s and early 1800s both showed the depths of intellectual and theoretical disagreements in the early American republic. Views of pluralism were no exception; Locke and Montesquieu were among the most important influences on early American political thought, and by now we can understand that this generated certain ambiguities.

We have already encountered Paine's more or less thoroughgoing rationalism. The other leading thinkers of the American Revolution and founding were somewhat more ambivalent. Ideas about the balance between central state power and other social institutions in a society where the central state was being newly created were necessarily somewhat different from those in any ongoing European polity. Consider Benjamin Franklin, a great founder and joiner of associations, not least the Freemasons; indeed he accompanied Voltaire to the latter's Masonic initiation. In his pre-revolutionary hopes for a federated British empire resembling the later Commonwealth, he showed

---

[75] Jennings, *Revolution and the Republic*, p. 164. See also Jennings, "Constant's Idea of Modern Liberty," in *The Cambridge Companion to Constant*, p. 88.

himself as uninterested as Burke in the abstraction of unitary and undivided sovereignty. Committed though he was to modernity and to enlightened patterns of thought, enlightened absolutism held no appeal for him and rationalized unity did not interest him. Still, the home rule for Pennsylvania for which he fought was democratic home rule, not the power of the local elites (in this case the Penn and Quaker oligarchy). He had a chief hand in drafting the revolutionary Pennsylvania constitution, the only early American constitution to radically reject the ideas of separation and balance in favor of a dominant and unicameral legislature—and, for that reason, the only one to find approval from the Parisian *philosophes* of the day.

We have already discussed Jefferson, whose late-in-life embrace of Destutt de Tracy's works was philosophically compatible with much that came before. Of the American intellectuals he was the most closely engaged with the French *philosophes*—closer than Paine, who knew little French, or than Franklin, who had fewer ambitions as a social philosopher however much he enjoyed being feted by the Parisian intelligentsia. Jefferson was a partisan of the French Revolution, witnessing its early stages as ambassador and consulting with Lafayette about the drafting of the Declaration of the Rights of Man and Citizen. Custom held little appeal for him; "the dead have no rights," and so rightfully social institutions ought to be abolished and recreated every generation. The radical contractarianism of the Declaration of Independence was not out of character. All of this coexisted with a commitment to limits on central state authority and to robust local and state self-government that, if it was intermittent, nonetheless seemed fervent when it manifested. And his views about the local power of the white master over black slaves are famously so conflicted as elicit explanations that are psychological rather than philosophical in nature. In Europe, and about Europe, Jefferson was a faithful Enlightenment and revolutionary rationalist; in and about America, the rationalism that animated his high-level political philosophy sat uneasily with other ideas.

James Madison never expressed any enthusiasm for the work of Tracy, or any of Jefferson's disdain for Montesquieu, despite his personal and intellectual closeness to his mentor. The influence of Montesquieu on the Federalist Papers is well known and indeed apparent on the latter's surface.[76] This was in part a rhetorical strategy, since the Federalists had an interest in neutralizing the anti-Federalists' invocation of Montesquieu's small-republic thesis.[77] But it was not only strategic; Madison continued to draw on Montesquieu for his understanding of federations throughout his career. As late as his end-of-life

---

[76] See Anne Cohler, *Montesquieu's Comparative Politics and the Spirit of American Constitutionalism* (Lawrence: University Press of Kansas, 1988), among many others.
[77] See my "Beyond Publius."

argument against nullification he treated Montesquieu as a source of insight about federalism and the diversity of laws among the states.[78] Madison, like Constant, disagreed with the small-republic thesis—but, also like Constant, he disagreed in the direction of arguing that a large republic could be sufficiently pluralistic to simulate the benefits of the ancient constitution, *not* in the direction of arguing that a large republic could be made homogenous, virtuous, and institutionally simple like a small republic.

The account of factions given in Federalist 10 is not strictly about associational pluralism; factions are collections of voters vying to control one level or another of government, not groups that govern themselves. But the distinction is easily overdrawn. Madison's argument here combines insight about the oppressive potential of local homogeneity and local majorities with an unusually strong endorsement of heterogeneity and plurality in political life. Local factions left to their own devices will act unjustly; but the solution is not to empower a central state that can overawe them. Rather it is to extend the size of the republic and multiply factions to make it difficult to assemble a majority coalition in favor of any particular partial interest.

This balancing approach is further developed in Madison's most important contributions to *The Federalist* on the relationship between the federal center and the states, numbers 45 and 46.[79] Here he argues that the federal center can safely be given increased power, precisely because citizens' loyalty so naturally lies with the more-local thicker community of their various states. The ties of affection and sentiment to state governments mean that the people would tend to be too passively trusting of them. But in a compound republic, that loyalty to the states becomes a virtue rather than a vice; it ensures that there will always be those keeping a watchful eye for government overreach or partiality. This is an endorsement of central power, but not one that could coherently call for the destruction or dissolution of the states, or even the civic education of the people to devalue their attachment to the states. If they did so, the channeling of loyalties toward productive constitutional ends would break down. The argument is strongly Montesquieuian, and anticipates both Burke's critique of the replacement of provinces with *départments* and Constant's defense of local patriotism.

Madison, it must be remembered, deeply distrusted the state governments as they had come to operate from 1776 through 1787. Although he drafted the Constitution that the Philadelphia Convention approved, he lost a number of fights he viewed as crucial to limit the states more thoroughly; his own preferences were for a more centralized order than the one he did so much

[78] Madison, "Nullification," in *Letters and Other Writings of James Madison, Fourth President of the United States*, IV: 395–425 (1835–6) (Philadelphia: J.B. Lippincott & Company, 1865), p. 424.
[79] Here I draw on my "Federalism, Liberalism, and the Separation of Loyalties."

to create. That could lead us to think that the argument in numbers 45 and 46 was offered in bad faith, but it need not. Madison does not say that citizens *should* be more loyal to the states, or that their loyalty arises out of good governance. He predicts that they *will* be, for reasons of proximity and familiarity. This sentiment, like the sources of faction, is a fact to reckon with and make use of. The urge to protect one's local community will keep the citizenry mobilized and jealous of their liberty, even if the local communities when left to their own devices would threaten it. His work with Jefferson on the Kentucky and Virginia Resolutions a decade later was thus perhaps not so radical a change of heart as it has sometimes been portrayed. Those resolutions against the Alien and Sedition Acts were the *Federalist 45–46* mechanism in action. Given the (reasonable) view that those acts were unconstitutional and violations of freedom, Madison and Jefferson drew on the available social resource for opposing them, the states.

Perhaps the most theoretically interesting and the best-known disagreement between Jefferson and Madison highlights the latter's Montesquieuian attitudes, his ongoing desire to draw on habitual sentiment for political purposes, and his concomitant doubts about reliance on abstract reason. In *Federalist 49*, against Jefferson's argument (in the *Notes on the State of Virginia*) in favor of frequent recourse to constitutional conventions, Madison argues that this would

> deprive the government of that veneration, which time bestows on every thing, and without which perhaps the wisest and freest governments would not possess the requisite stability...In a nation of philosophers, this consideration ought to be disregarded. A reverence for the laws, would be sufficiently inculcated by the voice of an enlightened reason. But a nation of philosophers is as little to be expected as the philosophical race of kings wished for by Plato. And in every other nation, the most rational government will not find it a superfluous advantage, to have the prejudices of the community on its side.[80]

Or, as he asked Jefferson in correspondence in response to the latter's call for the cancellation of all laws and constitutions once every generation, "Would not a Government so often revised become too mutable to retain those prejudices in its favor which antiquity inspires, and which are perhaps a salutary aid to [even] the most rational Government in the most enlightened age?"[81] Madison placed little faith in the pure enlightened rationalism of his fellow Virginian, or of the latter's French associates.

---

[80] Madison, "No. 49," in *The Federalist Papers*.
[81] Madison, Letter to Jefferson, February 4, 1790, in James Morton Smith, ed., *The Republic of Letters: Correspondence between Jefferson and Madison 1776–1826* (New York: W. W. Norton and Company, 1995), p. 650.

John Adams' early essay on the Stamp Act controversy, "A Dissertation on the Canon and Feudal Law" (1765), rests, in Enlightenment fashion, on a denunciation of both, "the two greatest systems of tyranny." They were mere excuses for the warrior nobility and the Catholic clergy to exercise despotic power. Education and equality, Calvinism and Commonwealth ideals, seemed to him the organizing principles of American life. He valued Greece and Rome, not the German forests, as the home of liberty, and Puritan America as leading the way to recover it for modernity. Crucially, Adams took "feudalism" to be a system that *culminated* in absolute monarchy, not a source of resistance to it; the Stuart monarchs stood as the example of those who united the canon and feudal law.

Adams took the Puritan and commonwealth tendencies of New England as characteristic of America as a whole. An illiterate American, he wrote, "is as rare an appearance as a Jacobite or a Roman Catholic, that is, as rare as a comet or an earthquake"—despite the longstanding continued existence of a substantial Catholic community in Maryland. He disdained the "party" "consisting chiefly not of the descendants of the first settlers of the country, but of high churchmen and high statesmen "imported since"—that is to say, among others, Anglicans. In other words, the young Adams had the Puritan–commonwealth congruence view that was the counterpart of James I's monarchy–episcopacy congruence view.[82]

By the mid-1770s, Adams' intellectual approach seemed to be quite different, partly in response to developments on the British side of the Revolutionary crisis. The Blackstonian insistence that there could be no *imperium in imperio* was itself a symptom of state consolidation and the fading away of ancient constitutionalism in British politics. For the next generation Americans were to show creativity in thinking about *how* sovereignty and jurisdiction might be divided, on their way to developing a federalist constitution;[83] but they committed no novelty in the bare idea that they could be, and Adams argued against the Blackstonian position. His *Novanglus* essays were the most sustained and influential ancient-constitutionalist brief for the American cause in the imperial conflict. Adams drew on the whole history of disputes about provincial liberties in composite monarchies, and defended the autonomy of the American provinces against Parliament's absolutist pretensions and absurd insistence on undifferentiated sovereignty. His arguments ranged from the provinces of Spain to the Channel Islands, with the most attention

[82] John Adams, "A Dissertation on the Canon and Feudal Law," in George W. Carey, ed., *The Political Writings of John Adams* (Washington: Regnery, 2000[1765]), p. 12.

[83] Gordon S. Wood, *The Creation of the American Republic* (Chapel Hill: University of North Carolina Press, 1969); Forrest McDonald, *States' Rights and the Union: Imperim in Imperio, 1776–1876* (Lawrence: University Press of Kansas, 2000); Alison LaCroix, *The Ideological Origins of American Federalism* (Cambridge, Mass.: Harvard University Press, 2010).

devoted to Wales, Scotland, and Ireland. The colonies' own various charters had constitutional standing, and the colonies had severally and corporately endorsed the Glorious Revolution, just as Scotland had. Indeed, he emphasized, the revolution had taken place separately in the American colonies, where Stuart-appointed royal governors who had revoked colonial charters were overthrown, and the ancient charters had been reclaimed.[84]

It is a commonplace to say that the pre-*Common Sense* revolutionaries appealed to "the rights of Englishmen." But this gives an incomplete picture, emphasizing only the appeal to common law and Magna Carta procedural rights that had been suspended by the Coercive Acts of 1774, or else to the right not to be taxed without representation. Adams, like Franklin, preemptively rejected any solution that would have involved sending outnumbered American representatives to Westminster; it was provincial autonomy, not representative participation in a unitary sovereign legislature, that they sought. And so they were in the at-first-glance odd position for Whigs of emphasizing the colonies' direct personal attachment to the crown and actively denying the supremacy of Parliament. Like pre-Union Scotland had had, like the Channel Islands still had, and like dependent Ireland should have had, the colonies had the right to complete internal self-determination and lay outside the jurisdiction of the local English Parliament at Westminster.

Adams' shift toward pluralism and away from Enlightenment simplicity was an enduring one. The constitutional theories he developed in the 1770s and 80s, his advice to the new states on adopting constitutions, his work on the Massachusetts constitution, and his *Defense of the Constitutions of the United States* against their *philosophe* critics, unfailingly emphasized the dangers of unified and simple forms of government. The separation of powers, bicameralism, and mixed government were his fixed principles; the unicameral and unitary democracy recommended by the *philosophes* was, to his mind, the civil war-prone anarchic democracy of ancient Greece. It was better to draw on the centuries of experience with mixed and balanced governments, with Britain as the best pre-American example. The primary flaw with the British constitution as it then existed was, he said, the misallocation of representation in the Commons, rather than the existence of the Lords or the monarchy. Adams, in his contrarian way, seemed to have moved away from his commonwealth republicanism of 1765 as the American republics developed. Indeed, his *Defense* is best known today for being out of step with its time. A few years earlier it would have been the encapsulation of American constitutional theory, but by the time it was published Adams' countrymen

---

[84] Adams, *Novanglus*, in *Political Writings*.

were abandoning the idea of mixed government (with its implication that, e.g., Senates were like the House of Lords and meant to represent the propertied few) in favor of a more thoroughly democratic grounding for checks and balances.[85] But for Adams himself, the distaste for simplicity and abstract rationality persisted.

During the 1790s, when the Federalist and Democratic–Republican factions were hardening into parties for which republican theory still did not have space, Adams was among those who blamed party division (specifically, the Jacobin Club) for French Revolutionary excesses. But unlike Washington—who imagined a direct connection between the Jacobins and the Democratic–Republicans, and condemned "self-created societies" as insurrectionary—Adams was careful to remember the value of freedom of association. He said that such societies must be "circumspect," not that they must be prohibited, and even in the midst of the controversy took "it for granted that political clubs must and ought to be lawful in every free country."[86]

Even during his late-in-life correspondence with Jefferson, when they avoided political disputes in the spirit of their reconciliation, he could not resist indirect tweaks by way of the Enlightenment:

> No man is more sensible than I am of the service to science and letters, humanity, fraternity, and liberty, that would have been rendered by the encyclopedists and economists, by Voltaire, D'Alembert, Buffon, Diderot, Rousseau, La Lande, Frederic and Catherine, if they had possessed common sense. But they were all totally destitute of it . . . We all curse Robespierre and Bonaparte. But were they not both such restless, vain, extravagant animals as Diderot and Voltaire?[87]

And to Madison he expressed the view that "Condorcet's Observations on the twenty-ninth book of the Spirit of Laws; [and] Helvetius, too, in his Letters to Montesquieu, printed in Mr. Jefferson's translation of Tracy" are among "the most pedantical writings that ages have produced." Of their fascination with simple, unitary, and undifferentiated governments, he asked,

> Is not despotism the simplest of all imaginable governments? Is not oligarchy the next, aristocracy the third, and a simple democracy of twenty-five millions of men the fourth? All these are simple governments, with a vengeance. Erect a house of a cubic form, one hundred feet square at the base, without any division within into

---

[85] The classic discussion is Gordon S. Wood, *The Creation of the American Republic*.

[86] Letter to Abigail Adams, December 14, 1794, in Charles Francis Adams, ed., *Letters of John Adams, Addressed to His Wife* (Boston: Little and Brown, 1891), p. 171. The letter continues, "I belonged to several in my youth, and wish that I could belong to one now. It would save me from the *ennui* of an evening which now torments me . . ." These were the bored evenings of Adams' time as Vice-President.

[87] Adams, Letter to Jefferson, March 2, 1816, in *The Works of John Adams, Second President of the United States* (Boston: Little, Brown and Co., 1856), vol. 10, pp. 211, 213.

chambers, parlors, cellars, or garrets; would not this be the simplest house that ever was built? But would it be a commodious habitation for a family? It would accommodate nothing but a kennel of hunter's hounds.

Better wisdom was to be found elsewhere:

I am not an implicit believer in the inspiration or infallibility of Montesquieu. On the contrary, it must be acknowledged, that some of these philosophers have detected many errors in his writings. But all their heads consolidated into one mighty head, would not equal the depth of his genius, or the extent of his views...When a writer on government despises, sneers, or argues against mixed governments, or a balance in government, he instantly proves himself an ideologian.[88]

Adams' turn away from his early views toward a modified Montesquieuian-ism may have left him perpetually out of sync in an increasingly democratic age; but it contributed to at least one enduring institutional development. Anglican or Episcopal churches in the new United States faced obvious diffi-culties in complying with the internal religious rules of the Church of England that demanded, among other things, that clergy swear ordination oaths of allegiance to the King. After the war ended, the Church of England petitioned for legislative relief for the American clergy. As ambassador to Britain, Adams actively interceded in support of the needed changes in British law, on behalf of American Episcopalians who sought the right to create bishops on Ameri-can soil who would not have to swear such oaths. He indeed provided specific reassurance that this would *not* engender controversy and opposition in the way that the pre-revolutionary episcopal dispute had.[89] For the Massachusetts Puritan commonwealthman who had blasted the canon law and episcopal ecclesiology, this was a remarkable change. Parliament enacted the Consecra-tion of Bishops Abroad Act in 1786, just a year after the Treaty of Paris. By 1789 an Episcopal Church in the United States was created that was subject to the Archbishop of Canterbury yet owed no allegiance to the British crown. This was the first such creation of an autonomous national church within the Anglican framework, and so in a sense the origin of the complex federative Anglican Communion that exists today among national churches tied to the Archbishopric of Canterbury but not to the British state.[90]

---

[88] Adams, Letter To Madison, April 22, 1817 in *the Works,* vol. 10, p. 256–7. Note the dismissive use of "ideologian," at a time when "ideology" and its derivatives were uncommon words.

[89] James Grant, *John Adams: Party of One* (New York: Farrar, Straus and Giroux, 2005), p. 319.

[90] Only in a sense; the [Anglican] Churches of Ireland and Scotland were corporately distinct from the Church of England, and so Anglicanism already had a somewhat federated structure. But it was a structure wholly within the political organization of the United Kingdom; it was the creation of the American church that broke that political link.

The Society of the Cincinnati

At the close of the Revolutionary War, the Continental Army's officer corps created a new veterans' association: the Society of the Cincinnati,[91] divided into thirteen branches by state and soon joined by a fourteenth for France. The Society's membership was restricted to those who had served as officers of the Continental Army for three years, or for the French branch, as a high-ranking officer in the French armed forces. Membership was to descend through the line of eldest direct male heirs. Members were entitled to wear a badge bearing the bald eagle; the badge was designed by Pierre L'Enfant, later the planner of the District of Columbia. The French branch made a gift of an elaborate diamond-encrusted eagle badge for the presidency of the American branch. George Washington was, naturally, chosen as the group's first president in 1783; he remained in that office until his death. (Hamilton succeeded him.) The Society pledged mutual friendship and communication, charitable support of officers' widows and orphaned children and others in need, and support of the union.

The Society quickly became a topic of bitter controversy. A perpetual society of high-ranking military officers and veterans looked suspiciously like the foundation of an aristocracy; membership even passed down through primogeniture. Moreover, the officer corps' pensions were a significant financial liability of the Confederation government. Many found it easy to believe that the Society was formed to influence Congressional tax and spending policy for their own benefit. At worst, a *corps* of military officers might overthrow constitutional government. The French branch compounded these worries, connecting the American officer corps to a foreign aristocratic monarchy. Adams, Jefferson, Madison, and Franklin—all ineligible for membership—each criticized the Society, at least in private. In public, this became the first great newspaper and pamphlet dispute of the postwar era. Town meetings and state legislatures passed anti-Cincinnati resolutions, from warnings that members would be viewed with disfavor in elections to threats to expropriate the Society's branches' treasuries. Many of the recurring styles of anti-associational argument were in play at the same time: the Society was incongruent with democratic republican government, entangled with a foreign power, likely to accumulate resources that would be outside of public control, and a self-interested conspiratorial faction.

[91] Markus Hünemörder, *The Society of the Cincinnati: conspiracy and distrust in early America* (New York: Berghahn Books, 2006); Minor Myers, Jr., *Liberty without Anarchy: A History of the Society of the Cincinnati* (Charlottesville: University Press of Virginia, 1983); Wallace Evan Davies, "The Society of the Cincinnati in New England 1783–1800," 5(1) *The William and Mary Quarterly third series* 3–25, 1948.

The uproar prompted Washington to propose far-reaching reforms: the abolition of heritable membership, the chartering of each state branch by state legislatures, and state supervision over their treasuries and expenditures. Despite Washington's support, the reforms failed; they required unanimous consent of the state branches, and only eight of thirteen agreed. The New Hampshire branch denounced what they took to be the surrender to unfounded objections and defended freedom of association in terms that are especially striking when we remember that Washington was a prominent Mason:

> The institution of Societies, establishing of funds, and wearing of Badges of the respective Orders will readily be acknowledged a right claimed and exercised by the Citizens of this and every other free Country, and if wearing the emblems of our order establishes a Rank of Nobility contrary to the [Articles of] Confederation we can see no reason why the badge worn by the free-masons does not as effectually do it.

Special objection was made to the idea that "we should tamely submit to give up into the hands of the respective Legislatures the small funds we established with the price of our blood."[92]

The acutely reputation-conscious Washington, recognizing defeat, announced his decision not to serve as President again, and decided not to attend the next general meeting—in Philadelphia in the summer of 1787. He even told Madison that this would mean he could not attend the Constitutional Convention, as he could neither be seen to endorse the unreformed Society nor be seen to snub his fellow officers by being in Philadelphia and *not* attending. Eventually, he relented; and once in Philadelphia felt that he could not refuse the Society. He did not attend its meetings, then or thereafter, and insisted that his presidency would be only symbolic; he took no further part in its affairs. During the Convention, concern was strong that the Society would have a role in politics so outsized as to constitute a "danger and impropriety." This was a reason to avoid popular election of the President, as the Society would "in fact elect the chief Magistrate in every instance," a remarkable thing to say in a convention that included more than twenty members including one in the presiding chair.[93]

Washington's inattention, the legacy of the controversy, and rapid social change and migration contributed to the Society's rapid atrophy from this

---

[92] July 4, 1785, in *Collections of the New Hampshire Historical Society*, volume 6 (Concord: Asa McFarland, 1850), p. 300.

[93] Elbridge Gerry, session of Wednesday, July 25, 1787, in James Madison, *The Debates in the Federal Convention of 1787 which Framed the Constitution of the United States of America*, Gaillard Hunt and James Brown Scott, eds (Buffalo, N.Y.: Prometheus Books, 1987[1840]), p. 323.

point forward. Arguably the first major nationwide political dispute of the newly independent United States left little long-term impact. But it showed something of the shape of disputes about associational life after the demo- cratic revolutions, a foreshadowing of the disputes that would be so central to the French Revolution and its aftermath. Organizations' failure to be congru- ent with the government of the polity, their apparent fracturing of national unity, and their potential for independent wealth, could be viewed just as skeptically by democratic states as they had been by monarchies.

8

Centralization in a Democratic Age: Tocqueville and Mill

Up until now some of the discussions in this historical survey have focused on thinkers whose inclusion as liberals might be contested. Lord Acton (to whom we will return) denied that any of the pre-revolutionary French thinkers qualified: "all these factions of opinion were called Liberal: Montesquieu, because he was an intelligent Tory; Voltaire, because he attacked the clergy; Turgot, as a reformer; Rousseau, as a democrat; Diderot, as a freethinker. The one thing in common to them all is the disregard for liberty."[1] There are reasons to think of Burke as a conservative, and of the Americans as various kinds of republicans. Destutt de Tracy, though probably indisputably a liberal, is relatively obscure today. This chapter, however, centers on two unarguably canonical and liberal theorists: John Stuart Mill and Alexis de Tocqueville.

Mill and Tocqueville were contemporaries,[2] mutual admirers, and, for a time, friends. Their respective works are very different in style, method, and fields of inquiry. "There are many differences," Mill accurately observed, "between your way of seeing things and mine, as you hold much more than I do to the past, and above all to its religious aspect."[3] But much unites them. They were both centrally preoccupied with the relationship between democracy—inevitable and overall desirable—and liberty. They both caution against the deadening, homogenizing effects of modern society. The fear of a kind of mass social conformism haunts the work of each, and they share a concern for the fate of the outstanding and original individual. "One of your

---

[1] Lord Acton, *Lectures on the French Revolution* (Indianapolis: Liberty Fund, 2000[1910]), p. 16.

[2] They were almost the same age, but Tocqueville began his political writing much earlier and died much younger. As a result, there is an asymmetry in their intellectual exchange. Mill wrote a substantial review essay of each volume of *DA*, and wrote a letter in response to *ORR*; but Tocqueville died just as Mill's most important work on political philosophy was beginning. He lived to receive a copy of *Liberty* but not to comment on it; *Representative Government, Utilitarianism*, and *Subjection of Women* were published over the subsequent ten years.

[3] Mill, letter to Tocqueville, December 15, 1856, in Mill, *Collected Works, vol. XV*, my translation.

great general conclusions," Mill wrote in response to *The Old Regime and the Revolution*, "is exactly that which I have been almost alone in standing up for here [...] namely, that the real danger in democracy, the real evil to be struggled against... is not anarchy or love of change, but Chinese stagnation and immobility."[4]

The diagnosis of "soft despotism" in volume II of *Democracy in America* is not identical to that of Victorian sameness of Mill's *On Liberty*, but there is a real commonality between them. Both endorse the post-revolutionary spread of democracy, and greatly sympathize with the democratic experiment in America, but think they must write somewhat against the spirit of an egalitarian age in defense of liberty. This suspicion of the mediocrity of a democratic modernity ties them together in what Alan Kahan has called their shared "aristocratic liberalism."[5] Moreover, according to Mill's own testimony late in life, Tocqueville's writings directly influenced his own opinions on some of the questions at the heart of this study.[6]

These shared moral and social concerns cast into sharper relief the very real differences between their points of view.[7] Questions of group life and group power, centralization and decentralization, lay near the heart of both men's thought. And attention to these questions allows us to see the pattern of difference between them. With all of the qualifications and nuances that one would expect of thinkers of their sophistication, Tocqueville consistently sees the world of intermediate and local groups as a check on or alternative to centralized state power, while Mill's view is quite different; he is always alive to the threat of local and in-group tyranny.

> Any despotism is preferable to local despotism. If we are to be ridden over by authority, if our affairs are to be managed for us at the pleasure of other people,

---

[4] Mill, letter to Tocqueville, May 11, 1840, in *Collected Works, vol. XIII*, p. 434.

[5] Alan Kahan, *Aristocratic Liberalism: The Social and Political Thought of Jacob Burkhardt, John Stuart Mill, and Alexis de Tocqueville* (Oxford: Oxford University Press, 1992). The phrase is fair, if it is emphasized that the relevant meaning of *aristos* is "the excellent" or "the best," not "the hereditary nobility," for whom Tocqueville had only qualified sympathy and Mill had none. Even so, I find the phrasing unfortunate, because *rule by* the best was none of Tocqueville's concern and not much of Mill's.

[6] The relevant passage from Mill's *Autobiography* will be discussed later. I pause here to say that we have some reason not to take the passage entirely at face value, and nothing in this chapter will turn on whether Mill in fact felt himself to have been influenced by Tocqueville or not. See H. O. Pappé, "Mill and Tocqueville," 25(2) *Journal of the History of Ideas* 217–34, 1964. For an earlier opposing view, see Terence Qualter, "John Stuart Mill, Disciple of De Tocqueville," 13(4) *Political Research Quarterly* 880–9, 1960.

[7] I am not concerned in this chapter with their differences on questions of foreign policy, though biographically these were probably the most important: Mill judged Tocqueville to be too much in the grip of French chauvinism, and too supportive of the French tendency toward national braggadocio and aggression to make up for national insecurity. Tocqueville's defense of the colonization of Algeria on the grounds that it gave the French a grand project to concentrate on was not to Mill's liking. This difference seems to have ended their years of warm and frequent correspondence, with no letters being exchanged for several years and only a few after the gap.

heaven forefend that it should be at that of our nearest neighbours...To be under the latter would be...to be the slave of the vulgar prejudices, the cramped, distorted, and short-sighted views, of the public of a small town or group of villages.[8]

In this chapter I show, first, that Mill and Tocqueville carry forward the basic contrast in views about intermediate groups in liberal thought we have seen in previous generations. Mill is not blindly a rationalist, nor is Tocqueville a narrow pluralist; but the difference in orientation between them is real. This will involve both a bird's-eye view of major themes from the *corpus* of each and special attention to some points of close contact between them. Second, I suggest that their respective rationalist and pluralist orientations shape some of their most enduring contributions and insights. Even more than the other contrasting thinkers studied in Part II, I find Mill and Tocqueville impossible to simply choose between. Each was fundamentally right about important questions, but for reasons that left them wrong on or blind to others, and in ways that made their views difficult to reconcile. Mill's understanding of the despotism of the patriarchal family and Tocqueville's appreciation for the way that intermediate groups could check the despotism of the democratic bureaucratic state are both crucial insights that a complete liberal theory should incorporate; but they drew those insights from rival understandings of the social world.

Mill was right that there were many differences between the two. One crucial difference seems to have been as basic as this: Tocqueville believed that France exemplified the modern European condition, while Mill thought it exceptional. Even where their interests converged, as Mill pointed out, basic differences remained about history and time: Mill often thought in terms of what would bring progress about, or at least make it possible, and usually looked forward, while Tocqueville worried about loss and decline, and often looked back.

When looking at the same historical trends, the same developments over the preceding centuries, Mill welcomed the expansions of state power as progressive and liberating, emphasizing the local power that was checked or abolished. Tocqueville focused on the state power that was created, and worried about the steady attenuation of liberties. The same pattern is evident looking forward. Mill could admit the reality of the French over-centralization that so concerned Tocqueville, only to immediately predict that this would prompt an overreaction that would leave France in danger of too *little* central state power. In other words, the future could turn out well or poorly, but if it turned out poorly that was more likely to be because of decentralization than over-centralization.

---

[8] John Stuart Mill, "Centralisation," in *Collected Works*, p. 606.

Tocqueville on Associations and *Corps*

The animating concern of Tocqueville's two greatest works is that the conjoined historical movements toward equality and centralization will leave despotism impossible to resist and freedom impossible to defend. He was clear in *DA* (though the American canonization of Tocqueville is prone to overlook this) that his concerns were either European or universal, not narrowly American. In the penultimate chapter of Volume 1 he refers to both the mores that once kept government limited, and to the institutions that did so, such as

> the prerogatives of the nobility, of the authority of sovereign courts, of the rights of corporations, or of provincial privileges, all things which softened the blows of authority and maintained a spirit of resistance in the nation ... political institutions which, though often opposed to the freedom of individuals, nevertheless served to keep the love of liberty alive in men's souls with obviously valuable results ... When towns and provinces form so many different nations within the common motherland, each of them has a particularist spirit opposed to the general spirit of servitude; but now that all parts of a single empire have lost their franchises, usages, prejudices, and even their memories and names and have grown accustomed to obey the same laws, it is no longer more difficult to oppress them all together than to do this to each separately.[9]

Here we not only see a *précis* for his study of the French old regime decades later; we also find by implication the animating questions of *DA*. Have the Anglo-Americans so far avoided this descent into servility? If so, how, and what can be learned from them about how to maintain liberty in a democratic age? In old regime France he saw the gradual erosion of intermediate bodies by a centralizing and homogenizing power that became almost irresistible as it aligned with the world-historical force of democratization. In the France of his own day he saw what he took to be the direction of the modern world: democratic equality and statist centralization reinforcing each other and grinding down freedom, distinctiveness, and accomplishment. In contemporaneous America he saw a democratic society that was resisting these trends, in part thanks to local government and to voluntary associations. But in the American future he saw the possibility of "soft despotism" of homogeneous mediocrity and centralized bureaucratic paternalism.

While both works offer famously complex and multi-causal accounts, group life and decentralized government figure prominently in each. The Americans benefited from their institutions of local self-government and from their mania for forming voluntary associations. And the French old

[9] Tocqueville, *Democracy in America*, J. P. Mayer, ed. (New York: Harper & Row Publishers, 1969 [1835/1840]), henceforth *DA*, pp. 312–13.

regime, by the time of the Revolution, was ready to collapse into a democracy that eventually yielded Bonaparte's despotism in large part because the Bourbon kings had centralized the state so dramatically, undermining urban liberty, provincial liberty, and the privileges of the *corps intermédiaires* so effectively.

Tocqueville openly committed himself to ancient constitutionalist historiography. Medieval Europe was everywhere much the same, with provincial liberties and urban self-government coexisting with feudal privileges and assemblies of the Estates. But—and this is the central thesis of the book—that shared order was eroded and replaced by a centralized state gradually over the course of early modernity, not suddenly by the Revolution. By the eighteenth century, "the ancient constitution of Europe" was "half-ruined everywhere"[10] and thus no longer able to check absolutist monarchs. At the highest level of abstraction, Tocqueville attributes this to the increasing equality of condition over the later Middle Ages and early modernity, a change in historical stage from feudal inequality to democratic equality. "The nobles were already beaten down and the people had not yet risen; the former were too low and the latter not high enough to hinder the movements of power."[11] Germanic customary law had been supplanted by Roman civil law, a "law of servitude," opportunistically deployed across the continent by monarchs set on establishing their "absolute power" "on the ruins of the old liberties of Europe."[12] Tocqueville offers a history of royal suppression of provincial liberties, urban self-government, and guild and corps privileges, as well as of the deliberate Bourbon undermining of the social role of the nobility.

The decayed institutions of the eighteenth century created a paradoxical situation for the old regime. On the one hand, they were unloved, indeed often detested. A nobility that no longer had any useful purpose in the countryside retained feudal privileges and immunity from taxation, and the wealthy urban classes naturally resented them for it. Moreover, they served to divide people against each other. While all were becoming more alike in social fact, they remained sharply legally and politically differentiated, and mutual antagonism resulted. But such freedoms as remained, such limits on royal absolutism as still existed, were thanks to these unloved institutions. They

---

[10] *ORR*, p. 103.   [11] *ORR*, p. 259.

[12] *ORR*, p. 258. This talk of "ruins" echoes Burke's admonition to the French revolutionaries: "Your privileges, though discontinued, were not lost to memory. Your constitution, it is true, whilst you were out of possession, suffered waste and dilapidation; but you possessed in some parts the walls and in all the foundations of a noble and venerable castle. You might have repaired those walls; you might have built on those old foundations" (Burke, *Reflections*, p. 35). Conversely, Voltaire held that Catherine the Great could improve Russia rapidly because "it was easier to erect a building than to repair one whose ruins would still be respected" (Voltaire, "Laws," in *Philosophical Dictionary*, in *Political Writings*, p. 22).

"preserved the spirit of independence among a great number of subjects, and inclined them to stiffen their necks against abuses of authority."[13]

And so Tocqueville emphasized the role of the prerevolutionary *corps intermédiaires*, at the same time that he described the inevitability of their decline. Like Montesquieu and Constant before him, he acknowledged their privileges and prerogatives to have been often (as Montesquieu put it) "odious in themselves," and he thought that they became progressively more intolerable as French society became leveled and homogenized. The *esprit de corps* found in the nobility, the clergy, the lawyers, and each city's bourgeoisie, their commitment to the group's privileges and rights of self-rule, provided them with both the motive and the means to resist royal despotism. About the *parlements* in particular, Tocqueville thought much as Constant had; their role in government "was a great evil which limited a greater one." Tocqueville writes about the dissolution of the *Parlement* of Paris in 1771 much as Constant had written about the Chalotais affair of 1765 that set it in motion. All of the *parlementaires* accepted their loss of status "without a single one of them personally surrendering to the royal will," inspiring other judges and lawyers to stand with them and refuse to cooperate with this suspension of legality. However socially unjust their position was, the *parlementaires* proved themselves to be courageous and committed defenders of liberty and the rule of law: "I know of nothing greater in the history of free nations than what happened on this occasion."[14]

Mill on Centralization and Local Despotism

Mill, by contrast, was deeply concerned with local power in all its varieties. He was intellectually committed to a balance between centralization and decentralization, and abstractly aware that central state power could be a threat to liberty. But as a rule he had far greater faith than did Tocqueville in the ability and propensity of state power to rationally check in-group tyranny. The usual situation was, Mill thought, one of local injustice that could be corrected only by those who had knowledge and the disinterestedness of distance. "Obedience to a distant monarch," he wrote in *Considerations on Representative Government*, "is liberty itself compared with the dominion of the lord of the neighboring castle."[15] In *On Liberty* he diagnoses the human inclination to "like in crowds," the temptation to live using no faculty other "than the ape-like one of imitation," as a fundamental threat to freedom and progress. That

---

[13] *ORR*, p. 172.   [14] *ORR*, p. 178.

[15] Mill, *Considerations on Representative Government* (1861), in *The Collected Works, vol. XIX*, p. 416.

generates a kind of spontaneous tendency toward oppression that must be deliberately overcome. That tendency is the primary object of critique in *OL*: conformism, the desire to suppress eccentricity and to reinforce what a social group already thinks. While Mill does oppose laws and regulations that violate individual liberty, he views such laws as more or less epiphenomenal; it is the underlying social attitudes that must be combated. The tyranny of the majority, though "vulgarly" feared primarily "through the acts of public authorities," often operates through social pressure. The resulting "social tyranny" may be

> more formidable than many kinds of political oppression, since, though not usually upheld by such extreme penalties, it leaves fewer means of escape, penetrating much more deeply into the details of life, and enslaving the soul itself. Protection, therefore, against the tyranny of the magistrate is not enough; there needs protection also against the tyranny of the prevailing opinion and feeling, against the tendency of society to impose, by other means than civil penalties, its own ideas and practices as rules of conduct on those who dissent from them; to fetter the development and, if possible, prevent the formation of any individuality not in harmony with its ways, and compel all characters to fashion themselves upon the model of its own.[16]

This introductory section to *On Liberty* suggests that social tyranny is primarily a feature of the majority of a whole society, as in our image today of Victorian England's cultural conservatism; this leaves the impression of something supra-local. But the "other means" involve countless micro-level social interactions, acts of personal judgmentalism and neighborly disapproval. This in turn suggests that the enforced "rules of conduct" could differ from one spot to the next without making much difference. Combining ideas from *On Liberty* and elsewhere, we can identify a kind of unfreedom that always especially excited Mill's concern: the enforcement of such soul-enslaving, individuality-stunting norms through the oppressive combination of public opinion and local personalized power. The patriarchal husband in a patriarchal society is exemplary. His personal despotic power, all the more abusive because it is so personal, is both created and aggravated by the fact that its exercise conforms with social expectations.

In his mature thought Mill was committed to flourishing human diversity and to a complex, emotionally rich, understanding of human psychology. He was a pluralist about both moral motivations and, as Isaiah Berlin put it, "the ends of life."[17] Humboldt and Coleridge inspired him in ways that marked a break with not only Bentham but also the rationalistic elements in

---

[16] Mill, *On Liberty* (1859), in *The Collected Works, vol. XVIII*, p. 220.
[17] Isaiah Berlin, "John Stuart Mill and the Ends of Life," in *Four Essays on Liberty*.

Enlightenment thought that Tracy built upon.[18] He was not, in other words, a "rationalist" for certain meanings of that word. But the diversity he endorsed was individual, not associational or communal. The local group with its own internal norms and local authority structures was a source of perennial unease for Mill. His rationalism concerned "that one among the political questions of the age which bears the strongest marks of being destined to remain a question for generations to come—Centralisation; or in other words, the limits which separate the province of government from that of individual and spontaneous agency, and of central from local government."[19]

Rationality in governance was almost always to be found in the distant center, which alone could be trusted to control local despotisms that kept humanity in backward ignorance. When he endorsed decentralization, local authority, and group life at all, it was only in sharply delimited and tutelary ways. He begrudged churches as well as universities for their tendency to encourage their own "system" and "particular set of opinions" at the expense of seeking "truth ardently, vigorously, and disinterestedly."[20] A diversity of opinions at the *individual* level, right and wrong, facilitated the search for truth, or so he argued in *OL*. But organizations and institutions and groups committed to their own opinions impaired it, by discouraging the growth of the inquisitive individualistic mind. This is the all-important limitation on his Humboldtian embrace of diversity. The dissenting churches stood just as condemned as the established church for preferring their own doctrine to the truth, and for educating their members to do likewise. Mill was willing to entertain the thought that intermediate groups or local government could serve an educative purpose, helping to prepare individual persons for further intellectual development. But toward intermediate groups as sites of resistance to the state, or as spaces in which persons might live content with familiar values, or as social contexts that could generate local elites and local power, Mill was unsympathetic if not overtly hostile.

Mill worried that even a democratically governed locality might be effectively dominated by local elites: aristocrats or their descendants, priests,

---

[18] Mill met Tracy in 1821 and mentioned him in a draft of the *Autobiography*, but in 1869 acknowledges with seeming embarrassment not having read either his *Political Economy* or the work on ideology of which it was a part. Letter to Cairnes, December 4, 1869, in *Collected Works*, vol. XVII. Contrast Mill on Constant, whom he appreciated especially as an advocate of freedom of the press: "The death of Benjamin Constant is a misfortune to the world. France, since the first revolution, has not produced his equal, taking into account purity of purpose, popular principles, and talents as an orator and politician." *The Examiner*, December 19, 1830; *Works*, vol. XXII, p. 809. Tocqueville, by contrast, never acknowledged Constant in print and may never have read him, an absence that was conspicuous even in his own time. See George Armstrong Kelly, *The Humane Comedy* (New York: Cambridge University Press, 1992), ch. 1, overview and for very plausible speculation as to why this might be.

[19] Mill, "Centralisation," in *Collected Works, vol. XIX*, p. 581.

[20] Mill, "Civilization" (1836), in *Collected Works, vol. XVIII*, p. 141.

wealthy businessmen. Unlike the intellectuals, bureaucrats, and lawyers at the center, local elites tend to come from such uneducated groups. They moreover tend to win election in single-member parliamentary districts. (His support for the Hare system of voting draws in part on the same arguments that motivate his support for weighting the franchise by education.) The locally powerful are well known, and may already command some respect for their leadership positions outside elected politics. They bring a base of support that can be mobilized in an election. And, as Adam Smith argued in *The Theory of Moral Sentiments*, there can be a strange kind of sympathetic engagement with the rich and powerful: they are visible to us, and seem to live well, and that can be enough by itself to excite admiration. So, even if in consensual ways, local elites can gain control of local government, which they will predictably use (in part) to entrench and extend their own power.

Mill said of himself that he learned from Tocqueville to moderate his views about local government. In his own Britain, he wrote in his *Autobiography*, he thought that,

> [c]entralisation was, and is, the subject not only of rational disapprobation, but of unreasoning prejudice; where jealousy of Government interference was a blind feeling preventing or resisting even the most beneficial exertion of legislative authority to correct the abuses of what pretends to be local self-government, but is, too often, selfish mismanagement of local interests, by a jobbing and *borné* local oligarchy. But the more certain the public were to go wrong on the side opposed to Centralisation, the greater danger was there lest philosophic reformers should fall into the contrary error, and overlook the mischiefs of which they had been spared the painful experience. I was myself, at this very time, actively engaged in defending important measures... against an irrational clamour grounded on the Anti-Centralisation prejudice: and had it not been for the lessons of Tocqueville, [I might] have been hurried into the excess opposite to that which, being the one prevalent in my own country, it was generally my business to combat. As it is, I have steered carefully between the two errors, and whether I have or have not drawn the line between them exactly in the right place, I have at least insisted with equal emphasis upon the evils on both sides, and have made the means of reconciling the advantages of both, a subject of serious study.[21]

Mill offers a fine, succinct analysis of the intellectual difficulties with steering a middle path. But it is easy to make too much of this tribute to Tocqueville's memory and to his own moderation. He offers, notably, no example of his newfound balance. In retrospect he still refers to his old opponents as having had a mere "prejudice." While Tocqueville may have thought that he had shown the perils of over-centralization in general—with France and America as exemplars—Mill seems to have drawn the narrower lesson that

---

[21] Mill, *Autobiography*, in *Collected Works vol. I*, ch. 6, pp. 202–3.

France is over-centralized. Through most of his career the possibility of over-centralization in Britain, or in any political dispute in which Mill might take part himself, seems to remain purely hypothetical. The example of the decentralized Poor Laws (also, remember, singled out for criticism by Smith) stayed with him throughout his life.

His important but little-known 1862 essay "Centralisation" offers a fuller statement of his relationship to Tocqueville's concerns. There he is explicit that France has centralized too much, while also expressing the conviction that all enlightened French opinion was following Tocqueville on this point, so much so that the real danger henceforth was an overreaction against central state power. (If this was an odd view halfway through Napoleon III's imperial reign, it looks even stranger with hindsight; the Third Republic that followed subordinated the regions to Paris more firmly than ever, and Tocqueville fell into a long period of relative neglect in French intellectual life.)

The essay reviews one book by Camille Hyacinthe Odilon-Barrot on centralization in France, and two by Charles Brook Dupont-White: one on centralization and one on state action and individual freedom. Through much of the review he treats "the question between governmental or central, and private or local, action" as one question, though he distinguishes the public/private and the central/local dichotomies before the end. Since he thinks Odilon-Barrot's critique of centralization represents the orthodox opinion among French intellectuals and, more importantly, among his English readers, he spends little time on it; the majority of the essay engages with Dupont-White. This is valuable for our purposes, as the latter offers an especially stark kind of rationalist liberalism, and the essay lets us see Mill's relationship to the view.

Dupont-White argues that, as human societies progress, the sphere of state action and the scope of state power necessarily expands, not contracts. Mill maintains that this sometimes rests on a confusion. Before there were railroads or joint-stock corporations, there was no need for legislation regulating either, so in that sense progress necessitates more laws. But it does not necessitate more expansive state power; the new laws need not be intrusive ones, and certainly ought not to create intrusive bureaucratic authority. The ordinary courts, he thinks, can enforce general laws without requiring new forms of executive enforcement agencies.

More broadly, he is unsurprisingly unsympathetic to the view that progress entails increased state intervention at the expense of "individual and spontaneous agency." However, Mill enthusiastically endorses Dupont-White's related claim that social progress often *consists of* increased state power. As Mill approvingly summarizes Dupont-White's view:

The first and greatest duty of the State, in all stages of society, is to protect the weak against the strong. Now, the operation of Progress is to give to the State ever new duties of this description to discharge. We can look back to a time when the State exerted very little power over the great majority of the community. But is it supposed that because the State did not, nobody else did? Quite the reverse. The State did not concern itself about the multitude, because they were under the absolute power of masters, who could be made responsible for them. Law and government recognised, as legally existing, only the few in authority: the slave-masters, the heads of families, the patriarchal chiefs of tribes or clans. Improving civilisation changes this state of things—relieves man from the power of man, and brings him under that of the law. Has not the State necessarily a wider range of action, when it is expected to protect the slave, the wife, the child, the debtor, instead of leaving them to the will and pleasure of masters, husbands, fathers, and creditors? These primitive superiors once had power of life and death over those who were subject to them. *It was the State which freed the weaker party from this despotism. The State alone could have done it, and on the State rests the duty of doing it, wherever it still remains to be done. All this is admitted, and forms no part of the debateable ground.* [...] As long as any wrongful authority is exercised by human beings over one another, the State has still the duty of abolishing it. As long as any, even necessary, authority can be tyrannically abused, it is incumbent on the State to repress and punish the tyranny.[22] [emphasis added]

The same philosophy of historical change is expressed in *On Representative Government*, this time making explicit that the state power that is needed to break the power of local authorities is despotic, not democratic:

[M]any a people has gradually emerged from this condition by the aid of a central authority, whose position has made it the rival, and has ended by making it the master, of the local despots, and which, above all, has been single. French history, from Hugh Capet to Richelieu and Louis XIV, is a continued example of this course of things. [... To the king] the eyes of all the locally oppressed were turned; he was the object of hope and reliance throughout the kingdom, while each local poten-tate was only powerful within a more or less confined space. At his hands, refuge and protection were sought from every part of the country against first one, then another of the immediate oppressors. His progress to ascendancy was slow; but it resulted from successively taking advantage of opportunities which offered them-selves only to him. It was, therefore, sure; and, in proportion as it was accom-plished, it abated, in the oppressed portion of the community, the habit of submitting to oppression. The king's interest lay in encouraging all partial attempts on the part of the serfs to emancipate themselves from their masters, and place themselves in immediate subordination to himself. Under his protec-tion numerous communities were formed which knew no one above them but the king. Obedience to a distant monarch is liberty itself compared with the dominion

---

[22] Mill, "Centralisation," in *Collected Works vol. XIX*, p. 589.

of the lord of the neighboring castle; and the monarch was long compelled by necessities of position to exert his authority as the ally rather than the master of the classes whom he had aided in affecting their liberation. In this manner a central power, despotic in principle, though generally much restricted in practice, was mainly instrumental in carrying the people through a necessary stage of improvement, which representative government, if real, would most likely have prevented them from entering upon.[23]

In other words, Mill breaks with Dupont-White's robust equation of state power with social progress *only for already mature and enlightened societies*. Once a society has reached moral and intellectual adulthood, its *further* growth will both encourage and be encouraged by greater freedom from state action. But prior to such adulthood the reverse is true. Progress depends on both more powerful and more despotic central states, both in the European past and in the non-European present.

This view should not come as much of a surprise after recent decades' attention to Mill's views on imperialism and nationalism. What he calls, in *On Liberty*, "the permanent interests of man as a progressive being" regularly trump his commitments to individual freedom, to representative government, or to self-determination, for peoples he deems insufficiently advanced. The various aspects of freedom are instrumentally useful to those "permanent interests" among civilized peoples. Their individual freedom of speech and debate allows them to progress toward the truth, as their participation in democratic politics allowed them to learn and to enlarge their minds. But those who are not civilized would use their freedom in ways that would impede their own progress. And so, on questions of military intervention in the affairs of other peoples,

> [t]here is a great difference [. . .] between the case in which the nations concerned are of the same, or something like the same, degree of civilization, and that in which one of the parties to the situation is of a high, and the other of a very low, grade of social improvement.[. . .] [N]ations which are still barbarous have not got beyond the period during which it is likely to be for their benefit that they should be conquered and held in subjection by foreigners. Independence and nationality, so essential to the due growth and development of a people further advanced in improvement, are generally impediments to theirs. The sacred duties which civilized nations owe to the independence and nationality of each other, are not binding towards those to whom nationality and independence are either a certain evil, or at best a questionable good.[24]

---

[23] Mill, *Considerations on Representative Government*, in *Collected Works vol. XIX*, p. 416.

[24] Mill, "A Few Words on Non-Intervention" (1859), in *Collected Works, vol. XXI*, p. 118. It should be noted that Tocqueville endorsed both an English imperial civilizing mission for India and a French one for Algeria, though his support for the latter seemed to owe at least as much to the sheer desire to see France accomplish something of greatness. Mill found *that* an unworthy goal,

Those for whom "nationality and independence" are an evil are sometimes Europeans:

> Nobody can suppose that it is not more beneficial to a Breton, or a Basque of French Navarre, to be brought into the current of the ideas and feelings of a highly civilized and cultivated people...than to sulk on his own rocks, the half-savage relic of past times, revolving in his own little mental orbit, without participation or interest in the general movement of the world. The same remark applies to the Welshman or the Scottish Highlander, as members of the British nation.[25]

Notwithstanding this disdain for Celtic savages (or for Russian serfs, whom he also considered too backward for immediate freedom), the greatest import-ance this kind of argument had for Mill was undoubtedly that of justifying British rule in India. For peoples who were unused to obedience or attached to tribal or kinship rather than "national" communities, despotism was indis-pensable for raising them up and preparing them for—eventually—national freedom. They had to be settled down by force. For peoples who were *too* accustomed to obedience and who had fallen into stagnation, societies "in which, there being no spring of spontaneous improvement in the people themselves," despotism was again indispensible—not to teach basic habits of discipline, but to break the power of backwardness. But everything depended on the quality of the despot. A stagnant country would only prod-uce an occasional Peter the Great out of its own system by chance. But a distant, rational, and civilized imperial power could supply such enlightened despots "constantly," and thereby

> ought to be able to do for its subjects all that could be done by a succession of absolute monarchs, guaranteed by irresistible force against the precariousness of tenure attendant on barbarous despotisms, and qualified by their genius to antici-pate all that experience has taught to the more advanced nation. Such is the ideal rule of a free people over a barbarous or semibarbarous one.[26]

There is an apparent contrast between Mill's writings on India and his various writings and activities with respect to the rights of Africans, slavery, and government in the West Indies.[27] The backwardness and servility of Indians was not, on Mill's account, biological or racial: it could and would be overcome in time. But it was so deeply rooted that it would take generations to overcome; they would not be ready for freedom in the foreseeable future. In

---

and criticized Tocqueville sharply for it, seeing in it a mere desire for national glory. That was undoubtedly present, but so too was Tocqueville's perpetual fear of the mediocrity of spirit that could characterize democratic modernity. See Jennifer Pitts, Introduction, in Pitts, ed., Alexis de Tocqueville, *Writings on Empire and Slavery* (Baltimore: Johns Hopkins University Press, 2001).

[25] Mill, *Considerations on Representative Government*, in *Collected Works vol. XIX*, p. 549.

[26] Mill, *Considerations on Representative Government*, in *Collected Works, vol. XIX*, p. 567.

[27] See Pitts, *A Turn to Empire*.

the debates about Africans, however, Mill championed racial equality, and bitterly opposed those who claimed that Africans were unsuited for freedom. The first round of this dispute involved the prominent conservative social critic Thomas Carlyle, who coined the phrase "the dismal science" to describe the liberal economists' support for abolition and free labor rather than the (supposed) community of interest between master and slave.[28] His writings actively defending slavery and black inferiority elicited a response from Mill in 1850, "The Negro Question."

After the 1865 Morant Bay rebellion in Jamaica was crushed with the massacre and executions of hundreds of black peasants, Mill (along with Herbert Spencer, John Bright, and Charles Darwin, among others) formed the "Jamaica Committee" to agitate for criminal charges against Governor John Eyre. Arrayed on the other side were prominent critics of liberalism including Ruskin, Dickens, and Carlyle. Carlyle had had a public exchange with Mill on race some time before, and he continued the old dispute with an overtly racist defense of Eyre.

Though Mill stood unambiguously for racial equality in the Jamaican case, his writings on empire are rife with characterizations of Indians as too immature for freedom. But notice this similarity: in the case of Jamaica, Mill effectively championed central state supervision over the local despotism of the plantation economy and the local state apparatus run for the benefit of plantation-owners. In the case of India, he advocated strong English central rule that would educate and enlighten those who would otherwise inevitably be subject to local oppression. In one case the local oppressors were white and English; in the other, they were Brahmin or Muslim. But in either case, the solution to local unfreedom lay in London. As Pitts notes, Mill's remedies lay in "tightening *metropolitan* constraints on unrepresentative local legislatures, rather than aspiring to render the Jamaican government more accountable to its subjects."[29]

In short, Mill's pervasive concern with the entwined problems of local despotism and local backwardness offered him reason to prefer distant power strong enough to overcome them. Local rule, small-group loyalties and membership, and adherence to custom were necessarily stultifying, at odds with the interests of man as a progressive being; and forcible inclusion into a great kingdom, nation, or empire at least might point the way toward intellectual uplift. Only in already-advanced societies could the reins be

---

[28] Thomas Carlyle, "Occasional Discourse on the Negro Question," *Fraser's Magazine for Town and Country*, December 1849, pp. 672–3. Carlyle had earlier used the word "dismal" in an account of Malthus' theories of population, and this has often been mentioned as the origin of "dismal science"; but the full phrase appears in "Negro Question" and not in the commentary on Malthus. David M. Levy, *How the Dismal Science Got Its Name* (Ann Arbor: University of Michigan Press, 2001).

[29] Pitts, *A Turn to Empire*, pp. 157–8.

slackened—and even there, only in ways that are instrumentally connected to Mill's vision of moral and cognitive development. It is well known that Mill advocates weighted voting to allow the less educated to develop their civic skills without too much damage to the intellectual quality of political decision-making; the same is true for his concessions toward decentralization and associational life in advanced liberal democracies.

In his review of *DA* volume II, Mill finesses Tocqueville's arguments in favor of decentralization so that it is not

> inconsistent with obtaining a considerable share of the benefits (and they are great) of what is called centralization. The principle of local self-government has been undeservedly discredited, by being associated with the agitation against the new poor-law. The most active agency of a central authority in collecting and communicating information, giving advice to the local bodies, and even framing general rules for their observance, is no hindrance, but an aid, to making the local liberties an instrument of educating the people.[30]

He developed this into a full theory of carefully controlled decentralization in *Representative Government*. After emphasizing the "lower grade of intelligence and knowledge" in local governments and the "generally far less enlightened" public that monitors them, he admits that localities can have greater knowledge of strictly local details. In a well-ordered system, "the principal business of the central authority should be to give instruction, of the local authority to apply it. Power may be localised, but knowledge, to be most useful, must be centralised."[31] Naturally, Parliament must carefully regulate the tasks the local governments may carry out, not least so that local majorities do not oppress minorities or individuals. He offers as an example (nearly the only one) of legitimate local authority the setting of "the mere amount" of local tax rates—provided that Parliament dictate the kinds of taxes and the rules of assessment. The aim is educational, but Parliament must set only lessons that the citizen-students are able to learn.

Jon Elster observes that Tocqueville's discussion of the jury system is more or less entirely tutelary.[32] The jury as a "judicial institution" is, according to Tocqueville, defective and a remnant of England's barbarian past. But as a "political institution," it is "the most efficient way of teaching [the people] how to rule." Elster notes, however, that for jurors to learn the lessons Tocqueville wants them to learn from jury service, they must believe that they are engaged in a worthwhile judicial endeavor. They must aim at truth and

---

[30] Mill, "De Tocqueville on Democracy in America (ii)" (1840), in *Collected Works, vol. XVIII*, p. 169.

[31] Mill, *Considerations on Representative Government*, in *Collected Works, vol. XIX*, p. 544.

[32] Jon Elster, *Sour Grapes: Studies in the Subversion of Rationality* (Cambridge: Cambridge University Press, 1983), pp. 94–7.

justice. If they aim at their own self-improvement, the enterprise will fail and indeed becomes a kind of narcissistic farce. Tocqueville could be *right* about the educational benefits of the institution; but those benefits must be understood as side-effects, not as the purpose of the institution. They are "essentially"—that is, necessarily—"by-products." If they become central, they will disappear. If jurors came to think as Tocqueville did—that their work was judicially pointless but politically beneficial—then even the political benefits would end.

While Tocqueville often adverts to the educational benefits of one or another institution, it is exceptional for him to suggest, as he seems to about juries, that these are primary. For Mill, it is the rule. Tocqueville's understanding of the moral improvement worked by local liberties and local self-government is one that the participants could admit to themselves without psychological strain: out of the necessity of working together on matters of local importance, we have learned how to work together. The improvement of the participants aligns with the function they are performing. The local questions are important ones, and the importance motivates the participants, regardless of whether they notice their own improvement or care about it.

Mill's carefully parceled-out local administrative tasks, however, seem to run afoul of both Elster's concern about essential by-products and Bernard Williams' related critique of government-house utilitarianism.[33] If the participants in Millian local government notice the sharp limits on their authority and think to ask about them, they will find that the answer is: we have given you as much responsibility as is good for you.

Much the same is true of voluntary associations. In *Liberty*, Mill calls the benefits to private persons' "mental education," the advantages of "strengthening of their active faculties, exercising their judgment," and increasing their knowledge, "a principal, though not the sole, recommendation of... of free and popular local and municipal institutions; of the conduct of industrial and philanthropic enterprises by voluntary associations. *These are not questions of liberty, and are connected with that subject only by remote tendencies; but they are questions of development*" [emphasis added]. Taking part in such activities can take citizens "out of the narrow circle of personal and family selfishness" and habituate them "to act from public or semi-public motives, and guide their conduct by aims which unite instead of isolating them from one another."[34]

On Tocqueville's telling, Americans join voluntary associations because they want to accomplish some purpose, and to do so socially. And in a democratic age, persons are mostly powerless to accomplish great things on

---

[33] Bernard Williams, *Ethics and the Limits of Philosophy* (Cambridge, Mass.: Harvard University Press, 1986).

[34] Mill, *On Liberty*, in *Collected Works, vol. XVIII*, p. 305.

their own. "The first time that I heard in America that one hundred thousand men had publicly promised never to drink alcoholic liquor, I thought it more of a joke than a serious matter and could not see why these very abstemious citizens could not content themselves with drinking water by their own firesides." One can well imagine that almost anyone from France would react this way to this particular manifestation of Second Great Awakening American Protestantism! But

> in the end I came to understand that these hundred thousand Americans, frightened by the patronage of drunkenness around them, wanted to support sobriety by their patronage . . . One may fancy that if they had lived in France each of these hundred thousand would have made individual representations to the government asking it to supervise all the public houses throughout the realm.[35]

We know that the temperance movement was to culminate almost a century later in Prohibition, brought about not by hundreds of thousands of individual petitions to the government, but by the very organized political action of voluntary associations. But that's no part of Tocqueville's vision here, and the French equivalent is a *reductio ad absurdum* for his French readers, not a prediction. The point of the contrast for him is that the Americans choose voluntary association *instead of* the state to effect social improvement as they see it.

> Americans of all ages, all stations in life, and all types of disposition are forever forming associations. There are not only commercial and industrial associations in which all take part, but others of a thousand different types—religious, moral, serious, futile, very general and very limited, immensely large and very minute. Americans combine to give fetes, found seminaries, build churches, distribute books, and send missionaries to the antipodes. Finally, if they want to proclaim a truth or propagate some feeling by the encouragement of a great example, they form an association. In every case, at the head of any new undertaking, where in France you would find the government or in England some territorial magnate, in the United States you are sure to find an association.[36]

Of political associations as such, he says that they "are only one small part of the immense number of different types of associations found there"[37]—and not, he suggests, the most important part. In Mill's review of Volume II, by contrast, the associations he draws on to illustrate the importance of the category are anti-slavery societies, the Chartist "Political Unions," and trade unions, the first two of which were mainly concerned with changing state policy and the last of which was significantly so. Only for such directly political associations did he seem interested in the actual goal of associational life, rather than in its tutelary by-products.

---

[35] *DA*, p. 516. [36] *DA*, p. 513. [37] *DA*, p. 513.

Indeed, at the time Tocqueville was writing about associations in America, Mill penned an essay advocating the expropriation of charitable endowments in England, "The Right and Wrong of State Interference with Corporation and Church Property" (1833). He moderated this view in his late-career essay "Endowments" (1869), and offered a rare suggestion that Britain might go too far down the French route of centralization; but, tellingly, it was only educational endowments that he there defended.

In the earlier piece, Mill wrote in favor of the state's right to "resume" (nationalize) endowments granted to educational and religious foundations after some defined period following the donor's death. Mill denied that there could be *any* wrong in such seizures. The dead donor no longer owned the resources; the living persons associated with the institutions were merely trustees, not owners; and the organizations themselves owned the resources only by a legal fiction. The beneficiaries of, for example, an endowment in trust for education, Mill claimed, were the nation as a whole, which could eventually do with the trust as it wished. Mill invoked *mortmain* and the fear of tying up land in perpetuity; the fictional existence of the institutions; the progress of knowledge over the "poor wisdom" of our ancestors; and the prospect of a more rational use of the resources by deliberate decision.

He reserved special scorn for the defenders of the Church of England's property—which derived, after all, from an earlier state seizure of resources from the Roman Catholic Church. He allowed that charitable endowments of money (not land) should be permitted for the donor's lifetime and some time beyond, and that those dedicated to education in particular were an affirmative good. And he retained enough suspicion of state actors to insist that nationalized charitable funds should be deployed for socially beneficial purposes, where possible in a similar (though broader) vein to the original goal: endowments for alms should be reclaimed and used for the general betterment of the poor, educational endowments of particular schools as well as those of the Church to education as a whole—Church endowments having been intended to promote spiritual improvement, which today were known to come from a broad education!

He saw the likelihood that endowments would be seized simply to fund general or military expenses or service the national debt, and charged that this would sacrifice serious moral goods even though it violated no rights. But the main thrust of the argument was in favor of the resumption and/or repurposing of religious endowments to educational goals.

It was only in the face of an apparent proposal to prohibit private charitable organizations from working toward poor relief or education altogether, since these were public purposes, that Mill in the later essay perceived a doctrine breathing the very spirit, and expressed in almost the words, of the apologies made in the over-centralised governments of the Continent for not permitting any one to perform the smallest act connected with public interests without the leave of the Government. [I]t is time to enter a protest in behalf of those 'private persons' whose . . . liberty of making themselves useful in their own way, without requiring the consent of any public authority, has mainly contributed to make England the free country she is; and whose well-directed public spirit is covering America with the very institutions [schools] which her state of society most needs, and was least likely in any other manner to get—institutions for the careful cultivation of the higher studies.[38]

Other private associations Mill may have found useful only insofar as they provided a civic education to their members; other charitable endowments were legitimately seizable for educational purposes. Private educational associations and endowments, at least, could find Mill's approval for their own ends.

In light of all this, Mill's comments on Mormon polygamy in *On Liberty* are slightly surprising.[39] The religion itself seems to him "the product of palpable imposture." He expressly condemns polygamy as "a direct infraction" of the principle of liberty, as a way of "riveting the chains" that bind women. He characterizes it as retrograde: a turn from civilization toward barbarism, just the same categories that he routinely uses elsewhere to distinguish those entitled to freedom from those who are not. Yet he counsels restraint: "I am not aware that any community has a right to force another to be civilized"[40]—a statement all but impossible to reconcile with his views in "Non-Intervention" and *Representative Government*.

He makes sure to mention that the oppressiveness of Mormon polygamy is different only in degree from that of familiar monogamous marriage, but that charge of hypocrisy on the part of non-Mormons is not the core of his reaction. Mill is clear that he is repelled by the mood in which the Mormons are persecuted, and the hypocrisy of it. Europeans have long lived peacefully in a world where Muslims (and, according to Mill, Hindus and Chinese) practice polygamy; it is the sight of the practice among "persons who speak English, and profess to be a kind of Christians" that has triggered what we would now consider a moral panic. Importantly, the depredations the Mormons had suffered by the time of *On Liberty* were local ones: they were chased from one American state to another and their prophet was killed by an armed

---

[38] Mill, "Endowments 1869," in *Collected Works, vol. V*, p. 616.

[39] On this case, see Bruce Baum, "Feminism, Liberalism and Cultural Pluralism: J. S. Mill on Mormon Polygyny," 5(3) *Journal of Political Philosophy* 230–53, 1997; Mark Tunick, "John Stuart Mill and Unassimilated Subjects," 53(4) *Political Studies* 833–48, 2005.

[40] Mill, *On Liberty"* in *Collected Works vol. XVIII*, p. 291.

mob. He emphasizes the passionate persecuting spirit at work, both in America and in Britain.

> What here concerns us is, that this religion, like other and better religions, has its martyrs; that its prophet and founder was, for his teaching, put to death by a mob; that others of its adherents lost their lives by the same lawless violence; that they were forcibly expelled, in a body, from the country in which they first grew up; while, now that they have been chased into a solitary recess in the midst of a desert, many in this country openly declare that it would be right (only that it is not convenient) to send an expedition against them, and compel them by force to conform to the opinions of other people.[41]

The specific target of the passage is the British press, which turn to "the language of downright persecution" whenever they mention Mormonism and try to stir up hatred of it. He does not defend the freedom to enter into group marriages, though it matters to him that the Mormon women consent. Rather, he critiques the conformist spirit behind the (bizarre) idea that *Britain* should invade Utah as a "civilizade."

"The family," Mill wrote in his most important defense of liberty against local despotism, *Subjection of Women*,

> is a school of despotism, in which the virtues of despotism, but also its vices, are largely nourished. Citizenship, in free countries, is partly a school of society in equality; but citizenship fills only a small place in modern life, and does not come near the daily habits or inmost sentiments. The family, justly constituted, would be the real school of the virtues of freedom.[42]

In all of these cases—the family, the voluntary association, local government, traditional religion and government—Mill was concerned about the lessons that would be learned and the habits that would be inculcated. He saw all of these as schools in which persons would learn to be free and equal, or in which they would learn to dominate and be dominated. He was perhaps the major theorist most firmly committed to the idea of congruence discussed in Part I.

Tocqueville also saw a social world with countless schools. But he emphasized the lessons that would be learned *about interaction with, and especially resistance to, the state.* The person who stood up to state power for the sake of his group's privileges would know how to do so in other cases. The person in a leveled society who never faced any authority but that of the state would develop the habit of truckling to every official. He shared Mill's recognition that there could be something especially degrading in subservience to some local magistrate or bureaucrat; but for Tocqueville, this was just the local face

---

[41] Mill, *On Liberty* in *Collected Works, vol. XVIII*, p. 290.
[42] Mill, *The Subjection of Women* (1869), in *Collected Works, vol. XXI*, pp. 294–5.

of central state power, and the willingness to bow and scrape was due not to the official's local in-group status but to the institution of which he was the representative.

Tocqueville's views on the family in America thus show no evidence of Mill's concerns. He says that the "yoke" of marriage is stricter in Puritan America than in Europe, that the sexual division of labor between the domestic and public spheres is more sharply defined. The husband's house is "almost a cloister" and "inexorable public opinion carefully keeps woman within the little sphere of domestic interests and will not let her go beyond them."[43] He describes American marriages and the rules surrounding them as austere, strict, and severe, and writes repeatedly of wives' constraints, duties, sacrifice of freedom, and relinquishment of will.

But he means none of this as criticism. Rather, the democratic impulse which levels all social distinctions also does so with respect to the distinction between the sexes; it "does raise the status of women and should make them more and more nearly equal to men."[44] But, contrary to the imaginings of anti-democrats in Europe, that near-equality will not mean sameness or a diminution of male authority within the household.

Contemporary readers generally and rightly believe that Tocqueville showed real insight and understanding about the importance of voluntary associations and local government, and that Mill did so about the family. But I think Mill's correctness about the family, slavery, and the obnoxiousness of the local busybody flows from the same intellectual sources as his wrongness about nationalism and about the future of centralization, and to some extent about imperialism as well. And conversely, Tocqueville's view that intermediate groups might be the only viable check against despotism (whether monarchical and hard or democratic and soft) more or less necessarily obscured from his view the unfreedom within those groups themselves.

---

[43] *DA*, p. 592.   [44] *DA*, p. 600.

9

From Liberal Constitutionalism to Pluralism

The British Pluralists

British Pluralism[1] as an intellectual school is conventionally marked as beginning with the legal historian F. W. Maitland's translation of a portion of Otto von Gierke's work under the English title *Political Theories of the Middle Ages*, and his substantial introduction to that translation. The figures identified with it are Maitland himself, the historian of political thought John Neville Figgis, G. D. H. Cole, and Harold Laski, with Ernest Barker and John Dewey sometimes being identified as fellow-travelers and sometimes being thought of as the critics who helped to kill the school off (or maybe both in turn). Its intellectual high-water mark was, to my mind, attained with Figgis' *Churches in the Modern State*, a minor masterpiece on freedom of religion and association, though a case could certainly be made that Laski's trio of works, *Authority in the Modern State*, *Studies in the Problem of Sovereignty*, and *The Foundations of Sovereignty*, are cumulatively more important. The school is generally thought of as coming to an end roughly in the 1930s, with Laski's turn to more orthodox socialism, under criticism from Dewey and others, under the weight of its inability to articulate what a theory of competing sovereignties means, and under assault from a world turning to centralization at best and totalitarianism at worst.

British Pluralism has largely been omitted from our sense of the history of liberal thought in the nineteenth and twentieth centuries, and there are several reasons for this.

Cole and Laski, probably the most famous members of the school, in their pluralist moments were and understood themselves to be something like guild socialists and corporatists, and their interest in Pluralist ideas was tied up with an interest in critiquing liberal economics. Pluralism is thus sometimes

---

[1] I will use "Pluralism" and "Pluralists" in this chapter to refer to the British Pluralist school, to avoid confusion with the broader uses of "pluralism" and "pluralist" in the book.

remembered as a side in a controversy regarding the best character of social-ism, economic organization, and the Labour political movement that was displacing both the Liberal party and the dominance of a sort of liberal ideology. The associations that interested Cole and Laski were, above all, trade unions, and secondarily, organizations representing economic interests. Their importance to the development of a decentralist socialist tradition has, I think, overshadowed the other Pluralists' contributions to liberalism.

Similarly, the recovery of the Pluralists in the 1980s and 90s was led by scholars who were primarily interested in syndicalism, guild socialism, and neocorporatism, Paul Hirst being the most prominent.[2] Hirst, like (some-times) Cole and Laski but quite unlike Figgis or Maitland, was fundamentally interested in *economic* associations, trade unions above all. Avigail Eisenberg's work on the Pluralist tradition, which came many years into that recovery, was among the only works to take the Pluralists seriously as a source for thought about religious and cultural groups rather than primarily about labor unions or corporate economic interests—and the connection she established there (on which I mean to build) still has not been much taken up in the literature.[3]

The Pluralists wrote at an odd time for the *word* liberal, and only partly because of the collapse of the Liberal Party and the so-called "strange death" of Liberal England.[4] British liberalism as an *intellectual* movement was coming to mean the "new liberalism," distinguishing itself from its "old" predecessor with a newfound enthusiasm for state power in the service of material welfare and limiting the power of industrial corporations; and this in turn meant that the "old" liberals came to appear, and perhaps even to think of themselves as, concerned primarily with limiting state power in economic questions. The pluralists were emphatically not on either of *these* sides; Laski was not a New Liberal,[5] and Figgis barely commented on economic questions at all.[6] To a substantial degree, Maitland and Figgis were concerned with different ques-tions altogether. Even Maitland's youthful *A Historical Sketch of Liberty and Equality*, a conventional piece of liberal intellectual historiography that runs from Locke and Sidney through Smith and Kant to Mill and Spencer to show

---

[2] See, e.g., Paul Hirst, *From Statism to Pluralism: Democracy, Civil Society, and Global Politics* (London: Routledge, 1997).

[3] Avigail Eisenberg, *Reconstructing Political Pluralism* (Albany, N.Y.: State University of New York Press, 1995). See more recently Victor Muñiz-Fraticelli, *The Structure of Pluralism* (Oxford: Oxford University Press, 2014).

[4] George Dangerfield, *The Strange Death of Liberal England* (New York: Smith and Haas, 1935).

[5] See his criticism of the old liberals for their neglect of the "social question" *and* of the new liberals and their institutions for paternalism, in "The Problem of Administrative Areas," in *The Foundations of Sovereignty and Other Essays* (New York: Harcourt, Brace & Company, 1921).

[6] He makes a few remarks about industrial capitalism in *Churches in the Modern State*, but these are primarily examples of things that he thinks churches ought not to take corporate public stands on.

the development of modern understandings of its titular ideals, eschews the word "liberal" altogether except in quotations from others.[7] And so views that might have been understood as liberal, *simpliciter*, decades before or decades later, fell between the early twentieth-century cracks, because they were neither New Liberal nor Old Liberal.[8]

Also at fault is the tendency in the twentieth century to treat rationalist liberalism as the sum total of the liberal tradition, and often to treat rationalism in its various forms as so constitutive of liberalism as to override normative criteria. Think of the recurring tendency to treat Hobbes as a (or the) founder of liberalism, a tendency most often found among liberalism's critics, whether from the left (Macpherson), the right (Strauss), or elsewhere (Pettit). The liberal tradition came to be identified not with individualism as a normative conclusion, but individualism as a methodological premise. It came to be identified not with constitutionalism as a political practice, but with contractarianism as a foundational commitment. And it came to be identified not with religious freedom as a normative *sine qua non*, but with the subordination of the church to the state as a desirable aspect of the legal consolidation of modern states.

This blurring of the line between Hobbes and liberalism was well underway in the pluralists' own time. Constitutionalist, Whig, and common law skepticism about Hobbesian sovereignty was hard to come by, displaced by Blackstone's theory of parliamentary absolutism, Bentham and Austin's theory of sovereignty and legal positivism, and Dicey's synthesis of the two: a parliamentary Hobbesian sovereign. In any liberalism of which Hobbes is the source, the Pluralists have no place; and it's no great surprise for the Pluralists to have seen themselves and be seen as alien to the liberal tradition.

One idea does seem to distinguish the British Pluralists from the pluralist liberals such as Montesquieu and Tocqueville, the kind of thing Anglo-Americans often dismiss as Germanic mysticism and obscurantism: the doctrine of the *real personality* of groups, a doctrine that ran through Gierke's work[9] and was the major theme of Maitland's seminal introduction to Gierke. "Real personality" was an idea opposed in the first instance to the so-called concession theory of group personality: that corporate group life was a fictitious privilege granted by sovereign command. To followers of Hobbes and Austin, or to those who emphasized the imperial permission clause in the

---

[7] Frederic William Maitland, *A Historical Sketch of Liberty and Equality: as ideals of English political philosophy from the time of Hobbes to the time of Coleridge* (Indianapolis: Liberty Fund, 2000[1875]).

[8] On this point, see my "Liberalism's Divide, After Socialism—and Before."

[9] Throughout, references to Gierke and his work mean only the four volumes of *Das Deutsche Genossenschaftsrecht*, the last published in 1881. This is the work that influenced the British pluralists. Antony Black notes that his later work became much less liberal and pluralist, more statist and nationalist. Black, introduction to Otto von Gierke, *Community in Historical Perspective*.

corpus about forming associations, incorporation was a kind of dispensation from the sovereign, and corporate bodies would have only such privileges as the sovereign found convenient. Gierke insisted that the Germanic and Christian ideas of fellowship preceded the recovery of the Roman law and were more fundamental; persons joining together in shared bonds created something of independent social and moral significance, as real as individual persons. In varying ways, the British Pluralists picked up on this idea.

However much we argue that liberalism is constituted by moral rather than methodological individualism, the doctrine of groups as real persons will be a hard pill for some liberals to swallow. That the theory of real group personality gets tied up with an old-fashioned story about the necessary despotism of Roman law, and the necessary connection between Gothic customary law and freedom only makes things worse. For obvious reasons, by the mid-to-late 1930s, Anglo-American liberals ceased to be enamored of just-so stories that placed the roots of liberal freedom in the ineliminable character of the German *volk* and its offshoots such as the pre-Norman Anglo-Saxons. But that historiographic point is secondary; real group personality is the crux. I will return to this toward the end of the chapter, and argue that real group personality is not only reconcilable with pluralist liberalism but, understood in the right way, necessary for it.

Lord Acton

Despite all of these reasons for a distance between Pluralism and liberalism, there is something odd in our sense of the relationship of the two. To see this consider Figgis' and Maitland's relationships to Lord Acton, among the most quintessentially and even dogmatically liberal (as well as Liberal) political thinkers of nineteenth-century Britain.

Acton was a historian first, a theorist second—similar in that way to both Gierke and Maitland, and to an extent Laski.[10] He was Regius Professor at Cambridge and a major force behind the Cambridge Modern History. But he was a historian of undoubted normative commitments: close to Gladstone's Liberal government; deeply involved in intra-Catholic struggles about papal centralization, ultramontanism, and the First Vatican Council, on the side of the decentralists; and a committed federalist. He was elevated to the peerage by Gladstone, and wrote profound essays on the theme that he termed "the

---

[10] Laski was only occasionally appointed to history departments, but held that "no attempt at reconstruction of our present institutions is likely to be successful save insofar as it is deeply rooted in historical knowledge." Laski, *Foundations of Sovereignty*, p. ix.

history of liberty," though he never completed his projected unified treatment of the subject.

His "On Nationality" has acquired a minor place in the canon as a rejoinder to John Stuart Mill's treatment of the subject in *Considerations on Representative Government*. Mill's nationalism looked favorably on the desire to create nationally homogeneous states, whether by breaking up multinational empires or by assimilationism that led backward provincial peoples to identify with the state. Either way, the end result would be universal subjective identification with the same cultural–political community, the nation-state. As far as Acton was concerned, this was precisely the outcome to avoid. Those who subjectively identified with the state as the embodiment of their nation would be much too trusting of and enthusiastic about their state, easily coming to endorse political absolutism. National plurality, like religious plurality, encouraged people to keep some distance between their self-identification and their political membership.

Such division was needed in order to stave off the trend in the modern state toward centralization and absolutism under a democratic government.

> The modern theory, which has swept away every authority except that of the State, and has made the sovereign power irresistible by multiplying those who share it, is the enemy of that common freedom in which religious freedom is included. It condemns, as a State within the State, every inner group and community, class or corporation, administering its own affairs; and, by proclaiming the abolition of privileges, it emancipates the subjects of every such authority in order to transfer them exclusively to its own. It recognises liberty only in the individual, because it is only in the individual that liberty can be separated from authority, and the right of conditional obedience deprived of the security of a limited command. Under its sway, therefore, every man may profess his own religion more or less freely; but his religion is not free to administer its own laws. In other words, religious profession is free, but Church government is controlled. And where ecclesiastical authority is restricted, religious liberty is virtually denied. For religious liberty is not the negative right of being without any particular religion, just as self-government is not anarchy. It is the right of religious communities to the practice of their own duties, the enjoyment of their own constitution, and the protection of the law, which equally secures to all the possession of their own independence.[11]

Fortunately, Acton thought, the "true natural" antidote to this rising tide of democratic absolutism had been found: "the one immortal tribute of America to political science," a constitutional federalism of clearly divided sovereignty. The reservation of authority to states that could oppose the federal center

---

[11] Acton, "The Protestant Theory of Persecution," in *The History of Freedom and Other Essays* (London: Macmillan, 1907), pp. 151–2.

offers "at the same time the consummation and the guard of democracy."[12] Federalism offers "the most efficacious and the most congenial" check on democracy and majority government. It "limits and restrains the sovereign power by dividing it [...it] is the only method of curbing not only the majority but the power of the whole people."[13] He considered it *the* great modern constitutional discovery, that which might make the democratic republicanism that was inevitable in modernity safe for individual liberty.[14] This was the intellectual framework for his objection to Mill's advocacy of the unified democratic nation-state. He saw, as Mill did not, the threat to human freedom that could come from the democratic-nationalist exaltation of the unified state acting as the unified national people made manifest.

Acton's ability to see the pluralist value in federalism, however, badly distorted his own view in turn. Although an opponent of slavery, before the outbreak of the American Civil War he wrote derisively of the abolitionists and half-admiringly of the south. Like Tocqueville, he thought that the southern slaveowning class was a kind of paradoxical defender of liberty. In an age when the idea of governmental omnipotence was destroying the idea of individual rights, the slaveowners were unavoidably committed to limits on governmental power, and especially to limits on the power of the center. "I saw in State Rights," he wrote after the war, "the only availing check upon the absolutism of the sovereign will."[15] These words were part of an almost-fawning correspondence he initiated with Robert E. Lee.

Secession, he wrote, "filled me with hope, not as the destruction but as the redemption of Democracy. The institutions of your Republic have not exercised on the old world the salutary and liberating influence which ought to have belonged to them, by reason of those defects and abuses of principle which the Confederate Constitution was expressly and wisely calculated to remedy. I believed that the example of that great Reform would have blessed all the races of mankind by establishing true freedom purged of the native dangers and disorders of Republics. Therefore I deemed that you were fighting the battles of our liberty, our progress, and our civilization; and I mourn for the stake which was lost at Richmond more deeply than I rejoice over that

---

[12] Acton, "The Influence of America," in J. Rufus Fears, ed., *Essays in the History of Liberty* (Indianapolis: Liberty Fund, 1985[1877]), p. 211.

[13] Acton, "Review of Sir Erskine May's *Democracy in Europe*" (1878), in *Essays in the History of Liberty*, p. 84.

[14] And in this way he was more committed than was Tocqueville to the potential importance of formal political institutions; Tocqueville was more pessimistic about institutions' ability to check the historical tide. Acton dissented from Tocqueville's "despondency" ("Sir Erskine May's *Democracy in Europe*," in *Essays in the History of Liberty*, p. 84); and endorsed the view that "Tocqueville never understood the [American] federal constitution." ("Review of Bryce's *American Commonwealth*" (1889), in *Essays in the History of Liberty*, p. 396.)

[15] Acton, Letter to General Robert E. Lee on November 4, 1866, in *Essays in the History of Liberty*, p. 363.

which was saved at Waterloo"[16]—an astonishing statement for a nineteenth-century Englishman to make.[17]

As an aside, this is an especially vivid example of the ways in which pluralism as a point of view or analytical lens (in this case, rationalism in others) offers insights and blind spots that are hard to pull apart. Acton's pluralism and federalism allowed him to see what Mill could not: that the rise of nationalism in Europe, the principle that nations ought to be states and vice versa, was illiberal and dangerous. His understanding of institutional pluralism and competition lent real depth to his understanding of religious liberty. And those same insights led him to analyses of the U.S. Civil War that were not merely wrong, but carefully and thoughtfully wickedly wrong. He identified the cause of the Confederacy as the cause of freedom, even knowing slavery to be evil; and he thought this with firm commitment, for many years. I suspect that the lenses through which we look at the social world let us focus on some features especially sharply but at the cost of blurring others. The lenses that best let us see centralization and state power may distort our picture of local and intragroup power, and vice versa. In the final chapter of this book I will offer reasons for doubting that the tension between rationalism and pluralism could even in principle be overcome or synthesized away. This is something less than that—a psychological difficulty, not a logical or sociological impossibility—but it is important to keep in mind.

Acton and the Pluralists

Figgis and Maitland were Acton's junior colleagues, not his students, but described themselves as deeply under his influence. Figgis' *Churches in the Modern State* includes an appreciation of Acton as an appendix; and it was Figgis who first edited and published posthumous collections of Acton's essays, with a coauthored intellectual biography-*cum*-personal appreciation as the introduction to the collection *Essays on the History of Freedom*. Maitland likewise wrote a moving celebration and obituary upon Acton's death.[18]

---

[16] Acton, letter to General Robert E. Lee on November 4, 1866, in *Essays in the History of Liberty*, p. 363.

[17] Lee's reply left no room for the halo that later Lost Cause nostalgia would put on his head. Sounding as if the Confederacy had not lost the war but had agreed to an equal truce which the Union now violated, he declared himself content with the end of slavery, but vehement in his opposition to incipient Reconstruction. If the war had settled the question of the permanence of the union, then the former Confederate states could not have their readmission to the union made conditional on ratification of the Fourteenth Amendment. He insisted that the Black Codes must not be tampered with and suffrage must remain a purely internal state matter. Acton offered no objection.

[18] *The Cambridge Review*, October 16, 1902.

Nor was this a mere matter of personal loyalty to a colleague. Figgis' book on *Political Thought from Gerson to Grotius* is shot through with references to Acton, especially approving of Acton's liberal moralized approach to history and intellectual history, and his embrace of conciliarism. Acton's advocacy of religious freedom, his opposition to the papal centralization that culminated in the First Vatican Council, and his devotion to federalism and decentralization in politics—these all complement and reinforce themes in Gierke, whose rediscovery of Althusius was all about building a German pedigree for federalism, and whose reconstruction of the intellectual shape of the Middle Ages moved freely back and forth between conciliarism in theology and constitutionalism in politics. For Gierke as for Acton, the intellectual and institutional history of freedom was deeply tied up with the intellectual and institutional history of decentralization, competing institutions, and multiple authorities checking one another. Maitland and Figgis learned these lessons from the Gladstonian liberal as well as from the German holistic medievalist; and they did not perceive there to be an essential conflict between the two.

Laski, who might be expected to have less sympathy than Figgis or Maitland with a Victorian antistatist liberal, devotes a chapter of his *Studies in the Problem of Sovereignty* to the contest between papal supremacy and its critics in the nineteenth century, a chapter centrally about Acton and filled with admiring evaluations like this: "To the study of a man who so strenuously devoted his life to the study of liberty it is difficult to approach without emotion. Acton's life was spent in repelling at once the claims of either Church or State to a unique sovereignty over the minds of Men."[19]

The British Pluralist school is too often treated simply as the reception of Gierke's Germanism in a British context. The most influential recent book on the pluralists, David Runciman's *Pluralism and the Personality of the State*, proceeds more or less in this fashion, mentioning Acton not at all. Indeed, almost none of the works studying the pluralists discuss their connection with Acton in any substantial way, except David Nicholls' *The Pluralist State*.[20] But Pluralism was Actonian liberalism and Germanist medievalism at the same time, with the two different idioms completely intertwined in their understandings of the priority of religious liberty, the centrality of conciliarism to

---

[19] Laski, *Studies in the Problem of Sovereignty* (New Haven: Yale University Press, 1917), p. 86. He elsewhere treats "the learning of Lord Acton" as an improbably high standard to meet, one that would need to be met in order to "do on the grand scale what Mr. Edward Jenks so brilliantly attempted in his 'Short History of Politics'." Laski, *Authority in the Modern State* (New Haven: Yale University Press, 1919), p. 20.

[20] David Nicholls, *The Pluralist State: The Political Ideas of J. N. Figgis and His Contemporaries* (New York: St. Martin's Press, 1975). In a way my complaint in this section amounts to the wish that Nicholls' book rather than Hirst's later work had launched the neo-Pluralist revival, such as it has been.

the intellectual and moral history of church government, and the evils of centralization in church or state.

A related mistake is to reserve the Pluralists for the intellectual ancestry of contemporary variants of socialism while reserving Acton for the intellectual history of market liberalism or some variant of conservatism (e.g. Hayek and Himmelfarb, two of Acton's recent enthusiasts). The particular intellectual habits of our own day encourage only socialists to see forbears in the pluralists, only conservatives to see ancestry in Acton, and, it sometimes seems, liberals to see no ancestors at all between Mill and Rawls; grasping the connection between Acton and the pluralists can help to overcome all of these errors.

Acton's federalism and Gierke's medievalism were perhaps compatible and combinable, but Acton himself was no medievalist.[21] Indeed, he was a forceful advocate of the historical narrative that has been dominant throughout modernity: that the ancients had discovered moral truth (in Acton's case, natural law) which was lost in superstitious servility of the Middle Ages, and then gradually rebuilt from Aquinas onward. While he was, literally, a Whig historian, he had little use for the Whig-historical narrative of ancient Germanic liberty confirmed in the Magna Carta and defining the true English law until it was subverted by the modern state of the Tudors and Stuarts. (It is, I suppose, difficult for a Catholic to feel wholly comfortable with that narrative.) For Acton, the Hobbesian sovereign state is an evil, but it is not a modern fall from medieval grace. What Maitland called "the federalistic structure of medieval society"[22] does not appear in Acton's own histories of freedom or federalism. Freedom of conscience is so central for Acton that he could not be anything but a post-Reformation modern. While he always opposed the modern centralizing state, he was also so deeply concerned with centralizing, corrupting papal power that he could not look to the Middle Ages and be happy just because there were no states to be found.

When Acton looked to the Middle Ages, he primarily saw the grand ideas that seem to us conspicuously political: natural law, religious persecution, the contest between would-be absolute kings and a would-be absolute church, and the idea of tyrannicide.[23] Certainly, he endorsed the traditional view that the conflict between church and empire allowed some freedom to grow in the institutional cracks; and he gave cursory due to the medieval origins of cities,

---

[21] I do not know how aware Acton was of the substance of Gierke's work. As far as I can tell, Acton mentioned Gierke only once in his writings, in passing. It is clear that Acton knew of the Germanist–Romanist disputes in historiography that provided the background to Gierke's scholarship. Those disputes, however, were not his.

[22] "Moral Personality and Legal Personality," in David Runciman and Magnus Ran, eds *State, Trust and Corporation* (Cambridge: Cambridge University Press, 2003[1905]), p. 66.

[23] "The History of Freedom in Christianity" (1877), in *Essays in the History of Liberty*, pp. 32–7.

parliaments, and the principle of representation for taxation.[24] But he seems to have seen these as accidents, not ideas. The recurring urge to "trace the free institutions of Europe and America, and Australia, to the life that was led in the forests of Germany," a trope of Whig medievalism for centuries, he dismissed as "desperate."[25]

Acton was a historian of ideas, Maitland a historian of law. The selections of Gierke chosen by Maitland for *Political Theories of the Middle Ages* were, despite the title, heavily jurisprudential. The modern student of political theory who looks to Maitland's famous introduction to that work for a statement of pluralist theory will likely be baffled by the dense discussions of doctrines of trust, corporate delicts, corporations sole, partnerships, and Roman and common law, to say nothing of the medieval ideas of *universitas* and *societas*. He commends Gierke to his compatriots' attention in this remarkable passage:

> Englishmen should be especially grateful to a guide who is perhaps at his strongest just where they must needs be weak: that is, among the books of the legists and canonists. An educated Englishman may read and enjoy what Dante or Marsiglio has written. An English scholar may face Aquinas or Ockham or even the repellent Wyclif. But Baldus and Bartolus, Innocentius and Johannes Andreae, them he has never been taught to tackle, and they are not to be tackled by the untaught. And yet they are important people, for political philosophy in its youth is apt to look like a sublimated jurisprudence, and, even when it has grown in vigour and stature, is often compelled or content to work with tools—a social contract for example—which have been sharpened, if not forged, in the legal smithy. In that smithy Dr. Gierke is at home.[26]

Maitland saw, both in England and on the continent, a rich and complex associational life that was always shaping legal ideas and doctrines. Since cities, guilds, monastic orders, parishes, and so on were real social actors with a real need to act corporately, common law and civil law alike were pushed to accommodate. In other words, where Acton noticed only political ideas and public law, with liberty arising accidentally, Maitland perceived legal ideas and private law, with the freedom of group life always being pressed from below.

The union of Actonian liberalism and Gierkean medievalism was thus not Acton's own project. It was, especially, Maitland's and Figgis'. It is this union that makes the British Pluralists so distinctive. Figgis, in his admiration for

[24] "The middle ages had forged a complete arsenal of constitutional maxims: trial by jury, taxation by representation, local self-government, ecclesiastical independence, responsible authority. But they were not secured by institutions..." "Review of May's *Democracy in Europe*," in *Essays in the History of Liberty*, p. 70.

[25] "Review of May's *Democracy in Europe*," in *Essays in the History of Liberty*, p. 69.

[26] Gierke, *Political Theories of the Middle Ages*, Maitland, trans. (Bristol: Thoemmes Press, 1996 [1900]), p. viii.

Acton, did attribute to the latter a kind of medievalism, and treated him as a forerunner of Gierke-inflected medievalist pluralism.

> There are, it is true, not wanting signs that his view of the true relations of States and Churches may become one day more dominant, for it appears as though once more the earlier Middle Ages will be justified, and religious bodies become the guardians of freedom, even in the political sphere. [...] His ideal of freedom as of the Church was in some respects that of the earlier Middle Ages.[27]

But notice: Figgis and Laurence here express their *own* view of medieval understandings of religion and freedom, and say that those understandings resemble Acton's views on religion and freedom. They do not attribute *to him* that view of the Middle Ages. They further note that any temptation to medievalism on Acton's part was checked by his moralism; he could not but judge older eras against his standard of justice, and this meant that the persecuting centuries could not attract him.

> The second tendency against which Acton's moral sense revolted, had arisen out of the laudable determination of historians to be sympathetic towards men of distant ages and of alien modes of thought. With the romantic movement the early nineteenth century placed a check upon the habit of despising mediæval ideals, which had been increasing from the days of the Renaissance and had culminated in Voltaire. Instead of this, there arose a sentiment of admiration for the past, while the general growth of historical methods of thinking supplied a sense of the relativity of moral principles, and led to a desire to condone if not to commend the crimes of other ages. It became almost a trick of style to talk of judging men by the standard of their day and to allege the spirit of the age in excuse for the Albigensian Crusade or the burning of Hus. Acton felt that this was to destroy the very bases of moral judgment and to open the way to a boundless scepticism. Anxious as he was to uphold the doctrine of growth in theology, he allowed nothing for it in the realm of morals, at any rate in the Christian era, since the thirteenth century.[28]

Maitland, like Acton, saw much of the danger in modern democratic life as originating in French Revolutionary doctrines: "It is always best to begin with France, and there, I take it, we may see the pulverizing, macadamising tendency in all its glory, working from century to century, reducing to impotence, and then to nullity, all that intervenes between Man and State."[29]

---

[27] Acton, *The History of Freedom and Other Essays*, p. xvii.
[28] J. N. Figgis and R. Laurence, "Introduction," in Acton, *The History of Freedom and Other Essays*, Figgis and Laurence, eds (London: Macmillan, 1907).
[29] F.W. Maitland, "Moral and Legal Personality," in *State, Trust and Corporation*, p. 66.

The Pluralist Theory of Group Life

Even once we appreciate the Actonian sources of British Pluralism, the problem of "real group personality" remains. How can that sort of metaphysical collectivism be brought into even a loose understanding of liberal thought? Part of what made Hobbes seem like a plausible liberal in the first place was the intuition that egalitarian individualism is a central feature of liberalism, combined with Hobbes' corrosive skepticism about groups standing on their privileges.[30] By contrast, Pluralism as an Anglophone intellectual movement was sparked by Maitland's introduction to his Gierke translation; the idea that groups have real existence that the state recognizes but does not create was its founding intellectual commitment.

I think that the most persuasive account of the theory of real group personality was given by Maitland, not in the introduction to Gierke, but in his later essay on *Moral Personality and Legal Personality* (1904).[31]

> If the law allows men to form permanently organized groups, those groups will be for common opinion right-and-duty-bearing units; and if the law-giver will not openly treat them as such he will misrepresent, or, as the French say, he will 'denature' the facts: in other words he will make a mess and call it law. Group-personality is no purely legal phenomenon. The law-giver may say that it does not exist, where, as a matter of moral sentiment, it does exist. When that happens, he incurs the penalty ordained for those who ignorantly or willfully say the thing that is not. If he wishes to smash a group, let him smash it, send the policeman, raid the rooms, impound the minute-book, fine, and imprison; but if he is going to tolerate the group, he must recognize its personality, for otherwise he will be dealing wild blows which may fall on those who stand outside the group as well as those who stand within it. For the morality of common sense the group is person, is right-and-duty-bearing unit. Let the moral philosopher explain this, let him explain it as illusion, let him explain it away; but he ought not to leave it unexplained, nor, I think, will he be able to say that it is an illusion which is losing power, for, on the contrary, it seems to me to be persistently and progressively triumphing over certain philosophical and theological prejudices.[32]

This account seems to me plausible and compelling. The plausible positivist rejoinder is that, if everyone knew that associations lacked legal personality,

---

[30] One account of Hobbes in this regard that I do admire, though I still dissent from its treatment of Hobbes as meaningfully liberal, is Richard Boyd, *Uncivil Society*.

[31] Laski's "On the Personality of Associations" seems to me torn between the view I attribute to Maitland here and the one I attribute to Figgis. Some might see that as a strength of the essay, thinking that it unites the two strands, though I think it fails to reconcile them; in any case it is a useful piece in its clear articulation of both. Laski, "On the Personality of Associations," in *The Foundations of Sovereignty and other Essays*.

[32] F.W. Maitland, "Moral Personality and Legal Personality," in *State, Trust, and Corporation*, p. 68.

i.e. could not enter into contracts or own property, then no one would treat them as right-and-duty bearing units. According to this argument, Maitland's assertion is question-begging, as are many arguments about law that rest on some idea of settled social expectations. Expectations about rules are endogenous to the rules actually adopted. If we had a different rule, expectations would adjust accordingly.

As I said, I think this is credible; but I also think that it is wrong, and its wrongness is a central pluralist insight. When persons join together to pursue projects in common, whether religious, cultural, educational, or recreational, and when they do so in ways that they mean to be more than ephemeral, several things more or less necessarily follow. One is that they adopt decision-making procedures, some ability for the group to act. This is perhaps the key step that differentiates a group from an association or organization. If we all happen to worship in the same way at the same place and the same time, our groupness suffices. But if we wish our union to outlast the first disagreement about time or place or manner or theological content, then we cannot rely on that happenstance; we will need a way to come to decisions, whether a simple majority voice vote or a complex system creating a self-perpetuating episcopacy with authoritative decision-making power or anything in between.

The simplest models are still compatible with groupness: at the end of a happenstance game of pickup basketball (or so I imagine), one of the players might say, "Same time tomorrow?" and then a majority of others say, "An hour later is better"; the first one goes along. That might be repeated over and over again, so long as each day the members of the group wish for it to carry on and value that more highly than they value the slight disruptions to their schedules necessary to accommodate the others. (Ephemera may be repeated and long term.) But come the day of a more serious disagreement—"Shall we admit this new player to our group?"—or a need to deal with outsiders—"I negotiate with you on behalf of my team about where and when we'll compete against yours"—the group may well find that it needs more than case-by-case agreement. It needs members to have committed to one another to be bound by collective decisions, or else to leave. At that point, the transition to association happens; the group becomes something else that can survive the departures of all of its founders, with a suitable provision for admitting newcomers, and something that can credibly engage with the outside world.

Something else that more or less necessarily happens in any collective enterprise beyond the simplest is that we will pool some resources and devote them to the cause. This demands the decision-making procedures just discussed: we all think that the project is worth sacrificing some of our separate funds, but we need some way to decide on how the funds will be used, on which of the many ways they might support the project will be chosen. It also requires the creation of offices and role differentiation: there must be a treasurer, and the treasurer must understand the difference between the treasury with which he's been entrusted and his personal wealth.

So long as the treasurer is more committed to our project, and to his reputation, than to the possible ill-gotten gains, we need nothing more than that understanding on his part. But suppose that we want more than that—as we will if our association grows too large for everyone to know the treasurer personally, or if the treasury becomes so large as to provide a temptation to even decent and honorable treasurers. We could each enter into a trust-like relationship with the treasurer, individually, and indeed trusts are an important legal instrument for the development of secondary institutions, much studied in that light by Maitland. But this is grossly inefficient for large groups, and moreover may be incompatible with our desire to pool resources. (I don't just want the treasurer to *hold onto my money for me*; I want it to *cease to be mine*, without thereby becoming his, personally.) The natural solution is to allow the association as such to own the funds, to be administered by whoever currently holds the office of treasurer, whose right to spend it is limited to associational business and ends when the tenure in office does. If the treasurer feels tempted, he knows that the association as such will have the legal authority to pursue him for misappropriation or theft.

That last steps required are: a) that the association as such be *understood* to own the funds, by its members and by the treasurer; and b) that that understanding be *legally recognized*, so that the law outside the group can make sense of the claim of misappropriation, and act accordingly. This is, I think, a basic set of social facts, and Maitland was right to see them as facts in need of recognition rather than simply responses to a preexisting positive rule.

When medieval Roman lawyers struggled with the question of whether guilds organized only by their members' consent were legal associations, what turned on the question was not whether the guilds would be "smashed," but whether they had personality.[33] When the members entered into a common enterprise and pooled some resources, what was the status of that pool? Who owned a guild-house? Who owned the guild treasury? These are problems for insiders and outsiders alike, not coherently resolvable without recognizing the associations as legal entities—in our sense, without recognizing their personality. And the history of the civilians' reconciliation to the guilds is one of recognizing a social reality. The Roman rule that no association was lawful unless it was created by the Emperor denatured the facts, and misdescribed the web of social relations that had been created in guild-heavy medieval cities. It was not the case that the Roman rule simply created social expectations around it; given the social fact of guilds, certain expectations

---

[33] Here I draw on Black's *Guilds and Civil Society*, as well as on Maitland's introduction to Gierke's *Political Theory of the Middle Ages*, p. viii.

spontaneously arose, and the lawyers' options were indeed to accommodate those expectations or else to "make a mess and call it law."[34]

Maitland's account here is as noteworthy for what it does not say as for what it does. In it, "personality" means only personhood in the legal sense or a direct moral analogy to that sense; it carefully has none of the romantic, emotional, or psychological associations we now attach to the word. More importantly, this account doesn't rely on any question-begging anthropomorphication. The attribution of personality does not make groups natural persons with human attributes, nor does it make groups ontologically prior to or superior to natural persons. It simply makes full sense of natural persons' freedom to engage in common projects, and the mechanisms they adopt for this. Both the "real" and the "personality" in "real group personality" risk being misleading to the contemporary reader. Maitland had no interest in metaphysics or spiritual essences; he was interested in the relationship between legal ideas and real social facts.

Contrast that with *Churches in the Modern State*. Figgis' book takes as its point of departure the then-recent Free Kirk of Scotland case, in which the House of Lords had ruled that a small conservative minority of that church who refused to sanction its merger with what they took to be a heretical group were, in case of schism, legally entitled to succeed to the previously unified church in the sense of owning its property. "What we find in this case [the Free Kirk case] is that the lawyers refused to consider the body as a Church, i.e. as a society with a principle of inherent life... They construed it as a mechanism, not as an organic life."[35]

Figgis says this kind of thing over and over again. But there is tremendous distance between saying that groups will be spontaneously socially viewed as persons in the sense of being right- and duty-bearers, and that the law ought to reflect this, and saying that groups are persons in the sense of having inherent life, much less organic life. The latter sort of anthropomorphism is actually important to Figgis' argument in the Free Kirk case. Among the attributes of natural persons is that they *grow*, they *develop*. They change over time in ways that are at least partly self-directed. They are capable, to use a word Figgis does not but might have, of *Bildung*. And it is these attributes of personhood that Figgis maintains the Free Kirk exercised. Its doctrine grew and developed, such that those who held fast to the original doctrine end by appearing schismatic. He cannot get to his desired condemnation of the outcome in the Free Kirk case just by relying on the thought that groups are and of right ought to be

---

[34] This emphasis on the priority of social reality over either philosophical purity or simplified legal doctrine was a central and recurring feature of Pluralist thought. Compare Laski's defense of Pluralism as *empirically* borne out, and critiques of sovereignty as a fiction and of the "facile brilliance" of Rousseau, in his *The Foundations of Sovereignty and Other Essays*, p. vi.

[35] J. N. Figgis, *Churches in the Modern State* (London: Thoemmes, 1997[1914]), p. 33.

right-and-duty bearers. He must insist that among the rights they bear is the right to *Bildung*.

Otherwise, there seems to be no reason why sociologically real groups, groups that insiders and outsiders interact with as if they had corporate life, could not be doctrinally committed to what they took to be unchanging truths. A contemporary majority of the members of the Free Kirk differed in their theological views from the church's founders. Why must that mean that "the church" as a corporate entity had matured and changed "its" mind? Why could it not mean that they had left a church that remained committed to "its" views? Either outcome could be compatible with the thought that the church had an ongoing independent existence over time, which was no mere concession from the state. I suppose that in a pluralistic society, at least some associations and churches would fall on each side of the line. Some would be in some sense about the current commitments of their current members, and some would be in some sense about a founding set of beliefs. Some religious groups understand religious truth to be given at a single time and clear and unchanging, others understand it to be difficult and added to over time by the exercise of (e.g. Talmudic or casuistic) reason. Some understand a hierarchical authority structure to be religiously mandated, others hold with some version of congregationalism, and others view decision-making structures to be matters of moral or theological indifference. The *Bildung* model in effect insists that all churches, all associations, are *really* committed to evolution in religious doctrine and perhaps to congregationalism or majoritarianism in decision-making authority. This amounts to a failure of the Pluralists to be fully pluralistic—a failure brought on by a too-literal embrace of the "personality" concept, a reliance on what Runciman calls Maitland's "German" as opposed to his "English" theory of what group personality as a concept *meant*.

I have emphasized the Pluralists' debts to and enthusiasm for Lord Acton. By contrast, their treatment of Mill was far from effusive. Maitland credited Mill with reconciling the idea of freedom with that of variety or diversity, in a way that his Whig and contractarian predecessors had emphatically not done, and respected his contributions to political economy, but had little more to say about him. Figgis is openly dismissive of *On Liberty* in *Churches in the Modern State*. He notes that Mill's principles could seem to completely justify the religious liberty that is his main concern, but he maintains that Mill's arguments simply fail. Those who commit religious persecution often say that they do so because religious error is other-regarding: your propagation of your false beliefs leads to my temptation and the jeopardy of my soul. The distinction between self-regarding and other-regarding behavior is not only untenable, according to Figgis; it is positively dangerous to freedom of speech. He offers the Bible and the writings of Rousseau as examples of books the writing and propagation of which profoundly affected others, reshaping the world in "explosive" ways. If we make intellectual and religious freedom rest on the foundation that their exercise affects no one else, then they will be unsustainable. Figgis' own argument emphasizes the collective and corporate character of religious liberty: *my* freedom of conscience is not an individual and self-regarding freedom, but is inextricably tied up with *our* freedom to worship and inquire, together, in an ongoing structure.

As we have seen, Mill himself denied much that the Pluralists held dear, which should not be a surprise. He was prone to see group life as a manifestation of the regrettable human tendency to "like in crowds." In his essays on religious and educational associations, he denies that their ability to hold funds intergenerationally can be anything more than a convenience at best.[36] Early in his career he thought it actively inconvenient, and called for the nationalization of charitable endowments. Later, he still emphatically maintained that associations' corporate lives were a mere legal fiction, always subject to revision by the state as needed. This is precisely the view that Maitland's historical work on trusts, and Figgis' theoretical work on churches, was meant to combat.

An understanding of the evolution of a pluralist tradition within liberalism, from such older sources as Althusius and the monarchomachs through Montesquieu to Tocqueville and Acton, helps us see the British Pluralists' place in intellectual history in a different light. They (at least some of them) combined a strong normative liberalism about freedom of association and freedom of religion with a kind of sociological holism about group life.[37] For these followers of Acton as well as of Gierke, working with (and sometimes equivocating between) a sociological and a metaphysical understanding of the reality of group life, there was no conflict between defending the freedom of group life and defending the freedom of individual persons. Indeed, they understood themselves to be doing the latter precisely by way of doing the former.

---

[36] "Endowments" (1869); "The Right and Wrong of State Interference with Corporation and Church Property" (1833), both in the *Collected Works of John Stuart Mill: Essays in Economics and Society 1850–1879*, vol. 5.

[37] Here there is an affinity with some ideas from the denouement of the liberal–communitarian debate. See Charles Taylor, "Cross-Purposes: The Liberal–Communitarian Debate," in Nancy Rosenblum, ed., *Liberalism and the Moral Life* (Cambridge, Mass.: Harvard University Press, 1989); Allen Buchanan, "Assessing the Communitarian Critique of Liberalism," 99 *Ethics* 852–82, 1989.

Part III

"[T]he failure to have a fully satisfactory solution to these difficulties is not a failure of liberal justice, because the liberal is right. Self-definition is important, and it is also important to end wrongful tyranny. The tension that results from these twin principles is at the heart of liberalism, but it is a valuable and fruitful tension, not one that shows confusion or moral failure. In general, tension within a theory does not necessarily show that it is defective; it may simply show that it is in touch with the difficulty of life."

Martha Nussbaum, "The Future of Feminist Liberalism," *Proceedings and Addresses of the American Philosophical Association*, Vol. 74, No. 2 (Nov., 2000), pp. 47–79, 68.

10

The Constitution of Group Life

The core claim of this book is that a full liberal theory of freedom cannot do without the insights of either rationalism or pluralism, and yet these are probably impossible to fully reconcile. Liberalism emerged out of intellectual traditions that (rightly) saw centralized absolute monarchies as threats to freedom and that (rightly) worried about local, customary, religious, and feudal power. The rival dispositions to view either the central and rationalizing state or the local and ethically thick group as the primary threat to liberty draw on different sociological and psychological generalizations, not on logically exclusive philosophical claims. While they can't both be right as *comparative* generalizations about which threat is greater, each can identify genuine wrongs that the other has difficulty seeing, or seeing as early or as clearly.

The pluralist orientation has been the easier one for contemporary political philosophy to overlook. This is in part because of the neglect of ancient constitutionalism and its Montesquieuian, pluralist offshoots in the history of liberal thought. In order to make the case for the book's thesis, I have thus done somewhat more to recuperate and elaborate ancient constitutionalism and pluralist liberalism than I have rationalism and its antecedents. Moreover, my own normative views strongly lean toward the pluralist side. But, as I have said, this book is not a defense of pluralism, and its thesis is *not* that pluralism is correct. In the book up until now I have not written an all-things-considered defense of pluralist liberalism, even if I have sometimes defended its plausibility.

In this chapter and the next, however, I will let my own normative judgments show a bit more clearly. I think that the resources offered by social theory of the sort seen in Chapter 3 and by the historical work of Chapters 4–9 support the book's main thesis, but I also think that they provide resources that can help improve normative arguments. I still aim to offer relatively balanced accounts and will let rationalism have its say; but I will offer conclusions of my own. These should be understood as subordinate to, not overriding, the book's main argument, and I will return to that argument in the final chapter.

Intermediacy Affects Politics

We saw in Part II that relations between states and intermediate associations can be constitutionally fundamental, going to the organization of the whole political order. This much was agreed on by both ancient constitutionalists and state rationalizers. This necessarily pushes us to think of the interactions between central states and intermediate bodies as not only cases of the former acting on the latter by regulation or intervention, but also of the latter acting on the former. We must pay attention not only to associations' freedom from the state but also to their effects on political life. In this chapter I examine some of the ways in which intermediate groups come to exercise political or quasi-political power. It might seem that this is a series of arguments against pluralism: if groups exercise political power, they must be subject to constitutional constraints. But we saw a series of pluralist arguments in Part II that only make sense if intermediate groups can affect political life, from Montesquieu's theory of the *corps* in a monarchy to Acton's account of multinational federalism. Here I try to draw out some of those arguments about political power in a more general form. Intermediate groups are rarely *only* inward-facing associations, and the state never *only* acts under neutral bureaucratic imperatives or as the neutral agent of liberal justice.

One idea we saw many times among the pluralists surveyed in Part II was that local organizations and memberships could provide what Constant called the "germ of resistance" to state overreach. This indeed is a central thought of the pluralist liberal tradition: intermediate groups, from voluntary associations to the provinces of a federation, can provide institutional bulwarks that protect the freedom of their members against state intrusion. They provide organizational resources to their members, as well as providing an emotional focal point, something the defense of which they can rally around. This requires, however, that they have some capacity to act in politics, to affect political outcomes. A bulwark is literally a physical structure that can protect passively, like a wall; but bulwarks in political life are different. They cannot passively protect their members. Even if they offer jurisdictional separation— the ability to flee an unjust law by moving into a different set of rules—that separation must itself be politically defended.

This means that group pluralism, to be politically stable, must to some degree be *oppositional*. There is a way of talking about associational life that emphasizes a spirit of trust and common participation that it can help develop. But bulwarks depend on there being a sense of independence that makes it possible to say "no."[1] The former is routinely called "neo-Tocquevillean," though the latter plays a major part in Tocqueville's argument in *The Old Regime and the Revolution* (and, I would argue, a genuine part in *Democracy in America* as well). The approach that emphasizes only cooperation really shares more with Mill. Pluralist approaches emphasize the "germ of resistance," Montesquieu's aristocratic honor, Tocqueville's *corps* solidarity, and Acton's loyalties to church or nation rather than state.

This pluralist model of groups' defensive political action has a counterpart: a concern that their political action will allow them the offensive ability to capture the state.

Faction

I suggested in Chapters 2 and 3 that a group's legitimate internal authority generates a surplus of internal power. To the degree that it does so, *it also generates external power*. The details vary by political regime, but in any political system that is at all open, the ability to marshal support from a fixed group—votes, financial contributions, volunteer activity, organizational effort, and so on—is a key resource. Indeed, these are resources that overtly political associations such as parties and lobbying groups work constantly to gain. The stronger the association or group in its own sphere, the greater the political resources that are provided to it, as it were, for free.

Intermediate groups are thus often also, in Madison's sense, *factions*: segments of the population that share some interest or goal around which they might be mobilized for political purpose.[2] Small groups can engage in bureaucratic capture as that phrase is traditionally understood in political science, structuring policy to their (or their elites') advantage on questions that are too narrow to draw much public attention. Large groups, especially in a democracy, can shape political outcomes by shaping public opinion and education. A key source of rationalist distrust of conservative religious groups, from the Enlightenment through to current debates about political liberalism, has been the suspicion that they would form citizens who were uninterested in the preservation of liberal freedom. Pluralistic freedom could thus be self-undermining. Large groups would use the state to entrench their dominant position. Small groups would not only resist state power to protect their internal autonomy; they would use it to preserve in-group elite privilege and

---

[1] Michael W. Foley and Bob Edwards, "The Paradox of Civil Society," 7(3) *Journal of Democracy* 38–52, 1996.

[2] For a general argument treating the problem of groups in liberal thought through the lens of faction, and for studying arguments about faction in much greater depth than what follows, see Richard Boyd, *Uncivil Society*.

to enforce their boundaries against outsiders. Finally, there is a version of the problem of faction that informs pluralism as well: the realization that really existing states often *are* captured by some majority group, yielding further reason to distrust it when it intervenes against minority groups.

Let us consider each of these in turn.

The Illiberal Majority

For thinkers such as Voltaire and Tracy—as well as the young John Adams— the power that the Catholic Church held over its members was not only objectionable in its own right, though it certainly was that. They worried that the power of the Church was both self-perpetuating and socially regressive: politics would be shaped by public opinion that had in turn been shaped by a backward-looking and authoritarian church. For Tracy as for his less-liberal revolutionary colleagues, this demanded a rapid rupture with the past in the educational system in particular. Political freedom in the future depended on education in the present.

A kind of educational vanguardism seems to follow. Certainly, schooling cannot be left entirely in the hands of the majority's church; but if religious education and influence outside the classroom walls is powerful enough, then secular control over what happens inside them may not suffice. The dominantly large cultural or religious group thus cannot simply claim associational freedom and teach its norms internally; those norms will shape the political world. And so we sometimes see majority religions accorded less than full liberal freedom by a reformist state. This is true not only when the reformist state is aggressively secular, as in France and Turkey, but also in, e.g., post-independence India, where the reform of Hindu practices and the transformation of Hindu ideas has long been a major public goal of social reformers. (Caste is treated as a public matter, not, in the Western sense, a private religious practice.)

These questions have been important in political theory debates in the last several decades: debates about liberal neutrality and perfectionism, about political liberalism, and about civic education. In all of these literatures, some have argued that the liberal democratic state, having a legitimate interest in its own preservation, must have a legitimate interest in shaping the values and norms of its citizenry so that they will support the liberal public order. If a majority group (or even large minority groups) teaches internal norms that are incompatible with that, then their associational, cultural, and religious freedom may have to give way.

We have some reason to be skeptical of the strongest versions of this kind of claim. Liberal institutions, inasmuch as they exist in the world, did not come into the world without navels. They evolved out of or were created from the ashes of non-liberal or illiberal institutions and societies. That means that liberal institutions don't require the specially modeled liberal citizen to make them possible or functional. Religious tolerance and equality before the law sometimes seem like the kinds of things that a society can't accomplish institutionally without drawing on a citizenry that has internalized the relevant norms—legal equality follows on the shared belief in human moral equality, for example. But if that were so, we would never have taken such steps toward them as we already have.[3]

Even within an ongoing liberal society, things change. The relationship between institutional push and character development that is modeled in the unsustainability critique is unidirectional. The state molds people, and they become the kind of people it needs them to be. But the relationships among politics, society, and character seem to me vastly more complicated and cyclical than that. One generation rebels against the norms and mores of its parents, only to see its own rebellion rebelled against a generation later. Great Awakenings of religious belief give way to decades of secularization that look endless until they end. The gender roles and sexual norms of the 1950s were apparently much more conservative than those of the 1920s—then there were two decades of sexual revolution and women's liberation, decades that in turn gave way to something else again. In each of these cases there may be an underlying trendline that the decades fluctuate around. I think that has been true for gender roles, but doubt that it has been true for religious belief, at least in the United States. But the fluctuations are interesting even if there is a trendline; they belie any unidirectional model of where moral characters come from, and make it look improbable that moral characters at the large social level can be finely engineered by deliberate state action. The 1960s were not engineered by the state of the 1950s, nor did they arise out of some neglect on the part of the society of the 1950s of the need for civic education and character molding.

But none of that provides reason to doubt that a large group's internal norms have *any* educational effect; that would be very strange, and would imply that groups should be much more ephemeral than they are. A large religion is sure to have *some* ability to shape the norms and values of its members, or it could hardly have endured for long enough to be a large religion. In Chapter 2 I suggested that one reason for not resting content with the pluralist "pure theory" of free association was the ability of intermediate groups to take up all of the available social space. The problem of the illiberal majority faction is a related thought. In democracies, or even in

---

[3] See also Andrew Sabl, "Virtue for Pluralists," 2(2) *Journal of Moral Philosophy* 207–35, 2005.

non-democracies shaped in part by public opinion, the internal norms of group life can, and at least sometimes will, spill over into political life.

This need not mean that a majority faction deliberately aims to make the state an instrument of its own group. A religious majority can have real effects without seeking to create a theocracy. Gender equality is a particularly important example here. The conservative religious majority might scrupulously respect the separation of church and state, but—having learned deeply gender-inegalitarian norms in internal group life—have insufficient moral conviction about women's freedom and equality to support the laws and institutions that protect them. To put the point in the other direction: the liberal concerned about women's freedom and equality may have reason to worry about the internal gender norms of large intermediate groups. The range of actions that could follow from that worry vary widely, from public statements and symbolic criticism[4] to limitations on in-group education to aggressive restriction of cultural, religious, and associational freedom, e.g. requiring gender equality in the priesthood.

Minority Group Capture

It is a commonplace of political science that small coherent interest groups can secure legal and political victories disproportionately often, on topics of greater importance to them than to the majority. The paradigmatic case is that of a narrowly targeted subsidy: the benefit to the recipients can be great enough to justify their political efforts, while the costs are so widely diffused that no one has enough incentive to mobilize against them. But subtler administrative and bureaucratic outcomes than straightforward subsidies exist, and their cost can be even harder to trace. And even considerable publicity may not avail against sufficiently concentrated effort.

Sometimes this will enable an intermediate group as a whole to gain access to the institutional resources of government. The Satmar Hasidic sect of Jews who have come to dominate the village of Kiryas Joel, New York, have captured the municipal government and the state funding that goes with it. Even in the face of repeated successful First Amendment challenges to the creation of a public school district organized to allow them to educate disabled children at state expense (other children attend private religious schools), the New York state legislature continued to shape the rules to their benefit until finally

---

[4] See here Corey Brettschneider, *When the State Speaks, What Should It Say? How Democracies Can Protect Expression and Promote Equality* (Princeton: Princeton University Press, 2012).

a form was found that could pass judicial muster.[5] At first glance this is remarkable; the Satmar community is unpopular in neighboring villages, far out of step with majority norms in New York, and very small. But a small group willing to vote in a very unified manner, and strongly committed to one issue, can have political impacts far in excess of its size. Few others are sufficiently motivated to be single-issue voters against them, but they are strongly motivated to be single-issue voters in defense of their use of the municipal form.

Sometimes, too, mechanisms such as these serve the internal authority figures, elites, or dominant subgroups who are best able to marshal the group's political resources. Remember the suggestion in Chapter 3 that external pluralism can generate in-group power in a number of ways. One of these is that the position of intermediaries from a small group is greatly enhanced by the presence of a dominant outside group; another is that the latter may well create in-group hierarchies so that it has convenient intermediaries at all. Across much of the non-European world, European colonizers created king-like chiefs in societies that had had more complicated, pluralistic, or egalitarian governing structures beforehand. Their internal power was externally constituted in the first instance. But even without such an origin, the dynamics of a small group's political interactions with the state can often result in state strengthening of in-group hierarchy.

In countries where family law is differentiated by religious community, such as India, this has been a frequent concern. Although the Indian state engages in deliberate liberalization and reform of Hindu customs, something of the reverse is true with respect to minority religions. The codes that the British left behind to govern Muslim and Christian family and inheritance law have rarely been reformed, and legislation about them has generally been responsive to the concerns of conservative group leaders. Famously, when the courts attempted to reform the inegalitarian Muslim law governing alimony in the Shah Bano case, conservative Muslim religious and legal leaders were able to mobilize so strong a backlash that the government substantially restored the *status quo ante* with legislation. Christian divorce law in India remained largely what it had been since the 1860s, including serious gender inequalities about property settlement and fault-based grounds for divorce such as adultery, and including no possibility of no-fault divorce even with mutual consent, until 2001.

Restrictive membership rules for Indian tribes in the United States and Canada, discriminating on the basis of religion, blood quanta, or gender (e.g. the children of men who marry non-Indians, but not of women who

---

[5] On Kiryas Joel, see Jeff Spinner-Halev, *The Boundaries of Citizenship: Race, Ethnicity and Nationality in the Liberal State* (Baltimore: Johns Hopkins University Press, 1994).

do so, gain tribe membership) arguably have a similar political dynamic. The contemporary meaning of governing power within tribes or bands is in large part set by the settler states; the states also control many of the resources which the tribes or bands are then permitted to use or distribute. All of this shapes the incentives and opportunities of local indigenous leaders to define membership in their own interests, whether to keep the number of claimants on resources small or to concentrate group authority in those who keep to a conservative version of group identity (e.g. a traditional religion).

The Majoritarian State

Earlier we considered a rationalist perspective on the idea that states, rather than acting autonomously, could be significantly swayed by a majority group's internal norms: states may need to act to reshape the majority culture so as to generate enough support for liberal and democratic norms to maintain the constitutional order. But from a pluralist point of view this is just the wrong conclusion to draw. It is, one might think, the normal condition for states to be captured by a majority group, and to have a standard tendency to promote that group at the expense of others. This is typically true of the *Staatvolk* in a nation-state. When judging the rights of ethnocultural or linguistic minorities, the state is not a neutral arbiter, even imperfectly seeking to balance the associational rights of group members against the rights of internal dissidents or minorities. It is, at best, a flawed judge, opportunistically and hypocritically applying standards to minority groups that the majority itself could not meet. Here again gender equality provides an important example: forms of gender inequality that the majority finds exotic and alien are disproportionately scrutinized, while those that are familiar become invisible.[6]

Similarly, a minority's public displays of religious symbols may be characterized as violations of the norm of a secular public sphere, while the majority's are treated as cultural background. In Québec, a commission on the accommodation of religious minorities co-chaired by Charles Taylor was convened in the wake of disputes over, among other things, Muslim women's headscarves. The one recommendation of the report that was promptly acted upon, in a fashion, was the idea of removing the crucifix that has hung in the provincial legislature's meeting hall since the repressive Franco-like right-wing government installed it in the 1930s. On the very day the report was released,

---

[6] See Anne Phillips, *Multiculturalism Without Culture* (Princeton: Princeton University Press, 2007); Sarah Song, *Justice, Gender, and the Politics of Multiculturalism* (Cambridge: Cambridge University Press, 2007).

the legislature unanimously voted to reject that recommendation; public headscarves might jeopardize religious freedom, but the crucifix was cultural "patrimony," and supposedly not a religious symbol at all.

At worst, the state captured by a majority group is not just a flawed judge but an actively malicious one. Policies toward indigenous peoples by settler states, often enough pursued in the name of freeing individual persons from tribal restriction or backwardness, have routinely aimed at the destruction of indigenous cultures and the expropriation of indigenous lands. The imposition of individually allotted property on American Indian tribal lands by the Dawes Act in the late nineteenth century, for example, purported to liberate individual Indians from a communalism that kept them all back. But the size of the allotments was deliberately fixed to be far below the total lands being divided, so that huge portions of Indian Country were taken out of Indian hands altogether and opened to white homesteading. A pluralist would think that relevant to a contemporary assessment of settler states purporting to protect the freedom of indigenous persons against the rules and customs of their groups—a common claim in cases including gender-inegalitarian and religiously restrictive membership rules, tribal restrictions on alcohol, initiation and punishment practices, freedom of speech and gender equality claims against traditional rules governing secret lore, and disputes arising under the U.S. Indian Civil Rights Act.

Territory and Government

Ancien régime provincial liberties and urban liberties were constitutively territorial; the privileges of the clergy, of guilds, or of aristocrats were not. Federalism is essentially territorial; Freemasonry is not. The dichotomy is somewhat overdrawn, of course. The privileges of the clergy as persons were closely tied up with the privileged status of church lands; monastic orders were orders of persons, but persons living physically together and governing their physical space; Freemasonry is administratively federated among geographic regions.

But there are clearly differences, at least of degree, and perhaps differences in moral kind. This is in part because territorial bodies necessarily involve *rule over non-members or non-consenters. Cuius regio, euius religio* is a doctrine of religious pluralism, from the perspective of the Holy Roman Empire, but it is not a doctrine of religious liberty; it necessarily involves non-believers in one faith being caught on territory that officially belongs to another. The territorial jurisdiction of ethnocultural minorities, for example in a federal region such as Québec or Catalonia, likewise involves rule over those who are not members of the group.

Not all territorial bodies are governmental. Most universities have a geographical core, a campus that houses academic and administrative functions and often houses a considerable share of students as well. Universities do not *rule* over non-members, but as their neighbors know, their territoriality entails substantial spillover and externalities. A university's choices about how to govern itself internally—how many students to admit, of what ages, whether to house them on campus, whether to allow fraternities and sororities, what rules will govern student life—have much more immediate consequences for those nearby than would the internal rules of a club or, usually, a church.

As has often been true when groups live side-by-side in crowded conditions, universities regulate their students' behavior in the interest of calm relations with outsiders. This is one of the ways in which pluralism generates internal power: a group that wishes to retain its autonomy against outsiders must be able to credibly commit to them that it can manage its members, and so it has to build up its ability to do so. (Traditional Jewish ghettos in European cities had to operate on the same principle; the ability to live freely as Jews depended in part on significant intra-communal surveillance and monitoring.) We often see universities not only building up dormitory or college residential capacity as a benefit for students, but also as a way to limit students' spread into the surrounding area. Indeed, some universities prohibit students from living in non-university housing altogether or limit their freedom to do so in various ways, in the interest of preventing them from disrupting the local housing market or from disrupting local peace and quiet with their social activities. But the fact remains that to some significant degree it is the corporate decision of universities whether or not to limit students in these ways. That is, the geographic space of the surrounding area is to a large degree governed by the university's decisions about its own space and its own members.[7] Residential associations have this ability to affect neighbors, as well as a kind of governing authority over non-members within, i.e. renters who lack a vote on association rules. Even the non-governmental territorial intermediate body has some real power to shape the lives of neighboring or encompassed non-members.

Such territoriality, whether governmental or not, has what should now seem like a familiar dual character. On the one hand, the territorial concentration allows for group life to flourish and provides the institutional and organizational resources for it to protect itself. The geographic concentration makes many forms of group life more sustainable even when it is not constitutive of the group's purpose (as in the case, for example, of an indigenous people whose self-conception is tied to a particular piece of land). A linguistic

---

[7] That does not, of course, mean that it is only a *burden* on them. The presence of the university may be of great benefit to a neighborhood, town, or city, socially, culturally, and economically.

minority can maintain a space where the language is spoken, heard, written, and read. A purposive organization like a university or a monastery can arrange the needs of daily life to support and serve its purpose, and can provide ongoing reinforcement to members of the worth and importance of the enterprise. And geographically concentrated communities have the possibility of becoming something like local social worlds,[8] which means that one can live in them in a variety of different ways, reducing the need to exit if one changes goals.

As far as organizational self-defense goes, even a territorial grouping without formal organization—think of an ethnic neighborhood in a city that might have a local business association and a local church but no governing structure—can gain the political weight to defend itself simply from dense local concentration and shared interest. A formal intermediate body like a university, or a governmental body like a city or province, has even more ability to do so. As Publius, Burke, Constant, and Acton all understood in different contexts, the sense that our group life is also our whole shared local world is a potent source of political motivation and organization, as well as an institutional base for counterbalancing pressure from outside.

On the other hand, that local concentration heightens power over members and generates real power over non-members. Both can be oppressive: Mill's local despotism of custom and opinion, or Madison's local majority faction. In the case of the non-members, if they are seen as part of the wider society's majority or dominant group, the exercise of local power can be especially sharp. It can be seen as a matter of group survival that local norms be protected against assimilative pressure from outside. Precisely in order to reduce exit by local members and reduce entrance or disruption by non-members, the locally powerful group may well act in ways that especially offend rationalist worries about individual freedom.

In light of all this, consider the recurring idea of "non-territorial federalism" associated with the Austro-Marxist theorists Otto Bauer and Karl Renner and the Hungarian liberal József Eötvös. The idea of organizing ethnocultural cleavages personally rather than territorially, allowing self-government and representation on a group basis that does not extend over non-consenting non-members, has an understandably enduring appeal. The rule over non-members makes group authority seem illiberal, coercive, and conflictual. But the advantages territoriality offers to group activities mean that we should routinely expect territorial concentrations to emerge and persist. Language communities, for example, are simply much more sustainable with a geographic core, and past some level of geographic dispersal are not sustainable

---

[8] Compare Will Kymlicka's idea of "contexts of choice" in *Liberalism, Community, and Culture* (Oxford: Oxford University Press, 1989).

at all. That geographic concentration will often afford the group local power even if institutions aren't organized in a way that formalizes it.

And the determined effort to free the local non-member from that local power can be highly disruptive of the ability of the group to conduct its own affairs. For example, the hybrid system of law in effect on American Indian reservations exempts non-Indians from all criminal and most non-criminal tribal jurisdiction, even though the reservations are territorial units. This leaves reservations unable to manage the externalities created by non-Indians' presence. Neither land use decisions nor basic local law and order can be maintained in a local patchwork; those who live in the area but are ungovernable by the local government become local disruptions.[9] If geographic concentrations do emerge and persist, that normally means that the group has at least some local governing power over non-members. Non-territorial federalism thus becomes *de facto* territorial. If this is prevented from happening—because the appeal of the idea of "non-territoriality" or the worry about group power is too strong—then the ability of the group to defend itself or even to persist may be destroyed by state action aimed at protecting local minorities and non-members.

Politics and Balance

What emerges from these discussions of bulwarks, factions, and territory is an understanding that group power to act in politics, or to refuse to be acted upon by the state, is not finely grained. Local, territorially concentrated group freedom becomes group power over non-members; protecting the non-members comes at a price to the group's legitimate freedom. Minority groups organizing to protect themselves can also organize well enough to capture an unjust share of state power, and the act of organization can worsen in-group hierarchies. Group members' freedom can be threatened by those in-group power relations, and yet the state's basic identification with the norms, cultural point of view, and interests of the majority can make it a deeply untrustworthy agency for the protection of members' freedom *against* their local rulers. All of this seems likely to be common. Against a state that is basically unfamiliar if not hostile, a minority group will be able to assert its local freedom only sometimes and only through concentrated political action. This will by definition advantage those who are able to organize and channel the group's political activities. These will often be those who were dominant in the group beforehand; when it is not, the process may well generate a new

---

[9] See my "Three Perversities of Indian Law," 12(2) *Texas Review of Law and Politics* 329–68, 2008.

internal hierarchy of those able to manage the politics of interaction with the state. The sustained simultaneous protection of the interests of subordinated group members against local domination *and* of the associational and cultural freedom of group members as such, even if conceptually possible, seems politically improbable. Political organization and political resources that are strong enough to protect group members' freedom against an unfriendly state may usually be strong enough to protect group elites' power in one way or another. Moreover, this dynamic can be self-reinforcing: the local institutions that enhance local authority also increase the capacity for political organization, making the capture of state policy toward the group that much more likely in the future. That is, institutional attempts to correct for state overreach in turn generate new sources of potential overreach. This seems to leave us without a vision of a social world in which freedom is seamlessly protected, a point to which we will return in the Conclusion.

11

Associations are Not States

In Chapter 2 we explored a congruence model of thinking about associational life, one that treated associations as subject to the constraints of justice and respect for rights that constrain liberal states. I argued there that this could not be sustained; intermediate groups are and ought to be purposive, in ways that both call for and legitimize substantive rules of conduct and belief, rules that would be illiberal if adopted as state legislation. This chapter returns to that idea, building both on the history of Part II and on the discussion in Chapter 10 of the entanglements between the intermediate sphere and political life. Perhaps the simple defense of group life against congruence depends too much on the idea of a small purposive group affecting mainly its own members; perhaps in light of organizational complexity and political effects, congruence is more plausible than it first appeared. Like Chapter 10, this chapter is written from a more overtly pluralist point of view than the rest of the book; it argues that neither challenge calls for a return to congruence.

Complex Associations

Many intermediate groups are themselves internally pluralistic.[1] Indeed I venture that *most* large groups are so. And by this I do not only mean that unincorporated groups like linguistic or cultural minorities encompass many formal associations and institutions, though this is true. Formal organizations themselves often contain internal associational spheres, ranging from voluntary associations' partly autonomous geographic chapters joined together federally to the student clubs (and, in a different way, the self-governing academic units) of a university to the array of geographically and purposively

---

[1] Here it is particularly important to remember that "intermediate" does not imply that groups are smaller than states, and that many of the groups under discussion are transnational.

differentiated associations (dioceses, religious orders, service organizations, educational institutions) within any sufficiently large religion.

The Roman Catholic Church is the example par excellence. Even at the time of its consolidation under a hierarchy headed by the Pope, it was made up of many independent monasteries and monastic orders as well as a separated order of lay priests. Indeed, since the rise of monastic orders and of substantially independent bishoprics preceded the Papal Revolution and the Great Schism, one should say of the Catholic Church what I said earlier about states: it came into the world already internally pluralistic, seeking to govern associations and institutions of various kinds that preceded it. The Papal "Revolution" was precisely an attempt to centralize authority and create a coherent lawmaking hierarchy where one had not previously existed. Today one would have to add to these, among many others, the worldwide networks of schools and universities associated with the Church, often through one or another religious order; and the non-monastic Jesuit order and Opus Dei, very different societies that share the feature of direct papal jurisdiction, placing them outside the supervisory capacity of the geographically organized secular clergy. What a liberal idea like "freedom of religion" means in this sort of context is not always obvious. Latin Mass traditionalists who reject the Vatican II reforms and movements to allow priestly marriage that ordain their own networks of clergy have both been disciplined or excommunicated. The Church hierarchy makes claims of religious freedom to oppose state regulations that would require Church-affiliated hospitals to offer contraception, or Church-affiliated universities to provide health insurance plans covering it; those who manage and operate those institutions sometimes disagree, and reject the claim of religious liberty being made on their behalf.

One of the most fascinating contemporary examples of a complex association is the Anglican Communion, a worldwide federation of national episcopal churches that have historic connections to the Church of England. The Archbishop of Canterbury is at the head of the episcopal structure, but lacks the Pope's scope for independent governing authority. The national churches are internally self-governing on many matters of doctrine and practice, and there is regular debate over *which* matters should be left to the national churches. The national churches themselves ordinarily adopt positions for their entire communions—that is, the doctrinal federativeness of the whole is not replicated within the national churches. A diocese must follow the rules of its national church. In recent years some conservative North American churches have sought to secede from the Episcopal Church of the United States and the Anglican Church of Canada, reconstituting themselves as the Anglican Church in North America (ACNA). Some have affiliated directly with the more-conservative Church of Nigeria—trying to make use of but at the same time fundamentally unsettling the federated structure of the whole body. The differences of doctrine are such that the overall structure would allow differences between national churches, but the American national church will not allow the same differences between dioceses. The Nigerian and several other national churches recognize ACNA as a fellow province of the communion, though it is still unsettled whether the overall Anglican Communion will do so, or how it can manage its traditional geographic federation if it does. The civil law is sometimes unavoidably entangled in these questions when, e.g., the seceding churches in Virginia sought to retain their historic church buildings, but were successfully fought by the Diocese of Virginia which considers them schismatics who have left (not revised) the church. Such church property cases have a long history of highlighting questions of complex association and of the meaning of religious liberty in corporate churches. The Free Kirk case in Scotland provided the occasion for Figgis' key contribution to pluralist theory, *Churches in the Modern State*; and during the Communist era, western branches of the Eastern Orthodox churches headquartered in Communist states (e.g. Russia, Serbia) sought to remove their branches from the traditional ecclesiastical structure.

In cases such as these, the question of how free an association is to have internal rules that differ from the general rules of the state is recreated in fractal form: how free is each group *within* the complex association to set internal rules that differ from those of the overall association? Within the Catholic Church, a monastic order is free to live according to internal rules that are much stricter than the rules governing membership in the church itself; but it does not follow that an individual monastery within a monastic order is free to set still-stricter standards than the order has ordained. Within the Anglican Communion, one national church may ordain women as bishops and another refuse to do so; but it does not follow that divisions within any given national church will have the same pluralistic freedom. And whether they do may itself be a question on which national churches differ, with some being much more domestically centralized than others.

Universities also form complex associations. Universities' internal pluralism is very old; the division into separate and partly self-governing Faculties or Colleges (e.g. of Law and of Theology) characterized universities' governance very early on. Indeed the division of a *university* (*universitas*) into *colleges* (*collegia*) offers our strongest continuity with the medieval Latin vocabulary about associations and pluralism. The kinds of internal plurality vary considerably from one university (and one university system) to another. The Colleges of Oxford and Cambridge are residential units that also directly employ professors, and that are not strictly demarcated by discipline.

Universities make many decisions about speech, speakers, associations, and ideas on their campuses; these are common sources of public controversy over university life. They may have rules governing all expression: for example, rules against hate speech, however understood.[2] They often have rules about what outsiders may be invited to speak on campus, or what lectures, conferences, and addresses will be entitled to take place in university settings or with the support of university funds. Religious universities sometimes prohibit, discourage, or refuse to fund or host speakers who oppose an important tenet of the religion: Catholic universities refusing to invite or support speakers who will defend abortion or homosexuality, for example. Some forbid religious proselytizing using university funds, whether by supported outside speakers or by religious student newspapers or magazines. Some take stands on national or international politics, refusing to support visiting lectures by outsiders on the basis of their political views.

Insofar as universities are complex associations, we again see that fractal pattern of freedom and group life arise. A widespread kind of dispute in American universities concerns the membership requirements of student clubs and associations. A conservative Christian student club wishes to exclude all gay and lesbian members, and all those whose religious views differ.[3] The university wishes to impose a rule of nondiscrimination on all of its clubs. Another, Catholic, university's student feminist society wishes to invite a speaker to campus to defend the moral permissibility of abortion; the university wishes to maintain its consistent view that abortion is abhorrent.

In both cases, one association or the other is going to be unable to order its internal affairs as it wishes. If the secular university were a simple association, it could clearly adopt an internal nondiscrimination rule. If the Catholic university were a simple association, it could clearly simply adopt, announce, and maintain its position on abortion. But they are complex associations, and it appears that their freedom of association conflicts with that of their members. A defense of thick associational rules seems indeterminate at best.

By the same token, a freestanding Christian or feminist association could clearly adopt the religious or ethical position it wished. A church may declare homosexuality sinful and reject nonbelievers; a feminist association may invite speakers to defend abortion. But in both cases, the students' claim of free association, free expression, or religious freedom conflicts with the university's ability to maintain its own commitments. To put it another way: it

---

[2] It is my view that *laws* against hate speech violate the right of freedom of speech—that is, I take the American First Amendment view and not the view common in the free speech jurisprudence of other liberal democracies. That means I think that if the congruence view were correct, university hate speech rules would violate freedom of speech. But of course the reader will know by now that I don't think that. For some readers, the force of the argument will be more apparent by reversing the hate speech examples; if you think that hate speech prohibitions are *required* to protect liberal equality, you might nonetheless think it an interesting problem whether universities could be justified in enacting a different balance of concerns domestically, and *refusing* to prohibit hate speech on campus.

[3] *Christian Legal Society v Martinez*, 561 US 2010.

seems that the students seek to maintain the same freedoms against the university that they have against the state—with the proviso that they normally wish the associations they form to be official university clubs, with the right to hold events in university space and to obtain university subsidies. The Christian club case is especially interesting for our purposes, because it highlights the way that the tension is present for individual students. Some students wish to be free to be gay or lesbian or atheist or Catholic while still having the right to join a club paid for by their tuition and student fees. And some students wish to be free to associate in a way that is dedicated to their conservative Protestant beliefs. When a club member is discovered to be lesbian and expelled, she will voice a complaint in terms of freedom; when the club is forced to adopt an open-membership rule, the original club members will do likewise.

Some universities refuse to allow or subsidize student groups of various political colorations; some refuse to allow student groups that apply political or religious membership tests. If a university insists that all of its internal associations themselves be, for example, non-exclusive in their membership—the so-called "all-comers" rules—there is a real similarity to the congruence view, or generally to rationalist skepticism of exclusive groups. But notice that the university, not the state, is imposing the group-skeptical rule. Universities are complex associations that reproduce group pluralism within themselves, and analogs of the rationalist–pluralist arguments reappear within complex associations.

I have suggested that intermediate associations could not coherently be expected to replicate the norms to which liberal democratic states are legitimately held; their internal rules will be norms that would be unjust if they were laws of a liberal state, and their purposiveness means that they cannot be neutral in the way that a liberal constitution should be. The question that arises with respect to complex associations is: do these considerations govern at the level of the umbrella association, or at a lower level? If we take freedom of association seriously, is it validly assertable *against high-level associations* in situations of complex association? When, for example, a legislature prohibits universities from adopting "all-comers" rules for student clubs, does it thereby *protect* freedom of association, or *impair* it?[4] When a diocese or a religious order, or a chapter of a federative association, takes a position contrary to that of its umbrella group, does it have an interest in associational freedom that the state should protect against the larger entity?

---

[4] All-comers rules at public universities have been prohibited in Virginia and Idaho. The all-comers rule at Vanderbilt, a private university, has been met with threatened legislative action in Tennessee on several occasions, but the legislation has not yet passed.

I think that legally cognizable associational freedom rightly vests in the overarching associations. Complex associations will often have *internal* reasons for respecting associational freedom in their domestic associational spheres, and those reasons will often resemble the reasons offered by liberal theories of justice for associational freedom from the state. But the resemblance is limited. Complex associations are still *purposive* associations: enterprise not civil, pursuers of the good not instantiations of the right. That they have internal reasons for creating (or allowing) internal associational spheres does not change this. Religious, cultural, and associational freedom—the freedoms to pursue goals and live lives in common—are best protected, not by seeking to aggressively protect each group of dissidents within a complex association, but by allowing a group's internal reasons and purposes to include internal complexity without sacrificing its autonomy.

I will devote the balance of this discussion to the case of universities, because it is universities rather than churches that most sorely tempt the confusion between complex association and state.[5] Universities seem the most state-like of complex associations; if even in their case freedom of association vests in the top-level group (the university) rather than the subordinate groups, if even the university is genuinely entitled to freedom of association in the governance of its internal affairs, then the same will most likely be true for, say, churches. The result is that states have sound reason to defer to the authority of the top level of complex religious associations rather than trying to vindicate the associational (or religious) freedom of dissident subordinate groups.

Universities and Liberal Justice

Churches as associations are defined by substantive commitments; they are shaped by their rules governing belief and practice. To have a religion is to have the possibility of orthodoxy and the possibility of heresy or apostasy, or their equivalents for religions that are centered on laws of practice rather than creedal belief. But, one might think, universities are paradigmatically *not* like that. The university at its best is defined around intellectual openness, the possibility of free exchange and free debate. Freedom of speech, of religious belief and inquiry, and of public debate are bound up with the mission of the

---

[5] I will also develop the argument ignoring the difference between public and private universities, a difference that is highly salient (I think too salient) under U.S. constitutional law. For most purposes herein the distinction does not matter. The all-comers rules which are the largest topic in what follows are constitutionally permissible but not constitutionally required at public universities, putting them on substantially the same legal footing as private universities as far as those rules are concerned.

secular university, as they are with the principles of liberal and constitutional democracy. Similarly, the prohibitions on various forms of discrimination that are so important to equal citizenship in the liberal state are at home in the *ethos* of a university, the dwindling number of single-sex colleges aside. There seems to be something importantly congruent between the principles of liberal justice and the values of university life.

One might therefore think that universities are more like states than they are like churches in fundamental ways. Churches must be free to distinguish between orthodoxy and heresy; neither states nor universities should do so. A church is devoted to an understanding of the truth and the good; the liberal state and the university should both be committed to open debate about such fundamental questions. Perhaps universities are best understood as something more like Oakeshottian civil associations than like enterprise associations. A university offers adverbial rules for how departments, faculties, centers, and schools govern their curricula and research agendas, not substantive rules on their content or conclusions. It offers adverbial rules to students on how to form and govern clubs of all sorts, in pursuit of a wide range of substantive interests and goals; it does not dictate those goals. Ideas and phrases from liberal political theory and constitutional law such as "viewpoint neutrality" and the unacceptability of "content-based" restrictions lend themselves easily to application in a university context. It is thus easy to start thinking in First Amendment categories when faced with intra-university problems, whether of academic or of associative freedom. In the associative cases of student clubs, this would mean a default presumption that clubs are free to restrict their membership, e.g. to co-believers or co-partisans for religious and political clubs, as well as a rule that they be free to invite such speakers as they wish to campus, to publish newspapers and magazines propagating their various views, and so on. The presumption of associative freedom might be defeasible, trumped for example by invidious discrimination that is irrelevant to the group's purpose and message (see *Roberts v Jaycees*, though I am a skeptic of both the result and the reasoning), but in the case of religious groups it would be especially strong. Blanket "all-comers" rules would be ruled out.

As the reader will have guessed by my use of conditional verbs, I think that the ideas laid out in the previous two paragraphs are mistaken.

To see why, first consider the meaning of "academic freedom." While easily confused with the rules of freedom of speech in the public sphere, academic freedom is actually a quite distinct value. On the one hand, it does not categorically protect the scholar's speech in the classroom. The instructor who turns the podium into a pulpit, who propagandizes and proselytizes to a captive audience of students, is not protected. Weber's argument in "Science as a Vocation" remains the right way to think about professorial responsibility. Academic freedom encompasses the freedom to *teach the subject*, including controversial views *within the boundaries of the subject* but with a duty to make clear that they are controvertible. In the ideal-typical university (i.e. not a seminary) that will never extend to propagandizing on behalf of one's own religion—a kind of expression that is central to the liberal constitutional right of freedom of speech. The structured, professional, power-and-authority-wielding context of an instructor's speech in a classroom comes with a structured professional ethic: one that includes wide freedom within the subject area but that is compatible with sharp limits on speech outside of it. Now, universities should be cautious in cases like this. The occasional incidental remark—say, the casual joke in front of a biology class that Republicans and Baptists may be frightened by the material—is not professional best practice but should not be punished. Pedagogical freedom and the free exchange of ideas in the classroom are genuinely important values and should have a pretty wide margin of safety around them. But those incidental remarks lie in the margin of safety, *not* in the core of academic freedom.

Much the same is true outside the classroom. Academic freedom as a *researcher* is the freedom to be judged only according to—but according to—the standards of an academic discipline. It means that, e.g., irrelevant political or religious tests will not be applied to assessments of scholarly merit. Whether my scholarly inquiries into political economy generates Communist conclusions, or I write letters to the editor in my free time espousing Nazism, as a scholar I will only be assessed *as a scholar*. The controversial speech in my free time, or the controversial conclusions generated by my research, will not be held against me in my professional capacity. "Unpopular" or "heretical" are ruled out as standards to apply. But there remain standards to apply, standards that are entirely foreign to the regime of free speech in the public sphere. Perhaps most obviously, scholarly fraud or misconduct—plagiarism, falsification of results, fabrication of sources—is utterly unprotected by academic freedom, and indeed normally constitutes grounds for disciplinary action up to and including dismissal even for tenured professors. Notice that plagiarism could not be criminalized under the First Amendment. If the work being plagiarized from was under copyright, then the copyright-holder might have grounds for a civil action—implying that the wrong was committed against the original author, not against the audience of readers. Uncredited but compensated ghost-writing would not even generate a private cause of action, and yet would still be scholarly fraud unprotected by academic freedom.

Less obviously but no less importantly, academic freedom is compatible with being judged according to disciplinary standards. It violates academic freedom to, e.g., refuse to tenure a candidate for promotion based on the political coloration of their research, but it does *not* violate academic freedom to refuse to tenure someone on the grounds that their published writings are mere political advocacy rather than scholarly research, or on the grounds that their scholarly research fails to meet a standard of quality. Questions of methodology are matters of disciplinary self-definition and self-government, and are legitimate. Academic freedom is not just the same thing as "free expression of ideas," and one of the salient differences is the application of methodological standards. Indeed to an important degree, academic freedom is a matter of the corporate autonomy of academic disciplines, not (or not only) the freedom of speech of individual researchers. *We political scientists*—or we philosophers or legal scholars or biochemists—have the authority and duty to assess one another according, and only according, to disciplinarily relevant standards of excellence in research. This is a kind of associative freedom, different in appearance from the associative freedom of co-religionists to judge one another's orthodoxy of belief and practice, but completely different in kind from any standard the liberal state may use in evaluating the speech of an individual citizen.

In short, academic freedom has some overlap of form and purpose with liberal freedom of speech, but it is genuinely not the same thing—more expansive in some respects, much more restrictive in others. It is the professional ethic of a purposive community, not a neutral and adverbial principle of justice.

Mutatis mutandis, the same is true of the associational freedom students have in the subsidized hothouse associational spheres that universities routinely make possible. It has overlap of form and purpose with liberal freedom of association in civil society, but the overlap is far from complete. Universities seek to foster intellectual debate and exchange of ideas by allowing students to form subsidized official clubs that are dedicated to one cause or another, to sponsor speakers and publish newspapers advocating those views, to meet together in associational settings to examine and pursue those ideas. (There are other goals for other kinds of clubs as well; most student clubs are recreational.) They harness students' energy and enthusiasm toward an educational end. This, too, is structured and purposive.

I do not think it obvious whether all-comers rules help or hinder these purposes; and the answer may not be the same for all universities at all times and places. One might reasonably think that they help: they foster *direct* engagement among students, discouraging segregation and ghettoization along sectarian lines. Students who spend all of their time associating with like-minded fellows may find themselves in echo chambers, deprived of exposure to disagreement and dissent. Insisting that clubs remain open to all students—political clubs to opponents, religious clubs to nonbelievers and dissidents, etc.—could be a way of ensuring genuine exchange. If students wish to sit in a room agreeing with each other—so this view would say—they are free to do so on their own; but if they are going to take advantage of the benefits of the university's cultivated associational sphere, they will have to encounter the disagreements that justify that sphere in the first place.

But there is much to be said on the other side as well. Especially for unpopular, minority, or novel ideas and practices, there is good reason for a protected time and space insulated from opposition. We want to explore an idea in some depth, in a way that requires building on shared premises rather than constantly rehashing responses to basic objections. We want to explore possible paths that our shared idea might take, in a provisional way that is not possible if our critics are likely to quote snippets of our discussion out of context. Our ideas are so unpopular that we are aware of criticisms and challenges all day, every day; association provides a moment of fellowship when we can recharge, encourage one another, share and explore reactions to those challenges, and so on. In the context of identity groups on campus (women's groups, ethnic minority groups, LGBT groups, etc.) this kind of thing is discussed under the name of "safe spaces." But the logic applies to beliefs and ideas as much as to identity.

If this is right, then the university's interest in allowing closed student clubs would not only be that it made the student members more comfortable. It would be that *the quality of intellectual exchange is enhanced* by allowing ideas to be developed, explored, and refined among those who share them. The expectation is that a vibrant campus life will be filled with moments of contact among people who disagree, and an educational purpose is served by allowing the disagreements to happen at progressively better intellectual levels.[6]

I do not claim to know the right way to balance these considerations, and doubt that they are best balanced in the same way in every context. But it should be noted that they are considerations, *not* about the abstract rights of the students, but about what organizational structure will promote the university's educational goals in lively on-campus exchange and debate. Like academic freedom, clubs' associational freedom is justified *and also shaped* by the purposes of university life. Opponents of all-comers rules who insist on students' associational freedom against the university just as if the university

---

[6] See here Cass Sunstein's "On Academic Fads and Fashions," 99 *Michigan Law Review* 1251, 2001, for a discussion of academic schools of thought, both within disciplines at large and at particular universities. The phenomena he discusses there can be highly productive, generating communities of like-minded scholars who can advance a research agenda quickly through mutual engagement; destructive, by encouraging an echo chamber and insulating the group's consensus from challenge; or both, simultaneously or in turn. It seems to me that the point is a general one: often new ideas can be formulated, explored, and refined in relatively closed settings, but closed settings can also encourage polarization, overinvestment in dead-end ideas, and extremism. Insisting on heterogeneous discussions at every stage can make discussions sterile, reducing everything to contentless least-common-denominator consensus; it can also prevent hothouses for bad ideas from developing. We must be willing to think in terms like "sometimes" and "it depends" about whether, when, and how group segregation can be productive of intellectual exchange.

were the same kind of entity as a liberal state are guilty of a serious category mistake. (The same can be said of *supporters* of all-comers rules who treat those rules as straightforward applications of the rules of non-discrimination and equal citizenship.)

Just as professors retain their normal freedom of speech *as citizens* (a professor of mathematics is as free to publish a ghost-written *novel* as anyone else is), so do students retain their associational freedom as citizens. Students at an all-comers campus are normally free to meet informally or to incorporate formally outside the university context. There are, however, exceptions to this; residential universities in particular sometimes claim authority over students' associational life even outside the sphere of subsidized student clubs. This happens most often in the context of fraternities and sororities or similar social organizations (e.g. Princeton's "eating clubs"). Both for reasons of managing town-gown relations and for reasons of structuring the social aspects of campus life, a number of universities have tried to limit or prohibit "Greek" organizations even when these are institutionally unaffiliated with the university. This too seems to me legitimate: a matter of residential colleges governing their settings by directly regulating student conduct, even when that "conduct" is "forming an association of a particular type off campus."

Residential colleges have many fewer behavioral rules than they used to; dress codes and parietal restrictions are long gone, and so much the better. But dress codes and dormitory parietal restrictions were both *legitimate* rules, notwithstanding the legal right of citizens to dress how they wish and to entertain visitors of the opposite sex in private residences. A college or university campus is an associational space, deliberately shaped in all sorts of ways to promote the university's purposes. Rules of student conduct that prevent Greek life from taking over the social life of a university may be prudent or imprudent, but they are legitimate.

In fact, public universities in the United States have been prohibited from banning Greek systems. Indeed, fraternities and sororities are singled out by federal legislation as retaining the associational freedom to be single-sex; even after *Martinez*, universities may not impose all-comers rules on them. *De facto* Greek systems are often deeply racially segregated as well; the restrictions faced by public universities relative to their Greek systems hobbles any attempt they might make to racially integrate their campus environments. The higher-level complex association is restricted so that freedom of association might be entrenched at a lower level.

In my view the better rule is that, in the complex association of a university, freedom of association vests primarily in the university itself. Claims of associational freedom made *against* the university—by official clubs, by unaffiliated fraternities, or for that matter by faculty members seeking to organize into a research center—should normally be made in terms of the university's own values and purposes, and indeed through the university's own internal decision-making processes, not in terms of citizens' liberal constitutional rights or through the courts. The same, incidentally, holds for freedom of speech in extracurricular settings. (I have already addressed academic freedom in curricular settings.) While normally a secular university[7] should not have viewpoint-based restrictions on, e.g., the sponsored speakers that student clubs bring to campus, its rules and its reasons here will differ from those of the liberal state. Sometimes they will be more permissive. In Canada, for example, it seems to me that universities have a duty in terms of their own values to disregard the hate speech regulations of the state. If the state wishes to punish a speaker after the fact it will do so, but the university's commitment to open debate should not be subservient to that prediction. But often they will be more restrictive. For example, a university may insist that speakers engage in question-and-answer exchanges with their audiences; it may reasonably decide that its educational purpose in subsidizing lecture fees and making its space available to outsiders is not fulfilled by bare lectures, campaign speeches, or sermons.

Liberal freedom is, in part, associational freedom: the freedom to join together under thicker rules than the liberal state could legitimately enact as laws, to bind ourselves together under authority structures other than the democratic constitutional state, to freely create organizations against which we can't then directly make liberal claims of freedom. Complex associations tempt many people into thinking otherwise, into applying the norms of constitutional liberal democracy to the internal affairs of these intermediate groups. But note that, *at most*, the complex association moves the purposive associations down a level; it does not show that one could coherently do without purposive associations. The university demonstrates that it is nonsectarian by neutrally allowing students to form their various religious groups—groups that, in turn, *are* sectarian. Complex associations, even universities, are purposive themselves. No clarity is gained by thinking of the university as a civil association. Like simple associations, and indeed like the sectarian clubs it may sponsor, it is an enterprise association; it encourages a domestic associational sphere for its own purposes, which are those of education and intellectual exchange.

---

[7] It is fairly widely acknowledged that religious universities may have content-based restrictions; Catholic universities need not subsidize or recognize pro-choice or LGBT student clubs, or host speakers whose talks will challenge fundamental Church doctrine. The institutional imperatives of *being a university* do push in the direction of a kind of intellectual openness, and indeed the Catholic universities that make up the most important sector of American religious higher education often do support quite robust debate and exchange—so much so that they are often challenged by co-religionists outside the universities, and sometimes by the Church hierarchy, for being too tolerant of speakers and speech that vary too widely from Church doctrine.

If this is true of universities, it is true of other complex associations as well. During the controversies between the Obama administration and the Catholic Church about the Patient Protection and Affordable Care Act (PPACA), the claims of the Church to be defending religious freedom were sometimes challenged by pointing to dissident Catholic groups such as the Leadership Conference of Women Religious (the association of Mothers Superior of orders of nuns in the United States) as well as by pointing to the general use of contraception by American Catholics. Since in fact individual Catholics overwhelmingly use contraception in the United States, their religious liberty was not, it was claimed, violated at all. While it may be that the infringement on religious freedom by PPACA was on net justified, these moves to try to deny that religious freedom was at stake *at all* were mistaken. Religious liberty is (in part) corporate: *libertas ecclesiae*, and this is so for reasons that are wholly compatible with liberal values, reasons grounded in the freedom of religious *persons* to associate in meaningful and authoritative ways. The freedom of the church is not diminished just because the church, for internal reasons, is a complex association; neither individual nor incorporated dissent impugns the corporate religious liberty found in the church itself. Dissidents remain citizens and persons, entitled to the rights of citizens and of persons; this limits what the church may do to *punish* their dissent. But *qua* members, they are subject to the church's internal rules and doctrines, and religious liberty is not served by allowing the state to opportunistically choose dissidents in order to break the liberty of the corporate whole.

State Action

Dissent can be silenced by a state exercising censorship, a university firing a professor or closing a student newspaper, a church excommunicating those it declares heretics, a cultural group shunning and isolating those who deviate from custom, a voluntary association removing officials or board members who publicly express their disagreement with the association's ideas, a homeowners' association prohibiting the posting or circulating of letters disagreeing with the board within the association's boundaries. In the United States the question of whether non-state actors are bound by such constitutional guarantees as the right of freedom of speech falls under the so-called "state action doctrine"; without state action, the right is not violated. In other countries, it is the question of whether constitutional rights have "horizontal effect" (from private actor to private actor) in addition to their "vertical effect" (between private actors and the state).

I think some version of a state action doctrine is a necessary part of construing liberal rights in a coherent way,[8] for reasons I have discussed. We cannot coherently claim the same general freedom and general right to equal treatment in the private sphere (and here I include the market as well as the associational sphere) that we have as against the state. But that is not to say that non-state actors cannot impede freedom of speech, or freedom.

More nuanced positions are possible between a rigid state-action doctrine and the demand for complete congruence, positions that emphasize one or another special feature besides statehood that could legitimate (public, constitutional) rights-claims. What follows are some of the considerations that might be brought to bear on whether some intermediate group's rules are relevantly similar to state action. Each is a reason for an exception to the general presumption in favor of associational freedom and the general validity of the state-action doctrine. Together they make possible a range of answers between the pure theory and congruence.

First, rights could be asserted against a non-state actor if it is especially large or powerful, or otherwise occupies a quasi-governmental role or social space. Some supporters of the idea that there is a free speech or free assembly right within the confines of private shopping malls have argued something like this: the courtyard of the mall has displaced the traditional town square as an important central meeting place, and so we must be able to exercise our rights of political communication within malls if they are to remain effective. The company running a company town, or an especially large homeowners' association, might similarly stand in for the state in a rights-claim. So might a church, especially a very hierarchical church that represents a large local majority: the Latter-Day Saints in Utah, the Catholic Church in many countries, Orthodox Christian churches in others. One could single out such large and powerful institutions and treat them something like the state, without necessarily running into the incoherence I identified in the congruence theory.

Second, one might apply a test, not of state action, but of what Rawls called the basic structure of society. Because the basic structure can manifest in many small loci of power rather than one large one, this is importantly different from the idea mentioned immediately above. No individual family is a large powerful social actor in that same way, but women can be systematically socially disadvantaged because of patterns of the gender division of labor that are reproduced in each family. If "the family" is one of the basic

[8] For opposing views see Mark Tushnet, "State Action, Social Welfare Rights, and the Judicial Role: Some Comparative Observations," 3 *Chicago Journal of International Law* 435, 2002; and Cass Sunstein, "State Action is Always Present," 3 *Chicago Journal of International Law* 465, 2002; Mark Tushnet, "State Action in 2020," in Jack M. Balkin and Reva B. Siegel, eds., *The Constitution in 2020* (Oxford: Oxford University Press, 2009); Gary Peller and Mark Tushnet, "State Action and a New Birth of Freedom," 92 *Georgetown Law Journal* 779, 2004.

organizing features of a society, then (on this line of reasoning) the fact that no individual family is large and powerful is immaterial. Unjust inequality is perpetuated through the basic structure of society, and one could resist that—demanding active state intervention within the structure of the family to prevent that perpetuation of inequality, for example. The traditional common law rule that both "common carriers" and places of "public accommodation" such as inns and restaurants were required to serve all-comers is similar. While inns and restaurants do not provide public goods strictly understood, and function perfectly well as private businesses, the overall social system of mobility that allows travelers to go where they are not known and trust that they will find accommodation is a basic feature of liberal society.[9]

And third, certain kinds of disadvantage or injustice could be singled out as being so pervasive and socially ingrained that the normal pluralism of the private sphere is unlikely to prevail, and respecting the state action doctrine is likely to mean that a caste system is perpetuated in the private sphere. One reaction in the southern United States to racial desegregation of public schools was to create Potemkin private academies. As private organizations rather than agencies of the state, they were (at that time) presumptively not subject to nondiscrimination rules. Restrictive housing covenants could in principle be a way of preserving the distinctiveness of neighborhoods, a kind of geographic pluralism. Against the background of the American racial caste system, they were a way to turn the private housing market into an instrument of that system (or, to put it another way, to prevent the private housing market from undermining it). The emphasis here is not on the size and power of the actor, or on the status of the actor *in general* as being part of the basic structure, but rather on the particular injustice at stake.

This offers a useful way to think about not only racial covenants and falsely private academies but also that of Bob Jones University. That Protestant university's internal rules against interracial dating led to its being denied tax-exempt status, first by the IRS and then by the U.S. Supreme Court.[10] That a private religious university should have restrictive rules quite unlike the rules of the liberal democratic state is normal. If the Bob Jones ruling stood for the general principle that such rules are illegitimate, then it would be incoherent in the way I have discussed. And Bob Jones University is neither a particularly powerful actor (in the way that, say, Harvard is) nor, probably, a part of the basic structure. But the ruling could be understood to stand for the coherent principle that the racial caste system is constitutionally distinctive in the United States, and that the state-action doctrine is at its weakest when private

---

[9] See Michael Walzer on mobility in "The Communitarian Critique of Liberalism," 18(1) *Political Theory*, February 6–23, 1990.

[10] *Bob Jones University v United States* (1983).

actors (even relatively unimportant ones) publicly endorse or maintain the system of racial supremacy. This uniqueness is recognized, among other places, in the doctrine that the Thirteenth Amendment "prevents the imposition of any burdens or disabilities that constitute badges of slavery or servitude," in addition to prohibiting slavery itself.

Each of these three offers a category of exception to the state-action doctrine: powerful actors, basic structures, or special pervasive injustice. It matters for their coherence that they are arguments about exceptions, not arguments to undo the basic rule. But in all three cases, the exception has to do with magnitude or importance. That means that any of these exceptions has the potential to swallow the rule, at least in the politically most salient cases. Broadly, I think that Anglo-American liberal readers will be inclined (as I am) to think that the third exception is justified in the context I described. But I suspect that Anglo-American liberal readers are generally skeptical of the French republican tradition of *laïcité*, prioritizing public secularism over private religious freedom. And defenders of *laïcité* might well argue in a similar way: the distinctive experience of French struggles for liberal democracy against a conservative politicized priesthood justifies a change in the normal rules of public and private. The schoolteacher wearing a nun's habit is not an individual person exercising her freedom of religion while happening to be involved in public employment; in that context (it is said) she symbolizes conservative religious domination of the public sphere, and creates an environment hostile to religious and intellectual freedom. While I can imagine finding this argument persuasive, I admit that I can't even imagine being persuaded to make the next leaps that are made. A nun-teacher joins the dominant religion to the state's authority; a Muslim student in a headscarf represents neither the dominant religion nor the state's authority. But others seem to be persuaded by that extension. More generally: the strategy of these three kinds of exceptions seems to preserve the background rule only in politically marginal cases. In precisely those cases in which some particular rationalizing or centralizing state is most likely to come into conflict with an intermediate group, because they are the politically most salient and sensitive cases, the "exceptions" risk becoming the rule.

Tushnet explicitly aligns the state-action doctrine with liberalism and resistance to it with social democracy—though he also suggests that the doctrine simply represents the kind of legal formalism that cannot survive the acid bath of legal realism. The legal realist can see that "the setting of each of the background entitlements is a result of state power that could have been exercised differently—that is, the result of policy and politics."[11] Tushnet

---

[11] Mark Tushnet, *Weak Courts, Strong Rights: Judicial Review and Social Welfare Rights in Comparative Constitutional Law* (Princeton: Princeton University Press, 2009), p. 189.

and Peller say that "[e]very exercise of 'private' rights in a liberal legal order depends on the potential exercise of state power to prevent other private actors from interfering with the rights holder," and so no "region of social life . . . can be marked off as 'private' and free from governmental regulation."[12]

I said in Chapter 3 that we should aim to think about groups as groups, rather than either as states writ small or as individuals writ large. If the exceptions to the state-action doctrine swallow the rule, then we have failed to distinguish between groups and the state. But that does not mean that a strong version of the state-action doctrine should be invoked to deny rationalist liberalism its due. If we fail to recognize that freedom can be implicated in the ways that groups govern their members, then we have failed to distinguish between groups and persons.

---

[12] Peller and Tushnet, "State action and a new birth of freedom."

Conclusion: Against Synthesis

I have argued that a liberal understanding of freedom is constitutively torn between a rationalist distrust of the local, the particular, and power embedded within group life, and a pluralist emphasis on the freedom found within and protected by group life against the power of the state. I have criticized various attempts to settle definitively for one or the other, or to redefine the distinction away. In these final pages I also offer reasons to doubt attempts to transcend the distinction and synthesize the two.

One might doubt the possibility of harmonization out of a general skepticism that different values can be brought together. This is pluralism in Isaiah Berlin's sense, the idea that the human good is intrinsically plural and can involve conflicts among irreconcilable truths. In one of his earliest statements of value pluralism, Berlin suggested that negative liberty would not always be compatible with other genuine and basic political values. There is no social world without loss, and we will often face the loss of either some morally desirable extent of negative liberty or some morally desirable extent of something else. Perhaps the arguments in this book mean that moral pluralism can characterize even what has been thought of as a single value such as negative liberty itself. Sometimes we will not be able to have the morally best degree of freedom of association and the morally best degree of protection against local tyranny.

This would have consequences for the structure of argument about particular cases. We cannot, for instance, simply point to the moral loss suffered by some relatively powerless or disadvantaged person within an association, religion, or cultural group and conclude that the group constitutes a local tyranny that must be dissolved or overruled by the state. Dissolution carries moral losses of its own. So, too, does the replacement of a procedural rule allowing local decision-making with one that allows outsiders to decide, on a case-by-case basis, when to substitute their judgment for the group's internal procedures. Moral pluralism also denies us access to Goldilocks' reasoning: the thought that if one theory or one course of action seems to go too far in one direction, another in another, that there must be some third alternative that happens to be just right. There may often be no such alternative, and we will only have a choice as to which losses to accept.

I am inclined to accept Berlin's idea, but do not intend the argument in this book to depend on it. The sheer possibility of value incommensurability does not show that it applies to every pair of values; neither is incommensurability the source of every impasse. The tension between rationalist and pluralist liberalism can be sufficiently generated by competing social and empirical considerations. It does not require that there be irreconcilable moral goods—say, autonomy and toleration—at the bottom. The complexity of the social world by itself generates genuine dilemmas and choices that entail losses. Berlin wrote that

> The notion of the perfect whole, the ultimate solution, in which all things coexist, seems to me not only unattainable—that is a truism—but conceptually incoherent; I do not know what is meant by a harmony of this kind. Some among the Great Goods cannot live together. That is a conceptual truth. We are doomed to choose, and every choice may entail an irreparable loss.[1]

The "conceptual incoherence" claim is the thesis of moral pluralism. But what he dismisses as a mere truism seems to me sufficient for our purposes. We cannot simultaneously attain all of the goods valued by pluralist liberalism and all those valued by rationalist liberalism, as a matter of social fact, regardless of whether it is coherent to imagine them coexisting or not.

Sometimes, however, a value conflict that cannot be resolved by compromise can be transcended. In order to cast doubt on the possibility of such an overcoming in this case, I will conclude by discussing a few possible strategies to seek it. All are in some way indebted to Hegel, the great philosopher of synthesis in general, and one especially concerned with combining both ethically thick social life with abstract universal principles, and life in corporate groups with life in the state. Hegel was purposely omitted from the historical survey in Part II in anticipation of this discussion. Some would deny that Hegel is properly a part of the history of liberal political thought, but there is no doubt that he appreciated both the freedom made possible by citizenship in a law-governed state and the freedom to live according to one's more particular ethical commitments and partial memberships.

While I cannot prove the negative, that *no* synthesis is possible, I will argue against all of these efforts at final reconciliation. There is a friction between group life and the state, even the liberal democratic state, a friction that does not admit of any stable resolution and does not admit of resolution at all

---

[1] Berlin, "The Pursuit of the Ideal," in Henry Hardy, ed., *The Crooked Timber of Humanity* (New York: Vintage Books, 1992), p. 13.

without moral loss. The relationship between state and groups is not one of reason and, say, culture, each of which could be assigned its proper place; reasons and culture suffuse both levels, but the reasons differ. The legitimate purposes of group life are not necessarily harmonious, either with each other or with the legitimate purposes of the state and of citizenship. Liberal constitutionalism itself partly depends on group life that is oppositional rather than harmonious. Moreover, as we have seen, the texture of social power is very uneven; this means that the boundaries between group life and the state cannot be fine-tuned as the synthesizing theories demand.

Note that it would not count as a synthesis of rationalism and pluralism to simply subordinate one to the other, for example by celebrating group life just so long as it receives autonomous endorsement from members and political enactment by the state. This denies pluralism at the outset. In what follows, by contrast, I think we find would-be syntheses that genuinely try to build on the contributions that both thick associational life and thin formal citizenship can make to freedom. Seeing why they do not succeed will help to illustrate the logical, sociological, and psychological barriers to complete harmonization.

Taylor and the "Long March"

In his various works on modernity and history,[2] Charles Taylor—both an important interpreter and, in key respects, a follower of Hegel—has returned several times to what he refers to as the "Long March." This is the centuries-long dissolution of the Great Chain of Being model of continuously hierarchical social relations, in which the cosmos is well ordered in a series of steps, from God's authority over angels through a king's authority over his subjects down to a patriarchal husband's authority over his wife and children. That model has gradually been replaced by one pervaded by a moral presumption of equal social relations. One of the last pieces of that transition has been the end of the presumed patriarchy of the family and its replacement by the companionate marriage of equals, in which wives retain their moral, political, legal, and economic status and equality. Democratic equality, once restricted to political relations among a subset of men, has now become a principle uniformly governing all across the social order.

After describing this process, Taylor writes: "Uniformity across niches is far from an obvious, common-sense requirement. Nevertheless, we have finally

---

[2] Principally, Taylor, *Sources of the Self* (Cambridge, Mass.: Harvard University Press, 1989); Taylor, *The Malaise of Modernity* (Toronto: House of Anasi Press Ltd, 1991); Taylor, *Modern Social Imaginaries* (Durham: Duke University Press, 2004); and Taylor, *A Secular Age* (Cambridge, Mass.: Belknap Press of Harvard University Press, 2007).

come to that uniformity: the long march has finally taken us there."[3] He emphasizes the links among that uniformity and liberal norms, a connection we have encountered in a number of contexts.

> These modes of imagined direct access are linked to, indeed are just different facets of, modern equality and individualism. Directness of access abolishes the hetero-geneity of hierarchical belonging. It makes us uniform, and that is one way of becoming equal... We can see right away that in an important sense, modern direct-access societies are more homogenous than pre-modern ones.[4]

Taylor explicitly contrasts the "direct access" society—in which, among other things, individuals directly access the state of which they are citizens—with the prerevolutionary world of intermediate bodies. Direct access is unmediated, immediate, and not in need of intermediaries. Protestantism is of a piece with this transformation; individuals gain the belief that they have direct access to the divine, and abandon their belief in the mediating institution of the Church. The long march is, in this sense, a march to the Protestantization of the whole social order.[5]

Taylor's view of processes like these is complicated, and not only because his view of Protestantism is complicated. He says that things could be otherwise: there is no presumption that modernization in non-western societies will tie together all the same bundle of ideas and practices that it has done in the Atlantic west. Individualism and the development of the market, egalitarianism and the rise of the modern state, the turn to natural science, the desacralization of the public sphere, the valuing of human rights, the development of a social world in which religion is a choice, and the development of a social world in which it is an infrequent choice: these do not all have to march in lockstep. Whereas traditional modernization theory was sometimes described as the idea that all *good* things go together in social change—democracy, development, secularization, education, women's rights—for Taylor, saying that it could be otherwise is meant to be hopeful: modern values he embraces and modern facts he welcomes do not necessarily entail the widespread abandonment of religious belief.

But Taylor does embrace these modernization stories as the history of the Atlantic west. All of those things have gone together, at least here. We can speak of a secular age succeeding other ages, we can see a long march of modernity and modernization. Like the stadial theorists, and like Hegel and Marx, Taylor sees an unfolding logic of at least this kind of modernity, a set of

---

[3] Taylor, *Modern Social Imaginaries*, p. 147.   [4] Taylor, *A Secular Age*, p. 211.
[5] Compare Steven Macedo, *Diversity and Distrust* (Cambridge, Mass.: Harvard University Press, 2000); Macedo, "Community, Diversity, and Civic Education: Toward a Liberal Political Science of Group Life," 13(1) *Social Philosophy and Policy* 240–68, 1996. Macedo offers a normative sociology of gradual Protestantization that corresponds nicely with Taylor's, though Macedo embraces these developments with much less ambivalence.

processes that move monotonically to tie the social world together in a crucial kind of whole.

Perhaps Taylor must think something like this. The theorist of the reality of shared understandings and social goods thinks that we aren't free to define very local social realities that are detached from wider universes of shared meaning. We are too thoroughly socially enmeshed for that. The secular age is an age of shared social meaning like any other: the age in which, for example, it is understood that religion may be chosen or not chosen, no matter how firmly any one of us holds to a particular view about what choice should be made. The shared social meaning of the era of the Great Chain of Being, when it was understood that patricide echoed regicide which echoed blasphemy, and that any of them upset that natural order in a much more profound way than mere murder, gives way. The shared social meanings of our era make it hard for us to imagine the idea that regicide could cause unnatural weather, as it does in Macbeth, as anything other than a poetic image.

Taylor's long march is a story of the synthesis of rationalism and pluralism. Our social groups are changed over time to match our political commitments. Egalitarian individualism becomes the rule across social spheres, so that we end with a real harmony between group and state, between local ethic and public justice, between plurality and rationality. I have mentioned Taylor's account of two models of civil society, one traceable to Locke, one to Montesquieu. The Lockean model is individualistic in its foundations and political in its structure: we come together as persons and create a political society unified by a set of juridical procedures. The Montesquieuian rests on group life and is social rather than political. The long march toward uniformity is a kind of Lockeanizing of Montesquieuian civil society. The norms of thick group life are gradually hollowed out and replaced by the thin, egalitarian, and juridical norms associated at least in principle with the liberal state.

But it seems to me there has been no such monotonic unfolding of the logic of western modernity, no teleological pull of egalitarian individualism transforming all social niches across the modern era.

Taylor argues that the uniformity of the modern age arose "not so much because of a natural drive to consistency" as out of the drive to *inclusion*, on the part of certain strata that initially were marginalized in the new order. "This is the last phase of the long march: on the one hand, the extension of the new social imaginary below and beyond the social elites who originally adopted it; and on the other, the extension of the principles of this new imaginary to other levels and niches of social life."[6] It unfolded, in other words, not simply due to the force of ideas (Taylor denies that his conception

---

[6] Taylor, *Modern Social Imaginaries*, p. 147.

of history is idealist in the pejorative sense sometimes used when discussing Hegel) but due to the political struggles excited by hypocrisy and non-isomorphism.

The isomorphism of the familiar is a powerful tendency. But it is not the only tendency. Recall James I's pronouncement that Presbyterian church government "as well agreeth with a monarchy as God and the Devil." He speculated that there would be a tendency toward uniformity in the direction of ecclesiastical governance; those who govern their church in a relatively egalitarian way will make bad subjects of a monarch. On the other hand, James' belief in a tendency toward uniformity was a self-undermining prophecy, as it led him to try to coerce uniformity in the direction of the structure of civil government. He sought to impose Anglican episcopacy on the Scottish church, to suppress Presbyterian ecclesiology and Calvinist theology. This naturally helped to sow skepticism about the monarchy among Calvinists who might not otherwise have felt it. States' suspicion of non-congruent, non-isomorphic associations, discussed in Chapter 3, is a source of pressure on the latter. The Society of the Cincinnati did not really survive its contact with this kind of pressure. But Calvinist Presbyterianism very much did.

Some of what Taylor calls "social imaginaries," once they take off, are strongly self-reinforcing. The bureaucratized modern state with its extractive and security apparatus is one such. The capitalist market is another. Once some people start seeing the world in terms of the security dilemma and realize the competitive gains that can be had through the bureaucratic state and its fiscal-military machinery, their neighbors are more or less forced to start doing so as well through competitive pressure or else by conquest and incorporation. Once some people start realizing the gains that accrue to the division of labor and the infinite fungibility of resources made possible by money and the market, it becomes constantly more difficult to withdraw from or even limit one's participation in the world of the market; the opportunity costs of doing so keep rising. Perhaps the modern state and the commercial market really do operate in iron-cage-like fashion: the social imaginary, once imagined, has a monotonic internal logic of expansion. I do not think that anything of the sort is true of association, culture, or religion. Indeed in those domains I think that movements in any one direction predictably generate counter-movements, for reasons that include the cycles of norms discussed in Chapter 10 and the drive to mutual differentiation discussed in Chapter 3.

The Freemasons emerged under a social order with which they were not isomorphic, and persisted under another social order with which they were also not isomorphic. Although pre-revolutionary Americans had been deeply fearful of the establishment of an Anglican episcopacy on this side of the Atlantic, and indeed the suspicion of it was a major contributor to republican revolutionary fervor, just such a structure was created while the ink was barely dry on the Treaty of Paris ending the Revolutionary War.

The same is true again for the rise of Mormonism out of Jacksonian America. The religious ferment in the early nineteenth-century United States was broadly democratic and egalitarian. Traditional religious authorities and elites saw their followers slip away. Charismatic leaders of revival meetings on the frontier did not depend on degrees from the elite east-coast training grounds of Protestant clergy. And the loose organizational forms of the Second Great Awakening limited the power that could be accumulated by many of the itinerant preachers. And yet one of the most effective charismatic religious leaders of the era, Joseph Smith, ultimately left behind an extraordinarily hierarchical new religion.

The "drive to inclusion" does not serve as the kind of unidirectional motor of history that Taylor envisions. I would go so far as to say: in-group egalitarianism has a strong tendency to be associated with sharpening boundaries between the in-group and the out-group. Adam Smith correctly foresaw that democratic republics would be slower to abolish slavery than would monarchies. In the latter, the gradual slope downward of social standing did not demand a bright-line distinction between the bottom caste and those immediately above it. But in *Herrenvolk* democracies such as Jacksonian America or Afrikaner South Africa, the elevated-to-equality status of the lowest class of the ruling race depends on its qualitative superiority to the subordinate race. I think that the same has often been true of the status of women: a woman in an aristocratic society could stand out in a way that was more difficult in a society based on the collective equal status of white men. A political actor like Madame de Staël might have been quite unthinkable in contemporaneous America.

And similarly, moves toward open-ended freedom and formal legality in the liberal public sphere predictably generate movements toward intermediate associations that provide more substantive content, more *meaning* for their members, than does the abstract state. More conservative religious groups thrive alongside a background culture and legal order that are increasingly liberal on, e.g., matters of sexual morality. Cities or towns (or private residential associations) offer local and distinctive lifestyles to mobile populations, letting people sort into local communities whose distinctiveness then becomes self-reinforcing. The dynamics of group pluralism can serve to accentuate distinctions between groups and hierarchies and conservatism within them. I do not suggest that these dynamics operate without resistance, that the sociology of group life is one of endless fragmentation and mutual differentiation. I only mean to suggest that these dynamics are among those in play, and that this denies us the natural harmonizing between public citizenship and group life that Taylor's long march seems to offer. The friction between states and associations is not one that the course of history will spontaneously overcome.

Rawls and the Morality of Association

A possible synthesis that operates mainly at the level of moral psychology may be found in the work of John Rawls.[7]

In *A Theory of Justice*, Rawls discusses associational life primarily as a stage in his developmental moral psychology, the stage between bridging the childish obedience to authority within the family and the principled commitment to justice and the right.[8] In associating with our fellows for a variety of purposes to which we have substantive commitments, in pursuing our conceptions of the good in common with them (to use language that Rawls doesn't in this context), we learn to think in terms of procedures and rules of fairness among equals. Our field of application gradually increases from the small association of the family to the large association of the "national community," at which point we are ready to understand justice as a demand of principle. This discussion is brief but important, and clearly indicates a harmony between the lessons learned in associations about how to interact with others and the eventual principles of justice. The idea that one might learn lessons of another sort—lessons of hierarchy or exclusion, or lessons of prioritizing the associational good over the political right—is never mentioned. In the well-ordered society, it seems, associations are congruent with the just state. While associational life is legitimately associated with the good (including with Aristotelian perfectionism) in a way that public justice is not, Rawls offers a sense of the relationship between the two that is not only compatible but involves the incorporation of the former into the latter.

Later, of course, Rawls sought to model the stability of the liberal state in a very different way, and one that was self-consciously attuned to the fact of religious pluralism. I think that Rawls' political turn drew on some of the same sensibilities that I have discussed in this book under the label of pluralist liberalism, and his rejection of autonomy-based comprehensive liberalisms as foundations for his theory of justice was an important move in reopening

---

[7] I am persuaded that Rawls' synthesizing impulse does owe something important to Hegel. His debt to Hegel was made explicit in his discussion of the reconciling task of political philosophy in the introductory pages of his *Lectures* on that topic, but it can be seen elsewhere as well. See Margaret Meek Lange, "Exploring the Theme of Reflective Stability: John Rawls' Hegelian Reading of David Hume," 1(1) *Public Reason* 75–90, 2009; Sibyl Schwarzenbach, "Rawls, Hegel, and Communitarianism," 19 *Political Theory* 539–71, 1991; Ragip Ege and Herrade Igersheim, "Rawls With Hegel: The Concept of 'Liberalism of Freedom'," 15(1) *European Journal of the History of Economic Thought* 25–47, 2008.

[8] John Rawls, *A Theory of Justice* (Cambridge, Mass.: Harvard University Press, 1971), pp. 467–72.

intellectual space for pluralism. But we may still be better off thinking of *Political Liberalism*[9] as another attempted synthesis, not as a turn to pluralism per se.

Rawls expressly limits his central analysis of pluralism to so-called *reasonable* pluralism, understood as the pluralism of comprehensive doctrines *that can generate support for justice as fairness*. While the language of an "overlapping consensus" might imply that the plurality of views comes first and the theory of justice emerges from what is shared among them, the reality is the reverse; the ("freestanding") conception of justice offers the metric by which comprehensive doctrines will be measured and found legitimate or wanting. And the holders of "unreasonable" comprehensive doctrines are entitled only to more or less grudging *modus vivendi*-style tolerance from the state. The moral psychology of "the morality of association" is still tacitly relied upon; genuine conflict between the moral lessons of our comprehensive doctrines and the moral demands of public justice cannot be admitted.

Moreover, the pluralism discussed in *Political Liberalism* is overwhelmingly a pluralism of *beliefs*. It is in that important sense individualistic. (Notice, again, the resemblance to a kind of Protestant ethos.) Not only are associations, institutions, and the dynamics of group life largely absent; so too is the pluralism of religious *practices*. There are good reasons for this; *Political Liberalism* is a moral argument, not a sociology, and it is concerned with the respect and disrespect shown to individual persons *qua* believers in a comprehensive doctrine. That is an important limitation on how pluralistic we should understand it to be.

Finally, the most direct discussion in Rawls' later writings of intermediate groups is entangled with a famously ambiguous discussion of justice and the family.[10] Having been criticized by Okin, among others, for his neglect of the family in earlier writings, Rawls sought to maintain the following distinction: the principles of justice do not directly govern relations within *a* family, a university, an association, a church, and so on. That is, he denied congruence; it is not "desirable, or consistent with liberty of conscience or freedom of association," that the public principles of justice be applied directly within group life. But insofar as the aggregate social institution of *the* family shapes the lives of citizens in a fundamental way, it forms part of the basic structure and as such *is* subject to the rules of justice; the same should be true of other aggregate social institutions such as universities. Rawls thus aims to combine associational and religious liberty on one hand with a firm commitment to not allowing associational life to impair citizens' liberty on the other.

---

[9] John Rawls, *Political Liberalism* (New York: Columbia University Press, 1993).
[10] Rawls, *Justice As Fairness: A Restatement* (Cambridge, Mass.: Harvard University Press, 2002), pp. 163–4.

Feminist critics were not satisfied;[11] the patriarchal family affects the fundamental prospects of women's lives from *within* each family, one at a time, and we cannot simultaneously immunize each individual family as a sphere of intimate association *and* regulate "the family" so as to ensure women's equal freedom. G. A. Cohen powerfully argued[12] that Rawls' persistent "wobble" in how to think about the family was symptomatic of a pervasive ambiguity in how Rawls thought of the basic structure (to which principles of justice apply) insofar as that includes social institutions outside the coercive apparatus of the state.

Cohen was, it seems to me, right about this. Rawls aims to respect a pluralistic liberty of association, including of intimate family association. He recognizes the cost to such liberty if all parts of social life are subsumed (as Cohen apparently thinks they should be) within the principles of public justice. But the basic structure, as Rawls defines it, is measured by its important social effects, and must include at least especially important associations and groups, including the family. It might turn out that the right amount of associational liberty is compatible with the provision of a just basic structure; but if so, that would be an improbable coincidence, not a necessary outcome. Rawls' wobble is preferable to Cohen's coherence; he is torn between two genuine liberal values, and does not want to do without either. But his theory is genuinely torn on this point; it aims at synthesis, and does not achieve it.

Hegel, Ethical Life, and Corporate Forms

Both harmonization over the course of history of the sort that we saw in Taylor and psychological reconciliation of the sort that we saw in Rawls are among the tools that Hegel uses in his ambitious attempt to overcome contradictions between public rational justice and group-based ethical commitments, between the Roman and Germanic inheritances of constitutional politics. Hegel believed that freedom can be reconciled with both abstract right and thick local ethics (and those with each other). His parallel thought at the level of social institutions looked to a harmonization of state and intermediate corporate bodies.

Hegel does not evince a rationalist hostility to ancient constitutions as such. In his essay on "The German Constitution," he deploys "the concept of the state" as a critical tool against the organization of the Holy Roman Empire—

---

[11] Susan Moller Okin, "Political Liberalism, Justice, and Gender," 105(1) *Ethics* 23–43, 1994; Martha Nussbaum, "Rawls and Feminism," in Samuel Freeman, ed., *The Cambridge Companion to Rawls* (Cambridge: Cambridge University Press, 2003).

[12] G. A. Cohen, *Rescuing Justice and Equality* (Cambridge, Mass.: Harvard University Press, 2008), pp. 116–35.

but he denies that "the concept of the state" is at odds with ancient consti-tutionalism. He recognizes the legal and jurisdictional multiplicity of pre-Revolutionary France in particular, and insists that France was nonetheless a genuine (indeed a powerful) state.[13] Variation in weights and measures, in customs and laws, in currency, in urban and provincial taxation: none of this detracted from France's essential character as a state. Neither did the division among classes and estates, or the inequality of their rights. Looking more broadly, he observes that neither religious nor linguistic uniformity has proven necessary for genuine statehood. In language that must surprise those who still think of Hegel as an apologist for Prussian centralized autoc-racy, he mocks "the pedantic craving to determine in every detail, the illiberal jealousy of all direction and administration by an estate, corporation, etc., of its own affairs, this pusillanimous carping at all independent activity on the part of the citizens," the insistence that no charitable activity be undertaken "unless it has first been not merely approved, but ordained, controlled, and inspected by the supreme government," that "the appointment of every village schoolmaster, the expenditure of every penny on a pane of glass" must be "examined, computed, corrected, and ordained by state, law, and government." In the affirmative, he states that "the centre, as the political authority and government, must leave to the freedom of the citizens whatever is not essential to its own role."[14] The man of system is held up to mockery. While he insists that *ancien régime* privileges and pluralities must be legally susceptible to deliberate legislative reform, he shows no hurry to sweep them away.

Nonetheless, of course, he is deeply concerned with unity, and the essay on the German Constitution is a call for a unified state—which requires unity of political judgment at the center, unified armed forces, and a shared national sense of commitment to that army. In his fuller political doctrine in *The Philosophy of Right*, he makes clear that this ultimate political unity should incorporate subordinate distinctions. Our membership in the rational state should be intermediated—primarily through our membership in corpor-ations, which represent us to and in the state itself.

Many real forms of institutional autonomy for intermediate groups also build the groups into the structure of government; recall the representation of towns and the Church in early parliaments and estates. But for two reasons,

---

[13] In this we see one piece of Hegel's very clear debt to Montesquieu. Michael Mosher has explored Hegel's connections to Montesquieu more generally in "The Particulars of a Universal Politics: Hegel's Adaptation of Montesquieu's Typology," 78(1) *The American Political Science Review* 179–88, 1984.

[14] Hegel, "The German Constitution" (1802), in *Political Writings* (New York: Cambridge University Press, 1999), pp. 22–3.

such institutional solutions do not transcend the tensions discussed in this book.

First, Hegel's corporations—it is perhaps more useful to think of them with the French *corps*, to help remember that they are not the modern business corporation, despite being organized by profession—seem to be conceived of as mutually exclusive in their memberships, like the constituencies or districts that elect members in existing legislatures. Citizens are conceived of as having their place in the Estates mediated by one *corps* per person, or else by their membership in an agricultural estate that is not organized into *corps* at all. The overlapping and cross-cutting memberships characteristic of liberal pluralism are incompatible with the model. In current single-member-district legislatures, each person votes in only one district to preserve fairness and equality of the franchise. Hegel's concern is very different; he thinks that one's *corps* membership organizes and in part constitutes the moral self. Belonging to a *corps* teaches individual persons to see an interest in common (the partial interest of their *corps*), grounds a morally worthwhile livelihood, and provides much of the structure of life in civil society (here remembering Hegel's special sense of that phrase). One could not meaningfully belong to more than one such *corps*, any more than one could really belong to more than one state.[15] And so the institutional problem of how to handle cross-cutting or overlapping memberships simply does not arise; the *corps* fit seamlessly together. But this is completely unresponsive to the facts of modern group pluralism. Conspicuously, it has room for neither cultural nor linguistic nor (perhaps "especially") religious groups, which cross-cut the *corps* and which are so prominent in contemporary understandings of group representation and mediated belonging. The state can tolerate those divisions,[16] but they will remain politically invisible; only the corporations exercise the fundamental purposes of intermediating our membership in the state and representing our particularities in the universal institution. Hegelian representation can provide an integrated structure of state and *corps*, but it cannot integrate public citizenship with the fluid subjective understandings of membership in various, and varying-over-time, associations.

This brings us to the second difficulty. Hegel saw no place for the feature of ancient constitutionalism so crucial to its uses by Montesquieu, Constant, and Tocqueville: the "germ of resistance" which our intermediate memberships provide us. The corporations represent us *to* the state, but cannot coherently protect us *from* it. Even in the relatively favorable discussion of *ancien régime*

---

[15] Again, in Hegel's sense, which is not falsified by the existence of dual citizenship in the real world.

[16] Up to a point. On the limits of Hegel's willingness to tolerate religious plurality, see Judith N. Shklar, *Freedom and Independence: A Study of the Political Ideas of Hegel's Phenomenology of Mind* (Cambridge: Cambridge University Press, 1976).

pluralism in "The German Constitution," that idea does not appear. Hegel's ambition to present us to ourselves in a unified way, to overcome our division against ourselves, does not allow for this kind of opposition between the institutions to which we belong. For our particular group to act to protect us against the universal state would count as a grave failure. This does not show that Hegel is wrong; but it does show that he does not somehow draw together rationalism and pluralism in a complete way. For all of his appreciation of the *corps*, of group life, and of local norms, it is finally always the rational and universal state that takes priority in his theory.

There is a genuine tension between the institutional realization of freedom to associate and of freedom within (or from) group life. Our consensual ways of joining together and pursuing our projects set and strengthen norms for those around us. They generate local surpluses of hierarchy and power that cannot be wholly tamed without harm to our cultural, religious, and associational freedom. The texture of social power is lumpy and irregular, and cannot be fine-tuned as the synthesizing theories demand. Liberty generates pluralism, which generates norms, norm enforcement, and local power, which limit freedom. Social groups provide organizational and political resources by which persons protect their freedom against the state; and those who hold in-group authority may then use those resources to enhance their own power, directly or through interaction with the state. And the ability to see freedom in our associational lives and power in the state all too often limits the ability to see power in associations and the possibility of freedom being enhanced by outside intervention—and vice versa. If we are concerned with liberal freedom, we are, I think, left with no choice but to reject synthesis—whether of intermediate groups' ethos with the state, or of rationalism and pluralism. This means living with a degree of disharmony in our social lives, our moral psychologies, and our political theory.

Bibliography

Acton, John. *The History of Freedom and Other Essays*. London: Macmillan, 1907.

Acton, John. *Essays in the History of Liberty*. Edited by J. Rufus Fears. Indianapolis: Liberty Fund, 1985.

Acton, John. *Lectures on the French Revolution*. Indianapolis: Liberty Fund, 2000[1910].

Adams, John. *The Works of John Adams, Second President of the United States*. Vol. 10. Boston: Little, Brown and Co., 1856.

Adams, John. Letter to Abigail Adams, December 14, 1794. In *Letters of John Adams, Addressed to His Wife*. Edited by Charles Francis Adams. Boston: Little, Brown and Co., 1891.

Adams, John. *The Political Writings of John Adams*. Edited by George W. Carey. Washington: Regnery, 2000.

Affaires de l'Angleterre et de l'Amerique. Paris: 1776–9.

Aligica, Paul Dragos, and Peter Boettke. *Challenging Institutional Analysis and Development: The Bloomington School*. London; New York: Routledge, 2009.

Althusius, Johannes. *Politica*. Edited by Frederick S. Carney. Indianapolis: Liberty Fund, 1995[1603].

Appiah, Anthony. *The Ethics of Identity*. Princeton: Princeton University Press, 2005.

Appiah, Anthony. *The Honor Code: How Moral Revolutions Happen*. New York: W. W. Norton, 2010.

Appleby, Joyce. "What Is Still American in the Political Philosophy of Thomas Jefferson?" *The William and Mary Quarterly* 39(2) (1982): 287–309.

Armitage, David. *The Ideological Origins of the British Empire*. Cambridge: Cambridge University Press, 2000.

Axelrod, Robert M. *The Evolution of Cooperation*. New York: Basic Books, 1984.

de Barante, Amable-Guillaume-Prosper Brugière. *Des Communes et de l'Aristocratie*. Paris: Librairie Française de l'Advocat, 1829.

Barry, Brian. *Culture and Equality: An Egalitarian Critique of Multiculturalism*. Cambridge, Mass.: Harvard University Press, 2001.

Baum, Bruce. "Feminism, Liberalism and Cultural Pluralism: J. S. Mill on Mormon Polygyny." 5(3) *Journal of Political Philosophy* 230–53, 1997.

Beales, Derek. "Philosophical Kingship and Enlightened Despotism." In *The Cambridge History of Eighteenth-Century Political Thought*. Edited by Mark Goldie and Robert Wokler. Cambridge: Cambridge University Press, 2006.

Berlin, Isaiah. *Four Essays on Liberty*. Oxford: Oxford University Press, 1969.

Berlin, Isaiah. *The Crooked Timber of Humanity*. Edited by Henry Hardy. New York: Vintage Books, 1992.

Berman, Harold. *Law and Revolution*. Vol. 1. Cambridge, Mass.: Harvard University Press, 1983.

Berman, Harold. *Law and Revolution*. Vol. 2. Cambridge, Mass.: Harvard University Press, 1983.

Besley, Timothy. "Political Selection." 19(3) *Journal of Economic Perspectives* 43–60, 2005.

Black, Anthony. *Guilds and Civil Society in European Political Thought from the Twelfth Century to the Present*. London: Methuen, 1984.

Black, Anthony. *Political Thought in Europe, 1250–1450*. Cambridge: Cambridge University Press, 1992.

Bloch, Marc. *Feudal Society, Vol. 2: Social Classes and Political Organizations*. Chicago: University of Chicago Press, 1961.

Bodin, Jean. *Six Books of the Commonwealth*. Translated by M. J. Tooley. Oxford: Basil Blackwell, 1955[1576].

Boyd, Richard. *Uncivil Society: The Perils of Pluralism and the Making of Modern Liberalism*. Lanham, Md.: Lexington Books, 2004.

Brettschneider, Corey. "A Transformative Theory of Religious Freedom: Promoting the Reasons for Rights." 38(2) *Political Theory* 187–213, 2010.

Brettschneider, Corey. *When the State Speaks, What Should It Say?: How Democracies Can Protect Expression and Promote Equality*. Princeton: Princeton University Press, 2012.

Brundage, James A. *The Medieval Origins of the Legal Profession: Canonists, Civilians, and Courts*. Chicago: University of Chicago Press, 2008.

Buchanan, Allen. "Assessing the Communitarian Critique of Liberalism." 99(4) *Ethics* 852–82, 1989.

Burke, Edmund. "Speech on the Petition of the Unitarian Society." In *Selected Writings and Speeches of Edmund Burke*. Edited by Peter J Stanlis. Washington, D.C.: Regnery Gateway, 1963.

Burke, Edmund. *Reflections on the Revolution in France*. Oxford: Oxford University Press, 1993[1790].

Burlamaqui, J. J. *The Principles of Natural Law, Vol. 2*. Edited by Petter Korkman. Translated by Thomas Nugent. Dublin: John Rice, 1776.

Campbell, Peter R. "Absolute Monarchy." In *The Oxford Handbook of the Ancien Régime*. Edited by William Doyle. Oxford: Oxford University Press, 2011.

Carlyle, Thomas. "Occasional Discourse on the Negro Question," *Fraser's Magazine for Town and Country*, December 1849.

Chambers, Clare. *Sex, Culture, and Justice: The Limits of Choice*. University Park, Pa.: Pennsylvania State University Press, 2008.

Chinard, Gilbert. *Jefferson et les Idéologues, D'après Sa Correspondance Inédite Avec Destutt De Tracy, Cabanis, J.-B. Say, Et Auguste Comte*. Paris: Les Presses Universitaires de France, 1925.

Christiano, Thomas. *The Constitution of Equality: Democratic Authority and Its Limits*. Oxford: Oxford University Press, 2008.

Cohen, G. A. *Rescuing Justice and Equality*. Cambridge, Mass.: Harvard University Press, 2008.

Cohler, Anne M. *Montesquieu's Comparative Politics and the Spirit of American Constitutionalism*. Lawrence: University Press of Kansas, 1988.

Constant, Benjamin. "Des Réactions Politiques." In *Œuvres Politiques*. Edited by Charles Louandre. Paris: Charpentier et Cie, 1874[1797].

Constant, Benjamin. *Journaux Intimes*. In *Œuvres*. Edited by Alfred Roulin. Paris: Gallimard, 1957[1829].

Constant, Benjamin. *Mélanges de Littérature et de Politique*. In *Œuvres*. Edited by Alfred Roulin. Paris: Gallimard, 1957[1829].

Constant, Benjamin. *The Spirit of Conquest and Usurpation and Their Relation to European Civilization* (1814), in *Political Writings*. Edited by Biancamaria Fontana. Cambridge: Cambridge University Press, 1988, p. 74.

Constant, Benjamin. *Fragments D'un Ouvrage Abandonné Sur La Possibilité d'Une Constitution Républicaine Dans Un Grand Pays*. Edited by Henri Grange. Paris: Aubier, 1991 [1810].

Constant, Benjamin. *Political Writings*. Translated and edited by Biancamaria Fontana. Cambridge: Cambridge University Press, 1993.

Constant, Benjamin. *Principles of Politics Applicable to All Governments*. Translated by Dennis O'Keeffe. Indianapolis: Liberty Fund, 2003[1806–10].

Craiutu, Aurelian. *Liberalism Under Siege: The Political Thought of the French Doctrinaires*. Lanham, Md.: Lexington Books, 2003.

Craiutu, Aurelian. *A Virtue for Courageous Minds: Moderation in French Political Thought, 1748–1830*. Princeton: Princeton University Press, 2012.

Crick, Julia. "*Pristina Libertas*: Liberty and the Anglo-Saxons Revisited." 6(14) *Transactions of the Royal Historical Society* 47–71, 2004.

Dangerfield, George. *The Strange Death of Liberal England*. New York: Smith and Haas, 1935.

Davidson, Ian. *Voltaire: A Life*. New York: Pegasus Books, 2010.

Davies, Wallace Evan. "The Society of the Cincinnati in New England 1783–1800." 5(1) *The William and Mary Quarterly* 3–25, 1948.

Diderot, Denis. "Essai historique sur la police de la France depuis son origine jusqu'a son extinction actuelle." In Diderot, *Œuvres politiques*. Edited by Paul Verniere. Paris: Garnier, 1963[1773].

DiMaggio, Paul J., and Walter W. Powell. "The Iron Cage Revisited: Institutional Isomorphism and Collective Rationality in Organizational Fields." 48(2) *American Sociological Review* 147–60, 1983.

Dixit, Avinash K. *Lawlessness and Economics: Alternative Modes of Governance*. Princeton: Princeton University Press, 2004.

Djin, Annelien de. *French political thought from Montesquieu to Tocqueville: Liberty in a Levelled Society?* Cambridge: Cambridge University Press, 2008.

Djin, Annelien de. "Was Montesquieu A Liberal Republican?" 76(1) *Review of Politics* 21–41, 2014.

Duff, P. W. *Personality in Roman Private Law*. Cambridge: Cambridge University Press, 1938.

Ege, Ragip, and Herrade Igersheim. "Rawls with Hegel: The Concept of 'Liberalism of Freedom'." 15(1) *The European Journal of the History of Economic Thought* 25–47, 2008.

Eisenberg, Avigail. *Reconstructing Political Pluralism*. Albany, N.Y.: State University of New York Press, 1995.

Ekman, Ernst. "The Danish Royal Law of 1665." 29(2) *The Journal of Modern History* 102–7, Jun. 1957.

Ellickson, Robert C. *Order Without Law: How Neighbors Settle Disputes*. Cambridge, Mass.: Harvard University Press, 1991.

Elliott, J. H. "A Europe of Composite Monarchies." 137(1) *Past & Present* 48–71, 1992.

Elster, Jon. *Sour Grapes: Studies in the Subversion of Rationality*. Cambridge: Cambridge University Press, 1983.

Epstein, Richard. *Bargaining with the State*. Princeton: Princeton University Press, 1993.

Fearon, James D. "Electoral Accountability and the Control of Politicians: Selecting Good Types Versus Sanctioning Poor Performance." In *Democracy, Accountability, and Representation*. Edited by Adam Przeworski, Bernard Manin, and Susan Carol Stokes. Cambridge: Cambridge University Press, 1999.

Figgis, John Neville, and Reginald Laurence. "Introduction." In Lord Acton, *The History of Freedom and Other Essays*. London: Macmillan, 1907.

Figgis, John Neville. *Churches in the Modern State*. London: Thoemmes, 1997[1914].

Floquet, Amable. *Historie du Parlement de Normandie. Tome 1*. Rouren: Edouard Frère, 1840.

Foley, Michael W., and Bob Edwards. "The Paradox of Civil Society." 7(3) *Journal of Democracy* 38–52, 1996.

Fontana, Biancamaria. *Benjamin Constant and the Post-Revolutionary Mind*. New Haven: Yale University Press, 1991.

Foucault, Michel. *Discipline and Punish: The Birth of the Prison*. New York: Pantheon Books, 1977[1975].

Foucault, Michel. *Security, territory, population: lectures at the Collège de France, 1977–78*. Edited by Michel Senellart. Translated by Graham Burchell. New York: Picador, 2007 [2004].

Frankfurt, Harry. "Freedom of the Will and the Concept of a Person." 68(1) *The Journal of Philosophy* 5–20, 1971.

Frug, Gerald E. "The City as a Legal Concept." 93(6) *Harvard Law Review* 1057–154, 1980.

Fuller, Lon. *The Morality of Law*. New Haven: Yale University Press, 1969.

Fuller, Lon. "Two Principles of Human Association." In *Nomos XI: Voluntary Associations*. Edited by J. Roland Pennock and John W. Chapman. New York: Atherton Press, 1969.

Fuller, Lon. "Human Interaction and the Law." In *The Rule of Law*. Edited by Robert Paul Wolff. New York: Simon and Schuster, 1971.

Galston, William A. "Two Concepts of Liberalism." 105(3) *Ethics* 516–34, 1995.

Galston, William A. *The Practice of Liberal Pluralism*. Cambridge: Cambridge University Press, 2004.

Garnett, Richard W. "The Freedom of the Church." 4(1) *Journal of Catholic Social Thought* 59–86, 2007.

Garsten, Bryan. "Constant on the Religious Spirit of Liberalism." In *The Cambridge Companion to Constant*. Edited by Helena Rosenblatt. Cambridge: Cambridge University Press, 2009.

Garsten, Bryan. "Religion and the Case Against Ancient Liberty: Benjamin Constant's Other Lectures." 38(1) *Political Theory* 4–33, 2010.

Gellner, Ernest. *Nations and Nationalism*. Ithaca: Cornell University Press, 1983.

Gellner, Ernest. *Conditions of Liberty: Civil Society and Its Rivals*. New York, N.Y.: Allen Lane/Penguin Press, 1994.

Gierke, Otto von. *Community in Historical Perspective*. Edited by Antony Black. Translated by Mar Fischer. Cambridge, Cambridge University Press, 1990[1868].

Gierke, Otto von. *Political Theories of the Middle Age*. Translated by F. W. Maitland. Bristol, England: Thoemmes Press, 1996[1900].

Gill, Michael B. *The British Moralists on Human Nature and the Birth of Secular Ethics*. Cambridge: Cambridge University Press, 2006.

Gordon, Scott. *Controlling the State: Constitutionalism from Ancient Athens to Today*. Cambridge, Mass.: Harvard University Press, 1999.

Grant, James. *John Adams: Party of One*. New York: Farrar, Straus and Giroux, 2005.

Greenens, Raf, and Helena Rosenblatt eds. *French Liberalism from Montesquieu to the Present Day*. Cambridge: Cambridge University Press, 2012.

Guizot, François. *The History of the Origins of Representative Government in Europe*. Edited by Aurelian Craiutu. Translated by Andrew Scoble. Indianapolis: Liberty Fund, 2002.

Hardin, Garret. "The Tragedy of the Commons." 162(3859) *Science* 1243–8, 1968.

Hardin, Russell. "Special Status for Groups." 6(2) *The Good Society* 12–19, 1996.

Hardin, Russell. *Liberalism, Constitutionalism, and Democracy*. Oxford: Oxford University Press, 1999.

Hardin, Russell. "Cultural Diversity and Liberalism." In *Political Legitimization Without Morality?* Edited by Jörg Kühnelt. London: Springer, 2008.

Hart, H. L. A. *The Concept of Law*. Oxford: Clarendon Press, 1961.

Haskins, Charles Homer. *The Rise of Universities*. New York: Henry Holt, 1923.

Hayek, Friedrich A. von. *The Constitution of Liberty*. Chicago: University of Chicago Press, 1960.

Hayek, Friedrich A. von. *Law, Legislation and Liberty*. Vol. 1. Chicago: University of Chicago Press, 1973.

Head, Brian. *Ideology and Social Science: Destutt De Tracy and French Liberalism*. Dordrecht; Boston; Hingham, MA: M. Nijhoff, 1985.

Hegel, Georg Wilhelm Friedrich. "The German Constitution." Edited by Laurence Dickey. Translated by H. B. Nisbet. Cambridge: Cambridge University Press, 1999 [1802].

Helfand, Michael A. "Religion's Footnote Four: Church Autonomy as Arbitration." 97(6) *Minnesota Law Review* 1891–1962, 2013.

Hertzberg, Arthur. *The French Enlightenment and the Jews: The Origins of Modern Anti-Semitism*. New York: Columbia University Press, 1968.

Herzog, Don. "Puzzling Through Burke." 19(3) *Political Theory* 336–63, 1991.

Hirst, Paul. *From Statism to Pluralism Democracy, Civil Society, and Global Politics*. London: Routledge, 1997.

Hobbes, Thomas. *A Dialogue Between a Philosopher & A Student of the Common Laws of England*. Edited by Joseph Crospey. Chicago: University of Chicago Press, 1997 [1681].

Hobbes, Thomas. *Leviathan*. 3 vols. Edited by Noel Malcolm. Oxford: Oxford University Press, 2012[1651].

Holmes, Stephen. *Benjamin Constant and the Making of Modern Liberalism*. New Haven: Yale University Press, 1984.

Holmes, Stephen. *Passions and Constraint: On the Theory of Liberal Democracy*. Chicago: University of Chicago Press, 1995.

Hont, Istvan. *Jealousy of Trade: International Competition and the Nation State in Historical Perspective*. Cambridge, Mass.: Belknap Press of Harvard University Press, 2005.

Horwitz, Paul. *First Amendment Institutions*. Cambridge, Mass.: Harvard University Press, 2013.

Hotman, François. "Francogallia." In Robert Molesworth, *An Account of Denmark: With Francogallia and Some Considerations for the Promoting of Agriculture and Employing the Poor*. Edited by Justin Champion. Indianapolis: Liberty Fund, 2011[1573].

Hulliung, Mark. *Montesquieu and the Old Regime*. Berkeley: University of California Press, 1976.

Hume, David. "Of the Original Contract." In *Essays, Moral, Political, and Literary*. Edited by Eugene F. Miller. Indianapolis: Liberty Fund, 1987.

Hünemörder, Markus. *The Society of the Cincinnati: Conspiracy and Distrust in Early America*. New York: Berghahn Books, 2006.

Israel, Jonathan. *Enlightenment Contested: Philosophy, Modernity, and the Emancipation of Man, 1670–1752*. Oxford: Oxford University Press, 2006.

Jacob, Margaret. *Living the Enlightenment: Freemasonry and Politics in Eighteenth-Century Europe*. Oxford: Oxford University Press, 1991.

James I, "The Hampton Court Conference" 1604. In *Constitutional Documents of the Reign of James I*. Edited by J. R. Tanner. Cambridge: Cambridge University Press, 1930.

Jaume, Lucien. *L'Individu effacé ou le paradoxe du libéralisme français*. Paris: Fayard, 1997.

Jaume, Lucien. *Tocqueville: Les sources aristocratiques de la liberté*. Paris: Fayard, 2008.

Jefferson, Thomas. *Thomas Jefferson, Writings*. Edited by Martin Segal. New York: The Library of America, 1984.

Jennings, Jeremy. "Constant's Idea of Modern Liberty." In *The Cambridge Companion to Constant*. Edited by Helena Rosenblatt. Cambridge: Cambridge University Press, 2009.

Jennings, Jeremy. *Revolution and the Republic: A History of Political Thought in France Since the Eighteenth Century*. Oxford: Oxford University Press, 2011.

Kahan, Alan S. *Aristocratic Liberalism: The Social and Political Thought of Jacob Burckhardt, John Stuart Mill, and Alexis De Tocqueville*. Oxford: Oxford University Press, 1992.

Kaiser, Thomas E. "Money, Despotism, and Public Opinion in Early Eighteenth-Century France: John Law and the Debate on Royal Credit." 63(1) *The Journal of Modern History* 1–28, 1991.

Kateb, George. "Hobbes and the Irrationalities of Politics." 17(3) *Political Theory* 355–91, 1989.

Kavka, Gregory S. "Why Even Morally Perfect People Would Need Government." 12(1) *Social Philosophy and Policy* 1–18, 1995.

Kelley, Donald. *The Human Measure: Social Thought in the Western Legal Tradition*. Cambridge, Mass.: Harvard University Press, 1990.

Kelly, George Armstrong. *The Humane Comedy*. Cambridge: Cambridge University Press, 1992.

Kibre, Pearl. "Scholarly Privileges: Their Roman Origins and Medieval Expression." 59(3) *The American Historical Review* 543–67, 1954.

King, Loren. "Liberal Citizenship: Medieval Cities as Model and Metaphor." 14(2) *Space and Polity* 123–42, 2010.

Kingston, Rebecca. *Montesquieu and the Parlement of Bordeaux*. Geneva: Librairie Droz, 1996.

Koch, Adrienne. *The Philosophy of Thomas Jefferson*. New York: Columbia University Press, 1943.

Koppelman, Andrew, and Tobias Barrington Wolff. *A Right to Discriminate? How the case of Boy Scouts of America v James Dale warped the law of free association*. New Haven: Yale University Press, 2009.

Kramer, Lloyd S. "Liberal Theory and the Critique of Bonapartism: Lafayette, Destutt de Tracy, and Benjamin Constant." 19(2) *Proceedings of the Consortium on Revolutionary Europe, 1750–1850*, 495–508, 1990.

Kramer, Lloyd S. *Lafayette in Two Worlds: Public Cultures and Personal Identities in an Age of Revolution*. Chapel Hill, N.C.: University of North Carolina Press, 1998.

Krause, Sharon. *Liberalism with Honor*. Cambridge, Mass.: Harvard University Press, 2002.

Kukathas, Chandran. *The Liberal Archipelago: a Theory of Diversity and Freedom*. Oxford: Oxford University Press, 2003.

Kukathas, Chandran. "Two Constructions of Libertarianism." 1(11) *Libertarian Papers* 1–14 (2009).

Kymlicka, Will. *Liberalism, Community, and Culture*. Oxford: Oxford University Press, 1989.

Kymlicka, Will. *Multicultural Citizenship: A Liberal Theory of Minority Rights*. Oxford: Oxford University Press, 1995.

Kymlicka, Will. "Justice and Security in the Accommodation of Minority Nationalism." In *The Politics of Belonging*. Edited by Alain Dieckhoff. Lanham, Md.: Lexington Books, 2004.

LaCroix, Alison L. *The Ideological Origins of American Federalism*. Cambridge, Mass.: Harvard University Press, 2010.

Lange, Margaret Meek. "Exploring the Theme of Reflective Stability: John Rawls' Hegelian Reading of David Hume." 1(1) *Public Reason* 75–90, 2009.

Laski, Harold Joseph. *Studies in the Problem of Sovereignty*. New Haven: Yale University Press, 1917.

Laski, Harold Joseph. *Authority in the Modern State*. New Haven: Yale University Press, 1919.

Laski, Harold Joseph. *The Foundations of Sovereignty and Other Essays*. New York: Harcourt, Brace and Company, 1921.

Lee, Daniel. "Private Law Models for Public Law Concepts: The Roman Law Theory of Dominium in the Monarchomach Doctrine of Popular Sovereignty." 70(3) *The Review of Politics* 370–99, 2008.

Le Roy Ladurie, Emmanuel. *The Ancien Régime: A History of France, 1610–1774*. Oxford: Blackwell Publishers, 1996.

Levey, G. B. "Equality, Autonomy, and Cultural Rights." 25(2) *Political Theory* 215–48, 1997.

Levy, David M. *How the Dismal Science Got Its Name*. Ann Arbor: University of Michigan Press, 2001.

Levy, Jacob T. *The Multiculturalism of Fear*. Oxford: Oxford University Press, 2000.

Levy, Jacob T. "Liberalism's Divide After Socialism—and Before." 20(1) *Social Philosophy and Policy* 278–97, 2003.

Levy, Jacob T. "Liberal Jacobinism." 114(2) *Ethics* 318–36, 2004.

Levy, Jacob T. "Sexual Orientation, Refuge, and Rights of Exit." In *Minorities Within Minorities*. Edited by Avigail I. Eisenberg and Jeff Spinner-Halev. Cambridge: Cambridge University Press, 2005.

Levy, Jacob T. "Beyond Publius: Montesquieu, Liberal Republicanism and the Small-Republic Thesis." 27(1) *History of Political Thought* 50–90, 2006.

Levy, Jacob T. "Federalism, Liberalism, and the Separation of Loyalties." 101(3) *American Political Science Review* 459–77, 2007.

Levy, Jacob T. "Not So *Novus* an *Ordo*: Constitutions Without Social Contracts." 37(2) *Political Theory* 191–217, 2008.

Levy, Jacob T. "Three Perversities of Indian Law." 12(2) *Texas Review of Law and Politics* 329–68, 2008.

Levy, Jacob T. "Montesquieu's Constitutional Legacies." In *Modernity in Question: Montesquieu and His Legacy*. Edited by Rebecca Kingston. Albany: SUNY Press, 2009.

Levy, Jacob T. "From Liberal Constitutionalism to Pluralism." In *Modern Pluralism: Anglo-American Debates Since 1880*. Edited by Mark Bevir. Cambridge: Cambridge University Press, 2012.

Lewis, C. S. *God in the Dock*. Grand Rapids, MI: Wm. B. Eerdmans, 1972.

Locke, John. *Two Treatises of Government*. Edited by Peter Laslett. Cambridge: Cambridge University Press, 1988[1689].

Lukes, Steven. *Power: a Radical View*. London; New York: Macmillan, 1974.

Macedo, Stephen. "Liberal Civic Education and Religious Fundamentalism: The Case of God v. John Rawls?" 105(3) *Ethics* 468–96, 1995.

Macedo, Stephen. "Community, Diversity, and Civic Education: Toward a Liberal Political Science of Group Life." 13(1) *Social Philosophy and Policy* 240–68, 1996.

Macedo, Stephen. *Diversity and Distrust: Civic Education in a Multicultural Democracy*. Cambridge, Mass.: Harvard University Press, 1999.

Madison, James. *Letters and Other Writings of James Madison, Fourth President of the United States. IV*. Philadelphia: J. B. Lippincott & Company, 1865.

Madison, James. *The Debates in the Federal Convention of 1787 which Framed the Constitution of the United States of America*. Edited by Gaillard Hunt and James Brown Scott. Buffalo, N.Y.: Prometheus Books, 1987.

Madison, James, Alexander Hamilton, and John Jay. *The Federalist Papers.* Edited by Clinton Rossiter. New York: Mentor Books, 1961.

Madison, James, and Thomas Jefferson. *Republic of Letters: Correspondence between Jefferson and Madison 1776–1826.* Edited by James Morton Smith. New York: W. W. Norton and Company, 1995.

Maitland, Frederic William. *The Cambridge Review,* October 16, 1902.

Maitland, Frederic William. *A Historical Sketch of Liberty and Equality: As Ideals of English Political Philosophy from the Time of Hobbes to the Time of Coleridge.* Indianapolis: Liberty Fund, 2000[1857].

Maitland, Frederic William. *State, Trust, and Corporation.* Edited by David Runciman and Magnus Ryan. Cambridge: Cambridge University Press, 2003[1905].

Mantena, Karuna. *Alibis of Empire.* Princeton: Princeton University Press, 2010.

McDonald, Forrest. *States' Rights and the Union: Imperium in Imperio, 1776–1876.* Lawrence: University Press of Kansas, 2000.

McIlwain, C. H. *Constitutionalism, Ancient and Modern.* Ithaca: Cornell University Press, 1947.

McWilliams, Susan. *Traveling Back.* Oxford: Oxford University Press, 2014.

Michels, Robert. *Political Parties: a Sociological Study of the Oligarchical Tendencies of Modern Democracy.* Eden and Cedar Paul, trans. New York: Free Press, 1962.

Mill, John Stuart. *Autobiography.* In *Collected Works of John Stuart Mill.* Edited by John Mercel Robson. Toronto: University of Toronto Press, 1977[1873].

Mill, John Stuart. "Centralisation." In *Collected Works of John Stuart Mill.* Edited by John Mercel Robson. Vol. 19. Toronto: University of Toronto Press, 1977[1862].

Mill, John Stuart. "Civilization." In *Collected Works of John Stuart Mill.* Edited by John Mercel Robson. Vol. 18. Toronto: University of Toronto Press, 1977[1836].

Mill, John Stuart. *Considerations on Representative Government.* In *Collected Works of John Stuart Mill.* Edited by John Mercel Robson. Vol. 19. Toronto: University of Toronto Press, 1977[1861].

Mill, John Stuart. "De Tocqueville on Democracy in America (ii)." In *Collected Works of John Stuart Mill.* Edited by John Mercel Robson. Vol. 18. Toronto: University of Toronto Press, 1977[1840].

Mill, John Stuart. "Endowments." In *Collected Works of John Stuart Mill.* Edited by John Mercel Robson. Vol. 5. Toronto: University of Toronto Press, 1977[1869].

Mill, John Stuart. *The Examiner,* December 19, 1830. In *Collected Works of John Stuart Mill.* Edited by John Mercel Robson. Vol. 22. Toronto: University of Toronto Press, 1977[1830].

Mill, John Stuart. "A Few Words on Non-Intervention." In *Collected Works of John Stuart Mill.* Edited by John Mercel Robson. Vol. 11. Toronto: University of Toronto Press, 1977[1859].

Mill, John Stuart. *On Liberty.* In *Collected Works of John Stuart Mill.* Edited by John Mercel Robson. Vol. 18. Toronto: University of Toronto Press, 1977[1859].

Mill, John Stuart. "The Right and Wrong of State Interference with Corporation and Church Property." In *Collected Works of John Stuart Mill.* Edited by John Mercel Robson. Vol. 5. Toronto: University of Toronto Press, 1977[1833].

Mill, John Stuart. *The Subjection of Women*. In *Collected Works of John Stuart Mill*. Edited by John Mercel Robson. Vol. 21. Toronto: University of Toronto Press, 1977[1869].

Mills, Charles W. *The Racial Contract*. Ithaca: Cornell University Press, 1997.

Molesworth, Robert. *An Account of Denmark: With Francogallia and Some Considerations for the Promoting of Agriculture and Employing the Poor*. Edited by Justin Champion. Indianapolis: Liberty Fund, 2011[1694].

Montesquieu, Charles de Secondat. *The Complete Works of M. de Montesquieu*. Dublin: W. Watson, W. Whitstone, J. Williams, 1777.

Montesquieu, Charles de Secondat. "Essai sur le goût." In *Montesquieu: Œuvres Completes*. Edited by Daniel Oster. New York: Macmillan Company, 1964[1757].

Montesquieu, Charles de Secondat. *Persian Letters*. Translated by C. J. Betts. Baltimore: Penguin Books, 1973[1721].

Montesquieu, Charles de Secondat. *The Spirit of the Laws*. Edited by Anne M. Cohler, Basia Carolyn Miller, and Harold Samuel Stone. Cambridge: Cambridge University Press, 1989[1748].

Montesquieu, Charles de Secondat. *My Thoughts*. Translated and edited by Henry C. Clark. Indianapolis: Liberty Fund, 2012[1720–55].

Mornay, Philippe de. *A Defence of Liberty Against Tyrants: A Translation of the Vindiciae Contra Tyrannos*. Edited by Harold Joseph Laski. Translated by Hubert Languet. London: G. Bell, 1924.

Mosher, Michael A. "The Particulars of a Universal Politics: Hegel's Adaptation of Montesquieu's Typology." 78(1) *The American Political Science Review* 179–88, 1984.

Mosher, Michael A. "What Montesquieu Taught." In *Montesquieu and His Legacy*. Edited by Rebecca Kingston. New York: State University of New York Press, 2009.

Muñiz-Fraticelli, Victor. *The Structure of Pluralism*. Oxford: Oxford University Press, 2014.

Myers, Jr., Minor. *Liberty Without Anarchy: A History of the Society of the Cincinnati*. Charlottesville: University Press of Virginia, 1983.

New Hampshire Historical Society. *Collections of the New Hampshire Historical Society*. Vol. 6. Concord: Asa McFarland, 1850.

Nicholls, David. *The Pluralist State: The Political Ideas of J. N. Figgis and His Contemporaries*. New York: St. Martin's Press, 1975.

Nozick, Robert. *Anarchy, State, and Utopia*. New York: Basic Books, 1974.

Nussbaum, Martha C. "The Future of Feminist Liberalism." 74(2) *Proceedings and Addresses of the American Philosophical Association* 47–79, 2000.

Nussbaum, Martha C. "Rawls and Feminism." In *The Cambridge Companion to Rawls*. Edited by Samuel Freeman. Cambridge: Cambridge University Press, 2003.

O'Brien, Conor Cruise. *The Great Melody: A Thematic Biography and Commented Anthology of Edmund Burke*. Chicago: University of Chicago Press, 1992.

O'Brien, Karen. *Narratives of Enlightenment: Cosmopolitan History from Voltaire to Gibbon*. Cambridge: Cambridge University Press, 1997.

O'Connor, Thomas. "Jansenism." In *The Oxford Handbook of the Ancien Régime*. Edited by William Doyle. Oxford: Oxford University Press, 2011.

Oakeshott, Michael. "Rationalism in Politics." In *Rationalism in Politics and Other Essays*. New York: Basic Books Pub. Co., 1962.

Oakeshott, Michael. *On Human Conduct*. Oxford: Oxford University Press, 1975.

Ober, Josiah. *Democracy and Knowledge: Innovation and Learning in Classical Athens*. Princeton: Princeton University Press, 2008.

Okin, Susan Moller. *Justice, Gender, and the Family*. New York: Basic Books, 1989.

Okin, Susan Moller. "Political Liberalism, Justice, and Gender." 105(1) *Ethics* 23–43, 1994.

Okin, Susan Moller. *Is Multiculturalism Bad for Women?* Edited by Joshua Cohen, Matthew Howard, and Martha Craven Nussbaum. Princeton: Princeton University Press, 1999.

Orwell, George. *The Road to Wigan Pier*. New York: Harcourt, Brace, 1958.

Ostrom, Elinor. *Governing the Commons: The Evolution of Institutions for Collective Action*. Cambridge: Cambridge University Press, 1990.

Ostrom, Elinor. "Social Capital: A Fad or a Fundamental Concept?" In *Social Capital: A Multifaceted Perspective*. Edited by Partha Dasgupta and Ismail Serageldin. Washington, D.C.: World Bank, 2000.

Paine, Thomas. *Rights of Man, Common Sense, and Other Political Writings*. Edited by Mark Philp. Oxford: Oxford University Press, 1995.

Pappé, H. O. "Mill and Tocqueville." 25(2) *Journal of the History of Ideas* 217–34, 1964.

Parthenay, Jean-Baptiste Desroaches de. *The history of Poland under Augustus II, which contains the great dispute between that prince and the princes of Conti and Sobieski for the Crown: with the other important transactions of his life*. Translated by John Stacie. London: W. Lewis and F. Cogan, 1734.

Patterson, Orlando. *Freedom in the Making of Western Culture*. New York: Basic Books, 1991.

Peller, Gary, and Mark Tushnet. "State Action and a New Birth of Freedom." 92(4) *Georgetown Law Journal* 779, 2004.

Pettit, Philip. *Republicanism: A Theory of Freedom and Government*. Oxford: Oxford University Press, 1997.

Pettit, Philip. *A Theory of Freedom: From the Psychology to the Politics of Agency*. Cambridge: Polity, 2001.

Phillips, Anne. *Multiculturalism Without Culture*. Princeton: Princeton University Press, 2007.

Pincus, Steven C. A. *1688: The First Modern Revolution*. New Haven: Yale University Press, 2009.

Pirenne, Henri. *Medieval Cities: Their Origins and the Revival of Trade*. Translated by Frank Halsley. Princeton: Princeton University Press, 1969[1925].

Pitts, Jennifer. "Introduction." In *Writings on Empire and Slavery* by Alexis de Tocqueville. Edited by Jennifer Pitts. Baltimore: Johns Hopkins University Press, 2001.

Pitts, Jennifer. *A Turn to Empire: The Rise of Imperial Liberalism in Britain and France*. Princeton: Princeton University Press, 2005.

Pocock, J. G. A. *The Ancient Constitution and the Feudal Law; a Study of English Historical Thought in the Seventeenth Century*. Cambridge: Cambridge University Press, 1957.

Pocock, J. G. A. "Burke and the Ancient Constitution: A Problem in the History of Ideas." 3(2) *The Historical Journal* 125–43, 1960.

Pocock, J. G. A. *The Machiavellian Moment: Florentine Political Thought and the Atlantic Republican Tradition.* Princeton: Princeton University Press, 1975.

Pocock, J. G. A. "The Myth of John Locke and the Obsession with Liberalism." *John Locke: papers read at a Clark Library Seminar, 10 December 1977.* Edited by J. G. A. Pocock and Richard Ashcraft. Los Angeles: William Andrews Clark Memorial Library, University of California, 1980.

Pocock, J. G. A. "Cambridge Paradigms and Scotch Philosophers: a study of the relations between the civic humanist and the civil jurisprudential interpretation of eighteenth-century political thought." In *Wealth and Virtue.* Edited by Istvan Hont and Michael Ignatieff. Cambridge: Cambridge University Press, 1983.

Pocock, J. G. A. *Barbarism and Religion, volume 1: The Enlightenments of Edward Gibbon, 1737–1764.* Cambridge: Cambridge University Press, 1999.

Pocock, J. G. A. *Barbarism and Religion, volume 2: Narratives of Civil Government.* Cambridge: Cambridge University Press, 1999.

Poggi, Gianfranco. *The State: Its Nature, Development, and Prospects.* Cambridge: Polity Press, 1990.

Pufendorf, Samuel. *On the Duty of Man and Citizen According to Natural Law.* Edited by James Tully. Translated by Michael Silverthorne. Cambridge: Cambridge University Press, 1991.

Putnam, Robert D., Robert Leonardi, and Raffaella Nanetti. *Making Democracy Work: Civic Traditions in Modern Italy.* Princeton: Princeton University Press, 1993.

Qualter, Terence H. "John Stuart Mill, Disciple of de Tocqueville." 13(4) *Political Research Quarterly* 880–9, 1960.

Rahe, Paul. "The Book That Never Was: Montesquieu's Considerations on the Romans in Historical Context." 26(1) *History of Political Thought* 43–89, 2005.

Rahe, Paul. *Montesquieu and the Logic of Liberty: War, Religion, Commerce, Climate, Terrain, Technology, Uneasiness of Mind, the Spirit of Political Vigilance, and the Foundations of the Modern Republic.* New Haven: Yale University Press, 2009.

Rasmussen, Dennis. "Burning Laws and Strangling Kings? Voltaire and Diderot on the Perils of Rationalism in Politics." 73(1) *The Review of Politics* 77–104, 2001.

Rasmussen, Dennis. *The Pragmatic Enlightenment: Recovering the Liberalism of Hume, Smith, Montesquieu, and Voltaire.* Cambridge: Cambridge University Press, 2013.

Rawls, John. *A Theory of Justice.* Cambridge, Mass.: Harvard University Press, 1971.

Rawls, John. *Political Liberalism.* New York: Columbia University Press, 1993.

Rawls, John. *Justice As Fairness: A Restatement.* Cambridge, Mass.: Harvard University Press, 2002.

Rawls, John. *Lectures on the History of Political Philosophy.* Edited by Samuel Richard Freeman. Cambridge, Mass.: Belknap Press of Harvard University Press, 2007.

Raz, Joseph. *The Authority of Law: Essays on Law and Morality.* Oxford: Oxford University Press, 1979.

Raz, Joseph. *The Morality of Freedom.* Oxford: Oxford University Press, 1983.

Resnick, David. "Locke and the Rejection of the Ancient Constitution." 12(1) *Political Theory* 97–114, 1984.

Richter, Melvin. "Comparative Political Analysis in Montesquieu and Tocqueville." 1(2) *Comparative Politics* 129–60, 1969.

Richter, Melvin. "The uses of theory: Tocqueville's adaptation of Montesquieu." In *Essays in Theory and History: An Approach to the Social Sciences*. Cambridge, Mass.: Harvard University Press, 1970.

Richter, Melvin. "Montesquieu and the concept of civil society." 3(6) *The European Legacy: Toward New Paradigms* 33–41, 1998.

Ridder-Symoens, Hilde de. *A History of the University in Europe, Vol. 1: Universities in the Middle Ages*. Cambridge: Cambridge University Press, 1992.

Robbins, Caroline. *The Eighteenth-Century Commonwealthman: Studies in the Transmission, Development, and Circumstance of English Liberal Thought from the Restoration of Charles I until the War with the Thirteen Colonies*. Indianapolis: Liberty Fund, 2004.

Roche, Daniel. *France in the Enlightenment*. Cambridge, Mass.: Harvard University Press, 1998.

Rosanvallon, Pierre. *The Demands of Liberty: Civil Society in France Since the Revolution*. Cambridge, Mass.: Harvard University Press, 2007.

Rosenblatt, Helena. *Liberal Values: Benjamin Constant and the Politics of Religion*. Cambridge: Cambridge University Press, 2008.

Rosenblum, Nancy L. *Membership and Morals: The Personal Uses of Pluralism in America*. Princeton: Princeton University Press, 1998.

Rosenblum, Nancy L. *On the Side of the Angels: an Appreciation of Parties and Partisanship*. Princeton: Princeton University Press, 2008.

Rosenblum, Nancy L. "Okin's Liberal Feminism as Radical Political Theory." In *Toward a Humanist Justice: The Political Philosophy of Susan Moller Okin*. Edited by Debra Satz and Rob Reich. Oxford: Oxford University Press, 2009.

Runciman, David. *Pluralism and the Personality of the State*. Cambridge: Cambridge University Press, 1997.

Russell, Conrad. "Composite Monarchies in Early Modern Europe." In *Uniting the Kingdom? The Making of British History*. Edited by Alexander Grant and Keith J. Stringer. London; New York: Routledge, 1995.

Sabl, Andrew. "Virtue for Pluralists." 2(2) *Journal of Moral Philosophy* 207–35, 2005.

Sabl, Andrew. *Hume's Politics: Coordination and Crisis in the History of England*. Princeton: Princeton University Press, 2012.

Salmon, J. H. M. "Catholic Resistance Theory, Ultramontanism, and the Royalist Response, 1580–1620." In *The Cambridge History of Political Thought, 1450–1700*. Edited by J. H. Burns. Cambridge: Cambridge University Press, 1991.

Saxton, Luther Calvin. *The Fall of Poland*. New York: Charles Scribner, 1851.

Schwarzenbach, Sibyl A. "Rawls, Hegel, and Communitarianism." 19(4) *Political Theory* 539–71, 1991.

Scott, James C. *Seeing Like a State: How Certain Schemes to Improve the Human Condition Have Failed*. New Haven: Yale University Press, 1998.

Scott, James C. *The Art of Not Being Governed: An Anarchist History of Upland Southeast Asia*. New Haven: Yale University Press, 2009.

Shackleton, Robert. "Allies and Enemies: Voltaire and Montesquieu." In *Essays on Montesquieu and on the Enlightenment*. Edited by David Gilson and Martin Smith. Oxford: Voltaire Foundation, 1988.

Shapiro, Ian. *The State of Democratic Theory*. Princeton: Princeton University Press, 2003.

Shennan, J. H. *The Parlement of Paris*. Ithaca: Cornell University Press, 1968.

Shklar, Judith. *Freedom and Independence: A Study of the Political Ideas of Hegel's Phenomenology of Mind*. Cambridge: Cambridge University Press, 1976.

Shklar, Judith. "The Liberalism of Fear." In *Liberalism and the Moral Life*. Edited by Nancy L. Rosenblum. Cambridge, Mass.: Harvard University Press, 1989.

Shklar, Judith. "Politics and the Intellect." In *Political Thought and Political Thinkers*. Edited by Stanley Hoffman. Chicago: University of Chicago Press, 1998.

Sidney, Algernon. *Discourses Concerning Government*. Edited by Thomas G. West. Indianapolis: Liberty Fund, 1990.

Siedentop, Larry. "The Two Liberal Traditions." In *The Idea of Freedom: Essays in Honour of Isaiah Berlin*. Edited by Alan Ryan. Oxford: Oxford University Press, 1979.

Skinner, Quentin. *The Foundations of Modern Political Thought*. Cambridge: Cambridge University Press, 1978.

Skinner, Quentin. *Liberty Before Liberalism*. Cambridge: Cambridge University Press, 1998.

Smith, Adam. *An Inquiry Into the Nature and Causes of the Wealth of Nations*. Edited by R.H. Campbell and A.S. Skinner. Indianapolis: Liberty Fund, 1981[1776].

Smith, Adam. *The Theory of Moral Sentiments*. Edited by R.H. Campbell and A.S. Skinner. Indianapolis: Liberty Fund, 1981[1790].

Smith, Adam. *Lectures on Jurisprudence*. Edited by Meek, Raphael, and Stein. Indianapolis: Liberty Fund, 1982.

Song, Sarah. *Justice, Gender, and the Politics of Multiculturalism*. Cambridge: Cambridge University Press, 2007.

Spector, Céline. *Montesquieu: Liberté, Droit, et Histoire*. Paris: Michalon, 2010.

Spector, Céline. "Was Montesquieu Liberal?" In *French Liberalism from Montesquieu to the Present Day*. Edited by Raf Geenens and Helena Rosenblatt. Cambridge: Cambridge University Press, 2012.

Spinner-Halev, Jeff. *The Boundaries of Citizenship: Race, Ethnicity, and Nationality in the Liberal State*. Baltimore: Johns Hopkins University Press, 1994.

Sproule-Jones, Mark, Barbara Allen, and Filippo Sabetti, eds. *The Struggle to Constitute and Sustain Productive Orders: Vincent Ostrom's Quest to Understand Human Affairs*. Lanham: Lexington Books, 2008.

Spruyt, Hendrik. *The Sovereign State and Its Competitors: An Analysis of Systems Change*. Princeton: Princeton University Press, 1994.

Staël, Germaine de. *Considerations on the Principal Events of the French Revolution*. Edited by Aurelian Craiutu. Indianapolis: Liberty Fund, 2008[1818].

Stein, Peter. *Roman Law in European History*. Cambridge: Cambridge University Press, 1999.

Steiner, Hillel. *An Essay On Rights*. London: Wiley-Blackwell, 1994.

Stone, Bailey. *The French Parlements and the Crisis of the Old Regime*. Chapel Hill: University of North Carolina Press, 1986.

Strayer, Joseph. *On the Medieval Origins of the Modern State*. Princeton: Princeton University Press, 1970.

Sunstein, Cass. "On Academic Fads and Fashions." 99 *Michigan Law Review* 1251, 2001.

Sunstein, Cass. "State Action Is Always Present." *Chicago Journal of International Law* 3, 2002.

Sunstein, Cass, and Stephen Holmes. *The Cost of Rights: Why Liberty Depends on Taxes.* New York: W. W. Norton, 1999.

Sutcliffe, Adam. *Judaism and Enlightenment.* Cambridge: Cambridge University Press, 2003.

Swaine, Lucas. "Deliberate and Free: Autonomy and Heteronomy in Political Deliberation." 35(1–2) *Philosophy & Social Criticism* 183–213, 2009.

Swann, Julian. *Politics and the Parlement of Paris Under Louis XV, 1754–1774.* Cambridge: Cambridge University Press, 1995.

Swann, Julian. "*Parlements* and Provincial Estates." In *The Oxford Handbook of the Ancien Régime.* Edited by William Doyle. Oxford: Oxford University Press, 2011.

Taylor, Charles. "What's Wrong With Negative Liberty?" In *The Idea of Freedom: Essays in Honour of Isaiah Berlin.* Edited by Alan Ryan. Oxford: Oxford University Press, 1979.

Taylor, Charles. "Atomism." In *Philosophical Papers, volume 2: Philosophy and the Human Sciences.* Cambridge: Cambridge University Press, 1985.

Taylor, Charles. "What Is Human Agency?" In *Philosophical Papers: Human Agency and Language.* Vol. 1. Cambridge: Cambridge University Press, 1985.

Taylor, Charles. "Cross-Purposes: The Liberal–Communitarian Debate." In *Liberalism and the Moral Life.* Edited by Nancy L. Rosenblum. Cambridge, Mass.: Harvard University Press, 1989.

Taylor, Charles. *Sources of the Self.* Cambridge, Mass.: Harvard University Press, 1989.

Taylor, Charles. *The Malaise of Modernity.* Toronto: House of Anasi Press Ltd, 1991.

Taylor, Charles. "Shared and Divergent Values." In *Reconciling the Solitudes.* Montreal and Kingston: McGill-Queen's University Press, 1993.

Taylor, Charles. "Invoking Civil Society." In *Philosophical Arguments.* Cambridge, Mass.: Harvard University Press, 1995.

Taylor, Charles. *Modern Social Imaginaries.* Durham: Duke University Press, 2004.

Taylor, Charles. *A Secular Age.* Cambridge, Mass.: Belknap Press of Harvard University Press, 2007.

Thompson, Martyn P. "A Note On 'Reason' and 'History' in Late Seventeenth-Century Political Thought." 4(4) *Political Theory* 491–504, 1976.

Tierney, Brian. *Foundations of the Conciliar Theory: The Contribution of the Medieval Canonists from Gratian to the Great Schism.* Cambridge: Cambridge University Press, 1955.

Tierney, Brian. "Religion and Rights: A Medieval Perspective." 5(1) *Journal of Law and Religion* 163–75, 1987.

Tilly, Charles. *Coercion, Capital, and European States, AD 990–1992.* Cambridge, Mass.: Blackwell, 1992.

Tilly, Charles, and Willem Pieter Blockman, eds. *Cities and the Rise of States in Europe, A.D. 1000 to 1800.* Boulder, Colo.: Westview Press, 1994.

Tocqueville, Alexis de. *Democracy in America.* Edited by J. P. Meyer. New York: Harper & Row Publishers, 1969[1835/1840].

Tocqueville, Alexis de. *The Old Regime and the Revolution*. Edited by François Furet and Françoise Mélonio. Translated by Alan S. Kahan. Vol. 1. Chicago: University of Chicago Press, 1998[1856].

Tomaselli, Sylvana. "The Spirit of Nations." In *The Cambridge History of Eighteenth-Century Political Thought*. Edited by Mark Goldie and Robert Wokler. Cambridge: Cambridge University Press, 2006.

Tracy, Antoine Louis Claude Destutt de. *M. de Tracy à M. Burke*. France: Imprimerie Nationale, 1790.

Tracy, Antoine Louis Claude Destutt de. *Observations Sur Le Système Actuel d'Instruction Publique*. Paris: Panckoucke, 1801.

Tracy, Antoine Louis Claude Destutt de. *A Commentary and Review of Montesquieu's Spirit of Laws*. Translated by Thomas Jefferson. New York: Burt Franklin, 1969[1811].

Tracy, Antoine Louis Claude Destutt de. *A Treatise on Political Economy*. Translated by Thomas Jefferson. New York: Augustus M. Kelley, 1970[1817].

Trevor-Roper, Hugh. "Some of My Best Friends Are *Philosophes*." 11(3) *The New York Review of Books*, August 22, 1968.

Tully, James. *Strange Multiplicity: Constitutionalism in an Age of Diversity*. Cambridge: Cambridge University Press, 1995.

Tunick, Mark. "John Stuart Mill and Unassimilated Subjects." 53(4) *Political Studies* 833–48, 2005.

Tushnet, Mark. "State Action, Social Welfare Rights, and the Judicial Role: Some Comparative Observations." 3 *Chicago Journal of International Law* 435, 2002.

Tushnet, Mark. *Weak Courts, Strong Rights: Judicial Review and Social Welfare Rights in Comparative Constitutional Law*. Princeton: Princeton University Press, 2009.

Tushnet, Mark. "State Action in 2020." In *The Constitution in 2020*. Edited by Jack M. Balkin and Reva B. Siegel. Oxford: Oxford University Press, 2009.

Van Kley, Dale. *The Religious Origins of the French Revolution: From Calvin to the Civil Constitution, 1560–1791*. New Haven: Yale University Press, 1996.

Vermeule, Adrian. "Selection Effects in Constitutional Law." 91(4) *Virginia Law Review* 953–98, 2005.

Voltaire. Letter to M. le Comte de Bernstorff, February 4, 1767. In *Œuvres de Voltaire*. Vol. 46. Paris: Chez Lefèvre Librarie, 1832.

Voltaire. "Très Humble et Très Respectueux Remontrance du Grenier à Sel." In *Œuvres de Voltaire*. Vol. 46. Paris: Chez Lefèvre Librarie, 1832.

Voltaire. "The History of the Russian Empire Under Peter the Great." In *The Works of Voltaire, a Contemporary Version*. Edited by John Morley. Translated by William F. Fleming. Vol. 18. 21 vols. New York: E. R. DuMont, 1901[1759/1763].

Voltaire. *Philosophical Dictionary*. In *The Works of Voltaire, a Contemporary Version*. Edited by John Morley. Translated by William F. Fleming. New York: E. R. DuMont, 1901[1764].

Voltaire. *Essai Sur Les Mœurs et L'Esprit Des Nations*. Tome 2. Edited by Rene Pomeau. Paris: Garnier Frères, 1963[1756].

Voltaire. *Letters on England*. Edited by Leonard Tancock. Harmondsworth, U.K.: Penguin Books, 1980[1726–9].

Voltaire. *Philosophical Dictionary.* In *Political Writings.* Edited by David Williams. Cambridge: Cambridge University Press, 1994[1764].

Voltaire. "The ABC." In *Political Writings.* Edited by David Williams. Cambridge: Cambridge University Press, 1994[1768].

Walzer, Michael. "The Communitarian Critique of Liberalism." 18(1) *Political Theory* 6–23, 1990.

Walzer, Michael. "Civil Society and the State." In *Politics and Passion.* New Haven: Yale University Press, 2004.

Walzer, Michael. "The Civil Society Argument." In *Thinking Politically.* New Haven: Yale University Press, 2007.

Ward, Lee. "Montesquieu on Federalism and Anglo-Gothic Constitutionalism." 37(4) *Publius: The Journal of Federalism* 551–77, 2007.

Weber, Max. "The Types of Legitimate Domination." In *Theories of Social Order: A Reader.* Edited by Michael Hechter and Christine Horne. Palo Alto: Stanford University Press, 2003.

Welch, Cheryl B. *Liberty and Utility: The French Idéologues and the Transformation of Liberalism.* New York: Columbia University Press, 1984.

Williams, Bernard. *Ethics and the Limits of Philosophy.* Cambridge, Mass.: Harvard University Press, 1986.

Williams, Bernard. "Political Philosophy and the Analytical Tradition." In *Philosophy as a Humanistic Discipline.* Edited by A. W. Moore. Princeton: Princeton University Press, 2009.

Wood, Gordon S. *The Creation of the American Republic, 1776–1787.* Chapel Hill: University of North Carolina Press, 1969.

Zakaras, Alex. "John Stuart Mill, Individuality, and Participatory Democracy." In *J. S. Mill's Political Thought: A Bicentennial Reassessment.* Edited by Nadia Urbinati and Alex Zakaras. Cambridge: Cambridge University Press, 2007.

Index